The Way of the Yoginī

The Way of the Yoginī

The Way of the Yoginī

The Secret teachings of the Goddess
As transmitted by Niṣkriyānanda

Translation, notes and commentary by David Dubois

Table des matières

xii

Preface

In June 1990, I discovered the *Sūtras of the Mad Master*, or *Vātūla-nātha-sūtra*, translated into French by Lilian Silburn. I was immediately fascinated by that Zen-like teaching, and I began to wonder: who was this Mad Master, and who were the Yoginīs who transmitted to him thirteen sacred utterances?

Later, in 1995, I encountered the *Secret Teachings of the Yoginī*, or *Chummā-saṃpradāya*: 105 utterances, illuminated by Sanskrit verses attributed to one Niṣkriyānanda. They were mentioned by Navjivan Rastogi in his work on the "Krama school"—of which these teachings form the foundation. Yet I had no clue as to the precise content of the Secret Teaching or how it connected with the *Mad Master's sūtras*.

In 2007, a book-length article by Alexis Sanderson presented the first in-depth study of this material, including several *chummās* (secret utterances), Sanskrit verses from the *Illumination*, and even a tentative translation with a Sanskrit version of some of the Thirty Secret Songs. I then surmised that the *Secret Teachings* might be an expanded version of the *Mad Master's Sūtras*.

In 2011, Navjivan published a partial Sanskrit edition of the text, transcribed from a Kashmiri manuscript.

But everything changed for me in September 2022, when my teacher, Mark S. G. Dyczkowski, gave me a transcription of a Kashmiri manuscript from the Benares Hindu University library. Though it lacked the first page, it was otherwise complete and coherent to the end.

1

It was then that I began translating it—both into French and into English. The French version, which includes some additional translations and more detailed commentaries, was published in June 2025.

This English version is accompanied by my commentaries. First, you will find a relatively close translation with explanatory notes. Then follow more personnal *Reflections* on each *chummā*, accompanied by a freer, more interpretive rendering.

Please note that there are thus two translations of the *Secret Teaching* in this book: one closely aligned with the Sanskrit text, and another that explores alternate translations and interpretations of the same words.

I have not included here two other versions of the *Secret Teachings of the Yoginī*. The first—*The Mad Master's Sūtras*—has already been translated into English by Mark S. G. Dyczkowski. The second—the *Kaula-sūtras*—may be the subject of a future publication.

I have tried my best to remain faithful to the text. But Sanskrit—the "Language of the Gods"—is famously subtle and difficult. I trust that any errors or oversights will be noted and corrected by those more learned than I.
Since Sanskrit is also highly laconic, I have added words in parentheses to ease comprehension.

The book is structured in three parts:

1. An introduction to the tradition of the Yoginī. You may skip this if you prefer to dive directly into the *Secret Teaching*s.

2. A raw translation with notes. This section may not be easy reading for those unfamiliar with scholarly Sanskrit translation.
3. Reflections and a second, freer translation. If you are new to this kind of material, or not especially drawn to Sanskrit, consider beginning here.

Feel free to navigate the book as you are inspired. You can jump to the section that attracts you most—or open the book at random. Let me be clear: while this book is based on primary sources, by far it is not a strictly academic work. It draws from both scholarly and experiential knowledge, but its ultimate aim is awakening—that is, love.

Finally, I would like to dedicate this book to my teachers: Armand Dubois, Isidore Dalla Nora, Pierre Magnard, Hemendranath Chakravarty, Amritanand Sarasvati, and Markji, whose lives of devotion I strive to emulate.

Why this book?

From the dawn of time, human beings have sought to understand their place in the cosmos, to find meaning in life, and to explore their relationship with the divine. This book is a small contribution to that timeless search by bringing to light a spiritual lineage that remains largely unknown yet profoundly relevant: the oral teachings of the Yoginīs—women of exceptional insight who, over a millennium ago, shared a vision marked by clarity, autonomy, and depth.

Long obscured by history, their wisdom returns to us like a distant echo of a hidden spiritual legacy.

One compelling idea lies at the heart of this work: what if these teachings were the foundation of what came to be known as Kashmiri Śaivism—one of India's most intricate and luminous philosophical systems, which emerged around the year 1000 CE? Deeply rooted in the Tantric tradition, this lineage delves into the essence of consciousness, the experience of inner freedom, and the realization of divine unity. At a time when Śaivism is enjoying renewed interest globally, rediscovering its earliest sources is both timely and transformative.

What sets this tradition apart is that it was cultivated and carried by women—yoginīs[1]—who were not only spiritual practitioners but also revered teachers. They embodied a sacred vision that was both radical and intimate. In a world where women have long been sidelined from spiritual authority, these radiant presences remind us that genuine wisdom transcends gender and cultural boundaries.

Their teachings, often delivered in poetic, enigmatic, and paradoxical form, call for an uncompromising freedom— freedom of being, freedom of thought, freedom of spirit. While grounded in Indian soil, this message is not tied to any culture or era; it speaks directly to the human heart. It also conveys a feminine perspective on the sacred, one that resonates powerfully today, especially in light of the growing collective yearning for a reconnection with the sacred feminine. Yet this teaching is not a system or belief—it is a living process, a direct experience of truth that is universal, timeless, and deeply human.

Why now? Because we live in an age where many of our old certainties are crumbling. The intellectual and moral

---

[1] I use capital "Y" when the Yoginīs are sacred beings or awakened women.

frameworks that once guided humanity are proving inadequate in the face of today's existential challenges. The teachings of the Yoginīs invite us to reevaluate how we relate to divinity, to freedom, and to the essence of who we are. They open the way to a sacred land, both raw and clear—one that blends awareness, beauty, and a renewed sense of harmony with the rhythms of life.

This book is a call to remember a wisdom that, though ancient, is vividly alive. To hear the voices of these women who, through centuries, have carried a message of awakening, courage, and inner grace. May we allow their breath to reach us today, to illumine our path, and to rekindle the flame of inner liberation.

An Introduction to the Yoginī Path

The Tale of a Yogi and His Encounter with the Yoginī

Once, there lived a yogi whose heart blazed with a singular longing—to transcend human limitations and awaken supernatural powers. He had been initiated into the Kaula lineage, an esoteric stream flowing from the heart of Tantra, where ecstasy, spontaneous embodiment, and reverence for feminine power merged into one path. This sacred way rested upon three core practices: the breath as gateway, the gaze as initiation, and space as revelation.

Having been admitted into the divine circle of Yoginīs, of Śiva and Śakti, the yogi set out to meet the Yoginīs not as mythic figures, but embodied in living women. These elusive beings, shape-shifting witches, were said to bestow rare gifts: powers and flight beyond the laws of matter, or even full awakening.

So he wandered—from shrine to sacred ground—those places said to pulse with the presence of the Goddess. According to legend, they were born where fragments of the Goddess's body fell upon the Earth. These sanctuaries were hidden from the eyes of the uninitiated, safe from the judgment of orthodox power. The rites practiced there were often defiant, even scandalous: offerings included cow flesh, dog meat, and—so the whispers claimed—human remains. There was wine, strong and sacred. And sexual union, especially with women deemed impure by the caste system. In brahmanic society, where purity and hierarchy reigned, these acts were unthinkable.

Devoted beyond measure, the yogi lived in ceaseless veneration of the Yoginīs, both divine and incarnate. Clothed like a wild forest man, adorned with human bone, carrying the trident and smearing his skin with sacred ash, he walked in the image of Śiva. Like Bhairava—fierce and free—he made his home among black dogs in cremation fields, haunted by ghosts and outcasts. At night, he performed the most secretive rites in the company of other initiates, exchanging the mysterious signs called *chummās*. He lived with intensity, drawn into the most hidden currents of Indian spiritual traditions centered on Kālī and her fierce sisterhood.

Yet something in him remained unsatisfied. A fever haunted him—a hunger, a sense of something just beyond his reach. Despite countless mantras, visions, and ecstatic trances, a whisper told him that true grace, real freedom, still eluded him.

One day, in a southern sanctuary known as the "Sublime Mountain," he sensed a presence. There, above him, sat a silent man on a rock. Instantly, the yogi knew: this was no ordinary person. He was a realized being, a *siddha*. He asked his name, his lineage. But the man gave no answer. His gaze, rimmed in dark kohl, was fixed on the sky, vast and open. Suddenly, their eyes met—and in that moment, the yogi was thrown into another realm. He collapsed, as if his being had been cut at the root.

He felt himself dissolve into infinite space—luminous, conscious, boundless. It was not a state, but a pure presence, beyond knowing, beyond all teachings or traditions.

When he returned to ordinary awareness, he knew he had been transformed. What he had just experienced was the true initiation—the grace beyond form. It was so simple, yet beyond words, like the final light of day melting into the horizon.

He looked again at the realized master, who now held a book. But his eyes still searched only the sky. The yogi followed his gaze. In the golden haze of dusk, the sky shimmered—and then, something emerged. A figure. The vastness itself took shape. A Yoginī. The yogi knew at once: she was *the* Yoginī—Bhairavī, the Goddess, the limitless Presence. Terrifying, beautiful, and tender beyond imagining. She was the scream at the center of life's anguish—and the silent rapture that makes life possible.

Smiling, she looked at the yogi, who still thought himself master of her mysteries. "Your grand experiences," she said softly, "are but shadows..." Then she revealed the heart-teachings—the whispered words, riddles, and inner symbols of the Yoginīs. The most hidden transmission of all. A tradition so secret that even the gods miss it.

Through this transmission, the yogi came to remember: he was the reincarnation of Durvāsa, the legendary sage known for his fury. His pride, born of karma and spiritual prowess, had kept him from surrender to the Presence. But now, he tasted the joy of non-doing—*Niṣkriya Ānanda*, Bliss Beyond Action, became his new name, his true self. And he became the central figure in this luminous lineage.

He remained there with his fellow initiates. One day, another seeker arrived—another yogi who had also encountered the Realized Master. His name was Vidyānanda—"the Bliss of Wisdom." He too had wandered, chanting and fasting in wild devotion. When Vidyānanda asked to receive the Yoginī's oral transmission, Niṣkriya shared with him the one hundred and five *Chummās*, the secret symbolic pointers of the path, along with a commentary—the *Prakāśa*—written in the sacred language of Sanskrit. He also shared the Thirty

Secret Songs, composed in the hidden tongue of the Yoginīs—songs so potent they remain untranslated, and we do not include them in the present book.

These teachings, two facets of the same oral wisdom, became the *Chummā-saṅketa-prakāśa*—the *Revelation of the Secret Signs of the Yoginīs*—the very text we translate and try to illuminate in this book.

Later, Niṣkriyānanda and Vidyānanda distilled the essence into thirteen aphorisms: *The Sayings of the Mad Master* (*Vātūla-nātha-sūtra*), accompanied by a brief exposition. A further version—*the Kaula Sūtras*—was shaped by later disciples. Thus, four forms of the Yoginī's oral wisdom emerged, all born of the Realized Master's gaze and presence.

This collection—rediscovered in the early 21st century after a millennium of silence—is what we now call the *Oral Corpus of the Yoginīs*. Though its influence can be felt in the deepest layers of Kashmir Shaivism and non-dual Tantra, it has remained hidden, unnamed. Yet it integrates all: body and mind, heart and breath, intellect and eros, the feminine and impersonal space, the flesh and the formless.

This book offers, for the first time, the living voice of that teaching—the Yoga of the Goddess, called in the texts "the highest of all yogas."

Let us briefly summarize the texts that make up this corpus—different versions of the same oral teaching:

1. The 105 *Chummās* and their Elucidation (*Prakāśa*) by Niṣkriya.
2. The 30 Secret Songs.

3. The 13 Aphorisms of the Mad Master and their Explanation.
4. The *Kaula Sūtras*.

Only the first version, the most extensive one, is translated here.

How to Approach This Book

Translations can seem intimidating—and with good reason. Sanskrit language is known for its complexity, and the pages are filled with unfamiliar terms, footnotes, and words that appear difficult to pronounce.

But there's no need to worry. Here are a few suggestions to help you enjoy *The Secrets of the Yoginīs* in the most enriching way.

If you feel the need for some background, you may read this introduction in full or simply focus on the sections that are of interest to you.

Each translation is accompanied by footnotes, including quotes from previously unpublished Sanskrit sources. These notes offer new, precise, and valuable insights. However, they may also interrupt the flow of your reading. That's why I suggest beginning with the translations alone. Read them without the notes first, even if the meaning seems unclear. The purpose is not to accumulate information but to allow the words to settle into you, like a slow infusion. Read gently, with no rush. It's better to read only a little and let it echo within you. Don't stare at the finger, give your full attention to the moon.

At times, you may feel drawn into the Presence itself, into the quiet depth of your heart. If that happens, stop reading. Follow that inner pull. That moment is the book's true purpose: not to inform, but to transform and reconnect you to the infinite Good.

I also recommend journaling your impressions. Take notes. Let the words of the Yoginīs stir your own reflections and insights. You may be surprised by what arises. Explaining something is often the best way to understand it. If questions emerge or if you would like to share your experiences, please feel free to contact me (see at the end of this book). Living exchange is the heart of transmission. The 21st century may become a time of isolation… unless we choose to use our technologies to forge new, meaningful connections.

If you'd like to engage with the sanskrit verses or words, take your time. Listening is the best way to learn—the rhythm and tone of Sanskrit don't translate easily into written guides. Until then, a few simple tips: any vowel marked with a line, like "ā," is long—don't be afraid to stretch it. "U" is pronounced "oo." "Ś" sounds like "sh," as does "ṣ" (with the tongue curled toward the palate; like all consonant marked with a dot below). "S" is always sharp, like a double "s." There are no "z" or "f" sounds in Sanskrit. The key is to go slowly and pronounce with exaggerated care and accent. Sanskrit flows like tango.

The translations strive to stay true to the meaning I've grasped from the original (and I make no claim to perfect understanding!), while still offering a readable version. At times, a single Sanskrit word is translated in multiple ways, or paraphrased into fuller English expressions. Similarly, an English word might reflect several Sanskrit terms. Contrary to popular belief, Sanskrit isn't significantly more polysemous than other languages. Most of its words have multiple meanings, which is common. What makes Sanskrit unique is its brevity—it often says more with less. This is why added clarifications appear in parentheses. Feel free to ignore them as you read.

My *Reflections on the Chummās* offers more depth and accessibility than the raw translations. If you find the notes challenging, that's a good place to begin.

For those interested in historical context or questions around authorship, dating and manuscripts, see Appendix 1 and 2 at the end of the book.

And finally: don't hesitate to open to a random page. Trust the Yoginīs to guide your steps.

Who Are the Yoginīs?

The Yoginīs are far more than mythical figures or exotic symbols—they embody a potent and fearsome duality. At once awe-inspiring and enigmatic, even feared like spirits of the night, they are also keepers of the deepest spiritual mysteries and guardians of inner awakening. These divine feminine beings are often said to dwell in liminal, untamed places—cremation grounds, thresholds of life and death— where transformation silently unfolds. It was in these sacred, marginal spaces that the yogi, later known as Niṣkriya, hoped to encounter them.

As the story goes, his journey eventually led him to a revered sanctuary in the South of India, known as the "Mountain of Glory" (*Śrī-Śaila*). There, within a network of hidden caves north of the sacred peak[2]—ideal for secretive practice—he entered the shadowed realm of Kaula rituals. These transgressive rites defied mainstream social codes, involving wine, bodily fluids, and other elements deemed impure by orthodox standards.

There, he met the figure who would change everything—a mysterious master who radiated a silence deeper than words. Known only as *Mauni-nātha*, the Lord of Silence, this sage revealed a truth that shattered all previous assumptions: the Goddess is none other than one's own consciousness, and the Yoginīs are not external deities but subtle forces within the body – and yet not the body as we believe it to be. This insight marked the beginning of an extraordinary transmission. We described this event above in a fiction of sorts, but based on what we know. This might have taken place around 800AD.

The silent master imparted to him the oral teaching of the Yoginīs—a collection of 105 secret utterances (*Chummās*) woven with paradox and poetic insight into the wisdom of non-doing (*niṣkriyā-jñāna*). From that moment, the yogi received the name *Niṣkriya Ānanda*, "Bliss of Effortlessness." He himself recounts this transformative moment at the opening of his text, *The Revelation of the Secret Words/Signs/Symbols of the Yoginīs* (*Chummā-Saṅketa-Prakāśa*). Our current translation, based on four rare Kashmiri manuscripts miraculously rediscovered, offers a glimpse into that living transmission, though the very first page remains lost—a fitting veil of mystery over the beginning of the tale... The Source is beyond – or before – words.

---

[2] Those caves still exist. They are known as the "Akka Maha Devi caves", from the name of a South-indian Yogini who is said to have practiced later on in this place, north of *Śrī-Śaila* in what is today the land of Andhra.

The text begins in a blaze of intensity. In the presence of the silent Master, Niṣkriya receives what the Kaula tradition calls "the gaze of power" (*śakti-pāta*). This moment is likened to a spiritual thunderbolt—a radical break that brings the seeker to his knees. But this collapse is no defeat; it is the supreme initiation, the most direct gateway to freedom within Kaula Tantra's already esoteric framework.

Here, liberation is not a distant promise of heaven after death. It is an immediate recognition: the divine is already here—within consciousness, within the very cells of the body. The body is not seen as a limitation, but as a condensed flow of divine awareness—a crystallized stream of sacred Presence.

Following this awakening, Niṣkriya Ānanda is immersed in a direct experience of unspeakable magnitude. He attempts to describe it through paradox: a presence that is as vast as space, yet vibrantly alive in all things; a bliss unlike any known joy, untouched by seeking and unbounded by effort. It cannot be taught, and yet it is ever accessible. Though beyond words, it hums in the primal syllable "a"[3].

The *Secret Sayings* of the Yoginīs (as we could as well translate their title), received from the Realized or Silent Master, are not teachings to be grasped intellectually. Like Zen koans, they are riddles meant to crack open the mind and draw us into direct experience. They are pointers in whispers from a vibrant sky.

This is not merely the tale of a man chasing magical powers—it is the account of a meeting with the Real, the

---

[3] *A-kathya* means also "What cannot be told" of spoken. Hence, the 105th teaching of the Yoginī is… silence.

Heart of the Yoginī. Through Niṣkriya's journey, we are reminded that ultimate freedom lies in a radical realization: the body, awareness, and the divine are one. And this teaching—more than a thousand years old—resonates now more than ever.

The Great Tree of Tantra

This book introduces, for the first time in over a thousand years, a rare and powerful teaching transmitted by a mysterious yogi named *Niṣkriyā-ānanda-nātha*—his full initiatory title. The name *Ānanda-nātha* is traditionally used for initiates within the Kaula tradition, the most secretive branch of Tantra, which includes the worship of the Goddess. It means "one who takes refuge in bliss," a phrase that hints at the centrality of sacred sexuality—since *ānanda*, in Sanskrit, has referred to erotic pleasure since the time of the Vedas, the oldest body of Indian scriptures. Interestingly, this same title was later adopted by ascetics of Advaita Vedānta, a renunciate tradition that renounces precisely what *ānanda* originally implied. Even the ten "orders" in their monastic hierarchy partly mirror the initiatory lodges of the Kaulas. Though the Vedāntins removed all physical elements, traces of the Kaula tradition still survive in their structure.

To understand the exceptional nature of what Niṣkriya passed down, we must first situate him within the spiritual landscape of India and within the broader "Tree of Tantra".

What is Tantra, really?

Tantra is, before anything else, a worldview—a deep knowledge. It holds that everything arises from a single, infinite consciousness, which expresses itself in limitless forms. This supreme awareness folds in on itself, becoming individualized in countless ways—appearing to herself as insects, animals, gods, and humans. Every living being is thus the infinite, contracted into form. And from this limited state, consciousness naturally longs to return to its unbounded essence. This return takes place through experience and, ultimately, through the integral wisdom that Tantra reveals.

The key idea is this: all is ecstatic consciousness. And it is by complete freedom that this boundless awareness limits itself, becoming embodied and identified with form. While other Indian non-dualist schools also proclaim "all is consciousness," Tantra places unique emphasis on delight, freedom, and bliss—especially the expansion of self through sensory awakening.

This vision embraces all aspects of existence—nothing is cast out. In Tantra, unity doesn't mean negating multiplicity. That's why its practices include not only study, ritual, meditation, and yoga, but also dance, song, pilgrimage, and embodied devotion. The body, heart, and mind are woven together in a cyclical journey—one of return to the Source and rebirth from it.

But what is Tantra in practice?

To keep it simple: Tantra is a spiritual stream rooted in Hinduism. Though Buddhist and Jain forms of Tantra also exist, this book focuses on its Hindu origins.

Like many spiritual systems, Indian traditions often divide life into two paths: renunciation or engagement. Tantra's originality lies in reconciling them. It offers a vision in which one can fully enjoy the world while remaining inwardly free. This is the ideal of *liberation in this very life*—not merely after death, and not through denial of the body.

Tantra is thus a spiritual movement that seeks both worldly fulfillment (pleasure, health, wealth, family) and liberation—both after death and in embodied life. Unlike earlier traditions that viewed the body as an obstacle, Tantra insists that the body is the temple of the divine, the seat of sacred power, and the field where truth is revealed.

Where mainstream Indian paths emphasize detachment from the world, from sensuality, from art, from women and pleasure, Tantra affirms the opposite: for the initiated, everything—including what society deems impure—can become a doorway to awakening.

Initiated into what?

Initiation is the great Door of Tantra. Opening into what ? Into comprehensive knowledge—an understanding that embraces all layers of reality. According to Tantra, the so-called orthodox Vedic or Brahmanic traditions preserve aspects of truth but only in fragments. They perpetuate the illusion that opposites must be chosen between: body *or* spirit, pleasure *or* renunciation, feminine *or* masculine. Tantra, in contrast, sees all polarities as expressions of one undivided living reality.

Fragmented knowledge breeds fear and limits power. Of course, this is part of the game consciousness plays with herself. But the more complete our insight, the more we are able to integrate worldly forces—including the body—into our awakening.

How is Tantra structured?

Following the great master Abhinavagupta, we can imagine Tantra as a vast tree. It grows from a common trunk—revelation from the divine, named here *Eternal Śiva*—and unfolds through multiple branches, each a new revelation, increasingly refined and powerful.

Practically speaking, one can progress through a series of initiations. Each opens a higher level of spiritual freedom—not only the "freedom from" conditioning (*negative liberty*), but also the "freedom to" act, feel, desire, and create (*positive liberty*). These two are not in conflict, but are two expressions of the same essence—consciousness, which is, by its very nature, freedom. So free, in fact, that it can manifest itself and forget itself in the same act. It can do what is impossible. Why? For the wonder of it all.

The further we climb the Tree of Tantra, the more the feminine reveals itself. At the lower levels, Śiva dominates—as the shining, pure, white Eternal Śiva. The Goddess appears as his Throne. Even here, though superior to mainstream Hindu and Buddhist doctrines, this level still respects social codes, especially the dualism of pure and impure that defines caste and conduct.

According to that orthodox worldview, only a small portion of humanity belongs to the four sanctioned castes. The rest—outsiders, untouchables—are seen as unworthy. Purity is everything. Life is pure; whatever moves away from life—saliva, bodily waste, death—is impure. This is why, in traditional India, even drinking vessels become defiled after use.

Understanding this cultural dualism is crucial, because higher Tantric teachings challenge it. In non-dual Tantra, there is a *practice of non-duality* itself. Not just an understanding. What is "not two"? - Pure and impure. Thus, what is rejected by Brahmanic society is embraced here—not just for shock value, but because all is life, all is sacred, all is consciousness. Awakening consciousness out of her fearful dreams.

In Śaiva Siddhānta—the so-called "final doctrine" of Śiva, which is in fact the "trunk" of the Tantra tree—a kind of dualistic cosmology persists: God, inert matter, and individual souls are seen as separate and eternal. Liberation means freeing the soul from matter, through divine mantras - angels sent in our world to save us through the ritual of initiation. But this freedom is usually reached only after death, by living a life of purity, vegetarianism, and celibacy.

This is the paradox: in traditional Indian thinking, purity is equated with weakness. Real power accepts impurity. Hence, the transgressive practices and the cremation-ground sub-culture of female-centered Tantra. Women, because of menstrual blood and reproductive power, symbolize both impurity and immense potency. That potency was long seen as dangerous—hence Manu's (the First Man) command to keep women under male control.

He used the term *svatantrā*—independent—which becomes, in higher Tantra, a sacred ideal.

But at the heart of the matter lies a contradiction: if life is pure, how can that which generates life—sex and menstrual blood—be impure? This unresolved tension sits at the core of Indian civilization.

The Yoginīs answer it—not through theory, but through lived experience and embodied wisdom. Their teachings offer the key to this paradox. And it is to them that we now turn.

The Teaching of the Yoginīs

At the highest levels of the Tantric tradition lies the teaching of the Yoginīs. The higher one climbs this great tree of Tantric wisdom—which, let us recall, encompasses all forms of knowledge—the more the feminine principle reveals its prominence. Yet, as we've seen, femininity has long been associated with impurity, even though it should be revered as sacred. Tantra exposes this contradiction and resolves it by affirming the supremacy of *power*.

In Sanskrit, that power is called *śakti*—a term that also designates the dynamic, creative force of the divine, often personified as the Goddess. The Tantric paths that recognize and celebrate this feminine energy are called *śākta* traditions, meaning "related to Śakti." And the manifestations of her energy are the Yoginīs.

Thus, non-dual Tantra is inherently *śākta*—feminine in its essence. The *tantras* themselves, the scriptures that convey this sacred knowledge, are most often structured as dialogues between the Divine Masculine and the Divine Feminine. In these texts, the Goddess—appearing as the supreme Yoginī—holds the central role. She is the source of wisdom, the sovereign of the Yoginīs, and the embodiment of awakened power.

Who And What Are the Yoginīs?

Yoginīs come in many forms. On the earthly level, they are sometimes described as the restless spirits of women who died in tragic circumstances—especially during childbirth or acts of violence such as sexual assault. Like ancient Furies, they may seek vengeance, often by possessing vulnerable beings, particularly children. Tantric texts offer methods for protection against these spirits through rituals involving *mantras* and offerings that may include blood or alcohol. Even today, in some regions, buffaloes are sacrificed in ceremonies invoking the Goddess as Queen of the Yoginīs. In such contexts, the term *yoga* is associated with sexual union, since the fury of these entities is often said to arise from traumatic or violated intimacy. Though the blood offered to them is seen as impure, it is believed to carry immense power.

This raises a profound question: Is impurity powerful *because* it is impure? Or is impurity a misunderstanding—a projection of fear onto raw power born of ignorance?

The Yoginī Tantra is deeply transgressive. It suggests that impurity holds a kind of sacred potency precisely in its violation of the norm. Yet within Tantra there is another path—distinct from, though intimately linked with, the Yoginī current. This is the Kaula tradition, sometimes even referred to as a "religion" (*dharma*) in its own right. It

presents itself as the hidden essence of all spiritual paths—
"the fragrance within all tantras, like scent in a flower."
Kula means family, specifically the mystical families of
Yoginīs, centered around the Goddess and her divine
consort. Male counterparts to the Yoginīs are known as
siddhas—realized beings. Though they may grant mystical
powers and insights, their ultimate purpose is spiritual
awakening, metaphorically called "the ability to fly
through the sky of consciousness" (*khecarī*).

Yoginīs are thus supernatural forces manifesting through
nature. Some appear as women, while others take female
form at will—one of their powers is *shape-shifting*,
including the power to transform others. They may pass on
their gifts—or, conversely, they may steal them. In many
stories, their most feared act is the theft of life energy itself.
Often likened to vampiric beings, Yoginīs are said to drink
blood or even consume human flesh. They resemble
witches, ogresses, and energy predators, depending on
how they appear or are encountered.

They are grouped according to their elemental affinities—
Yoginīs of the sky, earth, water, and mountains—and
gathered into countless spiritual clans, including the
terrifying *śakinīs* and the *ḍākinīs*, later made famous by
Tibetan Buddhism.

They live in spiritual lineages or tribes (*kula*), which is also
the root word for the Kaula tradition. In ritual, Yoginīs are
invoked within a mandala, a sacred circle surrounding their
Queen—an embodiment of the Great Goddess herself.
Each Yoginī represents one facet of this central deity.
When internalized in meditative practice, these mandalas
become *chakras*, the subtle "wheels" of energy within the
body. The Sanskrit word *cakra* also refers to spiritual
lineages or divine clans of feminine forces.

Within the microcosm of the human body, Yoginīs are the vital currents that sustain life—or, at times, drain it. They are the energies behind thought, memory, imagination, and even the ego itself. As such, they can nourish the soul—or turn against it. They may stir up inner torment through desire, anger, pride, or jealousy.

This makes the Yoginīs inherently ambivalent. One can never be certain whether their presence is benevolent or dangerous, spiritual or worldly. They may trigger visions of madness, or possess an individual—most often women—with overwhelming force.

They are, in essence, the wild and unpredictable faces of sacred power.

The Mad Quest for the Yoginīs

For the Tantric initiate, the highest aspiration is to encounter the Yoginīs—to receive from them either a supernatural gift or liberating knowledge leading to spiritual realization. A Yoginī may appear in the form of a woman—a young maiden, a courtesan, or ideally, an initiated and seasoned practitioner of yoga. The yogi and the Yoginī often travel together, moving from one sacred site to another in a journey that is both external pilgrimage and inner transformation.

Drawing from key tantric texts, Abhinavagupta, a great Tantra master from around the tenth century in Kashmir, explains that there are two fundamental types of encounters with the Yoginīs: those that are forceful, and those that are blissful.

In a forceful or *haṭha*-type encounter (as in *haṭha-yoga*), the Yoginīs exhibit a fierce or aggressive nature. In such cases, the practitioner must guard their body using *mantras*, as the Yoginīs are said to exploit subtle openings (*chidra*)—vulnerabilities like the eyes or the mouth—through which they can enter and possess the yogi. The mystical ability to enter another being's body, whether human or otherwise, is documented throughout tantric and yogic literature.

This siddhi, or yogic power, is believed to allow one to become effectively immortal, provided a viable host body is found. In theory, one can take over another person's body and displace their soul. However, while tantric ethics (yes, Tantra has its own moral codes) prohibit such parasitic acts—deemed demonic—it may be seen as acceptable if done for a noble or selfless purpose.

A famous legend about the ascetic Śaṅkara illustrates this. Engaged in philosophical debate with a married Brahmin, Śaṅkara seemed on the verge of winning. But the Brahmin's wife intervened, asserting her right to challenge him on the subject of erotic knowledge (*kāma*), a legitimate aspect of life alongside spiritual liberation. Śaṅkara, raised in renunciation, was completely unversed in love's arts. Faced with likely defeat—and thus marriage, along with all his disciples—he devised a clever solution.

With his yogic vision, he spotted a recently deceased prince. Entering the prince's body, he revived it and lived in the palace, learning about sensual experience firsthand. So enthralled did he become, however, that he forgot his mission. Alarmed, his disciples sent someone to sing a sacred poem before him, reminding him of his true nature: not the pleasures of flesh, but pure awareness. Awakened once more, Śaṅkara returned to his body and resumed the debate—ultimately converting both the Brahmin and his wife, who became his disciples.

This tale, while rich in metaphor, also highlights that many such narratives are told from the male perspective—men seeking women for mystical and sensual power. Yet, feminine Tantra is not misogynistic. Women are essential, active participants. They are initiates, practitioners, chanters of *mantras*, and ritual leaders. Ideally, they are awakened beings.

Tantric texts describe different types of women, often referencing their physical traits, but also recognize their potential to become spiritual masters or reveal new scriptures. For instance, the *Brahma-yāmala Tantra* mentions by name the woman who "brought down" the teaching into the world, along with her male disciples.

Significantly, the tradition in which Niṣkriya (or Niṣkriyānanda) stands—that of Kālī—was first revealed by a woman, Maṅgalā, also known as "Madam M." Several female masters of the lineage are also remembered by name. This is not incidental—it reflects the very heart of the Yoginī tradition. In Kaula Tantra, it is said that a woman can achieve in one month what might take a man an entire year. Man and woman are equally consciousness, but only the woman can *embody* that consciousness through the act of creation and giving birth. In this sense, she *is* Śakti. The Yoginī path goes beyond simple equality—it honors the unique, sacred potency of the feminine, both in body and in spirit.

Such teachings may echo ancient intuitions found in other cultures, but Tantra is unique in stating them so clearly.

Just as the goal of entering another's body (*para-kāya-praveśa*) is not about some magical power, but aims at liberation by realizing that one is not just *this* body, so too is union with a Yoginī not about sensual gratification, but spiritual awakening.

Indeed, the *knowledge of non-action (niṣkriyā-jñāna)* at the heart of these translated texts emerges from just such an encounter (*melāpa*)—a meeting that transcends ordinary sexual union. As stated at the beginning of each teaching, the true aim is the reception of a wisdom that goes beyond form—an intimate communion with the infinite.

The Symbols of the Yoginīs

How does one encounter a Yoginī?

In the case of a fierce encounter, the practitioner must first protect themselves through mantras and ritual offerings—usually of strong drink—and perform the rite in a secluded location, ideally one known to be haunted by spirits and unseen forces. When the Yoginī is willing to appear (a process that, according to some texts, may take up to six months), she often manifests in the sky. The initiate, now facing the extraordinary, is asked to draw blood from his thigh. If the Yoginī accepts this deeply embodied offering, she grants him his desire, unites with him, or even lifts him into the celestial realms, where he becomes a *siddha*, a perfected being, endowed with magical abilities and spiritual realization. If not, he perishes—either consumed or drained by her.

In the case of a gentle encounter with a benevolent Yoginī, the practitioner may proceed freely, guided by pleasure (*kāma*)—a sacred expression of the divine source and a path back to it. Through union with his celestial consort, he may conceive a "child of the Yoginī" (*yoginī-bhū*), destined for enlightenment and communion with these sacred dancers. He may also receive powers or an initiatory transmission. This initiation occurs through the sharing of vital and bodily fluids. In this context, the transmission is quite literally "oral," as the Yoginī transmits from her *lower mouth* (*adho-vaktra*)—also referred to as the *mouth of the Yoginī* or *mouth of impurity* (*picu-vaktra*).

One key to this meeting is testing the practitioner's relation to what society calls "impure." If he hesitates, if disgust or doubt clouds him, it means the grace has not awakened in him—he remains bound to ordinary dualities. But if he unflinchingly drinks from a skull filled with wine and sexual fluids, he is deemed ready. In that moment, ideally, he attains instant spiritual awakening. He directly realizes that sexual power is not impure—it is life's own sacred force in its most immediate form. The divine is life itself; thus, how could sex be impure?

Beyond the act lies the deeper recognition: the individual soul (*jīva*, "that which lives") awakens to its divine essence—it perceives itself as the source of all, as creative power (*śakti*) freely manifesting. What exists is freedom, life, consciousness, creative flow. For this reason, practices alone cannot bring about awakening. Enlightenment is not a result of karma, merit, or personal purification. As Abhinavagupta explains in the *Tantrāloka*, liberation arises solely from the absolute freedom of divine consciousness—this immediate presence, undeniable and mysterious, beyond all causality.

But there is another essential condition for an encounter with the Yoginīs: knowing their secret symbols (*chummā*), the signs of recognition (*saṃketa*). Like branches of a cosmic tree or segments of a mandala, Yoginīs are grouped into various clans (*kula*), each with its own unique identity and corresponding emblem—like a spiritual password. As in Gnostic visions of astral realms, mistaking these signs can be deadly; the sorceresses of the sanctuary may devour or destroy any seeker, man or woman, who fails the test.

A Kaula scripture titled *Introduction to the Play of the Clan* (*Kula-krīḍā-avatāra*) declares: "Whoever knows the signs of recognition and enters the sanctuaries in search of supernatural powers or spiritual fulfillment (*siddhi*) will receive them, directly from the mouth of the Yoginī."

Another key passage from the *Ciñcinī-mata-sāra-samuccaya* (10.25) uses the term *melāpa*, which means "meeting," "feast," or "celebration," in close connection with *chummā*:
"My beloved, I shall now speak of another secret feast where the Yoginīs appear."[4]

This *melāpa* may be a group rite—an ecstatic banquet or orgiastic gathering, culminating in trance and bodily merging. But as we've seen, it can also be an intense solo encounter, a meeting with fierce Yoginīs after prolonged mantra recitation, often in cremation grounds at night. The practitioner offers food, drink, or ideally, his own blood—drawn from the left leg or arm. This act expresses the leap into the unknown that true awakening demands.

In return, the Yoginīs transmit the *chummās*, the hidden keys. The practitioner becomes a *Bhairava* or a *Rudra*—

---

[4] *punar anyaṃ pravakṣyāmi cchuṣmā (chummā) melāpakaṃ priye.*

fully awakened. In some accounts, he may even transform into a Yoginī himself (!). The tantra that details such rituals is known as *The King of Tantras* (*Tantra-rāja-tantra*), the most feminine of all tantric scriptures. Its deities are women, and it affirms that access to the Absolute comes through their grace.

Still, Abhinavagupta (in *Tantrāloka*, 28) distinguishes two kinds of *melāpa*:
– *Priya*—the "sweet" meeting, where the Yoginīs are desirable, gentle, and erotic in nature.
– *Haṭha*—the "fierce" meeting, in which the practitioner risks death or energetic consumption.

In both cases, knowing the *chummās* is essential—it's a matter of life and death. These signs correlate literally with the moon's phases and with Yoginī clans. But symbolically, they refer to:

1. the merging of sensory rays into the space of awareness, and
2. the fusion of physical forms into unity.

Thus, to meet a Yoginī is rare, dangerous, and sacred. But its reward is incomparable: absolute awakening.

The Tradition of Goddess Kālī

Within the Kaula stream, there are multiple branches—each aligned with a cardinal direction. According to the influential tantra *The Essence of the Tamarind Teaching*, four Kaula traditions exist. The *Oral Teaching of the Yoginīs* belongs to the northern tradition, associated with Kālī. It is the most secret, and the most centered on the feminine. Here, there is no longer a God, only the Goddess and her Yoginīs—the divine energies. For without the Goddess, God is nothing; he cannot even know himself.

This highest branch of the Tantric Tree is marked by several distinctive features:

1. It is transmitted orally.
2. It was revealed by women.
3. It includes both solitary and collective sexual yogas.
4. Its imagery is intense, even terrifying—especially in its depictions of Kālī (though you should note that the familiar icon of Kālī with the protruding tongue differs from the Kālī of the Yoginī tradition).
5. It is preserved in a unique set of texts—both tantras (a word that means literally "a book") and secret scriptures—such as *The Secret Signs/Sayings of the Yoginīs* (*Chummā-sampradāya*).
6. Its philosophy is non-dual and idealist ("all is consciousness"), but inclusive—embracing the body, the world, and women—unlike Advaita Vedānta, which excludes all three.

This tradition is known by several names:

- *Oral Transmission* (*mukha-āmnāya* or *vaktra-āgama*)
- *Kālī's Path* (*kālī-krama*, or simply *the Krama*)
- *The Complete Truth* (*mahā-artha*)
- *The Teaching of the Goddess* (*devī-naya*)
- *The Secret Tradition* (*rahasya-āmnāya*)
- *The Revelation of the Mistresses of the Sanctuary* (*pīṭha-īśvarī*), or of the Yoginīs
- *The Teaching* (*mata*)

- *The Tradition of the Secret Teachings* (*chummā-sampradāya*)

Its primary scriptures include:

1. **The Tantra-rāja-tantra** – "The King of Tantras" (24,000 verses), whose fourth section, *Mādhava-kula*, linked to Kṛṣṇa, is a separate tantra and a key source on sexual yoga.
2. **The Devī-pañca-śataka** – "The Five Hundred Verses of the Goddess," which also exists in shorter versions (250 verses, 150 verses), and the *Yoni-gahvara-tantra*, all of which describe a Kuṇḍalinī yoga based on inner Sun, Moon, and Fire, and the myth of Desire as the source of all.
3. **The Ūrmi-kaula-ārṇava** – "The Ocean of Energy and the Wave."
4. **Chapter 7 of *The Essence of the Tamarind Teaching*** (*Ciñcinī-mata-sāra-samuccaya*) – preserving two works by Niṣkriyānanda (not translated here) that detail the Cycle of the Goddess's Twelve Projections (*Kālikā-krama*), later foundational to Kashmir Śaivism.

Alongside these tantras are many poetic teachings and hymns passed down by realized masters.

To better navigate this vast lineage, the Tree of Tantras is shown here as a "map." At its summit—or root, form another angle—stands the tradition of Kālī or the Krama, the living core of the Goddess's revelation:

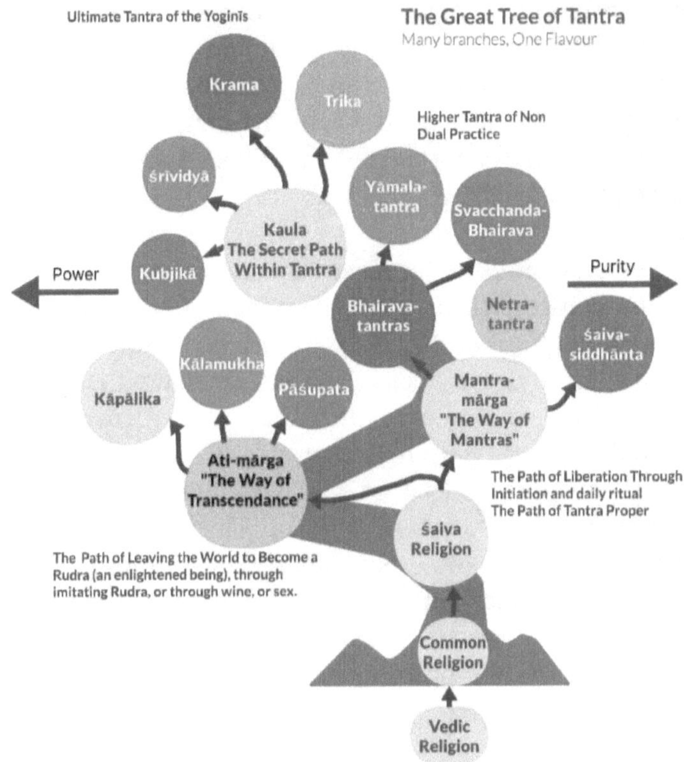

Sacred Wine or the Liquid Absolute

The Kaula tradition – of which the Kālī Yoginī Transmission is the highest branch - stands apart from more conventional forms of Tantra by placing emphasis not on external ritual, but on direct inner experience. That said, the historical development of Kaula traditions reveals that completely abandoning ritual was not easily achieved in the highly ritualized culture of India. Even yogic practice often becomes a form of internalized ritual—

mental offerings replace physical ceremonies, directed toward deities of the Tantric pantheon. Modern Kaula traditions like Śrīvidyā, with its famous *maṇḍala* of interlocked triangles, continue to maintain intricate and formalized rituals, comparable to those found in other Tantric paths.

However, within the broader Kaula stream, the Kālī tradition marks itself by a notable rejection of outer ritual. For example, the *Vijñāna-bhairava-tantra*, a foundational text of this lineage, declares in its opening that ritual practices are nothing more than "scarecrows for children"—empty activities for minds still caught in worldly concerns. Indeed, in Kālī's Tantra, one finds few of the standard elements of classical Tantra: no elaborate deity visualizations, no ornate *maṇḍalas*—at most, simple red or indigo circles drawn with powdered pigment. What does remain are *mantras* and *mudrās*—sacred sounds and symbolic gestures or postures that channel divine energy.

Over time, however, it seems that ritual forms crept back in. Surviving manuals of *Kālī-krama* liturgy demonstrate this return, though they continue to focus heavily on *mantras*, which remain central to all tantric systems. Tantra, after all, is often called the *path of mantras*, and its theology, metaphysics, and symbolism all revolve around these sacred utterances. Additionally, the Kālī tradition took root in southern India, particularly in Kerala, where thirteen temples correspond to the thirteen forms of Kālī. While rituals are performed at these sites, the original emphasis on inner realization appears to have faded in many local expressions of the tradition.

Regardless of these evolutions, Kaula Tantra retains its ceremonial aspect, especially in the form of the "three mysteries" (*brahman*). These are frequently referenced in the texts translated here. The three are wine, meat, and sexual union—called *brahman* because each one reflects an aspect of expanded consciousness. Practitioners of these mysteries are known as *brahmacārīs*, reinterpreting a term that, in orthodox contexts, implies celibacy, but here means the exact opposite.

Among the three, wine occupies a central place. The Yoginīs themselves declare, "The wine of the Kula must be drunk." But what is meant by this?

The Kaula Kālī Tradition of the Yoginī passes down grace through three modes:

1. direct, wordless transmission;
2. oral instruction; and
3. ritual initiation.

This third form of transmission revolves around the three sacred substances—sexual fluids, meat, and wine—the expansive manifestations of divine awareness. Sexual fluid represents the *effect* of this expansion—the blossoming of embodied consciousness. Meat and wine are its *causes*, since *brahman* in this context is the unfolding of awareness as delight (*ānanda*). Strictly speaking, all three are facets of one reality: *brahman* is expansion, is consciousness, is bliss.

If wine is unavailable, one may substitute it with other fermented drinks—made from barley, honey, or sugarcane—though wine remains the ideal. It is known as the "nectar of the left-hand path," associated with the Goddess (*vāmā*, both beautiful and sinister), into which the sexual fluids of both partners are immersed and which is then used to anoint the ground, the *maṇḍala*, and ritual implements—bells, vessels, ladles, incense burners. In

Tantric texts, wine is exalted as the divine in liquid form, the *absolute* that can be tasted.

Originating from the Caucasus region, wine found its way to India and came to occupy a central role in non-dual Tantra. One scripture puts it plainly: "In this (Kaula) rite, the wise will use substances forbidden in all other paths, soaked in the Nectar of the Left."[5] This nectar—*amṛta*—is none other than wine. The Kaula tradition affirms that while other substances (like beer or mead) are acceptable, wine alone is the shining radiance of divine energy, free from limiting beliefs. It is pure nectar, overflowing with conscious pleasure and light.

Thus, every initiate is obliged to drink it. Failing to partake at least once monthly on a sacred day is grounds for losing one's initiation and returning to a profane state. Failing to drink daily requires atonement. "The best," the texts say, "is to drink each day."[6] Wine is not optional; it is consciousness made drinkable. One can perform the worship of awareness using wine alone—but not without it. Importantly, only fermented drinks are permitted. Distilled spirits are never mentioned.

On this foundation, wine becomes a living metaphor for the nourishing, intoxicating power of awakened consciousness. Just as wine dissolves inhibition, the turning of awareness back onto itself dissolves limitation. Without trying to fix or improve the body, it is transformed—becoming divine, fluid, radiant, and free. It is for this reason the Yoginīs insist: drink the wine.

---

[5] *Tantrāloka* 29, 10.
[6] Quoted by Jayaratha *ad Tantrāloka* 29, 11-13.

Sacred Touch – The Essence of the Goddess Path

Sparśa, or touch, lies at the very heart of the Kaula tradition. But what does this truly mean? What role does touch play in this lineage that prioritizes direct experience over intellectual or ritual formalism? Let us explore a few reflections—grounded in precise references (don't be daunted by the Sanskrit!)—because much confusion and even falsehood circulates today around the so-called "Tantric touch." My aim is not to criticize in detail what is now promoted as "Kashmir massage" or "Kashmir yoga," two expressions that, to my knowledge, have no roots in authentic Tantra. Rather, I want to clarify the profound and specific importance of touch within Tantra—especially in the path of the Goddess.

In a now-famous passage, Abhinavagupta—the great synthesizer of Tantra, Kaula, and its two main streams, Trika and Krama—states that, unlike the other senses, touch never obstructs the expansion of consciousness.

Indeed, as the inner energy awakens, each sense can generate divine sensations: colors, radiant forms, fragrances, celestial sounds, extraordinary tastes. While these experiences can briefly draw the practitioner inward, they eventually become distractions—the mind clings to them, and expansion halts. Even Patañjali, the classical author of the *Yoga Sūtras*, recognized this dynamic. Meditation is thus a useful method, but it can also become a mirror of illusions.

Touch, however, is different. It supports consciousness in its unfolding. This is because it is not separate from the vibratory field that is the very body of awareness. One of the first signs of awakening is often described as the sensation of an ant crawling across the skin. Furthermore, touch plays a central role in "sexual yoga," referred to as the "primordial sacrifice" (*ādi-yāga*) or the "secret practice" (*rahasya-caryā*). One of the unique paradoxes of this path is that it honors both the intimacy of touch—especially erotic touch—and the transcendence of all contact, the pure sensation of boundless, ungraspable awareness.

Yet these are not separate: sexual touch and the felt sense of consciousness itself arise from the same pulse (*spanda*), like waves on a single sea. That vibration is Consciousness, the Goddess. In Sanskrit, *sparśa* means not just touch, but also sensation, whether pleasant or painful. It does not only refer to contact between two surfaces—it can also be "non-dual," a spontaneous shiver of life itself, the living pulse of Presence projecting herself into her own infinite space.

Another metaphor for this subtle feeling is *anāhata*—the "unstruck sound"—which also appears in the oral teachings of the Yoginīs. According to the *Kramasadbhāva Tantra* (2.86a):
"The supreme awareness of touch is revealed in the sacred banquet (*melāpa*, shared by the Yoginīs and Kaula adepts)."[7]

When *sparśa* is paired with a negation (e.g., *a-sparśa*), it typically refers to the inner space of awareness—the void that is both origin and container of all phenomena, all feelings. This motif appears repeatedly in the *Chummās*:

- In *chummā* 79, the dissolution of all things is described as "terrifying within the sky of ultimate non-sensation."[8]

---

[7] *melāpe militā sā vai sparśasya paramā citiḥ.*
[8] *bhīmam asparśa-parama-ambare.*

- In 14, the "wine of the Kula" is "not the result of ordinary contact."
- In 52, tactile experience becomes an entryway to mystical freedom: "for one who is absorbed in the sensation of total awareness."[9]
- In 55, consciousness is defined as a "powerful sensation."[10]
- In the final *chummā*, number 104, duality vanishes in a state "beyond all contact": "beyond sensation, untouched, without even the slightest trace of duality."[11]
- And in the text's closing lines, the Absolute is described as "the unfolding of a contactless sensation, the original Ground"[12].

Thus, *sparśa* joins both meanings: literal touch and inner sensation. In the *Ciñcinīmāta*, a treasure trove for the *Kālīkrama* teachings, Kaula practice is described as "immersed in the vibrant flow of felt nectar, without needing physical penetration."[13]

Initiation "eternally bestows the grace of realization; it is divine sensation itself."[14]

In the *Kaula Sūtras*, the sage Durvāsa—understood to be a form of Rudra or Śiva—is described as *sparśa-kāmasūḥ*—"one who fulfills all desires through a (simple) touch."

In the more rhetorically refined anonymous *Mahā-naya-prakāśa*, consciousness is described as "a wondrous astonishment of transcendent bliss, born of pure

---

[9] *mahā-vimarśa-saṃsparśa-samāviśtasya.*

[10] *sparśa-vibhavā.*

[11] *asparśe sparśa-hnutā svalpa-asaṃparkato 'bhitaḥ.*

[12] *a-sparśa-sparśa-vistāram adhiṣṭhānam apūrvakam.*

[13] *nirāveśa-sparśa-rasa-spanda-nisyanda-kandarā.*

[14] *ājñā-siddhi-pradaṃ nityaṃ divya-sparśa-svarūpakam* (9.103).

sensation."[15]
It "devours duality through inward touch"[16].

This advanced teaching presents *sparśa* as an intermediary experience—between the world of limitation and fully awakened consciousness. It is the true aim of so-called orgiastic rituals, of which "the point is the transcendence of both visual and tactile pleasure."[17] This work ultimately critiques sexual yoga, seeing it as a teaching aid, a lesser trick for those not yet able to grasp higher truths.

In the older *Mahā-naya-prakāśa* of Arṇasiṃha, the goddesses are the divinized senses—each wave of perception a ripple of conscious energy:
"The goddesses appear in sequence within the vast, unfathomable ocean, clearly visible as the waves of conscious sensation"[18].

As *Khecarī*, the freely moving goddess, she is "the sensation that moves through the sky of awareness, without fixed dwelling, entirely naked: such is the mudrā called Khecarī"[19].

Ultimately, the goddesses are described as:
"always manifesting in the center of the state beyond contact"[20],
and our true nature is:

---

[15] *tan-maya-sparśāt parānanda-camatkṛtiḥ* (1.15).
[16] *bhakṣayaty āntara-sparśād* (2.23).
[17] *darśana-sparśa-sambhoga-virāma-udrekataḥ—*.
[18] *itthaṃ devyo nirāveśa-mahārṇava-kramoditāḥ| tattvataḥ sparśa-saṃvitti-laharyām antare sphuṭam* v. 37.
[19] *yā sparśā sparśa-gagane carantī nirniketanā | sarvāvaraṇa-nirmuktā mudrā sā khecarī smṛtā* v. 102.
[20] *devyaḥ prathante satatam asparśa-pada-madhyagāḥ* (v. 181).

"beyond both touch and its absence, transcending even the absolute."[21]

Finally, the *Vātūlanātha Sūtras* (3) confirm that the Absolute is total freedom because it is "utterly untouched by either sensation or its absence"[22].

Thus, in essence, sacred touch—*sparśa*—is the living heart of the Goddess's path.
It propels the practitioner into the current of awakened consciousness and eventually carries them beyond all form, into an experience so intimate and expansive that it defies all naming.

The Death of Death, the Swallowing of Time

When I asked one of my masters why Benares was so sacred, he answered that it is because it is the city of Death. And, I must say, corpses (both human and non-human) are everywhere. But Death is liberation, freedom from grasping and self-identification. That is why the Cit of Death is the City of Liberation.

In the secret teachings of the Yoginīs, emphasis falls not on creation but on dissolution: Death. While the other major Kaula tradition, *Trika*, celebrates emergence and manifestation, the path explored in the text we translate here points resolutely toward absorption and withdrawal. Awakening, in this lineage, is described as the death of Death itself.

---

[21] *sparśāsparśa-padātīta-rūpatvād vigatottaraḥ* (v. 223).
[22] *sparśāsparśa-prathā-parivarjitopacārāt.*

Consciousness is, by nature, evanescent—it consumes the very phenomena it gives rise to. Inhalation absorbs exhalation; exhalation dissolves into silence. The sun consumes the moon, day overtakes night, and this cycle repeats in countless ways. When consciousness fully awakens, it devours even impermanence—it *swallows the act of swallowing*. Time, the great devourer of all, is itself absorbed. Mental constructs, choices, hesitations, and moral dilemmas (*vikalpa*) are incinerated in the fire of blossoming awareness.

All things are burned away—in other words, as Kṣemarāja explains, "everything is digested as the Self" (*ātmā-sākṣāt-kṛta*), just as fire transforms wood into its own nature. Consciousness is inherently oriented toward awakening; it is compelled to digest, assimilate, and return all things to itself. Its essence is *to devour* (*grāsa-ghasmara*). Between ordinary and awakened consciousness, the difference is not one of kind, but of intensity—yet in both states, consciousness continuously "feeds" on experience. Every moment is both emergence and disappearance. To perceive something is to erase everything else. The birth of one object implies the dissolution of others. This *disappearance* is their reabsorption into the unified field of awareness.

For instance, when I focus on a conversation in a café, all other noises recede. This fading is not annihilation—it is their return to the ocean of consciousness, like waves falling back.

Yet so long as one remains unenlightened, the same patterns re-emerge again and again. This is *saṃsāra*, the painful cycle of birth and rebirth. One might, following the metaphor of fire or digestion, assume that once all fuel is consumed, the flame dies. But consciousness, though it extinguishes everything within it, cannot itself be extinguished—for, who would remain to witness its end?

The Teaching of A, the Path of A, and the Power of Negation

Beyond its daring rituals and symbolic transgressions, the Kaula tradition—and its highest expression in the path of Kālī—delivers a profound teaching of awakening. But awakening to what? To the recognition of our essential nature, and that of all things. The world, the body, the senses, and even thought: everything is consciousness. This consciousness is not static—it is a dynamic intelligence that creates the ceaseless cycles of arising and dissolution.

To do so, it plays a cosmic game: it forgets itself. It denies its wholeness in order to appear as fragment—identified with "this" body, caught in a world that seems separate. In other words, we are the infinite Being that has chosen, in freedom, to mask itself in limitation.

How is such a paradox possible? Because consciousness is not merely light—it is power in motion. It is the freedom (*svātantrya*) to do what seems utterly impossible. As the Kashmiri masters say in the traditions of *Spanda* and *Pratyabhijñā*, consciousness has the power to appear as absent, even though that very absence is only possible through its presence! This paradox—of being and seeming not to be—lies at the heart of Tantric insight. It is also what gives rise to wonder.

According to the Yoginīs, *camatkāra*—the awe-filled thrill of recognition—is the essence of experience. In Tantric philosophy, even while we are caught in the illusion of being a limited individual, something in us always knows that we are more. We pretend not to know, but the knowing never leaves. This "conscious forgetting" is also the mechanism of imagination, of fiction, of play. Just as we can immerse ourselves in a story while still knowing it's not real, so too we live our lives with a silent background awareness that there is more—something fuller, more intimate, just beyond reach.

This sense of the beyond, of an ungraspable presence behind all phenomena—even pain—is called *ānanda*, bliss, and *camatkāra*, the ecstatic "yes" of consciousness to its own self-discovery through the unending highs and lows of life. These terms, found throughout the Yoginī teachings, later became central in the Kashmiri Shaiva tradition, especially in the work of Abhinavagupta.

It should by now evident that many key concepts of Kashmiri non-dualism, once thought to originate in Kashmir, were already fully developed in the earlier and more secretive Kālī tradition. *Spanda* (vibration), *camatkāra* (delight), and even the framework of *pratyabhijñā* (recognition) all appear in these earlier Yoginī texts.

One core symbol of this teaching is the Sanskrit letter A— both a phoneme and a metaphysical key. Several Yoginī aphorisms (called *chummās*, or sometimes *sūtras*) refer to the A, not just as a sound, but as a doorway to the unspeakable. The word *a-kathya*, often translated as "indescribable," can also mean "that which is to be spoken through the A." In this way, the A becomes the cipher of the Absolute.

The A is the first sound in the Sanskrit alphabet. And Sanskrit, in the Tantric worldview, is not an ordinary language. It is the crystallized vibration of divine speech—the very breath of awakened awareness. In the Kaula branch called *Trika*, the alphabet itself is seen as the matrix of all mantras, the source not only of language but of manifestation itself.

Each sound of the alphabet is traditionally classified according to its point of articulation in the mouth. All phonemes are expelled breath, originating in the chest—symbolic of the heart, the eternal core of consciousness. The closer a sound is to the heart, the less differentiated it is. And so, the sound A is the least formed, the most essential—it is pure, unmodified breath. It represents consciousness in its original fullness: Being that is aware of itself as all beings.

Śiva (being) and Śakti (awareness) are not two, but one, just as flame and heat are inseparable. The A gives voice to this wholeness without break.

Yet this Absolute is not static. Unlike inert objects—fixed and unchanging—consciousness can shift, evolve, and take on infinite forms without ever ceasing to be itself. When I perceive a landscape or undergo transformation, the "I" remains. This power of change without loss is called *svātantrya*, the freedom to manifest without dependence. The term itself fuses *sva* (self), *tan-* (expansion) and *-tra* (instrument, tool). It is the power of self-expression that depends on nothing but itself. According to the Tradition, this is what we are living just now, but without realizing it fully.

Thus, the A becomes a seed-mantra (*bīja*) containing the whole of reality – and beyond. Just as the peacock's egg holds in potential the intricate patterns of its future feathers, so too the A holds all phenomena within it. In the *Bhagavad-gītā*, Krishna declares, "Among sounds, I am the A." And while Krishna is typically seen as an avatar of Viṣṇu, in the Kālī tradition he is understood as an emanation of the Goddess herself. The *Mādhava-kula Tantra*, a core text of this path, depicts the divine as Narasiṃha, the Man-Lion form of Viṣṇu, and his consort as Lakṣmī—the abundance at the heart of all things. From this perspective, the famous *Gītā* is a Yoginī scripture!

The Goddess has many names, yet one of her most profound is *A-nāmā*—She whose name is A, or more precisely, She who has no name. She is the unsayable (*An-ākhyā*), the one who eludes capture in language. As the philosopher Henri Bergson said of the mystical: it cannot be said, and yet we cannot stop speaking of it. So we speak in negations. Thus, the Goddess is "She who cannot be spoken"—yet who calls forth all speech.

In this way, A is not just a sound. It is the silent womb of language, the matrix of manifestation, the gateway to mystery.

Remarkably, this symbol also appears at the heart of Buddhist tradition. In Mahāyāna Buddhism, the ultimate reality is vast, indivisible space—radiant and without edge. It is symbolized by A. One version of the *Heart Sūtra*, a central Mahāyāna text, consists of just one letter. You've guessed which one: A. It represents the *dharma-dhātu*, the field from which all things arise.

The meditation on A continues today in Japanese esoteric Buddhism, known as *Ajikan*—"the contemplation of A." Practitioners visualize a black A inscribed inside a white moon, written in a script derived from ancient Indian calligraphy. In *Dzogchen*, a Tibetan tradition closely aligned with the teachings of Kālī, the A similarly symbolizes the absolute. It appears in the *guru yoga* practice, where the disciple merges with the awakened state of the teacher.

And so we might ask: If A is so central in both traditions, did Buddhism influence the Yoginī path? Or was it the other way around? This rich and provocative question is where we now turn.

Buddhist Influence?

The identity of Tantra lies more in its symbols than in fixed dogmas. Buddhism, conversely, draws its core identity primarily from doctrinal positions rather than symbolic imagery. As such, it has historically found it easier to incorporate non-Buddhist symbols while resisting external dogmatic frameworks. Most notably, the concept of a permanent Self—arguably a necessary metaphysical postulate—has never been fully absorbed into Buddhist thought, precisely because its foundational principle is that of *an-ātman*, or non-self: no abiding self, no stable identity exists in persons or in things. Reality is a flux of momentary phenomena—ephemeral yet complete in each instant, like flashes of total presence that vanish as they arise.

This essential Buddhist idea has been expressed in many ways, likely because it is inherently challenging. If there is no intrinsic nature anywhere, only fleeting appearances, then language and meaning lose footing... Concepts become mental constructions—shared delusions, hallucinated consensus. Some Buddhist thinkers even questioned whether the notion of "otherness" itself holds any ground. Everything arises dependent on everything else, like reflections in a hall of mirrors. This is the heart of *śūnyatā*, the doctrine of interdependent emptiness.

One of the key formulations of this idea is *niḥ-svabhāva*—"without inherent existence" or "absence of self-nature"—alongside *niḥ-svarūpa*, "without self-essence." Paradoxically, these terms define Buddhism precisely through the assertion that nothing has definable essence. No other Indian tradition has adopted these expressions; even concepts like *nirvāṇa*, often misunderstood, found broader acceptance.

It is thus startling to find these very expressions appearing in the teachings of the Yoginī Kālī—in the voice of the supreme Goddess herself, within the most esoteric, intimate oral transmission, one even said to elude the awareness of Eternal Śiva himself...

How is this possible?

Indeed, some of the most characteristically Buddhist language is found in the texts of the Kālī tradition—and virtually nowhere else in the Indian Tantric corpus. Take, for instance, this verse from the *Devī-dvyardhaśatikā*, a scripture of the Kālī Tradition:

"Consciousness that is not an object of knowledge, that devours time, is present in all things in the form of Time.

A state of emptiness, she is No-self, the entry into the state of repose twelve finger-widths above the fontanelle. "[23]

The term *nair-ātmikā*—formed from *nir-ātmā*, a variant of *an-ātmā*—is one of the doctrinal pillars of Buddhism. You can scarcely find a more explicitly Buddhist expression.

Much of the vocabulary throughout the Kālī tradition echoes *Yogācāra* or Buddhist idealism, in which "everything is mind" (*citta-mātra*). This mind, however, is not a static awareness but a flowing stream—a dynamic flux. And this is precisely what the Yoginīs teach: consciousness is a living flow, a *krama* (a sequence or progression), which is also the name of the Goddess's tradition. Consciousness is not an inert substance but a self-renewing process. Its identity (*ātman*) is to be *without fixed identity*—to remain unfixed, uncontained. It shapes itself into bodies and thoughts, yet remains free to disidentify at any moment. Thus, consciousness manifests moment to moment, always afresh.

From this, we find verses in the Yoginī teachings that could easily be mistaken for Buddhist Tantras:

"(Consciousness) dwells in the transcendent union of pairs of opposites, which unfold as subject and object — the equality found in the fusion of sexual fluids within the ebb and flow of the great embrace."[24]

But the influence cuts both ways. As Professor Alexis Sanderson has shown, the higher one climbs in the

---

[23] *cidam aprameyāṃ samastabhāvāntare kālarūpām* || *129* || **nairātmikāṃ** **śūnya**pada *yātāṃ dviṣaṭkaviśrāmapade praviṣṭām|*

[24] *grāhyagrāhakavisphāradvandvamelāpake pare |* *mahāmaithunasaṃghaṭṭasāmarasyapade same* || *47* ||.

hierarchy of Buddhist Tantras, the deeper the Kaula influence becomes. For instance, in *Mahāmudrā*—perhaps the most refined Buddhist Tantric teaching—the presence of Kaula elements is unmistakable. A verse by a Kashmiri Buddhist monk reads:

"Ha! Conquering all objects,
The consciousness of the five gates (the senses)
Is from the beginning without form—
The mighty Lāmā, pure innate ecstasy (*sahaja*)."[25]

This could easily be rendered into Yoginī Kālī language by simply substituting *sāhasa* ("spontaneous", "unexpected") for *sahaja*.

Notably, this Buddhist phrase *niḥ-svabhāva*—"without intrinsic nature"—is rejected by Abhinavagupta, the most influential philosopher of Tantric Śaivism[26]. Yet in the Yoginī tradition, it appears prominently:

"The sages declare that the Transcendent is always realized and devoid of self-nature.
'I am That'—through this realization, one enters That."
(Chummā 74)

Although this expression does not occur in the *Chummās* themselves, it does appear in the *Ciñcinīmata-sāra-samuccaya*, a core Kaula text transmitting the Kālī teachings in its Chapter Seven. There, we read:

---

[25] From the *Seven Branches of Awakening*, attributed to the Kashmiri monk Śākyaśrībhadra, as found in the *Collection of the Seventh Karmapa*, text 52, and translated from Tibetan by Karl Brunnhölzl in *Sounds of Innate Freedom*, vol. 3, p. 172, translation modified. Note that this poem is different form the Mahāyāna poem attributed to that same master.
[26] *Vimarśinī* on kārikās 2, 4, and 10: *na hi niḥsvabhāvaṃ vastu bhavati* — "For a thing without an inherent nature does not exist."

"Without form, she perceives the complete destruction of all phenomena in sequence.
She is known as the 'empty womb surrounded by rays of the sun.'
She is (empty) because **she has no self-nature**."[27]

Here, consciousness is the fertile void from which all appears. Though infinitely generative, it remains ever-clear, ungrasped, and unchanging in essence. Realizing this is to awaken beyond death and time, because this consciousness—this unbounded presence—is who we truly are.

This vision also echoes Buddhist teachings on the "reality beyond being and non-being." Things are not *being*, because they vanish like dreams. Yet they are not *non-being* either, since they appear vividly. Consciousness, too, is neither material being nor a pure void: she shines (*prakāśa*) as lucidity herself and as everything. Symbolically, she is "hungry" (*kṛśā*), never confined by any appearance; yet she is also "full" (*pūrṇā*), as she contains all phenomena within herself.

Thus, consciousness is beyond the binary of "existence or non-existence". Rather, she is synthesis, "this *and* that". Utpaladeva, great Tantric philosopher and Krama adept, wrote:

"It is true that all things follow one of two paths: to be or not to be.

---

[27] *bhāvābhāvakṣayakṣīṇaṃ yaś cinoty aśarīriṇaḥ | sā cidā* **niḥsvabhāvatvād** *sūryakulakṛṣodarī || 7/171.*

But I bow to the Third Path, the marvelous, the Auspicious One (Śiva)!"[28]

Abhinavagupta echoes this: the union of fire and water, impossible in the physical realm, is made possible in consciousness. We can effortlessly imagine a liquid fire. Why? Because consciousness knows both presence and absence—it is the luminous ground of all dualities.

And this same radical notion—*niḥ-svabhāva*—is explicitly stated in the *Kaula Sūtras*, the pith teachings of the Yoginīs:

"The final state of consciousness and of phenomena is the absence of inherent nature." (*Kaula Sūtra* 50)[29]

Nowhere else in Indian Śaiva or Śākta traditions (centered on Śakti, the Goddess) is this Buddhist insight affirmed so directly. This verse alone would lead a reader to assume the teaching was Buddhist—this is perhaps why Śivopādhyāya, a 17th-century Tantric scholar, felt compelled to reframe the *Vijñāna Bhairava Tantra* (which draws on Yoginī teachings) in non-Buddhist terms. He even went so far as to reinterpret the Buddhist Perfect Wisdom (*Prajñāpāramitā*) as an embodiment of Kālī herself.

The *Kramasadbhāva Tantra*—a central Kālī text—uses *niḥ-svabhāva* six times, including this line:

---

[28] *Hymns to Shiva* 3, 1.
[29] *bhāvabhūtasaṃvidām ante* **niḥsvabhāvatā**paryavasānam || 50 ||.

"Behold the ungraspable, untouched space of absence of essence!"[30]

And in the *Mahānaya Prakāśa* of Arṇasiṃha, we read that the Absolute:

"sustains the essence of awakening (*unmeṣa*), peerless and devoid of self-nature."[31]

From all this, we may say the following: Buddhism offered India a radical vision—one that challenged essentialist metaphysics and shook Hinduism from its dogmatic slumber. Tantra, in turn, took this insight and refined it, integrating it into a vision that remained faithful to its own experiential and symbolic spirit. This dynamic interplay between rival traditions is not incidental—it reflects the deeper play of consciousness as it explores itself through denial and discovery.

On a personal level, we too confront this drama. As Jung described, we all wrestle with our "shadow"—the inner resistance to owning our divine potential. Like Sartre's notion of "bad faith", we sabotage ourselves, evading the freedom we fear. We blame karma, fate, trauma. We become clever at defending our limitations.

Tantra personifies these conflicting energies as Yoginīs—ambivalent forces that can either uplift or obstruct us. To ignore them is to remain powerless. To know them is to reclaim our wholeness. Yoga, from *yuj*, "to unite," is this reintegration. And as the philosophy of Recognition

---

[30] *niḥsvabhāvanibhau paśya nirlakṣaṃ niṣprayojanam* || 3, 93a ||.

[31] *niḥsvabhāvaniraupamyaparonmeṣasvarūpabhṛt* || *182* ||.

(*Pratyabhijñā*) insists: nonduality cannot be realized without first facing duality—our own inner split.

Only a sacred marriage—*a fire-union*—can transmute our shadow into embodied wisdom. This union is called *kula*—the sacred family, the totality of being. Hence the *Kaula* tradition invites us to move beyond the sterile pursuit of purity—whether physical, moral, or ideological—and embrace instead the harmony of the reconciled Yoginīs.

This balance, *khecarī-samatā*—equanimity in the open space of awareness—is also a reconciliation with the masculine, the realm of outer form. Then, and only then, union arises—limitless, ecstatic, free from confusion. A blissful knowing we are forever invited to taste.

To summarize:

Even though Buddhism borrowed symbols, rituals, and practices from Tantra, it also left a lasting impact on the Kālī tradition, which later gave rise to Kashmir Śaivism. Among the shared insights:

- All is consciousness.
- Reality is a projection of consciousness, like a dream.
- Subject and object duality can be transcended.
- Consciousness is without fixed nature—clear and spacious like the sky.
- It is neither being nor non-being, but lucidity itself.
- Tantra replaces the pursuit of purity with the quest for integration.

Dissolution and the Transcendence of Opposites

Since consciousness is devoid of fixed structure, without any inherent form, and escapes all definitions and imagery, it follows that the tradition centers its focus on emptiness and dissolution.

The theme of dissolution arises from the very first *chummā*. All modes of knowing (*jñāna*)—whether perceptions or thoughts—are said to dissolve into the ultimate, intangible space. Ordinary life is viewed as a contraction—a crystallization of energies such as fear, doubt, and guilt. The dissolution of these demonesses becomes an expansion into the open sky of Presence, untouched and pure.

Yet, negating duality is not enough, for what is merely excluded returns all the stronger. The more one reacts to one's reactions, the more one is entangled in their inertia. As the Krama master Rāma declares, "The mountain of duality is hard as diamond! Even perfect concentration cannot destroy it."

So what then is the way through? Love. Only love—the power to unify—can reconcile the Yoginīs in conflict, along with the polarities of masculine and feminine, subject and object. Love-making becomes the sole action that has the capacity to tame or transmute these inner demons, for their life depends on our unconsciousness. Union of awareness and space is love-making, is union, yoga.

But where do these conflicting forces originate, if all arises from the same consciousness?

Consciousness manifests. And in what form? In all forms, and their opposites. It arises as both presence and absence, as creation and reabsorption. Therefore, it transcends every polarity. It is the essence of all things, yet reducible to none. Thus, it stands beyond the deepest division: that between "my body" and "the world," between the perceiving self and the perceived object.

"There exists a constant relation
Between subjectivity and objectivity.
All this dissolves
Into egoless awareness.

In the crystal-clear omnipresent space
That truly lies beyond all things.
This absolute relationship is called
'Non-relation', for it never fluctuates."
(*ad Chummās 51*)

Once more, the words of Utpaladeva, the great Tantric philosopher, echo this vision:

"What is not must differ from what is.
Being is distinct from non-being, O Lord!
But You are beyond both being and non-being—
You are their hidden essence."[32]

This "2+1" schema lies at the heart of Indian spiritual thought. It invites us to move beyond binary thinking—*either/or*—into a dialectic of *both/and*: the ternary rhythm of thesis, antithesis, and synthesis.

In the West, this mode of thought is reflected in the Christian Trinity, itself inspired by the Greek philosopher

---

[32] *Hymns* 3, 18.

Proclus and the Platonic lineage. In India, it finds its most refined expression in nondual Tantra, with Krama as its secret root. Why is this important? Because thought naturally locks itself into false dilemmas—dead-end binaries that obscure deeper truths. Like a merchant pressing you with, "Take it or leave it!"

But distinctions are essential! Simply rejecting dualism isn't enough. That, too, becomes a form of dualism: opposing binary and non-binary thinking. To exclude an opposite is to remain caught within the pair. The harder you try to escape, the deeper you sink—like struggling in quicksand. The only way out is through integration: to include the opposite, to see duality as the dance of unity. This is the key secret of Tantric philosophy, as preserved by the Yoginīs.

Practically speaking, the body can only be transcended by passing through it. And this is precisely what life itself does—life, another name for consciousness, which roots itself in embodiment yet is never limited by it. When a couple gives birth to a child, that life exceeds them, without denying them. This explains one of the profound enigmas of this teaching: why is sexual yoga *commanded* (not merely proposed), even though the body is eventually to be transcended like an inert skeleton? Because the power to surpass the body originates within it—just as the seed contains the full-grown tree that surpasses it while including it. Awakening is an expansion, not a rejection. The energy of awakening flows in continuity with sexual energy—one movement unfolding in successive phases.

This vision—integrative, inclusive—is the ideal of the Kālī tradition: a total transformation of self and world into a dance of space-born energies, at once utterly simple and infinitely fecund. Consciousness is me, is us. And consciousness is absolute freedom—boundless, limit-transcending. But with such freedom comes the possibility of collapse, of falling into infinite prisons. That is *saṃsāra*, the ongoing cycle of joys and sorrows, the torment of being torn by what we do not fully know. Hence the necessity of awakening—of pursuing knowledge to its end: love. Perhaps pure love is the only true purity.

This is why the oral teachings overflow with paradoxes—sleeping awakenings, luminous shadows, overfull emptiness. The most essential text here is *The Secret Sayings of the Yoginī*, the *Chummās*. Paradox becomes the very language of awakening, for the Goddess is both one and many, yet also beyond both. The Yoginīs themselves—*they/she*—use all grammatical genders in their speech, flowing from masculine to feminine to neuter within a single phrase. Let us now turn to this living breath, still warm from the mouths of the Yoginīs. But don't expect secrets you can memorize or recite. Only the heart speaks to the heart. And the only secrets that escape are those whispered by lovers' lips.

In conclusion, it's worth pausing to note a striking echo of this feminine transmission in an enigmatic text from our own Western heritage. In 1945, a sealed library was discovered in Egypt: over fifty texts in Coptic, originally written in Greek. Among them, near a passage from Plato's *Republic*, appeared an astonishing work titled *The Thunder, Perfect Mind*. Across ten pages, the Nameless Goddess proclaims herself through the transcendence of all opposites:

"I am the one who is honoured
And the one who is scorned.
I am the whore and the holy one.
I am the wife and the virgin.

Attend to my poverty and to my wealth!
I am the foolish and the wise.
I am the essence and the one without essence.
I am union and dissolution.
I am what everyone hears,
And I am the speech no one can grasp."

The same teaching shines through: a naked Presence, everywhere, expressing itself through the very opposites that conceal it. Like the Nameless Yoginī, *Anāmā*, this Goddess speaks not her name. Astonishing, the resonance across centuries and continents! And with this mystery as our threshold, we step into the sanctuary of the primal forces of truth, beauty, and goodness.

Translation

The Frame Story: Metting of Nishkriya with the Silent Master

[33]*...(ta)ddṛkpātamahodayāt | bhūmau sampatitaḥ kṣiprāc*

chinnamūla iva drumaḥ ||

... because of the power of his gaze falling (upon me)[34],
I fell quickly on the earth
like a tree cut at its root[35].

---

[33] The Berlin ms starts at folio 2r, the first folio is missing.

[34] Beside *śakti-pāta, dṛk-pāta*, the power of the gaze of the master, is a power of awakening in the Kālī-krama. See, for example: *gurudṛkpātasāhasāt | pīṭhakramādau sarvatra viśuddhistasya jāyate* (*Mahānayaprakāśa* I, 16), « For this (disciple), absolute purity is born in all the (cycles of consciousness) like the pīṭhas and so on, from the sudden/violent power of the gaze of the guru. » *gurudṛkpātapātrāṇāṃ samśayatrāsavicchide* (*Mahānayaprakāśa* VI, 25b) : « (This teaching) cuts the fear of the doubts of those worthy vessels who receive the powerful gaze of the guru. » The liberating power of the guru's glance, or of a siddha, a yoginī, or of any deity, is considered a direct cause of liberation. To receive the gaze of a liberated being is liberating. Jayaratha mentions it as a mean belonging to the 'no mean' (*anupāya*) category of means, along with receiving an impure and powerful substance. One may thus be liberated by sight, taste, touch, sound or smell. See *Tantrāloka* translated by Mark Dyczkowski, vol. two, chapter two, p. 3, note 6. There, Dyczkowski offers a long and fascinating account of this direct, embodied mean of awakening, from Patañjali to Swami Lakshmanjoo. See also the PhD thesis of Christopher Wallis *To Enter, to be entered, to merge: The role of religious experience in the tradition of Tantric Shaivism*. Like *āveśa*, which can be taken in both directions 'to enter' or 'to be entered', this gaze is liberating both when one is looked at by a liberated one, and when one looks at such a one. Action and passion are both causes of direct awakening. This may also be connected with the important practice of sky-gazing, taught in the *Vijñānabhairavatantra* and others, and found here when Siddhanātha gazes 'upward' to the sky where the Goddess appears. This 'steady' gaze is also certainly related to the practice of *bhairavīmudrā*.

[35] This expression is also found in *Devīdvyardhaśatika*, 191a : *tatkṣaṇāt patate bhūmau **chinnamūla iva drumaḥ**|*, in the context of describing the "piercing initiation" (*vedha-dīkṣā*).

niruttaropamā bhūmir bāhyāntaḥkaraṇojjhitā |
aprameyā nirātaṅkā kālākālakalottarā ‖ 2

adhāmadhāmavibhavā nirniketā kramākramā |
asparśaparamānandacamatkāraughanirbharā ‖ 3

nirānandā nirāveśā sadasadbhramavarjitā |
nirvikalpā avikalpā tu saṃvidujjhitadharmiṇī ‖ 4

prāptā mayā jhagity eva vāsanāñjanavarjitā |

I suddenly attained, all at once,
the plane beyond which there is nothing higher and without
compare[36],
free from the outer and inner senses,
not an object of knowledge,
free from pain and fear[37],
beyond the energies of time or eternity,
the glory of an abode without abode,
not located anywhere,
a process without process[38],
an overflowing flow of wonder[39]

---

[36] Here the sanskrit seems irregular. It should be *niruttara-**nir**-upamā*. This is,
to my knowledge, the only occurrence of the compound *niruttara-upamā*.
Perhaps we should read *nituttarottarā* "beyond the supreme" ?

[37] *Nirātaṅkā*: fearless, painless, feverless. *Ātaṅka* seems to mean first 'fever',
and then fever as a symptom of fear. Appears also in *Mahānayaprakāśa* by
Arṇasiṃha, 2b.

[38] Litt. "a process and not a process".

[39] *Camatkāra* is, of course, one of the important expressions of later Kashmir
Shaivism. Like others (see below n. 59), its presence attests to the importance
of the Kālī-krama as a source for the Pratyabhijñā philosophy. *Camatkāra*
appears four times in the *Prakāśa* commentary, and twice as *camatkṛti*, though
not in the chummās themselves. In fact, it is far from uncommon in the Krama
texts, to denote the mystical inebriation, the state of dizziness (*ghūrṇi*) induced
by the awakening of consciousness. It is absent from its main tantras, but it is
used five times in the *Mahānayaprakāśa* of Arṇasiṃha. The fact that it is

- the supreme bliss without any touch (*asparśa*[40]),
a bliss without cause[41],

---

absent from the Krama tantras seems to indicate, however, that it was borrowed from the terminology of poetics.

[40] Or without contact, sensation, feeling. This bliss is not born of sexual contact. It is a feeling that does not depend on another.

[41] *Nirānanda* litteraly means "without bliss". In Tantra, it seems to designate a negative bliss, born of rest and emptiness. Abhinavagupta defines it thus: *śūnyatāmātraviśrānter **nirānandātmikā** sthitiḥ* (*Mālinīvijayavārttika* II, 35b) : « A state 'without bliss'- a state of repose in pure emptiness ». However, in the context of the Krama, *nirānanda* designates ultimate bliss, beyond bliss and its absence. *Nirānanda* appears three times in our text, always with other negations. One of the main sources for understanding the paradox of *nirānanda* is the *Kramasabhāvatantra* : *namo'stu paramānande **nirānande** namo'stu te ||1/ 8 ||* "Homage to you, (goddess) who is supreme bliss, salutation to you, bliss without cause". That sort of passage tells us that *nirānanda* is certainly a kind of bliss, but it doesn't tell why this negative and paradoxical turn of words is used. In 2, 49a, we find *nityaśūnya**nirānande** ṣaḍcakre avyaye dhruve*, "in the eternally empty bliss without cause, in the six wheels, immutable (and) permanent." Here again, *nirānanda* is connected with emptiness. In 2, 119, we find a more telling formulation: *ānandaṃca **nirānandaṃ** sānanda(<ṃ) rakṣace * * *? |* "And you protect (?) bliss, bliss without cause, supreme bliss". Here *nirānanda*, which means literally "non-bliss", resembles expressions found in English like "antimatter", which designates a type of matter, but of a sort very different from, or even opposed to, the one we ordinarily know. In 3, 46, *nirānanda* qualifies the experience in the *dvādaśānta* : *dvādaśāntā **nirānandā***. More interestingly, in the *Ciñcinīmataṣārasamuccaya*, we find *nirānanda* associated with its opposite *sānanda*. In 2, 10a, among a series of rhetorical formulas: *sānandaṃ kiṃ [g: + n] **nirānandaṃ** nirlakṣaṃ [k gh: nilakṣaṃ] kiṃ [k gh: ki] salakṣakam* "What presence of bliss? what absence of bliss? What goal or absence of goal?" Here *nirānanda* is obviously taken in its negative, literal sense. But it certainly expresses a type of bliss, so transcendent and different from the bliss we usually experience, that it is strikingly called as "non-bliss", no unlike the "no-ships" of Frank Herbert or the negative formulations of negative theology found in Plato's *Parmenides*. We find exactly the same line in 4, 16a. Just after this line is an interesting passage explaining those paradoxical expressions : 15a g) *sphurāhlādodayaṃ [sarve: sphurat hlā-] nityaṃ satattvaṃ parikīrtitam || 4/18 || ye [sarve: nāsti] paśyanti [k gh: yaścadanti; kh: yaṃvadanti g: yesvadanti] paraṃ nityaṃtallayībhūtavigraham [gh: tallayabhūta-; g: - bhūtaṃ-] |sarvasamarasānandaṃ nistattvaṃ ca prakīrtitam || 4/19 ||cidacinmathanodbhūtaṃ [g: cidacit-] svasvabhāvarasodbhavam |sānandaṃ [g: sā * nda] taṃ vijānīyād [sarve: -yān] **nirānandaṃ** tu tanmatam [k gh:tanmanaṃ; g: tatmanaṃ] || 4/20 ||* "Those (yogins) see the arising of flashing joy, eternal, known as 'endowed with the principle'. And its body dissolved into that, (this) bliss of the equal taste of all is known as 'devoid of

without penetration,
free from the mistakes of "real" and "unreal",
(a perception) without conception, not a concept,
but rather empty of the attributes of perception[42],

the principle'. But (when) arisen from the churning of subject and object (*cidacit*), born from the flavor of one's own nature, one should know (what is) 'endowed with bliss' as 'devoid of bliss'". While the end of that passage is not clear to me, it clearly points to two types of bliss, with the *nirānanada* being more advanced, while ultimate bliss transcends any such hierarchy. In the *Kālikākulapañcaśatikatantra*, she is described as negative bliss in the middle of the sun of awareness: *phaṭkārāntā mahāghorā grasantā bhairaveśvarān |ravimadhye **nirānandā** cinmarīcyantabhāsikā ||5/22 ||* "(Clearly present) at the end of '*phaṭ*', absolutely awesome, devouring the Bhairava lords, she shines inside the rays of consciousness, devoid of bliss, in the middle of the sun". In its most common sense, *nirānanda* is the very opposite of *ānanda*. In the key passage from the *Cicinīmatasārasamuccaya* quoted above, it is contrasted with sānanda in a series of such oppositions: *salakṣa* and *nirlakṣa* "with and without goal", *sālamba* and *nirālamba* "with and without support". The meaning is quite clear: the real bliss is beyond bliss and absence of bliss. So, in conclusion, there appears to be two uses of *nirānanda*: one is the ordinary sense, or near to it, *nirānanda* as absence or lack of bliss. From a spiritual point of view, it can designate the peace devoid of positive bliss one experiences in deep sleep, as is suggested in Abhinavagupta's quote above. The second sense, used here in our text, is to mean a bliss beyond conditioned bliss, "ultimate bliss". Thus, *nirānanda* would be synonymous with *paramānanda*. In the *Ṣat-sāhasrikā-saṃhitā* (29/45cd-47), it is associated with practice of merging mind space in the space of awareness, and this in the ultimate space, which is the 'bliss of stillness'. Here, *nirānanda* is explained as *nirācāra-ānanda*, 'the bliss of stillness'. The *Śrīmatottara*, a tantra in the Kubjikā tradition, plays on the meanings and offers alliteration (repetition of the same sound) based on the verbal root -*car*: 'By the practice of the Yoga of Stillness, one obtains the fruit. She whose nature is movement (*cara*) moves, (and her movement is) divided into (downward) motion (*cāra*) and upward motion (*uccāra*). That should be known as Stillness (*nirācāra*). Stillness is not other (than this). (This is) where actions (*cāra*) cease along with the activities (*karman*) of speech, mind, and body. When a pure (*nirmala*) state arises, that is said to be Stillness'. The editor and translator of these lines, Mark Dyczkowski, explains: 'In other words, this Stillness is the highest condition of the movement of the breath when it has reached the summit of existence beyond the End of the Twelve above the head. The Bliss of Stillness (*nirānanda*) is the supreme bliss that is the ultimate end of all fettered existence' (The *Manthānabhairavatantra*, Introduction, pp. 101-102).
[42] "The attributes of perception": thoughts about things we perceive. Or "her attribute is being free from consciousness".

a state free from the stains of residual binding tendencies
(*vāsanā*[43]).

tatraiva bahukālaṃ tu sthito'ham niścalākṛtiḥ || 5

I remained there for
a long time, motionless.

akasmāt tu prabuddho'smi tatprasādavaśān manāk |
apūrvasaṃvidāhlādacamatkāreṇa ghūrṇitaḥ || 6

Indeed, I was suddenly awake, faintly,
inebriated[44] with amazement
- the joy of an awareness like never before[45],
under the influence of grace.

sthito'haṃ vismayāviṣṭo nityānandena nanditaḥ |
śāstraprapañcavimukto gatāhaṃpratyayo yadā || 7

I was standing (there),
overwhelmed with wonder, overjoyed by continuous bliss.
Freed from the ego,
I was (also) freed from the rambling of scriptures.

tadā mayā siddhanāthaḥ sampṛṣṭaḥ pustakānvitaḥ |
yā kācid bhūr mayā nātha durgamā tvatprasādataḥ || 8

anubhūtā nirātaṅkā tāṃ yathā sarvato'bhitaḥ |
saṃlakṣayāmi satataṃ tathā kathaya me prabho || 9

Then I asked that Siddha Nātha[46],

---

[43] Free form habits. No concepts and no traces of them.
[44] *Ghūrṇi* is one traditional sign (*pratyaya*) of the awakening of consciousness, but it doesn't appear often in the Krama literature.
[45] For a very similar use of *apūrva-*, see *Vātūlanātha-sūtra, maṅgalaśloka* 5.
[46] Siddhanātha could be a proper name or a title. Siddhanātha or "perfected lord" is often "given to the founder of a lineage or transmission. It is equivalent

who was holding a book (in his hand) :
'O lord ! that extraordinary state,
hard to access (and) free of fear
was experienced through your grace.
Tell me, Powerful One !
how I may experience it everywhere,
in every circumstance, without a break !'

mahātmanā tadā tena maunasthena viśeṣataḥ |
ūrdhve vyomni yataḥ kṣiptā dṛṣṭir akramanirbharā || 10

Then that great soul,
while remaining silent[47],
cast a steady and full gaze
to the sky above.

tadadhiṣṭhānatas tasmāt parākāśāt samutthitā |
śivasyābhinnarūpā tu parā vāg aniketanā || 11

By the power of his practice (of gazing into the sky)[48]

---

to the title Ādinātha or Mūlanātha. Thus, each sacred seat has its own Siddhanātha" (M. Dyczkowski, *The Manthāna-bhairavatantra*, note 38 to chapter 6). Here Siddhanātha appears to be a name for that master appearing in the sacred seat of Karavīra. Siddhanātha is Śiva, taking birth in each age to reveal Kaula knowledge. We find, like here in verse 26 (*siddhanāthena...bhāṣitaḥ*) the expressions *siddhanāthena bhāṣitam/kathitam/prakaṭīkṛtam/vimalīkṛtam.* In the *Ambā-saṃhitā* he is mentioned thus: "Then, in the terrible Age of Strife she, the three-eyed (goddess) Maṅgalā, descended into the Northern Cave (*uttaragahvara*) in the district (*viṣaya*) of Oḍyāna. Siddhanātha also (descended) there into (his spiritual) lineage (*santati*). Having thus flown up (*oḍḍīya*) in the body, he obtained lordship and so is famous in all respects by the name of the venerable Oḍīśa. The place there is Oṣadhiprastha and she is praised as the auspicious one of the universe" (*Introduction*, p. 155, quoting *Ambā-saṃhitā*, 10, 165b-166a). Maṅgalā is again connected with the sacred seat of Odyāna. Oṣadhiprastha is a penance place of Śiva (*Śiva-purāṇa*, II, 3, 18).

[47] Perhaps the same Mauninātha mentioned in the *maṅgala-śloka* of the *Kaula-sūtra*?

[48] The practice of gazing at the sky is a central Kaula practice, also found in Tibetant Dzogchen tradition. Hemenji Chakravarti told me it is a variation of

the supreme Voice without abode,
arose from that supreme space.
One with Śiva,

vaikharyantakulottīrṇā samastāśrayavarjitā |
bhairavī saiva vikhyātā nirniketasvarūpiṇī || 12

she transcends the whole manifestation (*kula*)
ending with Articulate Speech[49],
herself devoid of any support,
she is said to be Bhairavī herself, her essence without fixed
abode.

tadaiva bhairavirūpāṃ nirdhāmaparamāṭavīm |
sarvāvaraṇanirmuktāṃ lāti nityam abhedataḥ || 13

There and then, she gives Bhairavī's form[50],
the supreme wilderness[51] without a fixed abode,
freedom from all veils,
in a way that is always without divisions.

aṭavīlas samākhyāto nityoditakhamūrtibhṛt |
apūrvataracidbhābhis sāmarasyavapuḥ paraḥ || 14

Known as 'the Wild one'[52],
bearing the form of perpetually dawning emptiness,
supreme by virtue of the most novel manifestations of
consciousness,

---

the *śāṃbhavī-mudrā*. About this yoga of space, see my book *The Yoga of the Goddess* (forthcoming).

[49] According to Tantra, consciousness is Speech. She unfolds in four stages: 1) Supreme, 2) Intuitive 3) Discursive and 4) Embodied. The Articulated is the name of that fourth and last level.

[50] The Goddess transmits her own state: awakening.

[51] *Aṭavīm* is "a place to roam" (Monnier-Williams), a forest, the wilderness.

[52] The word *aṭavīla* is not known to me, but I surmise it is related to *aṭavī*. Maybe also to *ativela*, "exceeding due boundaries".

(his) body is the oneness of (all) flavors.[53]

54

provāca prahasan māṃ sa kim arthaṃ tvaṃ samuddhataḥ |

*śāstrajālam idaṃ kiṃ syād bhrāntir nādyāpi te **cyutā** ||15*

Laughing, (the Goddess) said to me :
"Why have you become so proud ?
What is the point of this net of scriptures[55] ?
Even now your delusion is not gone !"

paśyemāṃ pustikāṃ vipra siddhanāthakarasthitām |
asyāḥ pañcaphaṇo[56] yas tu sthito dṛḍhanibandhanaḥ || 16
pañcendriyamayīṃ śaktiṃ viddhi tāṃ kramapāraga |
valayau dvau sthitau yau tu tau jāgratsvapnavigrahau ||
17

(She continued :) "O brahmin[57]! look at this book
in the hand of the Siddhanātha :
know that the five laces
holding it tightly bound

---

[53] Note the shift in gender. Probably, it describes Siddhanātha. But this constant change is a feature of the Yoginī teaching.

[54] BHU ms starts here at : *cyutā* | 15, corresponding to folio 2v1 in *Mélanges*, p. 340, n. 360.

[55] This expression – *śāstra-prapañca* or *śāstra-jāla* – appears often in this text. It is found in *Timira-udghāṭana*, an early Kaula tract : **śāstrajālena** *mohitā<ḥ> na jānanti parānanda<ṃ> & kulajñānaparāmṛtam*, folio 28r, ed. Somadeva Vasudeva), "Confused by the cage of scriptures, they do not know supreme bliss, the ultimate nectar of Kaula knowledge". *Śāstra-parañca* is also found in *Vātūlanāthasūtra* ad 3 : *sarva**śāstraprapañco**ttīrṇātvād*, "because it transcends the rambling of all the scriptures". The theme of transcending scriptural knowledge of scholasticism, seems to be a part of Krama rhetoric.

[56] *Pañcaphaṇaḥ* is a metaphor for *kuṇḍalinī*. It suggests the five-hooded snake rising above prince Siddhārtha to protect him from rain, among others.

[57] A brahmin is a member of the highest caste. But it means also an initiated person, re-born (*dvija*) through initiation.

are the Power of the five senses,
o you master of the Krama (worship[58]) !
Its two binding rings are
the waking and the dreaming state.

imau yau paṭṭakau dvau tu tau śṛṇuṣva samāsataḥ |
ūrdhvapaṭṭakarūpas tu prāṇaḥ saptaśikhaḥ smṛtaḥ || 18

But hear in brief (the meaning of)
those two wooden covers:
The upper cover is the exhaled breath
with its seven flames[59].

adhaḥstha(S:ḥ) paṭṭako yas tu
sa(S:ṃ)sthito 'pānavigrahaḥ |
pravāhadvayarūpo 'yam[60] saṃsthito dvija tattvataḥ ||19

The lower cover
is the exhaled part (of breath).
That (energy) is actually present

---

[58] Niṣkriyānanda is described as being intent on Krama worship, alluding probably to the *pūjā* type of practice among the three practices of that tradition: *pūjā*, *kathā* and *saṃkrama*. Worship or *pūjā* is ritual practice with mantras and hymns, including the three elements of sex, alcohol and meat, as made clear in the anonymous *Mahānayaprakāśa*, 9, 35-48.

[59] *Prāṇa*, like *agni*, has seven flames. Here, those flames are also a metaphor for the five senses and the mind. Those seven flames appear also in the corresponding teaching of the symbolism of the book in *Vātūlanāthasūtra*, 3: *saptarandhrakramodita**saptaśikho**llāsātmakaḥ*, the arising of breath is "the manifestation of the seven flames arisen in due order from the seven openings". The tie between the seven flames of Agni and seven secondary energies is attested in tantras, and especially in Kaula tantras. Cf, for instance, *The Yoga of the Matsyendrasaṃhitā*, ed. and trans. Csaba Kiss, 4, p. 446, n. 556. And there, Time (=Death) is visualized within breath, a central practice in Śaiva and Kaula tantras: "Now visualizing Time in its entirety as consisting of days and nights, the Moon is known to be in Iḍā, the sun in Piṅgalā (...) The Suṣumnā is the consumer of Time" (42-45).

[60] Sanderson suggests *aham* instead of *ayam*. That double breath would be the double form of the *ego*.

in the form of that double flow[61], o twice-born !

kulakaulakramonmeṣarūpau[62] dvau paṭṭakau smṛtau |
udriktaśāntavisphārasamāveśamayo(S:au) tv imau || 20

Tradition has it that those two covers (of that book)[63]
are the unfolding of the procession of Śiva and Śakti[64].
But (in actual experience), they are complete absorption
in the expansion of the (one state, both) the risen and the
peaceful[65].

ūrdhvasthā pūrṇavibhavā śaktir unmeṣadharmiṇī |
adhaḥsthā kṛśadeheyaṃ grāsinī śaktir aiśvarī || 21

---

[61] The expression "double flow" is also used by Śiṭhikaṇṭha in his commentary
on the kashmiri *Mahānayaprakāśa*, *ad* verse 3, where it qualifies the two
nostrils: *rasanā**pravāhadvayaṃ** nāsāpuṭadvayaṃ.*

[62] *Kula-kaula-krama* : kula and *kaula* stands Śiva and Śakti together, or for
Śakti and her manifestation.

[63] This image of the book reminds us of the two wooden pieces used to kindle
a fire, specially un ritualized context. The practice goes back to Indo-European
roots. In the *Uddhava-gītā* (5, 12), it symbolizes the relationship between
master and disciple. Connected through speech, it issues forth the fire of
knowledge.

[64] The compound *kulakaulakrama* is used in the *Ciñcinīmatasārasamuccaya*
to describe the goddess: *īdṛgrūpadharāṃ [kh: -dharā; gh: -gu * dharā] devīm*
[sarve: devi] cintayet [sarve: cintayed] vyomamaṇḍale | kumārīṃ [gh:
*kumarī] sukumārīṃ [gh: sukumārīśca] ca **kulakaulakramā**gatām [sarve:*
-gataṃ] || 8/47 || "The goddess bearing those (four arms and three eyes)
should be visualized in the circle of the sky, (as) a virgin, very young and come
through the union of Śiva and Śakti". It is also found at the beginning of the
Devīdvyardhaśatika : *śrutaṃ sarvam aśeṣeṇa **kulakaulakramā**gatam|*
pañcaviṃśatibhedena kālibhedaṃ mayā śrutam || 8 || "I have heard all that
has come from the union of Śiva and Śakti, I have listened to the Kālī (or
"beginning with ka"?) revelation (*kālibheda*) together with (its) twenty-five
sections".

[65] Here, one would expect that Śiva would correspond to *śānta* and Śakti to
udrikta. That is, of course, if *kula* is Śiva and *kaula* is Śakti. But the order is
reversed, as it is in the first verse of the *Spandakārikā*. One finds a long
meditation on this by Kṣemarāja in his *Spandasaṃdoha*. *Śāntodita* is common,
but I know of no other example of this *udriktaśānta*. *Śāntodita* is part of the
Śaivasiddhānta vocabulary, and also appears four times in the
Pātañjalayogaśāstra.

Above stands Śakti,
(her) glory full and expanding.
Below is the devouring Śakti,
sovereign, her body emaciated.

bhittvaitat paṭṭakayugaṃ madhye paśya vimarśataḥ |
mahāśūnyātiśūnyaṃ tu kṣarākṣaravivarjitam || 22

Open this pair of covers
and behold the center with the power of awareness[66],
for that great Void beyond the void
devoid of "permanent" and "impermanent".

asparśa(S:ṃ) paramākāśaṃ nirniketaṃ niruttaram |
sarvottīrṇam anābhāsaṃ sarvatrāvasthitaṃ sadā || 23

It is without sensation[67], the ultimate space,

---

[66] *Vimarśa* is the hallmark word of the Pratyabhijñā. In our text it appears in the sense of "intense felling" or full self-awareness, as in *mahāvimarśasaṃsparśasamāviṣṭasya* « for someone who is fully entered in the feeling of self-awareness" (*ad* chummā 52). It appears twice in the *Ciñcinīmatasāra* where it designates the power of mantras (*mantravīrya*, 2,11 ; 5, 1 same line and 5, 5). But it is used in the *Kramasadbhāvatantra* as well. 1, 2 has *svavimarśadaśānibhā* "(consciousness) resembles the state of self-awareness". In 1, 36, the god asks the goddess *svavimarśabalena* "through the force of his awareness". In 2, 121, the goddess is *vimarśagrasanākulā* "eager to devour thoughts", or maybe consciousness itself ? And in 3, 71, she is pure, tranquil and *vimarśasthā* "standing in self-awareness". And in 6, 4, she must be worshipped always *vimarśataḥ* "with the strength of awareness". But we can notice that *vimarśa* doesn't seem to be associated with language, as it is in Pratyabhijñā, where the notion gets its main inspiration from the "grammarian" Bhatṛhari.

[67] According to Monnier-Williams, *sparśa* can mean "feeling, sensation", both pleasant and unpleasant. Beside the sense of touch and the notion of contact between two objects, tantric literature uses *sparśa* to express feeling, especially subtle ones like, for instance, the arising of energy within the body. It is like *pipīlasparśa* "the feeling of an ant" crawling on the skin. On *sparśa*, there is the study of Ernst Fuerlinger, *The Touch of Śakti*. In the Krama sources, we have first, in the *Kramasadbhāvatantra*, a passage describing how the goddess is present as sense organs : *melāpe militā sā vai sparśasya paramā*

citiḥ | ||*2/86a* || "Truly, supreme consciousness is gathered in union of touch", that is, in the center of touch. Here, it is the organ that is meant. In our text, it occurs nine times. In its negative sense, it always qualifies *ākāśa* "space". The ultimate space of awareness is beyond feelings. Thus, at chummā 79, the destruction of everything is *bhīmam asparśaparamāmbare* "terrible in the supreme sky beyond feeling". At chummā 14, the "wine of Kula" is *asparśasaṃbhavam* "not born of a contact" or not possible as an ordinary sensation, unlike ordinary wine. But *sparśa* as contact is attested at chummā 52, where freedom from ordinary food is *mahāvimarśasaṃsparśasamāviṣṭasya* "for the one who is entirely absorbed into contact with total self-awareness". But even here, *sparśa* could be taken as "full feeling". At chummā 55, awareness is *sparśavibhavā* "a powerful feeling". At 104, the final chummā, duality is destroyed : *asparśe sparśa (B:apsarśasparśa)hnutā (B:hrutvā<hnutam a) svalpāsaṃparkato 'bhitaḥ* || in the space "beyond feeling, devoid of feeling,
without even the faintest touch (of duality)". In the final part of the *Prakāśa*, the absolute is *asparśasparśavistāram adhiṣṭhānam apūrvakam* "the expanse of a sensation without touch,
the primordial ground". Here the two meanings of *sparśa* as contact and as feeling come together. In the *Ciñcinīmata*, the "house of western (Kaula) tradition" is *nirāveśasparśarasaspandanisyandakandarā* (3, 4a) "she who is rooted in the flow of the vibration of feeling and delight, without (needing) a penetration into (something else)". Later in that same text, describing one initiation process, it is said that this initiation is *ājñāsiddhipradaṃ nityaṃ divyasparśasvarūpakam* || *9/103* || : "It gives the accomplishment of the Command, it is a perpetual divine feeling". In the *maṅgalaśloka* of the *Kaulasūtra*, the teacher Durvāsa, who is Rudra incarnate, is *sparśakāmasūḥ* « one who fulfill desires by touch ». In the later and more sophisticated anonymous *Mahānayaprakāśa*, consciousness is *tanmayasparśāt parānandacamatkṛtiḥ* || *1/15* || "the wonderful miracle of supreme bliss because of a feeling filled with it". And *bhakṣayaty āntarasparśād* (2, 23) « she devours (duality) through an inner feeling". According to this text, *sparśa* is just an intermediary phase, to be transcended in what is the real goal of Krama practice, *darśanasparśasambhogavirāmodrekataḥ* "because of the (final) predominance of visual and tactile enjoyment being put to rest". The context indicates that *sparśa* means sexual pleasure. In the earlier *Mahānayaprakāśa* of Arṇasiṃha, he describes the goddesses of the divinized organs as waves of feeling: *itthaṃ devyo nirāveśamahāvarṇakramoditāḥ | tattvataḥ sparśasaṃvittilaharyām antare sphuṭam* || *37* || "Thus, the goddesses arise gradually from the great Letter without penetration. It is really clear in the waves of feeling awareness". One wonder if *mahāvarṇa* should not be emended to *mahārṇava*, so that it matches with the metaphor of waves arising in the ocean. Consciousness, as Khecarīmudrā, is *yā sparśā sparśagagane caranti nirniketanā | sarvāvaraṇanirmuktā mudrā sā khecarī smṛtā* || *102* || "she who moves as feeling in the feeling space, (but) without delimited abode, free from all veils : she is then remembered as the gesture of She Who Moves In Space". And so, those goddesses *devyaḥ prathante satatam*

without abode and with nothing above,
above all, beyond appearance,
ever and everywhere present.

sṛṣṭisthityupasaṃhārakālagrāsāntakaṃ param |
sarvāvaraṇanirmuktaṃ svasvarūpa(S:ṃ) svagocaram ||
24

It is the supreme at the end of the devouring of Time,
(that is, at the end of the cycles) of emission, existence and
resorption.
Freed from all veils, it is one's own essence,
the intimate field (of self-awareness)."

itthaṃ parataraṃ tattvaṃ sākṣātkṛtya mayā (a?)kramāt |
tyaktaṃ sarvam aśeṣeṇa śāstrajālaṃ samantataḥ || 25

Having thus directly and fully (*kramāt*)
realized the absolute principle,
I[68] then let go completely of all the trappings of scriptures,
without keeping anything.

tyaktaśāstraprapañcena siddhanāthena dhīmatā |
dṛṣṭas[69] *tu tatkṣaṇāt tena parituṣṭena(:absent from B)*
bhāṣitaḥ || 26

At that moment, the wise Siddha Nātha

---

asparśapadamadhyagāḥ || *181* || « show fully themselves in the heart of the
state beyond feeling". For, our true nature is *sparśāsparśapadātītarūpatvād*
vigatottaraḥ || *223* || « the absolute beyond, because its essence is beyond
(both) the states of touch and no touch", or beyond feeling and its absence. In
Vātūlanātha ad 3, that supreme state is also absolute,
sparśāsparśaprathāparivarjitopacārāt "because metaphorically, it is entirely
devoid of the manifestations of (both) touch and its absence". Sparśā is also
found in Kathā 3, "the Teaching on Multiplicity".
[68] "I" : Niṣkriyānanda.
[69] Here a conjecture could be : *dṛṣṭam* - "when Siddha Nātha had seen that
supreme absolute..."

who had (also) gave up
the lies of scholastic teachings,
looked at me and, pleased, said (to me, Niṣkriyānanda) :

yogyas tvaṃ sanmate putra durgame'smin mahākrame |
ityuktvā kṛpayāviṣṭo bodhayāmāsa māṃ prabhuḥ[70] || 27

"O son with a true mind ! hard as it is to obtain,
you are worthy of that Great Tradition (*mahākrama*)[71]."
Having said this, overcome with compassion,
the lord enlightened me.

kiñcic chummopadeśaṃ tu saṃketapadavistaram |
durbodhaṃ tu mahāyogipravarāṇāṃ samantataḥ || 28

There exists indeed an extraordinary secret instruction[72]
revealing entirely the secret state without abode with
detailed words and symbols (*saṃketa*),
but hard to understand completely,

---

[70] Note that the masculine *prabhuḥ* could address the Goddess. See, for
example, the first verse of the *Mālinīstava* where Śiva addresses the goddess
as the masculine *prabhuḥ* : *jaya tvaṃ... jñānaśaktiḥ **prabhur** devi*
(*Manthānabhairavatantra*, Kumārīkākhaṇḍa, edited and translated by M.
Dyczcowski, 4, 38, edition and translation vol. 4 and notes vol. 5). See there
note 44, p. 211 of vol. 4, from the *Saṃvartārthaprakāśa*, a commentary on the
Mālinīstava : *prabhur devī | prabhuḥ parameśvarī | paramaś cāsau īśvarīś ca
prabhur iti |* "The Lord is the goddess. The Lord (*prabhu*) is the Supreme
Goddess (*parameśvarī*). The lord is supreme (*parama*) and is the Goddess
(*īśvarī*)".
[71] That is, you are ready to receive the whole (*mahā*) tradition (*krama*), beyond
the practice of worship through sex, wine and meat. In chapter 7, of the
Ciñcinīmatasārasamuccaya, a chapter describing the Krama tradition, the
yogin practicing the Krama *pūjā* is described as *mahākramavicārakaḥ*
"inquiring into the great Krama" (223b) and *kālikramavicārakaḥ* "inquiring
into the Kālī-krama" (224b). This expression is otherwise quite common to
describe Kaula worship.
[72] Beside this text, the word *chummā* appears once in the
Ciñcinīmatasārasamuccaya, 2, 30a. See also TĀ, 4, 236. Kṣemarāja glosses
Svacchanda-tantra, 15, 1 *chummakāḥ* with *pāribhāṣikī sañjñā* "a technical
term", a secret place in the subtle body or a secret sign. See
Manthānabhairavatantra, Introduction, p. 361.

(even) for the best among the great yogis.

yatas   tasmān   mahoddāma(B:mahoddhāma)sāhasaṃ
padam acyutam |
samāruhya haṭhād asmi suprabuddhadaśānvitaḥ || 29

Thanks to that (secret teaching),
I have risen inevitably
to the imperishable state of Audacity, the great exuberance,
and so, I am endowed with full awakening[73].

ittham apy adbhute tattve siddhanāthaprasādataḥ |
prāptaṃ tvayā(S: mayā) tv(abs. in B) anirdeśyaṃ
vikalpaughavilāpakam || 30
yad apūrvataraṃ kiñcit tat te vakṣyāmy aśeṣataḥ |

In the same manner that
I received (it) by the grace of Siddha Nātha
in the wonderful state (described above),
I will tell you[74] entirely that
extraordinary original state,
even though it cannot be pointed out,
(for it) dissolves away the flow of doubts.

bhakto(S:bhrānto[75]) 'si sarvapīṭheṣu brahmaṇy eva sthitas
(S:avasthitaḥ) sadā || 31

---

[73] *Suprabuddha* is important term in the *Spandaśāstra*, which seems to have taken inspiration from the Krama. It is also an important teaching in the *Svacchandabhairavatantra*, 11. For one can be awake (*buddha*), well awake (*prabuddha*) and perfectly awake (*suprabuddha*).

[74] Probably Niṣkryānanda speaks here to his disciple Vidyānanda, as we can see in the *Ciñcinīmatasārasammuccaya*, VII, verses 38b-188. It recounts the transmission of the *mahā-kālī-krama* to Vidyānanda in the *pīṭha* of Śrīśailam. See also Appendix 1 below. For an edition and translation of that chapter, see Mark Dyczkowski, *Appendix to Tantrāloka IV*.

[75] The manuscript read *bhakto'si sarvapīṭheṣu*. According to Sanderson, that reading doesn't makes much sense, because *bhakta* is not usually constructed

You[76] practice devotion in all the sacred sanctuaries,
always dwelling in the (static) absolute[77].

tvayādyāpi na viśrāntiḥ samyag āsāditā parā |
sandigdhāṃ matim āśritya kiṃ paryaṭasi putraka ||32

Still, even now you have not
found supreme and total rest.
Remaining in doubt,
why do you err, o (my) dear son?

yogyas tvaṃ parame jñāne yatas tasmād alaṃ bhava |
pravakṣyāmi mukhāmnāyaṃ yathā prāptaṃ yathākramam
|| 33

Since you are worthy of the ultimate knowledge,
enough of that !
I tell you the oral tradition,
just as I received it, in that same order.

darśanāmnāyamelāpavarjitaṃ satatoditam |
pūjyapūjakasambandhaprojjhitaṃ paratattvataḥ || 34

Devoid of philosophies, traditions and secret gatherings[78],

---

with a plural locative. But we find *bhaktim... karoti* with locative in the context
of Niṣkriyānanda transmitting knowledge to his disciple Vidyānanda in the
seventh chapter of the *Ciñcinīmatasārasamuccaya*, verses 184b-186 : *tasya*
uttaradigbhāge.... **tatra**... *divyaguhā...* **tatra** *ārādhanakaṃ kṛtvā...* **karoti**
bhaktim *yogīndro...* So, there in that *pīṭha*, Vidyānanda *does* bhakti.
[76] Vidyānanda.
[77] Reading *brahmaṇi eva sthitaḥ*. Alternatively, one could read *brahmaṇye iva*,
'showing piety'. But then, the *saṃdhi* should probably read *brahmaṇya iva*,
not *brahmaṇy eva*.
[78] Wallis understands « beyond philosophy, beyond the [four] Kaula
traditions, [even] beyond the [scriptural] Krama teaching (*melāpa*) ». Melāpa
is a technical term often mentioned together with *chummā* and *āmnāya*. For
example, in *Ciñcinīmatasārasamuccaya*, 10, 25: *punar anyaṃ pravakṣyāmi*

it is always present and, from the supreme perspective,
it is free from the (dual) relationship
between the worshipped and the worshipper.

ekāgramanasonmeṣavimarśena mahāmate |
rahasyapadavistāraṃ vijñeyaṃ vitataṃ śṛṇu || 35

O wise one!
with a one-pointed mind and an expanding thought,
listen to what is to be known extensively,
with the detailed explanation of its secret words.

karaṇacakkta opho (ogho?) ḍitir abhasā kulakaulikapuṭayugmu vicāra | andaru vāhir ukāsiti sahasā paśśu majji śūnyata avikāra || 1

Pay close attention to the couple of Śiva and Śakti by looking clearly to the flow of the Wheel of the Senses. In-between inside and outside, Audacity expands. Look directly to unchanging emptiness![79]

aniketapustakakathā ||
The teaching of the book without abode[80]

[81]

---

cchuṣmā(<chummā) melāpakaṃ priye | "O dear one! I will tell another one: *chummā* and *melāpa*".

[79] Those thirty verses "of the secret tradition" seem to be in old kashmiri or another *prākṛta* language, a non-Sanskritic vernacular. The Author has interspersed them among his verses in Sanskrit. I offer here only very tentative translations of the first three. Each one is followed by a title. They seem to be related to the preceding of following *chummās*. And so, I have included and translated those "titles".

[80] These words, found below each of the thirty verses in vernacular seem to be kind of "titles". Here, the teachings of the Yoginīs are described not as *chummā* or *sūtra*, but as *katha*, "words" or *carcā*, "inquiries". One is reminded of the *logia* in the gnostic *Gospel of Thomas*.

[81] Rastogi'ms starts from here.

parataram aniketaṃ tattvamārgasthitaṃ te |
nirupamapadachummāsampradāyam samantāt || 36
svarasavaśatayāham tvatkṛpāghrātacittaḥ |
prakaṭataravacobhir darśayiṣyāmy āśu nūnam || 37

I will now, without further delay,
show you wholly, in most clear words,
and by the power of the taste of my (experience),
to you whose mind is touched by (my) compassion (for you),
that ultimate state without abode,
reachable by that path of truth,
the tradition of those secret teachings[82]
whose words are beyond compare.

---

[82] The *Chummā-sampradāya*. The name given here to the tradition of the Kālī Yoginī.

The 105 Secret Teachings of the Yoginī

liṅgu abhijñānu || *1*
The Sign is the sign of recognition[83]

yatremāḥ saṃvidaḥ sarvāḥ sabāhyābhyantaroditāḥ |
asparśaparamākāśe nirnikete pare śive || *38*

vyaktāvyaktapadātīte niḥspandānandasundare |
*līyante kramayogena tal **liṅgaṃ** saṃsmṛtaṃ param* || *39*

The tradition says that
the supreme Liṅga is that supreme Śiva,
that supreme space without dwelling[84],
devoid of sensation (*asparśa*),
beyond the manifest and the non-manifest,
beautiful with the bliss beyond vibration[85],
where all cognitions, whether from
inside or from outside, dissolve away gradually.

sarvātigaṃ tad evoccaiḥ prathitaṃ sarvagatvataḥ |
*sv**ābhijñāna**tayā nityaṃ jagattritayabhedataḥ* || *40*

---

[83] *Abhijñāna* in the sense of a sign of recognition, a token « serving as a proof for » (MW), just like in the story of *Abhijñāna-śakuntalā*. In other words, a symbol, a token of recognition for a meeting. Kṣemarāja tells also of such signs of recognitions or symbols (*abhijñānāni*) to be found in daily ordinary life (see *Pratyabhijñā-hṛdaya*, 12).

[84] Without abode, that is, without any special abode as a precondition. Consciousness, like space, doesn't dwell anywhere.

[85] *Niḥspanda* designates consciousness as a void that is the source of all powers, and specially of the enlightening power, as shown in that expression as found in the *Vātūlanāthasūtra*, *ad* 13, describing the power of the perfect master, who awakens his disciples *niḥspandānandasundaraparamaśūnyadṛgbalena* "through the power of a gaze that is supremely void, beautiful with a bliss beyond vibration". Here, like in *a-sparśa*, *spanda* denotes sexual contact or movement. *Niḥspandānanda*, like *asparśānanda*, is a bliss not born from sexual contact.

All-pervading (and) all-transcending,
it thus displays itself to noble beings,
as recognition of oneself,
everyday revealed as the three worlds.

*nijaparaśakti samuhu samarggo akamu mahoghe avaṭi
ayādhi |*
*samarākchepa śameti abharggopa bhavasāhasakośa a
anādhi || 2*

*The primordial treasury is experiential Audacity that
brings to peace the sun (of Consciousness) that absorbs
and projects, while merging all energies of oneself and
the other into the true path – a great desireless flow.*

sāhasakathā |
The teaching of Audacity

araṇi samudāyu || 2
(It) arises from the (union) of the two kindling sticks.

śivasyābhinnarūpeyaṃ śaktir akramataḥ parā |
proditā paramonmeṣarūpā svacchandacāriṇī || 41

This supreme Śakti
cannot be separated from Śiva.
She arises all at once,
a supreme opening, absolutely free[86].

*tayor **araṇi**manthānaḥ **sām**arasyamaho**dayaḥ** |*
saṃghaṭṭo yas tato jātā niṣkāmā dṛṣṭir avyayā || 42

---

[86] Consciousness "moves freely", according to her will. This is especially true
of Kuṇḍalinī manifesting in the body possessed (*āviṣṭa*) by her and showing
the traditional signs (*pratyaya*) of that penetration.

The churning of those two sticks[87]
is the infinite arising of the fused flavors (of Śiva and
Śakti).
From that rubbing[88]
is born the unblinking vision, free from desire[89].

***bahi yākhiti rāji niccu gagani tārācayu
śaśidinakarayutu | apariśacinnabhasadani
vikaca(vikasi? conj. S) raśmibindu acchutu || 3***

***In the outer (world) the stars, together with the Sun and
the Moon always shine in the open sky. In the same
way, the Multiplicity of the rays (of the senses) expands
in the abode of emptiness free of sensation -
Consciousness.***

vṛndakathā ||
The teaching of Multiplicity[90]

cakreśī melaku || 3
(Then follows) the union of the Goddesses of the Circle.

*tato 'nalpacidullāsaghana(R:cidullāso   yena)   sṛṣṭer
anantaram |*

---

[87] *Araṇi*(s) are two pieces of wood used in vedic ritual to kindle the sacred fire,
Agni. One piece is flat below and the other is above, like a stick. The sexual
symbolism is obvious. There is a third element not mentioned here, a handle
kept on the upper *araṇi*, to make it stable while whirling it like a spinning top
with the help of a rope. This action is called *agni-manthāna*, "churning for
fire".

[88] In *Tantrāloka* III, *saṃghaṭṭa* is equated with *spanda*, consciousness as
vibration. Together with *sāmarasya, spanda, sparśa, manthāna*, it belongs to
the lexical field of sexuality, central in Krama, together with the lexical field
of space, sky and void.

[89] In *Vātūlanāthasūtra ad* 8, *anicchocchalitam* "arisen without will" is
paraphrased with *niṣkāmatayā* "in a way that is without desire". So *niṣkāma*
means "spontaneous".

[90] On the Wheel of Multiplicity, an important set of Krama teaching, see
Mahārthamañjarī, 38.

nirāvaraṇanirdhāmaparamākāśavṛttayaḥ || 43

cakreśvaryo *raśmirūpā devatāḥ kulavarjitāḥ |*
nirniketapade'dvaite(B,BHU:śvete) **militā**
vyāptisaṃyutāḥ || 44

The Goddesses of the Circle[91],
endowed with pervasiveness,
gather in the non-dual spaceless space.
Bodyless, the deities of that assembly
are the activities
of the supreme spaceless space,
the transparent (space) from which arises directly
the playful manifestation of that abundant awareness.

udaya cakchakaraṇāvalimāgo niravayinijamarīci bharu
udayi | sonicu udayādika me avibhāge thyaviśśāma
ubhajavāno anayi || 4

dvādaśavāhakathā ||
The teaching of the twelve currents[92]

kālagrāsu || 4
(Those Goddesses) devour Time.

sṛṣṭyādikalanārūpo yatra akramacidambare |
kālas saṃhāram āpnoti **kālagrāsas** *sa ucyate* || 45

The "Devouring of Time[93]" happens

---

[91] The organs of senses and mind, embodied by the Yoginīs appearing in the sacred seat.

[92] Same teaching in *Vātūlanāthasūtra*, 10. The twelve are five sense organs with the mind, and fice organs of action with the intellect.

[93] *Kālagrāsa* – the Devouring of Time" - is a very important notion in Krama and Kashmir Shaivism. In the *Ciñciṇīmata*, the goddess is *viśvasyajananī yā sā* **kālagrāsā***valambinī* || 5/16 || "she who engenders everything (and) who is eager to devour Time". In the *Devīdvyardhaśatikā*, the goddess is

when (those deities of) division,
like (the goddess of) creation, take back Time
into the sky of timeless awareness.

karaṇakusumati || 5 (B:karaṅku sumāti)
The senses (create) flowers (offered to that space).

cidānandamayollāsam icchājñānakriyātmakam |
karaṇānāṃ *vapur yatra pūjārthaṃ(B:pūjraktam)*
puṣpatāṃ *gatam* || 46

(That resorption) is a manifestation of the bliss
that is consciousness,
a manifestation that is Will, Knowledge and Action.
That is the beautiful body of the senses,
where it (all) becomes an offering of flowers[94].

*yo pañcapapañca rūpa bahi andarikṣitipabhicī ye nicu
samabhāge* |*rū-aparggahuchoniti cisman diriyathe
amara ameya churandi sa bhāve* || 5

pañcāmarakathā ||
**The teaching of the five immortals (flows of
Consciousness)**

manumati   paricāraku || 6
(R:cāruta;BHU:manumatiparicārukta)

---

kalāgrasantīṃ *cidamaprameyāṃ samastabhāvāntare kālarūpām* || *129* ||
nairātmikāṃ śūnyapadena yātāṃ dviṣaṭkaviśrāmapade praviṣṭām|
"Consciousness that is not an object of knowledge, devouring Time, present
inside everything as Time, devoid of self, gone to the empty state, entered into
the resting state (at the end of) twelve finger width (above the head)". This
goes with the image of the Goddess eating all she has created, being both
"full", satiated, and emaciated, hungry. This echoes the metaphor of the full
and new moon found in Kaula scriptures and in Indian culture at large.
[94] Litt. "for the purpose of worship" (*pūjārtham*). That compound is found in
Ciñcinīmatasāra, 7, 44b, *ālikhen maṇḍalaṃ tatra krama**pūjārtham** uttamam*
"One should draw there the *maṇḍala* for the supreme goal of Krama worship".

The mind and the will become a servant (of that space)

grāhyagrāhakavisphāradvandvamelāpake pare |
*mahāmaithuna(R:mahābhairava)saṃghaṭṭasāmarasyapa
de same* || 47

manomatī *tu tatraiva* **paricārakatāṃ***(B,BHU:taṃ) gate* |
nirāvaraṇaciddhāmni (... last pada missing) || 48

In that supreme gathering of dualities,
in that expanse of the subject and the object,
in that equal state of union (arising) from
the friction of the great intercourse,
the mind and the will (*mati*) become
servants in that very (space,
the) abode of naked awareness…

vīra cayasi akṣesari nicaye sami āmelaku inirahetu |
**yo avirat tathyo nirupama akamanaye so saṃghaṭṭu
jayūna acetu** || 6

saṃghaṭṭakathā ||
**The teaching of vibration union (without compare and
desire).**

ahamiti ghaṭṭanu || 7
(He shines through) the friction/vibration of the "I"

tadā mitāmita(BHU:sitāsita)syoccair **ahaṃ***kārasya*
ghaṭṭanam |
ullaṃghanakramaḥ ko'pi vibhāti kalanojjhitaḥ || 49

Then, there is an intense vibration of the sense of "I"
- which is both limited and unlimited[95].

Through a transcendence of (all) processes [96],
that extraordinary one shines, free from division.

*Akama marīcinicayu sarasapanekamapripāṭī saditu
ameyu | ullaṃghiti nijapadu amanamane
vibhajiparamākāśu atheyu || 7*

ullaṃghanakathā ||
The teaching of transcendence.

phalu(B:phala) nirvānu || 8
The result is extinction (of bondage).

kvacin niruttarapade dṛṣṭatattvasya sarvadā |
phalād ahetukollāsād ūhā nirvāṇavāg bhavet || 50

Within that extraordinary absolute state,
when the truth is seen without interruption,
Intuition arises – word pointing to extinction -,
Because of the fruit (of awakening)
which comes about without a (visible) cause[97].

rami(R:rati) ekāyanu || 9
He delights on the one path

yatas tatas tu sarvatra sarvakarma yathā tathā |
kurvan nirāmayo vyāpī krīḍaty ekāyano'cyutaḥ || 51

---

[96] *Ullaṅghana*: an important term of the Krama vocabulary. It means "going beyond the conditioned states" through a movement of awareness (*vṛttyā*). In Pratyabhijñā, this is translated philosophically as a power to transcend the laws of nature and even logic: *yogīcchayā hi śiṃśapāpi avṛkṣasvabhāvā bhavet*, "for by the yogi's will, a rosewood tree can be deprived of its tree-nature" (*Īśvarapratyabhijñāvimarśinī ad* 2, 4, 10).

[97] One could perhaps emend -vāk "speech" to -bhāg "one who partakes". The compound *nirvāṇabhāk* appears, for example, in *Śivasūtravārttika* 3, 42, 4 : *mukto nirvāṇabhāg yataḥ* "he is liberated for the partakes in extinction".

As a result, one does everything
everywhere in whatever manner.
Pervading (all), one (remains) without blemish.
One plays, (but) on the one path[98], without falling.

Parādyā (a ?)vandhyā || 10
(R:parābhāvavandyā;B:parādyāvanvryā)
The supreme (level of speech) and the others become
fruitful

tataḥ svātantryato nityaṃ proditā avibhedataḥ |
*giraḥ **parādi**rūpiṇyo (B:yau) bhedābhedaprathātmikāḥ ||*
52 (last pada absent in R)

(One's) words arises from that freedom
without being separated (from it),
in the forms of the Supreme (speech) and so on,
a manifestation that is both
differentiated and undifferentiated.

akṣacakrodaye(B:o) 'pīha
niścalatva*(BHU:***niṣphalatva***)(sva:absent in R)rūpatām |*
prayātāḥ   paramavyomasvarūpā(d   apari: absent   in
R)cyutāḥ || 53

Even when the wheel of organs manifests in (daily life),
(one's words) are stable,
not falling at all
from that supreme space.

akka ca akama padā aniketana vāca caturvidhathi a u
avātī | ta sivannivanni avināśa acetana assaralahara-
amalāñī || 8

---

vākcatuṣṭayakathā ||
The teaching of the fourfold speech (that continues in awakened state).

nṛttagītaprathāsu || *11* (B:nṛttagītaprayāsu)
Dance and songs arise (from that space).

tato 'nuttaraciddhāmarūpe saty ucite(R:udite) śive |
dṛgādihastapādānta(R:āntara)rūpāṇāṃ saṃsthito 'kramāt
|| 54
*raśmīnāṃ ca tathā vācāṃ **nṛttagītodayo** 'mitaḥ |*
anāveśasamāveśavilās(BHU:vilasa)odayamantharaḥ || 55

Then, he abides beyond change (*akramāt*)[99]
in the state of Śiva,
the abode of absolute consciousness.
There, the rays of the senses, of the hands and feet,
as well as words, arise without limit
as dance and songs
- the slow arising of the play
of complete absorption without absorption[100].

ovallīyajanu || *12* (R:ovallī amanu;B:ovallī ajanu)

---

[99] This applies to all that is already present in the space of awareness. All the dances and songs, the forms and the names, are apparent self-transformations of that space. Time flows from eternity, or rather is the movement (*krama*) of an all-together-given reality. Utpaladeva tries to explain that intuition when he adapts the Sāṃkhya theory of causation, replacing inert matter with Consciousness. She is everything potentially, all at once (*akramāt*) and she self-transforms gradually - and that is Time.

[100] As often with those expressions we find in the Kālī-krama « language » (*sva-bhāṣā*, see *Pratyabhijñā-hṛdaya ad* 15 : **svabhāṣāmayeṣu kramasūtreṣu**), of the type « an X which is non-X », it means that « X » is not of the usual type. Here is meant a complete immersion of the faculties in the space which is the Goddess of Consciousness. But it is not « an immersion into » space, because space is always already present everywhere in everything. Thus, it doesn't penetrate « anew » and it is not a temporary trance, but rather the recognition of an ever-present fact.

The lineage is the (true) sacrificial offering.[101]

paramātmamaheśasya tarpaṇārtham āha (B:tarpaṇāt tu māhā...) | (R:absent)
anantecchākulollāsalaharīṇām akṛtrimam || 56

He tells the truth of the oblation
to the Great Lord who is (one's) supreme self:
the authentic (offering) of the infinite waves surging
from the transcendent ground which is will.

rūpādiviśvavisphārasaṃvinnicayavigrahāḥ |
ovallyaḥ *kathitās tābhir* **yajanaṃ** *kriyate param || 57*

All the embodiments of the expansion of awareness
- the universe made of forms and other (perceptions) -
are revealed as the (true) lineages (of master)[102].
Through them is accomplished the true (*param*) sacrificial
offering.

anubhavaśānti || 13
Peace (comes from devouring limited) experience.

ittham saṃsāracakre'smin ramamāṇasya lokavat |
jñātasvātmasvarūpasya nityatṛptasya kasyacit || 58
paramānubhavāhlādacamatkāreṇa sarvadā |
niyatā(R:nityā)nubhavagrāsāc chāntiḥ
saṃjāyate(B:manjayate) parā || 59

Thus, supreme peace finally happens
because limited experience is devoured[103]

---

[101] I take *ajanu* as (*ovallī*)*yajanu* and not as « birth », because in the
explanatory verses we find only *yajanam* and no *jananam*.
[102] See Jayaratha *ad Tantrāloka* 29, 39 : *ovallyaḥ jñānapravāhāḥ* « the
lineages are the flows of cognitions ».
[103] Again, the special teaching of the the Krama: experience is itself devoured
within the space of Consciousness. Or rather, there are two consciousnesses,

by the constant wonder
of the joy of that ultimate experience.
(And this happens) in this wheel of *saṃsāra*
for someone who delights (just) like (ordinary) people,
(but) who has known his true essence, his own Self,
(and) who is (therefore) always happy.

kulamadhu peyu || *14*
The kula-wine is to be drunk.

kulaṃ *proktaṃ parāśaktirūpam asparśasambhavam* |
peyaṃ *tad eva* **madyaṃ***(BHU:madhyaṃ) tu kalānāṃ*
pravilāpakam || *60*

Kula is said to be the supreme Śakti
not born from a contact.
That wine is to be drunk[104]
for it dissolves away the dividing forces.

śūnyātītavṛtti || *15*
(That happens through) an act that goes beyond (mere)
void.

sadaiva paramā **vṛttis**
sadasadbhrama(BHU:krama)varjitā |
satāṃ nirāb(R:v)ilā spandā **śūnyātītā** *sadoditā* || *61*

The supreme act is always going on,
free from the mistaken notions 'this is true' and 'that is
false'.

---

just like there are two egos. The limited consciousness is absorbed into
unlimited consciousness, herself absorbed into the transcendent Void.

[104] The topic of wine of fermented liquor is well attested in Kaula worship. It
is discussed in the anonymous *Mahānayaprakāśa* where it is mentioned nine
times. See also *Manthānabhairavatantra*, Kkh, chapter 46. Here, *madhu* and
madya might also allude to *madhya*, 'center', a fact perhaps confirmed by the
BHU ms reading.

For the true adepts, she is transparent:
the vibration beyond void, always present.

hatāhatobhayarave sa bāhyābhyantarodite |
layaṃ yāte sati, tadā saṃsthitā niravagrahā || 62

When physical and mental noises[105]
that arise, both outside and inside,
dissolves away, then that unstoppable (Goddess)
remains without inhibition.

anāmanidrā || 16
(She is) a nameless sleep.

niḥśeṣabhāvavibhavaprapañcaughaparikṣayāt |
*avācyatvād **anāme**ha **nidrā** śāntā parā smṛtā || 63*
parā mudrāmantranirīhakathā padatrayāntargatā |
(R says a line is missing here, but B and BHU concur)

Tradition says that she is a supreme and peaceful sleep[106]

---

[105] The compound *hatāhata* is further elaborated in *Vātūlanāthasūtra ad* 13.

[106] The topic of so-called "yogic sleep" (*yoganidrā*) is remarkable in Krama literature. It appears in the *Ciñcinīmata*, when describing the twelvefold Kālī : *vācām atītaviśrāntir yoganidrā gurormukhāt | labhyate ...|| 7/164 ||* "One obtains yogic sleep beyond speech from the master's mouth". Later in that same chapter about the Kālī tradition, the Goddess is said to be experienced through yogic sleep : *sphuraty antargatā ghūrmir anākhyaṃ spandam uttamam | cidaciccakramadhyastho yoganidrānubhāvitaḥ || 7/206 ||* "She shines clearly inside (as) dizziness, a nameless supreme vibration, standing in the middle of the wheel of things endowed with consciousness and deprived of it, experienced through yogic sleep". In a more general Kaula context, sleep is one of the signs (*pratyaya*) of the awakening of Consciousness : *ānandaś codbhavaḥ kampo nidrā ghūrmis tu pañcamaḥ | tattvaviddhasya deveśi pañcāvasthā pravartate || 9/42 ||* "For one who is pierced (by the awakening energy of Consciousness), o Mistress of the gods, the five states unfold : bliss, jumping (out of the body), trembling, sleep, and dizziness". That same verse also appears in the *Ūrmikaulaśāstra* 2, 232. That piercing and transmuting energy is the Command (*ājñā*) or the grace of the Goddess. It manifests as sleep when the yogin grasps the state in-between extremes : *sarvabhāvaṃ parityajya śāntabhūmau samāviśet | grāhyāgrāhyagrahāntastho vyoma(<ā)vyomāntarasthitaḥ || 9/49 || tadāhlādaparānando*

that has no name[107] here, because it cannot be expressed through words,
for (in her) the flow
of all the extended and mighty phenomena has entirely subsided, with nothing left.
She is (therefore) the supreme, the silent revelation
of *Mudrā*[108] and *Mantra* present in the three states[109].

gamiti viṣayukaraneśa riharitopabhavi khecaramudra ameya | cyovannarahi tu mantropajuniśitothi a-aparivitti nirīha adheya || 9

---

yoganidrātmabodhakaḥ | nidrāvasthā bhavet hy eṣā ājñāsiddhiḥ pravartate || 9/50 || "Abandoning all states, one shall enter the peaceful state, grasping (it) between what can be and what cannot be grasped, present between space and no-space. The supreme bliss of that delight awakens as yogic sleep. When yogic sleep happens, this realization of the Command happens". The idea of entering between sleep and waking is one of the famous awakening instructions of the *Vijñānabhairavatantra* : *anāgatāyāṃ nidrāyāṃ pranaṣṭe bāhyagocare | sāvasthā manasā gamyā parā devī prakāśate || 75 ||* "When sleep has not yet come (but) outer objects have disappeared, through reaching that mental state, the Goddess Supreme shines". The *Manthānabhairatantra* offers more signs of awakening, but sleep is still among them : "The eleven signs of attainment (*pratyaya*) (that manifest then) are (as follows). 1) trembling (*dhunana*), 2) possession (*āveśana*), 3) shaking (*kampa*), 4) sleep (*nidrā*), 5) rolling (of the eyes as if inebriated) (*ghūrmi*), 6) (the sensation of) ants (crawling on the body), 7) dancing on one limb, 8) (speaking in the Kaula) language (*bhāṣā*), 9) tears, 10) jumping like a deer and 11) roaring (like) a lion". (Dyczkowski 2009, p. 115, Kumārīkākhanda, 13,101cd-102). On the signs of awakening and progress, see also n.16, p. 58, *Notes to chapter 33*.

[107] The nameless Goddess is a recurrent topic of Kaula teachings. See Mark Dyczkowski, *Manthānabhairavatantra*, vol. 2, p. 101 : "Anāmā is a common name for Anākhyā in the texts of the Kālīkrama (...) 'Anāma' may simply mean in a non-technical sense that something is so subtle that it cannot be properly explained and therefore named like 'the inner Vow that has no name'. In a deeper sense, 'Anāma' denotes the ultimate transcendental reality, which is the source of manifestation and all that can be described and named but is itself beyond description and so is the Nameless, just as it is the Unwritable (*alekhya*). It may be the abstract Mahākaula free of all the polarities. So, it can apply to the God as well as to the Goddess".

[108] Mudrā is sacred gesture and inner posture, state of consciousness.

[109] The three states of waking, dream and sleep. Or, rather, the three phases (*tri-pada* "three steps") of projection, existence and resorption.

mudrāmantranirīhakathā || *9*[110]
The silent teaching of Mudrā and Mantra (being awakened Consciousness).

bhautiku dinu || *17* (R:bhautikthi dina)
The material world is the day (of Consciousness).

pṛthivyādimahābhūtakārye kāraṇasaṃyute |
*prodite tatra sarvatra **bhautikaṃ** tad **dinaṃ** smṛtam* || *64*

When the effect that are the (five) great elements[111]
- earth, etc. – together with the faculties
(that perceive and create them) is fully arisen,
then and always the tradition calls it 'day'.[112]

pakṣvākiśo || *18* (R:paksādhākiśo)
(When) the opposites (are dissolved, the Goddess is said to be) "emaciated".

*ātmātmīyagrahodreka**pakṣo** yatra layaṃ gataḥ |*
*nirnimeṣapadaṃ tasya **kṛśaṃ** grāsaikaghasmaram* || *65*

When the opposites that are the excess of grasping at 'me' and 'mine'
are dissolved, that is then one's "emaciated" state,
without opening[113] (to an outside world),

---

[110] The title of this *kathā* seems to be missing in B, R and BHU mss ; or, possibly, that title is *mudrāmantranirīhakathā*, and the rest of that line is marginal annotation ?

[111] This teaching on the elements is elaborated in *Vātūlanāthasūtra*, 6.

[112] The 'day' seems to correspond to the 'full' (*pūrṇā*) state of consciousness. Night is then the 'thin' or 'emaciated' state (*kṛśā*). In this last state, consciousness is eager to 'eat' or to devour all, while in the previous one she is replete and at rest.

[113] *Nirnimeṣa* appears also in the *Cittasaṃtoṣatriṃśikā*, 1. Generally speaking, *unmeṣa* and *nimeṣa*, keys terms of the *Spandaśāstra*, are used also in the Krama teachings.

where (Consciousness) is only eager to devour (everything).

rātrī āgamu || *19*
(Then,) night falls.

ekasmin sati kācit tu **rātriḥ** *samyak par***ā***gatā |*
sarvasaṃhārasaṃhārasaṃhartrī(BHU:hantrī) satatoditā
|| *66*

In that one (Consciousness) falls the night,
truly supreme,
(for) it is always fallen[114],
(a night) that is the resorber of the resorption of the resorption of all.

cidacidbhedavibhava(<vibhāga)prakāśagrasanākulā |
mahāśūnyātiśūnyeyaṃ nirlakṣyā advayavigrahā || *67*

She is mad with manifesting and devouring
the manifestation divided into
'conscious' and 'devoid of consciousness'.
That great Void beyond the void
has no mark to be pointed at, her body non-dual[115].

varṇāvarṇavibhāgaṃ tu yā rāti satataṃ kṣaṇāt |
rātris sā kathyate ghorā nirupākhyā akramākṛtiḥ || *68*

Always and at each instant she bestows[116]
the distinction between articulate sound and silence.
She is (thus) called 'night', terrible,
She cannot be described and is devoid of temporal form.

---

[114] It says 'risen', playing on paradoxes, as always in Kālī-krama teachings.
[115] Or "her body having no second" and, thus, being beyond compare.
[116] The Author gives here a traditional etymology of "night" : rātrī would come from the verbal root -rā "to give".

*yo mahābhūtāvali pañcaku avira tu yugmodavupatteku
visāsi | so vinivāriti akṣayu mukhagatu nityoditu
paranutu avabhāsi || 10* [117]

yugmakathā ||
**The teaching of the couples (of opposites among the five
material elements).**

murto kiñcīnā || 20 (R,B:mutto)
Nothing is (really) liberated.

*ity etasmin pare vyomni prathite sati sarvataḥ |
bhedābhedādivaicitryaṃ cidacidvigrahaṃ sadā || 69*

Thus, it is only in that supreme space,
manifested everywhere,
that the wonderful variety of what is different and
identical,
with (its) aspects endowed with or devoid of
consciousness, (exists).

na kiṃcid *api sarvatra* **muktaṃ** *yatra layaṃ gatam |
eṣaḥ ko'pi sadā bhāti nirantarataro'mitaḥ || 70*

Nothing is ever liberated in any respect
or dissolved away into somewhere (else).
It is (only) that extraordinary one
that shines (thus) always, absolutely uninterrupted[118]
(and) without limit.

---

[117] Verse missing in R.

[118] *Nirantarataraḥ* appears also for the sky in *Yogavāsiṣṭha*, IV, 43, 21, and is
glossed as *nirantarataram atyantaniravakāśam ambaraṃ* "The sky is (even)
more than without interruption – absolutely without any free room". Though,
it is strange to say that space has no free space. But the idea is that space, like
some solid rock, has nothing that can cut or interrupt it. It is the same with the
space of Consciousness.

citsvarūpo 'kramadṛśā saṃkṣayodayavarjitaḥ |
nistaraṅgo nirābhāsaḥ sarvābhāsāntaroditaḥ || 71

(Being) of the very nature of awareness,
he is without destruction or creation,
considering that he is without becoming,
without waves, without (this and that) appearance,
present inside all appearances (simultaneously).

pasaripasarimilitisiciccakka samañja bhuñjiti niju
upabhoguye pallaṭi asaṃvitti athakkasayathijau
khaṇḍamarīci mahogu || 11

khaṇḍacakrakathā ||
The teaching of the broken Wheel (of the Senses).

akulapaveśu || 21 (BHU:akulapavecu)
(Still), one enters into the transcendent (state).

nirāvaraṇanirdhāma(<ṃ,B:nibhāma) nirānandaṃ
nirāśrayam |
paraprakāśam aspandaṃ śāntacinmātravigraham || 72

Naked abode beyond abode,
beyond bliss and without support,
supreme light without vibration,
it is the embodiment of peaceful pure awareness.

nānāśaktikarasphāraviśrāntipadam acyutam |
niyatānubhavakṣīṇasvasvarūpaikagocaram || 73

Never failing, it is the state

where the vast expanse[119] of the rays
of the many powers (of the senses) comes to rest,
the exclusive domain of one's own essence,
where limited experience has been destroyed.

akulaṃ gurubhiḥ proktaṃ niḥsvabhāvaṃ sadoditam |
samo'(B:sa so')hamiti saṃgrāsāt(B,R:saṃkrāmāt)
praveśas tatra jāyate || 74

This is what the masters proclaim as 'transcendent',
devoid of a nature of its own, (but nevertheless) always
risen.
When (one is) devoured (into the feeling)
that 'I am equal (to that transcendent)',
then one becomes absorbed into that (transcendent).

sā e citi haṭhāniju āśayumajjivyomithicī sarasapane |
usigatagatava prabhājisa anāśayu ivigatālamba
caccacinu asane || 12[120]

nirālambakathā ||
The teaching of No Reference Point.

avasānabhūmi || 22
(That) is the final state.

bāhyāntarakrameṇemāḥ saṃvidullāsabhūmayaḥ |
yāḥ sphuranty asthirā nityaṃ bhedābhedaprathātmikāḥ ||
75

These states that are the manifestation of Consciousness

---

[119] *Sphāra*, "extensive, wide, large" is an important word of Kaula tradition
and, later on, of Kashmir Shaivism. In the *Ciñcinīmata*, the absolute is
praṇavasphārakaṃ "expanding as the vibrating (om)".
[120] Verse missing in R.

through the regular (phenomena happening) both outside
and inside,
shine as impermanent (but) without ceasing
—a display that is both made of differences and identities.

*tāsāṃ tu yugapat proccaiḥ sāmarasyavapur parā (last
pada missing in R)* |
*yā agādhollaṅghanād bhāti sā **bhūmiḥ prāntagā** smṛtā* ||
76

But the tradition says that their final state
is the supreme embodiment of (their) fusion
that shines intensely and all at once,
having transcended into the abyss (of the Absolute).

***iṣagati phoneta cida akamakame niravakāśapadipi a-
avatthi samarasarasaviccī agamagame agādha
kathanucinupadiparyanti** || 13*

***agādhakathā** ||*
The teaching on the abyss (of the Absolute).

avācyakathā || 23 [121]
(That) teaching is unspeakable.

etadbhūmyadhiroheṇa maunaṃ sañjāyate mahat |
śabdārthakuvikalpena varjitaṃ satatoditam || 77

When one rises to that (transcendent) state,
absolute silence happens,
free from the evil concepts of words and their meaning,
(but) always present (even in concepts).

*ata eva tu nirdiṣṭam **avācyaṃ kathanaṃ** param* |

---

[121] Verse missing in R.

atha akāreṇa vā vācyaṃ varṇāvarṇojjhitena ca || 78

Still, that is why the unspeakable teaching
is pointed out, (even though it is) beyond (words).
Or it may be expressed through 'A',
free from words and their absence[122].

**akatha kathāguru mukhasaṃcāre sānu mahāmartako ca
vijimbhi akitaka paravismaya anukāravu agamāvaṭipivo
samahakṣambi || 14** [123]

avācyakathā || 14[124]
The teaching on the unspeakable[125].

dehavināśanu || 24
Destruction of the body (happens then).

asmin sati śarīre 'pi **dehasya** *trividhasya yā |
vismṛtis sa* **vināśaḥ** *syād guruvaktraprasādataḥ* || 79

Even while this body is present,
there happens the destruction, that is,
the forgetting of that threefold body,
by the grace come from the master's mouth.

niruttarottaradaśā || 25 (R:*niruttarottarottaradaśā*)
(That) is the state beyond the absolute.

niruttarottarā *kācit kramākramavivarjitā |*
daśā *pūrvāgamagamād (BHU:pūrvagamād) vyajyate
nityanirmalāt* || 80

---

[122] Here I take *varṇa* as an equivalent for words, concepts and speech as a whole.

[123] Verse missing in B and R.

[124] Kathā missing in BHU, in B, present in R.

[125] Or "the revelation through the sound A".

(That) is the extraordinary state before and above the absolute[126],
devoid of change and permanence,
that manifests from the pure and always (present transcendent state)
that has happened due to the teaching revealed before (all others).

bhūtabhāvana kañcuka vilaye apāri anākhya
gaganiviśśāmu | satatodita kālākāla kṣayethyo
akaranakaranenicu avirāma || 15 [127]
[128]

Anākhyakathā (?) ||
The Teaching of the Inexpressible.

śrīnāthaprāptiḥ || 26
One reaches the true refuge.

śrīḥ śaktiḥ paramā proktā jagadvibhavanirbharā |
sasphurā nirdvayā yā tu tasyāḥ prabhur[129] *anuttaraḥ || 81*

The sublime Śakti[130], said to be supreme,
is full of the abundance of the world.
She manifests, (but) without (real) duality.
Her master is the absolute[131].

---

[126] I believe that here, 'absolute' (*nituttara*) means 'transcendent' (*akula*). The Goddess is before and above Śiva.

[127] Verse missing in R.

[128] The title of this *kathā* is missing, but possibly this verse and the following make a single *kathā*, as the next verse bears the mention *'padadvayena'* "in two verses".

[129] *Prabhu* is a synonym of *nātha*.

[130] Or "Śakti is 'the sublime'".

[131] Anuttara is here equivalent to *niruttara* and *akula*.

śāntātiśāntarūpo(R:śāntāntātiśāntarūpo;B:-rūpe) yaḥ sa
śrīnāthaḥ *smṛto'vyayaḥ* |
tadrūpatāsamāpāttiḥ **prāptis** *sā jāyate'calā* || 82

He is a peace beyond peace,
whom the tradition calls the true infallible refuge.
One reaches permanent
identification with his essence.

nirīhacarcā || 27
(This happens through) exercising without effort.

ceṣṭākāyaparispandaḥ saṃvidullāsacoditaḥ |
tena projjhitarūpeyaṃ niścheṣṭā **gatir** *ucyate* || 83

The movement of the body and (its) activities
arise as the manifestation of Consciousness.
Therefore, she is completely free (from those and)
she is called 'awareness without business'.

yā sā **nirīha***vācyeha kalpanāgrāsataḥ smṛtā* |
sati kṣobhe'pi sarvatra bhrājamānā sthitā sadā || 84

Here in this tradition, she is said to be 'without effort',
because she devours (all such) concepts.
Even when excited, she is always present,
shining in full.

lelihyacaryā || 28 (*chummā* and verses missing in R)
(This) is the practice of swallowing (the world).

*viśvaprapañcavibhavo līḍhan(ORL: ḥ)(B:līḍha)kālena
sarvadā* |
so'pi līḍho yayā samyak mahāsaṃhārasaṃvidā || 85

The rich expanse of the phenomena of the world

is always swallowed by Time[132].
That (Time) is itself swallowed entirely
by Consciousness which is Great Dissolution.

*saiveha satataṃ devī **lelihānā** sthitā**kramā** |*
aniruddhatayā sākṣād aparokṣā sadoditā || 86

This is her, the Goddess always
swallowing (Time)
without being interrupted (by time),
always directly present, unchanging.

paryantacchumma || 29
(This) is the final secret teaching.

*mahā**paryanta**sambodhapara**cchumma**mahodayaḥ |*
nānādarśanasaṃbhūtacarcābhiḥ
parivarjitaḥ(R:mahādbhutaḥ) || 87

The complete revelation of the supreme secret teaching,
the complete and final awakening,
is completely free from
the ruminations induced by the many philosophies.

vaktrād vaktrakramodbhūtaḥ(R:bhūta-)sāhasākhyo
mahādbhutaḥ |
kālākālobhayollāsasaṃkṣayāt satatoditaḥ || 88

(Rather,) induced by oral transmission,
it is the great wonder called 'Audacity',
always present because
il completely destroys (the alternative of) time and its
absence.

---

[132] Time or Becoming is none other than Consciousness.

anāśritiḥ || 30 (R:anāśriti)
One is without support.

*icchākṣobhodayamalair(R:layair) abhilāṣaiḥ samantataḥ
| varjitatvād ayaṃ samyaṅ
nistaraṅgā(B:a)prathātmikaḥ(R:nistaraṇgaprathātmikaḥ)
|| 89*

Because he is entirely free from desires
– those stains of excitement arisen because of will –
he is an entirely unmoving
expansion.

*niṣkāmo nirvikāraś ca sarv**āśrayavivarjitaḥ** |
sāmarasyarasāsvādasaṃcarvaṇarataḥ sadā || 90*

Without desire, he is without change,
devoid of all supports,
always intent on savoring
the joy of fusion.

pānthāvadhūcī || 31 (S: *panthā*)
(That) is a forsaken path.

*sarvatra rasamāṇo 'pi(S:ramamāṇo 'pi)
niyatāśrayavarjitaḥ |saṃvidullāsavibhavair
anirodhatayābhitaḥ || 91
prāpnoti vṛttim agamāṃ **pānthavat** tv **avadhūtikām** |
nirlepāṃ puṣkaradalasthitavārivad añcitām || 92*

Even though one delights everywhere,
one takes no fixed abode.
In no way stopped
by the abundant manifestations of consciousness,
one reaches the state that cannot be reached,
just like on a path forsaken (by all),

(but) stainless, (for) one walks on it
like water (glides) on a lotus leaf.

aṭṭuviṣayabhūmi aḍāvisadā
paracirggaganajannārajānāre |
apabuddha sa ehakatha apadāviparīto bhāsi apamāna ||
16 [133]

aṭṭāṭavīkathā ||
The teaching of the eightfold wilderness.

macci umaccī || 32
(Awareness) is excited and mad.

svasvātantryodayā tayā(B:udayatayā) nirvicāratvam
āgatā |saṃvin navanavollekharūpiṇī sarvabhakṣiṇī || 93

Consciousness doesn't consider (whether it is proper or
not),
because she arises by her own freedom,
drawing ever new pictures
and devouring all (of it).

yuktāyuktavicārais tu varjitā cañcalā sadā | yā sthitā
nirbharā saiva proccair unmanatāṃ gatā(S:unmattatāṃ
gatā) || 94

Indeed, she is free from having to enquire whether it is
fitting or not :
she is a fickle one.
She remains without limits,
and so goes into deep madness[134].

paramaṃ śivam ālokya tadvaśīkṛtacāpalā |

---

[133] Verse missing in R and B.
[134] Litt. 'mindlessness'.

mattonmattā *citiḥ khyātā satām(R:samāna) apracyutā tataḥ* || *95*

When she sees the supreme Śiva,
he tames that restless one.
That excited and mad awareness
becomes then unmoving for the sincere (adept).

sarvabhakṣagrāsakā || *33* (R:grasikā, B:grāsiku)
She swallows the one who devours all.

vṛttiprapañcarūpasya sarvagrāsaśarīriṇaḥ |
grasanāya uditāya(B:udyatāya) alaṃ
sāmarasyamahodayāt || *96*
tīkṣṇātitīkṣṇarūpeyam nirāvaraṇavigrahā |
saiveha kathitā kācit ***sarvabhakṣasya bhakṣikā*** || *97*

Because of the great manifestation of the state of fusion
that is eager to fully (*alam*) devour
the expanse of mental states
of the embodied beings who are (already) devouring all[135],
this extremely sharp (awareness)
whose body is naked
is revealed to be that extraordinary one
who devours the One who devours all.

bharitavyāpakā || *34* (R:-vyāpaka)
She pervades the fullness (that is Śiva).

iyam akṣīṇavibhavā saṃvittir aśarīriṇī | *(line missing in R)*
viśvaprapañcavisphāravṛttyullāsasamarpaṇāt || *98*
vyāpikā *tu samākhyātā nirāvaraṇadharmiṇī* |
*bhairavasya amitāloka****bharitasya*** *nirākṛteḥ* || *99*

---

[135] The individual subject is already « devouring » all, but to a limited degree only. See *Pratyabhijñā-hṛdaya*, sūtra 14.

This consciousness whose riches cannot be exhausted
doesn't have a (separate) body,
but she is rightly called '(all) pervasive'
because she offers the play of the operations (of senses and
mind),
the sudden expansion (*sphāra*) of the expanse of all things.
She is the pervading transparency of Bhairava,
Who is without form,
full of limitless manifesting light.

manana īśa tiśa kṣud(S:t)a āgūriti paramākāśapadi
thitikitti | vittipapañca(S:prapañcu) akāme(S:akame) |
pūriti bhuji niravakāśu avitti ǁ 17 [136]

devīcatuṣṭayakathā ǁ 17
The teaching of the four goddesses.

niṣkaraṅku yogu ǁ 35
(This) is the (best) yoga free from the skeleton.

karās trayodaśākārāḥ sarvākṣakṣobhavṛttayaḥ |
aṅkaṃ tu nirniketā yāḥ/ nirniketāyāḥ saṃvido
dehavistaram (Śivopādhyāya : -vistarāḥ) ǁ 100

The 'hands'[137] (or 'rays', *kara-*) are the thirteen rays (of
the sun of Consciousness),
the operations agitating all the faculties (of body and
mind).
As for the 'hook' (or 'ornament', *aṅka*), it is the expanse
of the body[138],
(made up of) the cognitions without abode[139].

---

[136] Verse missing in R.

[137] See *Vijñānavivṛti*, XX about *kara* and the traditional interpretation of
karaṅkinī-mudrā.

[138] *Aṅka* may also mean « body » in a secondary sense.

[139] For their « abode » is the space of abodeless awareness.

etat karaṅkam ākhyātaṃ (:point) (<début de proposition)
tasyāgrāsād(R:tasya grāsāt ; Śivopādhyā:prasād)
anāvṛtam |
niṣkaraṅkaṃ *samuddiṣṭaṃ nirālambaṃ*
nirāmayam(R:nirāśrayam) || 101
paraṃ **yoga***varaṃ guhyaṃ niyatadhyānavarjitam |*
nityaṃ bhāti nirāveśacetasām anirodhataḥ || 102

That is called the 'skeleton',
for it is naked, as it (is Consciousness that) devours (all).
Rightly designated as 'devoid of a skeleton'
(because) it is without (material) support and blemish,
it is the best yoga, the secret
devoid of any limited visualization.
It shines always for those
whose attention is not absorbed (into something else),
for (nothing) can stop it.

akāyakhecara || 36
One lives in space free from the body.

anenaiva sadā **kāya***(R:sadākāśa)saṃkalpakalanojjhitaḥ |*
*mitāmitadaśottīrṇacid***ākāśacaro** *bhavet || 103*

Through that very (yoga), one becomes
always free from the notions build around the body,
(and) one lives in the space of awareness,
beyond the limited and unlimited states.

akaraṇa khecarakaraṇa paveśeya
pabhavipathamapatibha agamagame | paramākāśapada
aviśeṣe sādhāmarahikhekalanicu akame || 18 [140]

---

[140] Verse missing in R.

khekalākathā || 18
The teaching on the energies of space.

bharitapūrṇā || 37
She is full of (bliss).

*yatas tu(R:yas tu) viśvavibhavaṃ **bharitaṃ** nirniketayā |*
yayā svatantrarūpiṇyā saṃvidā saiva sarvadā || 104
*akhaṇḍitanijollāsarūpatvāt **pūrṇa**vigrahā |*
paramānandaniḥṣyandanirbharā saṃsmṛtā amṛtā || 105

Immortal, she is rightly remembered as
full beyond measure of the flow of ultimate bliss.
Her body is always full because
her playful dance is undivided.
This is because she is free Consciousness,
without (fixed) abode,
filling the abundance
of everything.

pūrṇakiśī || 38
She is (both) full and emaciated.

*itthaṃ **pūrṇa**svarūpāpi mahāgrāsaikaghasmarā |*
*sarvottīrṇaviyadvṛttim atyajantī (BHU:abhyajantī) **kṛśā***
smṛtā || 106

Thus, even though she is full in her own essence,
she is also eager only to devour all.
Thus, the tradition says that she is emaciated as well,
because (while being full), she doesn't give up
her empty state beyond all.

śaścī akitakaphuraṇā rūpe niścamaśamuśita
andararājiśattipurā śivapadinī rūpi sajjimilitinārī
curubhāji || 19

ardhanārīśvarakathā ‖ 19
The teaching of the androgynous Lord.

lelihānā lāmā ‖ *39*
She is the source of spiritual realization[141] (because) she
swallows (everything).

kṛpādibhāvabhedasya(B:bhāvayogasya)   *haṭhād*
akramayogataḥ |
***lelihāna**tayā **lāmā** bhakṣakī yā tu sā smṛtā* ‖ *107*

Because she swallows forcefully
and all at once
the duality of feelings like affection,
she is Lāmā the Devouress, according to the tradition.

lānāt sarvasya jagato sāti(R:māti) sarvatra cābhitaḥ |
lāmā seha samākhyātā sarvagā sarvavarjitā ‖ *108*

Because she gives the whole world
everywhere and in every respect,
she is rightly called Lāmā in this teaching:
she is (both) in all and devoid of all.

sarvasaṃhāravṛttyaiva yā sarvaṃ sṛjati kṣaṇāt |
viśvatra vartate nityaṃ saiva lāmā parā smṛtā ‖ *109*

---

[141] Lāmā is the name of a group of yoginīs. They seem to have special practices
centered on sexuality: they « kiss » (*cumbikā*) and thus it is fitting to say that
Consciousness who « swallows » or « licks » everything is a lāmā yoginī. For
an example of lāmā as a kind of yoginī giving liberation, see
Ciñcinīmatasārasamuccaya,   8,   50 :   *karoti   vividhākārā
bhuktimuktiphalapradāḥ* | *vāmā lāmā tu sākinyā khecarī bhairavī smṛtāḥ* ‖ *8*
« According to tradition, the vāmās, the lāmās, the śākinīs, the khecarīs and
the bhairavīs are shape-shifting, giving both powers and liberation ». In the
Kularatnoddyota-tantra, the lāmā is « adorned with knowledge » : *lāmā
jñānānvitā tatra prajñā deyā svarūpataḥ* (6, 63b). They are listed in the
Khacakrapañcaka-stotra, 18 and 31.

She takes back all (into herself),
(just like) she emits all in one instant.
She always operates in everything,
so, she is remembered as the supreme Lāmā.

kedhinā || 40 (R:krodhinī)
She is (perpetual) wrath.

saiveha **krodhinī** *nityaṃ sarvasaṃhārikā yataḥ |*
kathitā tu tato'nādibodhavisphāraghūrṇitā || 110

She is always wrathful,
for she absorbs everything.
Indeed, it is said then that she is drunk
with the expansion of rootless awareness.

ubhayasṛṣṭi || 41
She is a double creation.

akalodrekarūpā yā svasvabhāvaikadharmiṇī |
kulavistārasaṃsthāpi(R:-yi)
bhāvabhedaprathātmikā(R:prathārpikā) || 111

She is abundant with undivided power / the power of "A".
Her only nature is her own nature.
Still, she is also present as the expanse of the whole,
she is the essence of the manifestation of the duality of
phenomena.

ubhayoḥ **sṛṣṭi***vibhavā bhedābhedamayī sadā |*
parā parāpara sṛṣṭiḥ soktā(B:moktā) śambhoḥ sadoditā ||
112

(To explain :) she is the evolution of both creations:

she is always both duality and unity.
Always active, she is said to be the supreme creation of
Śiva,
both superior (in unity) and inferior (in duality).

prāntakathāvadhi || 42
She is the ultimate final teaching.

yasyāḥ svatantrā prathate sṛṣṭir īdṛk(R:dṛk)svarūpiṇī |
nirāvaraṇanirdhāmasaṃvido 'nuttarākṛteḥ || 113

Her freedom - her creation - expands,
whose very nature is such,
from Consciousness without abode and veils,
from the manifestation of the Absolute.

*śāntātiśāntarūpeha(R:rūpā) saiva **prāntakathāvadhiḥ** |*
sadasadbhrāntisaṅkalparahitā saṃsmṛtāvyayā || 114

Here in this tradition[142], she is peace beyond peace,
the ultimate final teaching.
Devoid of concepts built on the mistakes
of "there is" and "there is not", she is changeless.

śūnyasaṅghaṭṭu || 43
(That) void is vibrating.

***śūnyā**tiśūnyaciddhāmni **saṃghaṭṭo** nityam āsthitaḥ |*
yas tena sarvasaṃhārasaṃhartrīti nigadyate
(BHU:nigadyana)|| 115

Vibration is always present
in the abode of awareness, Void beyond void.
Hence that (vibration) is called

---

[142] Rendering both *iha* and *saṃsmṛtā*.

'she who resorbs all resorption'.

nijajanmagrāsu || *44* (BHU:nijajanmagāsu,B:grāsu)
She devours what is born from her.

nānāsaṃvitkarollāsasvarūpasya **svajanmanaḥ** |
grāsakī *satataṃ bhāti kaivalyāt sarvagā citiḥ* || *116*

She manifests as she who always devours
what is born from her
- her own essence displayed as the many rays of
experiences.
Being transcendent, she is all-pervading awareness.

anicchiccha || *45* (R:anicchakaccha)
She is will that doesn't will (anything in particular).

abhilāṣeṇa saṃyuktā cidvṛttiḥ prathate tu yā |
saivehecchā samākhyātā viṣayagrāsalālasā || *117*

As for the power of awareness
that manifests together with desire,
it is rightly named 'will' in this (tradition).
It is an ardent desire to devour the objects.

tāṃ tyaktvā nityam amalā yā sphuraty aniketanā |
svasvarūpasamāveśacamatkāraikanirbharā || *118*

The one that shines, pure (and) without a fixed abode,
is that absolutely limitless state of wonder,
an immersion into one's own essence,
when that (state of desire) has been dropped away forever.

yatra saṃvinmahāvyomni nistaraṅge sadodite |
anicchecchā *samākhyātā kāpi sā sarvadoditā* || *119*

When she is in the great space,
waveless and ever present,
she is rightly called 'will without will',
extraordinary, always arisen.

akathanakatha || *46* [143]
(That) is the teaching of no teaching.

*tatra sākṣād **avācya**iva **kathā** kāpy udayaty alam |*
anuttarapadaprāptau vācā (<a)bhedagrahaḥ kutaḥ || 120

In that matter, that very (Consciousness) beyond speech,
arises directly as an extraordinary teaching,
able to reach the absolute state.
How could one grasp non-difference trough speech?

apūjapūja(R:ā) || *47*
(This) is the worship without worship.

pañcopacārikā pūjā kṛtrimā yā bahiḥ sthitā |
vilayaṃ tatra sā yātā kvāpy akramapade'game || 121

Outer worship with the five offerings is artificial.
She[144] dissolves away
in that extraordinary state
beyond Time (and) unreachable.

***apūja**iva samākhyātā sā **pūjā** paramāvyayā |*
nityoditamahāsaṃvitpañcavāhena ḍhaukitā || 122
aniketaparavyomaṃ bhairavasya avibhedataḥ |
akalpitamahājñānasamullāsena nirbharā || 123

That supreme and changeless worship
is aptly expressed as being absolutely no worship.

---

[143] R puts this *chummā* here.
[144] The worship, that is, Consciousness. Awakening is the true worship.

It is offered through the five flows
of great Consciousness ever present,
to the abodeless
Supreme sky inseparable from Bhairava.
Thus, she is beyond measure in her
playful manifestation of the great natural knowledge.

carācarajagadgrāsaniratah ko'pi sarvadā |
apūrvo'sau sthito'nalpah pūjanas satatoditah || 124

There is an extraordinary One,
always eager to devour the world, alive or not.
He is abundant worship always manifest,
primordial presence.

vyāpaka sarvabhakṣa ummaccī avadhūcīrāśita anirodhe
niravadhi rūpaka me asamaccī caryakā ca udayi
parabodhe || 20

caryāpañcakakathā ||
The teaching of the fivefold conduct.

amudramudra(R,B:ā) || 48
She is the gesture of no gesture.

karaṅkiṇyādimudrābhih kṛtakābhir vivarjitā |
vigrahagrahasaṃkocanirmuktā viśadākṛtih || 125

She is utterly free from (the five) artificial
gestures[145] like the 'Skeleton',
(for) her form is evident,
freed from the contraction of grasping at forms.

---

[145] Mudrā. In the Kālī-krama sources, we find a series of five such gestures
that are physical postures as well and induced states of the mind. In the
Jayadrathayāmala-tantra, for instance, those five are: Karaṅkiṇī, Krodhinī,
Bhairavī, Lelihānā and Khecarī.

*amudraiva smṛtā **mudrā** yatra pūjā mahotsave |*
jayaty akalpitas so'yam avaṭāṭaṅkaṭaṅkitaḥ || 126

(Hence,) the tradition remembers her as being
verily no gesture, a gesture where worship
happens in the Great Festival (of awakening).
Natural, this (gesture) unblemished by asperities obstacles
and traps[146], surpasses (all).

amantre(R:a) mantra || 49
He is the mantra of no mantra.

manaḥsaṃkalpakalanāsamūhair yo manāg api | na
spṛśyate hi saṃvitti glapanāt(B:r lapanāt) prathate yataḥ
|| 127

For, since that Consciousness that is
not at all touched by
the crowd of the dividing concepts of the mind
(still) spreads out through talking.

tataḥ ko'pi nirāveśarūpo'sparśo'svaraḥ sadā |
varṇāvarṇakalodrekavarjitaḥ satatoditaḥ || 128

Thus, he is always some extraordinary one
with no extraordinary state[147], no sensation and no sound.
He is not dominated by the division due to words and their
absence,
he is always actually present.

---

[146] Litt. « unchiseled by holes and crags ». Here we ought to remember India
was a culture where most people used to go by foot. Unevenness of the ground
as a direct consequence of bad karma is a special topic of Buddhism. On the
contrary, Buddha pure lands are said to be even, smooth and giving way below
the feet at each step.
[147] *Nirāveśa.*

anuccārya mahānādo hatāhataravojjhitaḥ |
vyāpī sarvagato **mantro(B:e')mantraḥ** *prokto niruttaraḥ*
|| 129

That great sound cannot be uttered,
free from the noise coming (both) from outside and inside.
He is all-pervasive, present in all, absolute,
said to be 'the mantra that is not a mantra'.

vannavihīnaniruttarukhassarujagasamūlapakitigā yatra
reka ukāra hakāra vikassaruvannacittra ciññeya vicitra
|| 21

gāyatrīkathā || 21
The teaching of Gāyatrī[148].

akaraṇe karaṇu || 50
It is a dance posture without (visible) cause.

karaṇais tāṇḍavādyair (one syllable missing, so -ādibhi ?)
anantaiḥ kṛtakais sadā |
dehaprāṇavinirvartyair(B:vinirdhantyair<vinirvṛttair)
ujjhito nityam āsthitaḥ || 130 (line missing in R)

He is ever present as freed from postures[149],
dances and other innumerable tricks
that come from
the body and vital energies.

akartavyam *idaṃ proktaṃ* **karaṇaṃ** *paramaṃ mahat |*
sarvendriyacidullāsāt svasvarūpaprakāśakam || 131

---

[148] Gāyatrī is a famous verse from the Veda, invoking the Sun as a symbol of
inner light.
[149] *Karaṇa*, a dance pose, of series of narrative gestures, because of the context
is obviously dance (*tāṇḍava*).

It is said that it cannot be 'done',
(for) it is the supreme posture/action.
It is the revealer of one's own essence,
for it is the playful manifestation of Consciousness
through all faculties (of body and mind).

***matimanuperiti karaṇasamargge ahamiti gahuhuravāṃ
na aśeśu | ko ca avitto budhna abhaṅge ummesabhāji
apaveśu || 22***

avṛttāntakathā || 22
The teaching without business.

asaṃbandhe sambandha || 51
It is a relation without relation.

*ahantedantayor nityaṃ sambandhas
sa(B:ṃ?)sthito'calaḥ | sarvo'yaṃ vilayaṃ yāti
nirahaṅkāracitpade || 132
sarvottirṇatayā samyak sarvage vimale'mbare |*
asaṃbandhaḥ *samākhyātaḥ* ***sambandhaḥ***
paramo'kramāt || 133

There is a permanent relation
between subjectivity and objectivity.
All that dissolves
in the state of awareness without ego,
in the all-pervading pure sky
that truly surpasses all.
This supreme relation is properly called
'no relation', for it doesn't evolve (*akramāt*).

***vigalanicuñña acuñña sa bhupāvividha padātha
sāthukavale u | āśayuciti sadā nīrūpā viccīvijuvirū
praghaṭṭeti || 23***

saṃghaṭṭakathā || 23
The teaching of vibrant union.

anāhāra(R:ā)tṛptiḥ || *52*
It is feeling full without taking food.

rūpādibhāvavibhavajñānād eva prajāyate |
tṛptiḥ *parā mahāsaṃvidbhairavasya sadā samā* || *134*

Supreme fulfilment of
the great Bhairava of consciousness
is always the same.
It arises just through the experience
of the abundance of phenomena like form.

anāhāra*daśāyogād dehaprāṇojjhitākṛteḥ* |
mahāvimarśasaṃsparśasamāviṣṭasya sarvataḥ || *135*

(It arises) without taking any food / by union with the state
of fasting,
for (that Bhairava) whose form is free from body and vital
energy,
who is always absorbed in the full feeling
of great realization[150].

adṛṣṭadarśanu || *53*
It is an invisible vision/philosophy.

antaḥkaraṇarūpe tu jñāne sarvatra saṃsthitam |
taduttīrṇa*mahāsattāsvabhāvaṃ jñaptilakṣaṇam* || *136*

There is an awareness/capacity for understanding
always present in cognition, in the inner organ,

---

[150] The presence of *ahantedantā, spanda, mahāsattā, svātantrya* and *vimarśa* makes one wonder whether this text is really by Niṣkriyānanda, that is, before Utpaladeva. If it is the case, then it is a game changer.

whose nature is Great Existence
that transcends this (mental cognition).

tenaiva satataṃ sākṣātsaṃsthitaṃ **darśanaṃ** *param |*
sarvabhāvapadārtheṣu paramaṃ nirniketanam || 137

For that reason, the supreme vision/philosophy[151]
is always and wholly present in full view.
It is the Supreme, without abode,
(even though it is present) in all things and phenomena.

grāhyagrāhakasaṃskāravitarkaparivarjitam(B:parivarja
nam)| saddaiśikamukhāyātasampradāyena gamyate || 138

Utterly devoid of subject, object,
of training[152] and reasoning,
it may be understood through the tradition
transmitted orally by a true teacher.

niruparāguparudhammu   anābilu   bhedābhedakalādi
acchutu | aviśīcī vigatarggahu avicalu buji-aghaharu
puṇyavimutu || 24

puṇyapāpakathā || 24
The teaching on virtue and vice.

acāru cāru || 54
He is (both) moving and unmoving.

nirāvaraṇacidrūpaghanād acyutavṛttitaḥ |
acāras tu samākhyāto vajravanniścalaḥ sadā || 139

---

[151] The presence of *vitarka*, *mahāsattā* and *padārtha* shows that *darśana* is to be understood as 'philosophy' or 'doctrine'. Those are words from the Nyāya school of Indian philosophy. Several terms are used in those verses that hint on Nyāya practice and its transcendence: *mahāsattā*, *jñapti*, *darśana*, *padārtha*, *vitarka*.

[152] *Saṃskāra*, "training, preparation, perfecting", like in *vikalpa-saṃskāra*.

Indeed, he is rightly described as 'unmoving',
for he is ever unmoving, like a diamond,
because he doesn't fall from
uninterrupted[153] naked awareness.

sa eva sarvasaṃvittivibha(B:-ā)ve svecchayā abhitaḥ |
caraty(B:carasya) **acāracāro** *'yam acyuto 'nāvilaḥ paraḥ ||*
140

That same one, (though) not falling, clear and
transcendent,
moves all around by his own will
in the expanse that is all awareness/in the expanse of all
experiences.
(So) he is (both) moving and unmoving.

vyomācāru || 55 (this *chummā* is missing in R)
She moves in the sky.

ittham sadaiva sarvatra paravyomadaśāgamā |
arkaprakāśavad bhāti pūrayitvā carācaram || 141

Thus, she is always and everywhere
revealed as the supreme sky.
Like the sun, she shines,
filling (all) that is living or not.

nirābhāsanirāveśanirānandacamatkṛtiḥ |
yā sparśavibhavā saiva **vyomācāra***gatiḥ smṛtā(R:sataḥ) ||*
142

Wonder without appearance,
without trance, without bliss,

---

[153] *Ghana* in the temporal sense of 'that which is without break of breach'.

she is a powerful feeling,
remembered by tradition as 'moving in the sky'.

sañcāru || *56*
There is a transmission.

mukhān mukhakramāyātaḥ sarvasaṃkalpavarjitaḥ |
vaktrāmnāyaḥ paro yo'yaṃ **saṃcāro***(R:')mitaḥ(BHU:eḥ)*
sthitaḥ || *143*

Going from mouth to mouth,
devoid of any personal choice,
this supreme oral tradition
is infinite transmission.

paryantu asāru || *57*
Ultimately, (phenomena) are without substance.

yatas tu citprakāso'yaṃ rājate tattadātmanā |
paramādvayavisphārarūpo'khaṇḍitamūrtimān || *144*

Since that light of awareness
shines as this and that,
—a supreme and non-dual expansion—
her manifestation is undivided.

nīlapītasitādyās tu varṇā grāhyabhuvaṃ śritāḥ |
*ye sarve te***'niśaṃ** *proccair* **niḥsāra***tvaṃ tato gatāḥ* || *145*

But since the colors, like blue, yellow or white
depend on the level of graspable (objective phenomena),
all of them are always and absolutely
without substance.

akalito saṃsāru || *58*
Saṃsāra (becomes) undivided.

bhedāḍambarasaṃkṣobhasvabhāvaḥ **kalanā***tmakaḥ* |
saṃsāraḥ *saṃsthito nityaṃ niyatagrahacetasām* || *146*

For those whose attention is conditioned in grasping,
samsara is always divisive activity,
by its very nature an overwhelming agitation,
the noise of duality.

prabuddhahṛdayānāṃ tu vikalpagrāsatas sadā |
anuttaraśivābhāsas sarvatraiva virājate || *147*

But, for those whose heart is well awake,
it shines always and everywhere,
as the appearance of absolute Śiva,
for (they) devour (all) concepts/dilemmas.

mithyābhimānu || *59*
Self-identification is false.

*dehaprāṇādy***ahaṅkāro** *mithya***iva** *svīkṛto janaiḥ* |
tattvatas tu sadā bhāti citsvarūpo 'vinaśvaraḥ || *148*

The ego that people identify with (phenomena)
such as the body, vital energy and so on, is verily false.
But in truth, (that ego) always shines
essentially as imperishable Consciousness.

guhyopadeśu || *60*
(This) is the secret teaching.

satataṃ bhrājamāno 'pi sarveṣāṃ sarvataḥ sadā |
guruvaktreṇa samprāpyo **guhyo** *'yam* **upadeśa***kaḥ* || *149*

Even though that secret teaching
actually shines in plain view,

always (present) for everyone,
one may get it (only) from the mouth of the master.

svapnabhramu || *61*
(The world becomes like) the delusion of a dream.

*anena prāptamātreṇa **svapnabhrānti**samo bhavet |*
bhāvābhāvaprapañcasya viśvavistāravibhramaḥ || *150*

Just by reaching this (secret teaching),
(the world[154]) becomes just like the delusion of a dream.
It (becomes) the confusion of the universal expanse
of the expanding lies[155] of presence and absence.

bhāva sabhāve sardha-avināśī sapanasabhāvanavi
ughanna | te ajanijaniravadhi agamapakāśī
idassadiṣṭikāci vipacchanna || **25**

ajātabrahmakathā ||
The teaching of the unborn Absolute.

chalāchala ūrmi || *62*
(BHU:phalāphalarūmi,R:ūmi,B:bhūmi)
It is a wave (on an ocean both) moving and unmoving/ both
true and false.

chalo(BHU:phalo) 'kasmāt samullāsas
tannāśe(R:nāśo')cchala ucyate |
*evaṃ **chalācchala**mayī sakṛd **ūrmiḥ** sthitā tu yā* || *151*

'Moving'/false because it manifests without a cause,
it is (also) said to be 'unmoving'/true when it disappears.
In this manner that (Consciousness) is present

---

[154] *Saṃsāra* and *ahaṅkāra* mentioned in chummās 58 and 59.
[155] *Prapañca.*

as a universal[156] wave, both moving and unmoving/both false and true.

samudrasyeva tattulyā viśvasthitir iyaṃ sthitā |
yataḥ samyaksamuddiṣṭā gandharvapuravat tadā || 152

The existence of everything
is just like (a wave) in the ocean.
Therefore, it is aptly taught
to be like a city in a cloud.

mahābhrāntisvarūpā tu niḥsārā kṛtakā abhitaḥ(R conj.:niḥsārā kṛtakā matā) | tasmān nātra grahaḥ kāryaḥ sadbhiḥ sattattvadarśibhiḥ || 153

This existence is a great delusion,
it is utterly constructed and devoid of substance.
Therefore, the true adepts who see reality
should not grasp at it.

nirāveśabhūmi || 63
(This) is a state without trance.

*ihāvaśiṣyate tasmād **bhūmiḥ** kācin nirāśrayā |*
*nistaraṅgatayā sākṣān **nirāveśā** niruttarā || 154*

Therefore, what remains according to this (teaching)
is an extraordinary state free from support,
absolute (and) without trance[157],
directly (experienced) as waveless.

asphura ulati(BHU:ulatti) || 64
She reverts[158] to non-manifestation.

---

[156] *Sakṛt.*
[157] There is no separation between deep meditation and daily life anymore.
[158] Hindī *ulṭā* « inverted », *ulṭī* « inversion ».

anantasaṃvidvisphārasphurattā layam āgatā |
yatra sarvojjhite dhāmni pare nityavikasvare || 155

The manifestation of the infinite expanse
of Consciousness dissolves away
in the all-transcending supreme abode
that is ever expanding.

asphurattā*svarūpe'smin sarvāvaraṇavarjite |*
saiva śaktir ihoddiṣṭā nirūpā vigatāvadhiḥ || 156

Within that essence without manifestation,
freed from all veils,
is this power pointed at here,
who is without form, without limits.

tadbalena yataḥ sarvam kālākālakalāvapuḥ |
sphurattām bhajate'nalpasvasvātantryamahodayāt || 157

It is by her strength that all,
embodied through the energies of time and eternity,
take part in manifestation,
(that is), because of the great rise of her own abundant
freedom.

akrama krama(R:-mu) || 65
It is a process without process.

bhinnaprathātmikā yāvad vṛttayo bahir āsthitāḥ |
*viṣayāharaṇaunmukhyais tāvad **krama** iti smṛtaḥ || 158*

When she manifests as duality,
(her) operations are outside.
Then the tradition calls this a 'process'

because (those movements) are turned towards grasping
objects.

taduttīrṇe pare yatra cidacidbhedavarjite |
*mahāvyomny advayatayā sarvo bhāty **akramas** tu saḥ ||*
159

When everything shines without duality
in the great empty sky, transcendent (and supreme),
devoid of the differences between
what is and what is not endowed with consciousness,
then he is 'without process'.

īdṛksvarūparūpo yo bhāty akramamahodayaḥ |
sa eva sarvatodik kaḥ kramaḥ ko'pi nirantaraḥ || 160

The one who shines with such an essence
is the great manifestation without process.
He is all-facing, so what process is this?
—An extraordinary uninterrupted process!

prāguktalakṣaṇe'nante śaktirūpe sadodite |
satataṃ saṃsthite sākṣāt saṅkalpakalanojjhite || 161

(This happens) in the infinite power
defined before, who is always actual,
present directly in full,
freed from the division of choices[159].

paramākāśapade nicu akame mama bhāve pasaro
apameyu | niśito vitti nicayu agamagame
ittalūkālukamuko adheyu || 26

(no *kathā* title here, neither in BHU nor in R)

---

[159] *Saṃkalpa.*

Paramākāśakathā (?) ||
The teaching of the supreme space.

alayu udayu || 66
He is without dissolving or arising.

padārthapralayo yatra svasvarūpodayas tataḥ |
akhaṇḍabhāvabhāso ya udayāstavivarjitaḥ || 162

That into which things dissolve,
that from which one's own essence arises,
is a manifestation that is not divided
into 'arising' and 'dissolving'[160].

athicī thiti || 67
She is an existence without existence / Standing in no-
stance.

bhedonmeṣasthitir yatra layaṃ yātā agame(R:')pade |
aprakampye nirākhyākhye sā asthitiḥ sthitir avyayā || 163

That existence which is the opening of differences
dissolves aways in the unreachable state,
unshakable, named "the Nameless":
that is the state not standing (anywhere, therefore)
imperishable.

saṃhārā sṛṣṭi || 68
She is (both) resorption and creation.

sarvasaṃhārasaṃhārapadāt sakalaniṣkalā |
svabhāvabhāvarūpeyaṃ sṛṣṭir ullasitā kramāt || 164

Following the state of resorption of resorption of all,

---

[160] *Asta*, to concur with the translation of *laya* as 'dissolution'.

she is (both) with and without divisions.
Naturally endowed with phenomena,
this creation arises gradually.

***adharapayodharamūlādhārita   acalitu   cighadirataṃ
avibhaccī || 27***
(... one line missing?)

rasatrayakathā ||
The teaching of the threefold taste.

vāyupithivi || 69
Winds becomes earth.

*calanaspandanoddeśarūpe(R em.:o,B:ī, Śr.: -rasī)
cañcalamūrtibhṛt |*
***vāyur** yas tena satatam āśyānatvam upāśritaḥ || 165
yatas tasmāt tu kāṭhinyarūpā **dharaṇir** ucyate |
viparītasvabhāvo 'yam akrameṇa vyavasthitaḥ || 166*

Wind is pointed out as movement and vibration,
he bears an unstable form.
Therefore, when he solidifies
completely,
he becomes hard
and is then called 'earth'.
(Wind and earth) have the opposite nature at the same time.

jalu jalanu(<jvalana) || 70 (R:jalajana)
Water becomes fire.

*dravarūpaṃ **jalaṃ** khyātam ādātuṃ tad yato 'kramāt |
agnidehaṃ tu tenaiva svīkṛtaṃ dhāmaśaktitaḥ || 167*

Water is known to be liquid,

since it becomes of that (form) in one instant[161].
But the body of fire digests this very (water),
because of the power of the abode of fire[162].

jaḍu ākāśu || *71*
Space is inert.

(R:y-)eṣāṃ caturṇāṃ bhavato yatrotpattilayau sadā |
vyomni *tat tu* **jaḍaṃ** *proktaṃ niścalatvād acetanam* || *168*

These four (elements) always
arise from and dissolve into space.
But (space) is said to be inert,
it is devoid of consciousness because it doesn't move.

viparītavṛtti || *72* (BHU:viparītachatti)
There happens (then) an inverted movement.

ākhyātā guruvaktrokta(BHU:ortha)yuktyeyaṃ **vṛttir**
akramāt |
viparītagamenoccaiḥ sākṣātkāratayoditā || *169*

That movement (of the four elements), once known all at
once
through the means told by the master,
arises directly (and) from above[163]
through an inverted movement.

kañcukasvarūpu || *73*
(Consciousness) is the essence of the restrictions.

---

[161] Its form is to change form in one instant.
[162] According to MW, *dhāman* can refer to the « site of the sacred fire ». Also, water first dominates fire, being the ocean above the fire of the End of Times. But eventually this Fire takes over.
[163] *Uccais*, the four elements operate 'from above', from the space element.

***kañcuko**nmeṣavistārarūpiṇī sarvagā sadā |*
viśvavaicitryacitrasya sūtradhāratvam āgatā || 170

Always present in all,
she is the vast expanse of the unfolding of restrictions[164].
She is the creator[165] of the wonderful painting
of the variety of everything.

māyīyu(R:-a)rūpu || 74
(Material) form is a magical illusion.

rūpaṃ *yad dṛśyajātaṃ tan **māyīyaṃ** bhedavisṛtam*
(R:bhedavistara, BHU:bhedavistṛta) |
[166]atāttvikaṃ paricchinnaṃ tat sattāvadhisaṃśritiḥ ||171

Whatever form is seen, that is a magical illusion,
an expansion of duality.
It is not real, it is limited,
it is the support of the limits of existence (at its grossest
end).

nairūpu || 75
(Reality) is formless.

---

[164] Restrictions like time, space and form.

[165] A *sūtradhāra* literally means one who holds the threads. It can be used to denote the puppeteer who hold the strings of a puppet, controlling its movements. The same name is given to the director of a play who holds the "threads" of the plot. It is also the name given to a draftsman or architect who plots a map or a geometric diagram or maṇḍala. Here it refers to the painter of a picture. That same metaphor is used at the start of the *Kaula-sūtra*, presented by Śitikaṇṭha as a summary of the teachings of Niṣkriyānanda: *ṣaḍdarśanavyatirikte 'rthe **sūtradhāra**bhuvaṃ śritaḥ | rudrāvatāro durvāsaḥ stūyate sparśakāmasūḥ ||* 'Durvāsa, the incarnation of Rudra, who desired (the reality) without touch, is praised as present in the reality distinct (and superior to that taught by) the six philosophies—he has entered the plane of the creator (*sūtradhāra*).'

[166] R ends here, but N. Rastogi quotes the colophon in its introduction, saying that he was told this colophon by Pandit Dīnanāth Yakṣa who claimed to have another manuscript, more complete.

Tad evaṃ bhautikaṃ rūpaṃ nirniketacidañcitam |
vibhāti nityaṃ tattvena (BHU:nītaṃ) **nīrūpaṃ**
paramārthinaḥ(<paramārthataḥ) || 172

Thus, material form is
Woven with abodeless Consciousness.
In reality, she shines without interruption,
being really formless.

avutto phala || 76
The result manifests without (a cause).

*a*hetukatayā(B:kathayā) anantaśākhaṃ yugapad akramāt
|
parāparavibhedais tu bāhyāntaravapuḥ sadā || 173
vṛtti*prapañcasampatti***phalaṃ** *prollasitaṃ mahat |*
anuptaṃ paracidvyomnas tadā āścaryāvahaṃ satām ||
174

(Then) the permanent essence of the outside and inside
(worlds), displayed both as superior and inferior,
manifests fully, simultaneously and all at once,
with infinite branches (and) without a (visible) cause.
This is the great miracle for the true beings:
the fruit that has not been sown
—the perfection of phenomenal states
of the sky of supreme awareness.

anaṣṭa(B:anaṣṭi)dṛṣṭi || 77
(Non-dual) vision (never) perishes.

bāhyasthā bhedarūpeyaṃ dṛṣṭir ābhyantarī(B:atyantarī)
tathā |
avibhedamayī bhāti nirmalā nirbhramā sadā || 175

That vision manifests as duality when standing outside.
When is stands inside,
it shines without duality,
always pure and without error.

asya dṛgyugalasya alam ākṣepakatayā gatiḥ |
tatas tu saṃsthitā tasmād etaduttīrṇalakṣaṇā || 176

The experience[167] of those two visions
is able to project (the states of bondage and liberation).
But then, she stands up, (awake as both).
Therefore, she transcends both.

*kācit tu paramā **dṛṣṭir anaṣṭā** suvikasvarā |*
nirniketanirātaṅkamahājñānodayātmikā || 177

Rather, she is an extraordinary ultimate vision.
She doesn't perish, she expands powerfully,
(for) she is the arising of Great Knowledge
without abode and without fear.

padma(BHU:chadma)vṛṣṭi || 78
She is (like) a rain of lotuses.

***padma(BHU:chadma)vṛṣṭir** iva uccais tu patitā saiva*
nityaśaḥ | sarvatra viśvavibhavavyāpinī paramādvayā ||
178

That (Consciousness) falls abruptly and eternally,
like a rain of lotuses,
pervading every corner of the universal expanse,
absolutely non-dual.

sarvanāśu(B:nāśtu) || 79

---

[167] *Gati.*

He is the destruction of all.

*yatra akramamahāpātāt **sarva**(BHU:parva)graham*
aśeṣataḥ |
svam(BHU:sve) jhaṭity ātmavibhavaṃ
dehaprāṇādisaṃsthitam || 179
tathā ātmīyam anantaṃ tu viṣayākṣādivistaram |
bhāvakṣayamaye(BHU:aṃ) bhīmam
asparśaparamāmbare || 180
*sāmarasyatayā nityaṃ **nāśaṃ** yāti samantataḥ |*
sa ko'pi niḥsamaśamaḥ śivo'nantaḥ paro'vyayaḥ || 181

He is that extraordinary being, peace beyond compare,
good, infinite, supreme, imperishable,
into whom all that is grasped
goes to total destruction in a manner of fusion,
because of that sudden and great fall (of the true vision).
All one's manifestation,
body, vital energy, etc.,
as well as all one's infinite expanse
of the organs and their objects
(dissolve) suddenly into the terrible
ultimate sky beyond feeling,
the destruction of phenomena.

grasanagrāsu || 80
(Even) devouring is devoured[168].

***grasana**syāpi saṃhartā mahā**saṃhāra**vigrahaḥ |*
duṣprāpaḥ sarvataḥ sākṣād dhaṭhayuktyā anubhūyate ||
182

---

[168] *Grāsa* or *grasana*, "devouring" belongs to the lexical field of eating, connected with (digestive) fire, the sun and the moon, breath, Time, death and the notion of impurity. The Kaula practice (to which the Krama belongs) aims at transcending those dualities. In this dialectical process, both polarities are dissolved, for the dissolving action it itself dissolved: Death dies, the time comes of the end of Time, emptiness is emptied, and so on.

He devours even devouring,
the embodiment of total resorption,
impossible to reach for anyone,
(but) directly experienced through powerful practice[169].

nirāvaraṇalābhu(BHU:lātu) || 81
He is the gain without veils.

*akṛtrimaḥ paro **lābho nirāvaraṇa**vibhramaḥ* |
ayam eva guroḥ samyagāśayo grāsaghasmaraḥ || 182

He is the supreme authentic gain,

---

[169] *Haṭha-yuktyā*. The adjective *haṭha*, "violent, with force", is used several times in this teaching, always with the idea of bypassing the conventional hierarchies, as in verse 30 with words like *Anuttara*. Abhinavagupta interprets it along Kaula lines in the *Parātriṃśikā-vivaraṇa*. In *chummā* 40, it is about "hastily swallowing all dualities", as in *chummā* 94. In the *Ciñcinīmata*, the energy of the Goddess pierces speedily to the supreme state : *haṭhakramaparāśaktirvedhayet [k: haṭhakramyaparāśaktivedhayes; kh gh: haṭha * * parā-] mānavigraham* | *vyomātītaṃ vyomapadam uditaṃ [gh: - mudinaṃ] bhānavīkramam* || *7/212* || "The supreme power of the inevitable (*haṭha*) process pierces the body of pride, beyond the sky, arisen (as) the state of the sky, the process of (spiritual) realization". Later in that same chapter on the Krama teachings, those verses gather all the important notions of the tradition: *viśvākāroditaṃ cakraṃ viśvasthityāvabhāsakam* | *viśvasaṃhārakas tejas tattejo grāsaghasmaraḥ* || *7/235* || *vividhena vibhāgena haṭhakramam anuttamam* |
karoti kramiko yogī sa yogī yoginīpriyaḥ || *7/236* || "The yogi who gradually manifests the wheel of all forms, who makes shine the existence of everything, who dissolves all; is the Splendor, the Splendor that is eager to eat in every way and in all its parts. It is the inevitable process, the Ultimate: the yogi who does this gradually is a yogi dear to the Yoginīs". In the *Kramasadbhāva-tantra*, the Goddess is eating all in the same way : *haṭharāvā arāvasthā rāveṇa haṭhabhakṣakī* || *2/28* || "She is a forceful cry in a state of silence, devouring forcefully (everything) through this cry". Later she is *abhāvena tu sā devī jñānena samatāṃ gatā* | *haṭhabhāvā svabhāvasthā aṭavyāṃ haṭhamadhyagā* || *2/36* || "the Goddess to be equalized by perception of non-being (between in- and out-breath) : she is inevitable (*haṭha*), standing as one's own nature, wild, living in the inevitable center". In fact, it can be applied to any process (*krama, pāka, kavalana, grāsa*) in order to stress its inevitability, its overpowering strength.

devoid of the veil of confusion.
He is the true meaning of the master,
that voracious devouring!

nirāloku prakāśu || 82
It is a light without light.

*bāhyāntaragataiḥ sarvair **ālokaiḥ** parivarjitam |*
*idam eva mahāsaṃvit**tejo**'nantaṃ sadoditam* || 184

Totally devoid of all
outer and inner lights,
this is the great light of Consciousness,
always present.

mahāsaṃhāranāśu || 83 (absent in B)
It is the great Destruction of destruction.

*idam eva **mahāgrāsagrāsakaṃ** kalpanojjhitam |*
tīkṣṇātitīkṣṇarūpiṇyā saṃvidā labhyate sphuṭam || 185

This is the great Devouring of devouring,
devoid of imagination,
clearly obtained
by extremely sharp awareness.

śivāśivanāśu || 84
It is the destruction of good and bad.

idam eva tu sarvasya bandhamokṣobhayātmanaḥ |
*śivāśivasya **saṃhantṛ**nistaraṅgaṃ nirantaram* || 186

This is the waveless, the uninterrupted
destroyer of good and evil,
of all that consists in the couple
of (polarized) bondage and liberation.

naṣṭe'kālanāśu || 85
In that destruction, (dependence on) absence of time is (also) destroyed.

saṃvitsaṅkalpakalanāsvarūpasyāntarasya yaḥ |
akālo *nirvikalpākhyasaṃvidrūpas tu* **bhakṣakaḥ** || 187

The absence of time that belongs to
the inner dividing energy of concepts withing Consciousness
is the form of Consciousness called 'without concepts',
(because) it devours (those concepts).

so'pi yatra **kṣayaṃ** *yāto nairapekṣyapade'game |*
sarvaśaṅkāvinirmuktas so'yaṃ ko'py avaśiṣyate || 188

But even that (Consciousness) is destroyed
in the independent state beyond reach.
This is the extraordinary one that remains,
freed from all fears.

diṣṭināśu || 86
(This) is the destruction of vision.

ayam eva tu **dṛk**chakteḥ *sarvasyā* **nāśa** *ucyate |*
niḥsaṅketaparajñānarūpo niravadhir mahān || 189

This is what is called the destruction
of all the power of vision,
the supreme knowledge without secret teachings[170],
the great limitless.

Rūha(BHU:ūha) cāru || 87

(This) is the rising progress.

ādyonmeṣaparākoṭivimarśa **rūha(<roha)** *ucyate* |
tatraiva caraṇaṃ **cāra***sthito 'yaṃ nityanirmalaḥ* || *190*

The realization of the ultimate degree
of primordial awakening is called 'rising'.
There verily is progress,
the eternally spotless unmoving progression.

acāru || *88*
(Thus,) not moving, (one acts).

itthaṃ nijāt parād(B:parā) rūpān **niṣkampaś(B:niṣkalāt)**
ceṣṭate punaḥ |
sarvaṃ karma sadā kurvan sarvatra samadarśanaḥ || *191*

Thus, without trembling, one acts anew
from one's own supreme essence,
doing everything always
with an equal vision everywhere.

avibandhamudra || *89*
(This) is the gesture without bonds.

*eṣā sthitā mahā***mudrā** *kulākulakalojjhitā* |
aniruddhā *sadā sarvaiḥ saṃvidunmeṣavibhramaiḥ* || *192*

This is the great gesture
free from the division into transcendent and immanent.
She is never blocked by any confusion
that unfolds from Consciousness.

avācyu saṃbandha || *90*
(This) is a relation beyond speech.

sarvottīrṇasvarūpeṇa saha nityam ayaṃ sthitaḥ |
*sāmarasyasvabhāvo 'sau **sambandho vāgvivarjitaḥ** || 193*

He is forever present
together with his transcendent essence.
That relation is a natural fusion,
(a relation) beyond words.

avitto prasādu || 91
(This) is grace immortal.

*ayaṃ **prasādaḥ** paramo bhāto nityaṃ svarūpataḥ |*
***avṛttā**nantamahimā*
sarvākhyaya(<ākhyāna,BHU:pyaya)vivarjitaḥ || 194

This is grace supreme,
shining eternally from one's own essence,
whose greatness is infinite and immortal,
is devoid of anything that can be given a name.

aniyatopadeśu || 92
(For,) the teaching is not limited.

***upadeśo** hy **aniyataḥ** sandehābhāvalakṣaṇaḥ |*
sāśrayānāśrayapadadvandvabhedair anāvṛtaḥ || 195

For the teaching is not limited,
as it is characterized by the absence of doubt.
It is not conditioned by the dilemma
of being 'with support' or 'without support'.

vāḍavokaraṇu || 93
The submarine fire destroys (the body).

nānāvṛttisamullāsaḥ pratyāvṛttitayā sadā |
*nigīryate tadā akāya**karaṇo vāḍavaḥ** smṛtaḥ || 196*

When the whole manifestation with its many movements
is persistently destroyed by turning back[171],
then the tradition calls it a 'submarine fire"
that destroys the body.

khamudrābhyāsu || *94*
(This) is the practice of the Gesture of space.

ayam eva sadā purvo heyādeyakramojjhitaḥ |
nirdhāmadhāmavibhavaḥ **khamudrābhyāsa** *ucyate* || *197*

That ever original (Consciousness)
devoid of the necessity[172] of taking and giving
is the expansion of an Abode without abode,
called 'the practice of the Gesture of space'.

jambukīkaraṇu || *95*
It is becoming like a coward.

sṛgālo 'nāśam āyāti pratyāvṛttyavalokanāt |
yathā tatheha paramāṃ niruttaracitiṃ sadā || *198*
samālokya haṭhād dehavistāro layam āgataḥ |
jambukīkaraṇākhyo 'sau khyātaḥ ko 'py akramakramaḥ ||
199

A coward escapes death
by looking backward.
Just like that, here when one (looks backward),
one sees fully the permanent ultimate (and) absolute
Consciousness
the expanse of the body
dissolves away by force.
This is known as 'becoming like a coward',

---

[171] Consciousness turns back on herself.
[172] *Krama.*

an extraordinary process without process.

āpāgāsu(<āṇava grāsu) || *96*
(When) individuality is devoured, (he becomes the Self).

āṇavā*dimalair vyāpto dehādigrahasaṃśrayāt* |
*ātmā tad***grāsa** *uditaḥ pārimityaparikṣayāt* || *200*

He is pervaded
by the impurities of individuality, etc.
because he grasps at the body, etc.
as support (on which awareness dwells).
When that is devoured,
he rises as the Self
because limitation
is totally destroyed.

sakalaharaṇu || *97*
Everything is removed.

samastaharaṇād *vāraḥ sa eveha gataḥ svataḥ* |
nirīho'yam akathyas tu sadasadbhramavarjitaḥ || *201*

Because everything is removed,
That very limitation[173]
disappears spontaneously in this (very life).
But this absence of desire cannot be taught,
(for) it is devoid of the mistakes of "there is" and "there is
not".

khi u khi u || *98* (B:khita khita)
It is devoured again and again.

---

[173] *Vāra.* Mark Dyckowski chose to translate *vāra* as "occasion", meaning
that the occasion for awakening appears (reading *āgata* instead of *gata*)
spontaneously, "because everything has been removed".

yad viśvavibhavaṃ citram īṣallīnaṃ svacitkaraiḥ |
*tad eva bhoktṛbhojyādibhāgād **bhuktam** ihocyate || 202*

The expanse of everything, (like) a wonderful painting,
starts dissolving because of (the rise of) the rays
of one's own Consciousness.
That same (expanse) is said here to be devoured
when (all its) parts, such as the eater and the eaten, (are
devoured).

caṭṭaniścaṭṭī || 99
(Breath is both) interrupted[174] and uninterrupted.

caṭṭaḥ prāṇavināśas tu niścaṭṭaḥ prāṇaghaṭṭakaḥ |
*sa eveha vinirdiṣṭaś **caṭṭaniścaṭṭi**(S:a)kodayaḥ || 203*

"Interrupted" because the breath disappears,
but (also) "uninterrupted", because the breath vibrates.
This (breath) is pointed out here
as the manifestation that is (both) interrupted and
uninterrupted.

lāhapavāhī || 100 (S:lāhapravāhī)
It is a flowing wave.

śaktyodayasthitisphāravigrahaṃ lāti yas sadā |
*tenaiva harati kṣiprād yato **lāhas** tataḥ smṛtaḥ || 204*

Its power constantly bestows (*lā*)
embodiment as the expanse of manifestation and
existence.
In the same manner, it suddenly removes (*ha,* that
embodiment).

---

[174] See MW *caṭana* : n. cracking, splitting and *cāṭayati-,* to break.

Therefore, tradition call it "a wave"[175].

sa eva pravahadrūpaḥ **pravāha** *iti kathyate |*
avināśasvabhāvo yo nirvitarkakramo 'kramaḥ || 205

That very (wave) is flowing
and so is called "a flow".
Its nature doesn't perish (for) it is not a process:
it is a process that may not be rationally investigated.

lāhapravāhikā *seyaṃ hānivṛddhimayī prathā |*
svabhāvagaganābhāsarūpācchinnaiva bhāsate || 206

This flow of a wave
is an expansion that is both retraction and expansion.
It shines as absolutely uninterrupted,
as the appearance of the sky of one's own nature.

yo apariśa paramagagana parathānā ca u **pīṭhapithyādi**
sa rūpa |
bhāsaniti na devī caya nānānijamarīci maya phurandi
arūpa || 28

pīṭhacatuṣkakathā ||
The teaching of the fourfold sacred seat.

tanughanu || 101
She is (both) thin and gross.

tanutvaṃ sarvasaṃhārāt(BHU:ś) citir yātā samantataḥ |
svatantrasṛṣṭivisphārād **ghana**tvaṃ tu samāśritā || 207

Consciousness becomes thin

---

¹⁷⁵ *Lāha* means a kind of lac in modern hindī. But it resembles the sanskrit
laharī 'wave' and the explanation given fits a flowing (*pravahat*) wave that
comes and goes away.

because all dissolve completely (in her).
She becomes gross when
(her) creative freedom unfolds.

ekasyā eva satataṃ kālasaṃhārasaṃvidaḥ |
parādvayācyutāvṛttiḥ khagākhyeyaṃ vyavasthitā || 208

From only one Consciousness
that resorbs Time, (all comes).
She is a state that doesn't fall, supreme and non-dual,
Standing well as 'the One moving in space'.

layathānā   urdhva   talayu   udayā   aparokṣepa
sarisamabhāve   puru   aniketanavicci   mahapalayāthyo
avibhinno savusadatta sabhāve || 29

layodayakathā ||
The teaching of merging and arising (within
Consciousness).

antā anta || 102
He is the end of the end.

antaḥ *smṛto vināśas tu tasy****āntas****ta(...missing) |*
śāstraprapañcakalanāvarjito bhāti sarvataḥ || 209

'End' means destruction.
But when that ('end') ends,
he shines everywhere, devoid
of the divisions of the lies of the teachings.

adhu ūdhu(B:adharūcu) || 103
He is (both) below and above.

adhaḥ *śabdena kathito vedyo rūpādivibhramaḥ |*

bhavabhedapadas tuccho(B:missing) rāgadveṣādiviplutaḥ
|| 210

'Below' means the knowable,
the delusion of forms and so on,
the plane of dualistic becoming,
empty, immersed in attraction and aversion and so on.

sa eveha samākhyātaḥ sarvottirṇas tv(B:missing)
anāmayaḥ |
*vyaktāvyaktadvayottīrṇa **ūrdhvaṃ** śivamayaṃ param ||*
211

That same one is here called 'transcendent',
without blemish, (because) is transcends
(the opposites of) 'manifest' and 'unmanifest',
it is the 'above', Śiva supreme.

*tathā ca ruruṇā proktam(BHU:rtham) **adhaḥ** śabdena*
tattvataḥ |
sṛṣṭisthityupasaṃhārarūpaṃ bhedatrayaṃ sadā || 212

And this it is said by Ruru (Bhairava)
that 'below' really means
the ongoing triple duality
of creation, existence and destruction.

*smṛtam **ūrdhvaṃ**(B:missing)   tu   sahasā   tadeveha*
aniketanam |
kālagrāsāntadehaṃ tu sarvadikkaṃ nirantaram || 213

'Above', here (in our teaching)
means that Audacity without abode
whose body is the complete dissolution of Time,
who is all pervading and without interruption.

diṭṭo niṭṭo || *104 (BHU:diṭhṭho niṭhṭho)*
He is destroyed (as soon as) seen.

ittham bhedamayaṃ sarvam
kālāgnyādi(BHU:ākālādi)śivāntakam |
*tattvena vyapadeśena sakṛd yad **dṛṣṭam** akramāt* || 214

In this way, all that is made of duality,
from bottom to top[176],
become seen, all at once, without transition,
through (this) true teaching.

*tatkṣaṇān **nāśam** āyāti tad evādvayacitpade* |
asparśe
sparśa(B:apsarśasparśa)hnutā(B:hrutvā<hnutam
a)svalpāsamparkato 'bhitaḥ || 215

From that instant onward, it is definitely
destroyed in the state of non-dual Consciousness
beyond feeling, devoid of feeling,
without even the faintest touch (of duality).

Conclusion of Niṣkriyānanda

pūjāsaṃkramakathanakrameṇākramaparaḥ |
pīṭheśvarīmukhāyātagīticarcāmahodayaḥ || 216
ko 'py anuttaracidvyomaprāpakaḥ satatoditaḥ |
vācyavācakasambandhanirmukto jayatād ajaḥ || 217

Excellent is that Unborn,
freed from the relation between word and meaning,
that extraordinary one, wholly risen,

---

[176] Litt. "from the Fire of (the End of) Time, up to Śiva ».

144

guide to the space of absolute Consciousness.

Devoted to what is beyond process
through the processes of worship, transmission and oral
teaching,
he is the great arising of the dialogue[177]
—the song revealed orally by the mistresses of the sacred
seat[178].

pañcādhikaśateneha padaugho yaḥ sthitaḥ paraḥ |
trimśaccarcārahasyena nirbharas tatra sarvadā || 218

Here that supreme flow of words
consists of one hundred and five (*chummās*)[179],
everywhere overflowing with
the secret of thirty talks[180].

carceyaṃ bhāti nitarāṃ samyaggarbhagatā samā |
vaktrād vaktrakrameṇoccaiḥ satāṃ hṛdi vijṛmbhate || 219

That dialogue shines to the highest degree,
equal with all that is in the womb (of consciousness).
It blossoms fully in the heart of true (adepts)
through oral transmission.

---

[177] *Carcā*, 'alternate recitation of a poem by two persons'. May allude to the thirty verses in the vernacular. Note that the last of these thirty verses comes right after this, in the Conclusion itself.

[178] The Yoginīs of the sanctuary of Śrīśaila in the South of India, or those of the cremation ground of Karavīra near Mingora, capital city of the Swat valley, in what is nowadays Pakistan, the Yoginīs led by Maṅgalādevī. Ten kilometers to the east of Mingora, lies today Manglor, also called 'manglawar', the 'door of Maṅgalā'. Perhaps the cremation ground of Maṅgalā was there? A Tibetan pilgrim of the 14th century tells us that at the entry of Uḍḍiyāna stood a sandalwood statue of Maṅgalādevī, among other sacred places. See Sanderson « The śaiva exegesis of Kashmir », in *Mélanges à la mémoire d'Hélène Brunner*, p. 267, n. 107.

[179] We count only 104 *chummās*. I believe the ultimate one is silence, fort the absolute cannot be expressed (*akathya*).

[180] The thirty verses in *prākṛta* language.

pīṭhāgatta peṭhī śarivadanāgīti kathāka mukta esa jhalakku anubhaveti nirupamacissadanā saṅkāmādi kurā u avikaghu || 30

gītikathā ||
The teaching of the song (of the Yoginīs).

evaṃ tattvaṃ vibhātīha śāntāc(B:ś) chāntataraṃ param |
pūjyapūjakapūjādivikalpaparivarjitam || 220

This principle shines here,
more peaceful than peace, supreme,
devoid of the fabrications
of a thing to be worshipped, a worshipper and worship.

sākṣātkāramahājñānayogadhyānādisaṃkṣayāt |
sarvatra sarvato nityaṃ kurvan(<kṛtam)napi viceṣṭitam ||
221
keṣāṃ cinmahatāṃ nūnaṃ satāṃ
a(BHU:vyut)kramacetasām |

Even though it is eternally accomplished
in all respects because (in it)
because the direct experience of Great Knowledge
has destroyed yoga and meditation,
(still) it is practiced even now[181]
by some extraordinary and true (adepts)
with a vast awareness and turned towards what is non
gradual.

ṣaḍbhir astrair mahodbhāsair ahaṅkāras tu garvitaḥ ||
222

---

[181] *Nūnam.*

*indriyākhyair   anantābhir   vāsanābhir   vivāsitaḥ
(B:vināśitaḥ) | yaḥ sa eva purā ahaṃ tu durvāsā nāma
viśrutaḥ || 223*

But, perfumed (*vivāsita*) with an endless number of habits,
the *ego* is proud with (its) six weapons of great splendor[182]
called 'the sense'.
That one (proud ego) is me, who was called 'Durvāsa'
in a previous life[183].

*yaḥ prākṣāptamahājñānasiddhanāthaprasādataḥ |
sa evāhaṃ tu saṃjāto niṣkriyo vigataspṛhaḥ || 224*

I am he who was graced by the Siddha lord
with the direct experience of Great Knowledge.
(And) this is me, who is (re)born as actionless[184],
(all) desires gone.

*nirahaṅkāraciddhāmavyāpī nityaṃ vikasvaraḥ |
sarvatra sarvataḥ sākṣāccaramāṇo 'py anāvṛtaḥ || 225*

(I'm now) all-pervasive as the abode of Consciousness
devoid of *ego*, always expanding.
Even though I move everywhere in all situations,
I am unconfined (in any place).

*svasvarūpasamāviṣṭo nirbhayaḥ saṃsthito 'calaḥ |
itthaṃ   rahasyam   atulaṃ(B:aṭṭālam)   nirbhayaṃ   te
prakāśitam || 226*

Absorbed into my own essence,

---

[182]The six senses: five, plus the mind (*manas*). This is a rather Buddhist
formulation.
[183] *Purā*. There is a play of words on Durvāsa, a legendary sage famous for his
bad temper, the verbal root -*vās* "to inhabit, stay" and *vāsanā* "habit, trace left
by repeated pas actions'.
[184] Niṣkriyānanda.

I'm well established, firm and fearless.
Thus, the secret beyond compare
(and) without fear has been revealed to you (Vidyānanda).

kāraṇair apy agamyaṃ tu niḥsandigdham anuttaram |
avināśam anāveśaṃ sarveṣāṃ satatoditam || 227

It is beyond even the reach of (ordinary) faculties,
free from confusion, absolute,
imperishable, without (limited) trance,
ever present to all.

asparśasparśavistāram adhiṣṭhānam apūrvakam |
tasmād etat samāviśya satataṃ niravagrahaḥ || 228

It is the expanse of a sensation without touch,
the Primordial Ground.
Getting henceforward absorbed into (that),
be ever without constraints.

unmanībhāvanirato vihara svasvatantrataḥ |
paramānubhavonmādacarvaṇonmattacetanaḥ || 229

Enjoy (life) freely,
fully in love with the state beyond mind,
your heart mad with savouring
the intoxication of the ultimate experience.

...loke krame ||
..in the way of world.[185]

vaktrād vaktreṇa vaktavyaṃ nedaṃ lekhyaṃ tu pustake |
[186]

śāstraprapañcaracanāvarjitaṃ hi yato 'bhitaḥ || 230

---

[185] A part is missing here.
[186] B stops here.

This should be told from mouth to mouth,
but not written in a book,
for (this teaching) is utterly devoid
of the order (found in) scholastic chatter.

The Conclusion of 'Anantaśakti' Vidyānanda, the
Compiler of the Oral Secret Teachings of the Yoginīs

ittham mukhāgamarahasya mahodayena |
pūrṇātipūrṇam amṛtaṃ paramārthasāram || 231
nirvartitaṃ munivareṇa rahasyagarbhaṃ |
śāstraprapañcakalanākalitaṃ paraṃ yat || 232

Thus, the overflowing ambrosia of the secret oral teaching
(of the Yoginīs)[187], fuller than full, the supreme womb of
secrets,
unfragmented by the divisions of scholastic lies,
the essence of supreme truth,
has been entirely revealed (in the human world)
by the great lord, the best of silent sages.

saṃsārasaṃbhrama(?<ṃ) ca ya(t)
pravibhāgabandhasaṃbandhasaṃkṣayagater
avikalpamūrtiḥ | sākṣādanāviladhiyā laghuvākkrameṇa
mudrādharas tu vidadhe tad anantaśaktiḥ || 233

Having destroyed (false) relations, bonds and divisions
of the delusion of saṃsāra,
I, (Vidyānanda), composed this text.
I am the embodiment of thoughtless (awareness free form
words).

---

[187] The *Chummā-sampradāya*, the Oral Secret Teachings of the Yoginīs, on
which Niṣkriyānanda composed a *Commentary* (*Prakāśa*) compiled here by
his disciple Vidyānanda.

(Nevertheless), I, who bear the mark (of the Absolute)[188],
endowed with infinite powers[189],
composed this (book) with those brief words,
thanks to (my) direct vision of the Wild One[190].

191

kālākālakalākalāpavibhavaṃ sambhakṣya cidvṛttito
bhittvājñānamahāndhakāram abhitaḥ
samyagdayātattvataḥ | udghāṭyāśu(R.:-aṃśu)
niruttarottaradṛśāc(R.:-ā) chummākhyasaṃketake
bhedābhedavivarjite nirupame proccaiḥ prakāśaḥ kṛtaḥ ||
234

Having devoured, through the operation of consciousness,
the expanse of all the energies in Time and beyond,
having pierced through the great darkness of ignorance,
completely, truly and out of compassion,
having unlocked (it) at once with an absolutely supreme
gaze,
the secret (oral) teaching called '*chummā*',
devoid of duality and unity, without equal,
has been revealed powerfully.

iti cchummāsaṃketaprakāśaḥ śrīniṣkriyānandaprakāśitaḥ
sampūrṇaḥ || ||

---

[188] And also, 'who bear the six insignia' of a Kāpālika ascetic—the skull bowl
and the trident among them. For we know, from the *Ciñcinīmata*, that
Vidyānanda indeed was an ascetic bearing those traditional signs.

[189] Ananta-śakti : this is the name of the Author of the Commentary to the
Vātulanātha-sūtra, a shorter version of the *Chummā-saṃpradāya*. Should we
understand that Vidyānanda is the Author of this shorter version and of its
Commentary? I believe so.

[190] The Wild One is Niṣkriyānanda, the Author of the *Chummā-saṅketa-*
prakāśa.

[191] This last verse is also recorded by R as being "according to P. Dinanath
Yaksh".

Thus, the *Illumination of the Secret Teaching*, revealed by
Niṣkriyānanda, is complete.

Colophon by the Scribe

saṃpreṣite cetasi hāritārthajñaptyai
mahājñānabhavatsakāśam |
yuktyā yayā vedyate(vedayute?) tadantas tat tattvavid
vetti vijṛmbhitaṃ te ||

When the heart is impelled to know the lost meaning,
the intimate presence of Great Knowledge
is known through the (right) mean, so that in the end
the knower of reality knows your expansion.

na dṛśyate tvatpratibhāsaśakteḥ
svapne'rthavaicitryanimittam anyat |
taddṛṣṭasāmarthyatayā sadaiṣā
viśvaprapañcaprathanaikahetuḥ ||

This is not seen because of your power of illusory
appearance,
(like) in a dream caused by the diversity of objects (as if)
other (than Consciousness).
(But) that (illusory power) is always the only cause of the
manifestation of universal phenomena (and discourses
about them)[192],
because of the efficiency of seeing (those appearances)[193].

divākaravatsasya || *śivāya namaḥ* ||
(This manuscript) belong to the son of Divākara. Homage
to Śiva!

---

[192] According to another meaning of *prapañca*.
[193] Here 'seeing' is another name for consciousness.

152

Reflections on the Chummās

What follows is not a scholarly commentary, but a series of personal meditations inspired by the *Chummās*—until the final one: silent awareness.

Plato once said that light blinds those who have lived too long in darkness. Accustomed to mistaking shadows for reality, unaware even of their own ignorance, such souls are first wounded by the brightness of truth. In the same way, dear reader, know that what we are about to approach is not conventional knowledge, but the wild, searing territory of the *Yoginīs*, whose sole and sacred desire is to pull us out of the cavern of forgetfulness.

It is essential to enter these teachings both cautiously and boldly. As Krishna reminds us in the *Bhagavad Gītā*, what seems sweet at first often turns bitter, while what first tastes bitter may become a nectar to those who persevere beyond their initial reactions.

We are stepping into a sanctuary—not a place of retreat, but a crucible of transformation. Let us proceed without presumption, but with steady resolve. Let us lay aside our assumptions and let silence speak. For it is only with a clear mind and an open heart that we can receive what the *Yoginīs* offer: the bare recognition of what we truly are.

Notice also that gender is not fixed here; it may even shift within one sentence, like the face of the Yoginī. "Gender-fluid," and yet it rests as the immovable ground of all genders and numbers. Still, this entire teaching is not concerned with "deconstruction," but rather with relaxing into infinite Goodness—the Nameless Goddess.

So let us enter.

1 – The Practice of Recognition: Space as the Symbol of Self-Awareness

yatremāḥ saṃvidaḥ sarvāḥ sabāhyābhyantaroditāḥ |
asparśaparamākāśe nirnikete pare śive || 38

vyaktāvyaktapadātīte niḥspandānandasundare |
līyante kramayogena tal liṅgaṃ saṃsmṛtaṃ param || 39

sarvātigaṃ tad evoccaiḥ prathitaṃ sarvagatvataḥ |
svābhijñānatayā nityaṃ jagattritayabhedataḥ || 40

The tradition says that
the supreme Liṅga is that supreme Śiva,
that supreme space without dwelling,
devoid of sensation,
beyond the manifest and the non-manifest,
beautiful with the bliss beyond vibration,
where all cognitions, whether from
inside or from outside, dissolve away gradually.

All-pervading (and) all-transcending,
it thus displays itself to noble beings,
as recognition of oneself,
everyday revealed as the three worlds.

Commentary

The sages tell us: what we seek, we already are. Yet we continue to search. Why?

Let's return to something so simple it's often ignored: falling asleep. Each night, the miracle occurs—everything fades. Our body, our thoughts, our worries, our sense of self. Gone. As in death, we keep nothing. Not even memory. And paradoxically, without this dissolution, we cannot survive. We surrender daily to this vanishing. The empire of our waking life, so fiercely defended, is handed over to the nothingness of sleep without protest. We long for it.

This pattern isn't limited to sleep—it plays out constantly. Every sensation, every thought, every moment we try to hold slips away. The taste of a pastry, a memory, a sudden noise—all arise and vanish. We live in a cycle of appearance and disappearance. But where do these moments go?

At first glance: nowhere. Yet there's a *witness* to this disappearance. Some presence perceives the absence, this quiet "Ah, it's gone." The Yoginīs (or the One Yoginī) point here. To a living presence that embraces both presence and absence. To the space of Consciousness, which is neither seen nor touched, but within which all is seen and felt.

This presence is the *liṅga*—the Sign. It is not a form or object, but a symbol. In some Indian myths, it's a column of light with no beginning or end, untraceable by the gods—our limited faculties. Usually, the *liṅga* is the emblem of Śiva, of God. But in the feminine vision of the Yoginīs, the sign is not vertical but spacious. *Ākāśa*, luminous space, unbounded. Śiva is this space. Your true nature.

And this is where things are turned upside down: this symbol of the divine, traditionally male, is revealed as a feminine openness. For Kālī is not merely the consort of Śiva—She is the origin of all, even of Him. Without consciousness, nothing can be experienced. Not even emptiness. Not even nothing.

All arises from the vastness of open awareness, and returns to it. Like waves on the sea. Buddhist wisdom calls space "the queen of metaphors"—rightly so. In Tantra, this space is the Queen herself. The Great Goddess. Kālī.

"All is impermanent," said the Buddha. And he inferred that "all is suffering". Yet impermanence is not a curse. It is a pointer—everything that vanishes *reveals* its source. That source is salvation. The sign. The mark of who we truly are.

The Yoginīs invite us to feel this rhythm: appearance and return. In every thought, every breath, lies the path back. Even Time, which devours all, becomes an ally. Impermanence is freedom.

This is why the Goddess is Time—*Kālī*, from *kāla*, time. She births and consumes simultaneously. To feel this is not annihilation—it is liberation. To feel her gentle hand even in the vanishing of a thought.

The tradition calls this *saṃsmṛti*—recollection. A sacred memory. The Goddess takes form as the Yoginī-circle, in the cremation ground, the body itself. That space is alive, and its crystallization is this very teaching.

Our five senses and mind—these are the Yoginīs. When their powers are turned inward, they become the source of wisdom. The cremation ground is the body, the arena of revelation.

This is not a doctrine—it is practice. When I rest my attention on the space around the body, not straining, the body dissolves into it. This space is the symbol of the Absolute—*anuttara*. Untouchable, *a-sparśa*, beyond contact.

Even the ritual of touch—the exaltation of sensation, even sexual ecstasy—is, in this lineage, only a gate. The deeper space is subtler than pleasure. It is not absence. It is radiant and alive. Not abstract, but embodied in everything.

It surpasses the duality of form and void. It is their common source. Whether I feel a sensation—or its absence—I am the source of both.

This dissolution is not an event. It's not something that occurs in a deep meditation. It is here, now, in ordinary life. The Goddess invites us to notice the dissolving of all things, to recognize them returning to the space that "I am". To rest in that.

To recognize. That's the key word. In the Tantric school of *Pratyabhijñā*—"Recognition"—it means more than gratitude. It is the moment I connect what I've only heard with what I see directly.

Like the story of the princess. She's heard of a prince, noble and virtuous. She dreams of him. Yet every day, she sees a man who seems plain. Until a page suggests: "Is he not the one?" She looks closer. The prince of her dreams... was before her all along.

She had never seen him for who he was. Because she believed such perfection had to be distant. And yet—everything changes, just by recognizing what was already there. Not by gaining something new. Just by truly seeing what is.

This is what recognition offers. Not a new world. A new look, direct with no filters.

The awakened state is not something to acquire. It's the awareness that the one experiencing all this—right now—is already free.

I don't become awakened—I realize I already am. Just as one stops searching for glasses… when they realize they're already wearing them.

This space, this *liṅga*, is the ever-present witness in which all forms arise and dissolve. It is limitless. Timeless. It is not "in" space. It *is* the space of wide open awareness.

The practice is simple: pay attention to this open field in which the three realms—earth, sky, and in-between—appear. These are not separate worlds. They are projections of the Goddess-consciousness, seen through the lens of individuality.

Each moment, I watch as my senses—my inner Yoginīs—create, and uncreate. I worship not through ritual, but by observing this sacred play.

This is the essence of the first teaching. The space is the sign. The space is the Self.

2 – The Union of Śiva and Śakti: Awakening Arises from Their Friction

śivasyābhinnarūpeyaṃ śaktir akramataḥ parā |
proditā paramonmeṣarūpā svacchandacāriṇī || 41

tayor araṇimanthānaḥ sāmarasyamahodayaḥ |
saṃghaṭṭo yas tato jātā niṣkāmā dṛṣṭir avyayā || 42

This supreme Śakti
is inseparable from Śiva.
She bursts forth spontaneously—
a manifestation of absolute awakening,
free in all her movements.

From their mutual friction,
like rubbing two sticks together,
rises the vast emergence of unity.
From this encounter is born
an unwavering vision, free of desire.

All things dissolve into the space of Consciousness. But how does Consciousness bring forth everything we see and feel?

After presenting Śiva as pure transcendence—almost beyond Consciousness itself—the Yoginī now unveils the union of Śiva and Śakti, the Goddess, as the source of all things and every experience.

This creative, sexual union is symbolized by the metaphor of two wooden pieces rubbed together to spark fire. One is vertical, spun with a small bow; the other, a horizontal plank with a hole, or a cross-shaped piece of wood called *svastikā*. Intuitively, we might think Śiva represents the vertical rod, evoking masculine erection. But strikingly, it is the Goddess who is described as active and upright, moving around Śiva, who is horizontal and passive. It's not the male sex stirring within the feminine matrix, but the other way around: the Goddess dynamically revolving around the stillness of Śiva. Consciousness, in motion, circles around Being, which is still.

This imagery echoes another powerful myth—the churning of the Ocean of Milk, from which arose ambrosia and other marvels. *Manthāna*, the act of churning, often recurs in Yoginī symbolism. The fire ritual, in both Indian and European traditions, merges these two myths: the friction that gives birth to fire, and the churning that yields immortality. Here, friction is life-giving. Specifically, it's the rubbing of inhalation and exhalation that lights the fire of vitality.

(Ritual Fire Ignition in Slavic Lands)

So, how does our everyday experience unfold?

We often live fragmented lives. We shift personas depending on people and situations. Inside, we're flooded with impressions, thoughts, images, and memories, all disjointed. One life contains many. Old memories appear like disjointed snapshots, leaving behind a sense of scattered mosaic. Our actions and words contradict each other. We do what we don't want and want what we don't do. We seem composed of conflicting energies. We are distraction, dispersion, contradiction—the breath's exhalation and inhalation in opposition.

161

This is why most spiritualities aim for harmony. That harmony involves simplifying and uniting our inner forces—reconciling body and mind, past and present— hoping to shape a fully integrated self. Others go further: not just unity, but absolute oneness, excluding all difference. Hence arises the temptation to set pure unity against worldly duality.

But Tantra offers a third path: not fragmented duality, nor sterile oneness, but *unity in diversity*—a reconciliation of opposites. And that arises through relationship. Utpaladeva, the great tantric philosopher, tells us: everything is relationship—not only in the world, but even within the Absolute.

The Absolute is not singular isolation. It is the union of two—Śiva and Śakti, God and Goddess.

Why? Because absolute singularity is barren. Creation requires polarity. We accept that nothing in this world exists in isolation: left implies right, up implies down, greatness is relative to something lesser.

Similarly, the space of Consciousness, while stable and independent, is itself a relationship between two aspects: space and sentience, vastness and sensitivity, sky and body. When I sit down, I sense my body as a radiant mass in space. This, too, is relation. This primal relation births *my* world. Creation is born moment by moment through interplay—between subject and object, between "I" and "this," between what I just felt and my response to it now—a chain of reactions, endless relations.

The original relation is that between body and space. "Body" here means the feeling of being, not the physical form seen by others. Body and space—like subject and object—are intertwined.

Usually, I overlook this. But when I awaken to space's presence, my sensitivity awakens. Energies bloom within. This is the supreme awakening—beyond the contracted states ruled by fear.

All is Śakti, the energy of consciousness. But this energy, this power to move and feel, is often frozen in fear: fear of others, of change, pain, loss, death, of duality. But when I sensorially open to visual, auditory, or tactile space, my sensations shift. I move from contraction to opening. The Sanskrit word for awakening evokes both "opening the eyes" and "blossoming." When attention turns to space, the body blooms like a flower.

A new relationship begins—between body and world, awareness and space, subject and object. A *friction* (*saṃghaṭṭa*) arises—an erotic fusion between senses and their objects. And from this friction is born the awakened experience, "unwavering vision"—a consciousness increasingly expanded, less and less captivated by the limited things it sees, in which it recognizes, wordlessly, its own creation.

Practically, this gaze is first awakened in meditation. I sit with wide-open eyes. My attention rests at the edge of my visual field. Immediately, my subtle body—the body of awareness—feels lighter, fresher, as if after a deep breath and an exhale of relief.

Another practice implied here is breathwork. Just as life is sustained by the friction (*manthāna*, a term also rich in sexual connotation) between inhale and exhale, so too does awakening arise from attending to the breath's turning points. When I place attention at the end of an exhale, attention lifts away from movement and expands into a blossoming presence—a wave of silent freshness that endures as long as distraction does not steal it.

And if I get distracted, I begin again, at the next breath. In this way, conscious silence extends and deepens. Awareness unfolds. Awakening happens—as sparks from the friction of breath, of life's opposing currents.

This new Śakti bursts forth *suddenly* (*akramataḥ*)—not through a process. That doesn't mean she is static like a rock. Unlike traditions that praise the immovable anvil, Tantra speaks of "ever-arising action," a *nityodita* presence—perpetual dynamism, for motion is the essence of Consciousness.

A new world emerges, described as the contents of a secret book. Earlier verses likened the energies of inhale and exhale to a book—one opened only when attention slips between breaths or thoughts.

This emergence happens all at once. It doesn't evolve, even if energies do unfold in Time. The fire kindled from the friction between body and space is transcendent, beyond Time. It permeates becoming but also surpasses it. This fire of presence is the soul of spiritual evolution—but it itself does not evolve.

From another angle, subject and object are like the two fire-sticks. The vertical one, spun with a cord, is the *liṅga*, the masculine. The horizontal one, with a hole, receives and grounds it. *Manthāna* means friction, but it also refers to churning milk into butter, or intense thinking to yield insight. In Indian myth, gods and demons churned the cosmic Ocean of Milk to extract treasures of Consciousness.

Tantric practice often involves this play of opposites: breath in and out, body and space, subject and object, and, of course, man and woman in ritual union. This *copulation* creates not only life or its fluid potential, but spiritual awakening.

In the *Trika* tradition—the "Triad," distinct yet complementary to that of Kālī—Śiva and Śakti, in union, give birth to all things, and especially to the individual. Beyond the divine couple lies the mystery of their child: the individual self.

Tantra destroys nothing. It transmutes. The individual, above all, is the field of awakening, because it is through the body that universal Consciousness contracts and individuates. And Tantric awakening is embodied (*jīvan-mukti*), and thus individual. Śiva and Śakti create a body that suffers if its origin is forgotten—but a radiant new body for one who sees, in that very body, the work of the God with the Third Eye together with the Daughter of the Mountain.

3 – The Re-Creation of the Senses: The Sovereign Ones of the Wheel Merge

tato 'nalpacidullāsaghana sṛṣṭer anantaram |
nirāvaraṇanirdhāmaparamākāśavṛttayaḥ || 43

cakreśvaryo raśmirūpā devatāḥ kulavarjitāḥ |
nirniketapade'dvaite) militā vyāptisaṃyutāḥ || 44

The Goddesses of the Circle,
endowed with pervasiveness,
gather in the non-dual spaceless space.
Bodyless, the deities of that assembly
are the activities
of the supreme spaceless space,
the transparent (space) from which arises directly
the playful manifestation of that abundant awareness.

Following the singularity of the first *chummā* and the duality of the second, we now encounter the multiplicity in this third phase—a progression mirrored in many spiritual traditions.

As the movements of the senses consciously dissolve into space, they reemerge, gradually transformed. But their nature shifts; they are no longer mere energies of a body perceived as separate, but become Yoginīs—divine energies that create and dissolve a world of infinite self-realization, transcending the grasp of ordinary understanding.

In the symbolic language of the tantras, the senses (including the mind) are referred to as the "Sovereign Ones of the Wheels." These Yoginī-goddesses are said to unite within the space that is their essence and living source. To unite is to engage in yoga; thus, these energies are "Yoginīs". From this point forward, the activities of the senses (and the mind) nourish the feeling of unity, rather than reinforcing the belief in a real separation between consciousness, body, and world.

These energies are omnipresent, infused throughout the all-encompassing space. This space, which is Consciousness herself, is the "place beyond place," for space is where everything occurs, yet it itself is not confined to any particular location—it is everywhere. The energies then merge back into their source, but this time with awareness.

Indeed, the energies of the senses dissolve into space each time we fall asleep, enter a blank state, faint, or lose awareness of the world. However, we usually experience this dissolution unconsciously, unaware of its significance and value. Before slipping into unconsciousness, we are already unmindful. Now, having been initiated (like a reset) into the wonder that is life, we observe these cycles of creation and dissolution with a supple ardour.

Practically speaking, I sit facing the sky, the sea, an open landscape, or simply allow my gaze to open in panoramic attention. In the space that then reveals itself, thoughts, perceptions, and other movements continue to arise, but with a different flavour. It is as if the inner and outer movements—the sensations, the thoughts—become translucent, allowing the "light" that is Consciousness to shine through. More than that: the movements (*vṛtti* in Sanskrit, meaning "whirlwind," hence "operation" of one of the senses) are unveiled as Consciousness within Consciousness, just as waves in the ocean are the ocean itself, made of the same liquid substance.

The entire body, composed of these whirlwinds of energy, begins to yawn, to open, as if carrying a lamp within, that desires to spread into space. The *liṅga*, the "sign" that is the body, gradually unites with space, like a block of salt dissolving in the salty ocean. The body we ordinarily know is a crystallization of the sap of Consciousness. Its hardening results from the forgetting of the boundless immensity. The contracted *linga* of the body merges in the expanded *linga* of space, the *linga* that *is* the Goddess in her original, eternal state.

When we are distracted by our own powers, light (manifestation) then contracts and takes on increasingly rigid forms. But when attention—that is, the awakening aspect of Consciousness—remembers space, this process reverses. From this blending of body and space, of masculine and feminine (*linga* and *yoni*), a presence emerges—fresh, new, beyond mind and body, beyond the senses and the solidity of the usual world.

4 – A Body That Slays Death: These Goddesses Devour Time

sṛṣṭyādikalanārūpo yatrākramacidambare |
kālas saṃhāram āpnoti kālagrāsas sa ucyate || 45

Time—encompassing the energies of creation,
sustenance,
and dissolution—recedes
into the boundless sky of timeless awareness.
This process is referred to as "Time being consumed."

In Sanskrit, the term *kāla* signifies both "time" and "death," reflecting the understanding that time inevitably leads to the cessation of all things. Tantra further posits that each ending heralds a new beginning. Cycles follow one another, with smaller cycles nested within larger ones, all encompassed by grander cycles of creation and dissolution. These cycles represent the breath of universal Consciousness itself—the embrace of Śiva and Śakti, whose friction manifests as *spanda*, the pulsation of the supreme Heart, the source of all that exists, yet itself unbound.

Time embodies change—the evolution of phenomena. Imagine if everything were to become utterly still; no events would transpire, rendering the passage of time indiscernible. Notably, our perception of time diminishes as internal changes slow: heartbeat, breath, and thought. Thus, decelerating physical and mental activities effectively slows time itself.

In Indian philosophy, time is said to devour all. It is deemed the supreme deity in the *Mahābhārata*, India's great epic, which lends its name to the subcontinent. Like Chronos, time is the ultimate sovereign, consuming all it engenders. Even other deities are not exempt from its grasp; all are eventually swallowed by Time's maw, synonymous with impermanence and destiny (*daiva*).

Therefore, mastering time equates to mastering that which governs all—a formidable endeavour. To slay the Slayer of all is to conquer death itself, transcending time.

How does one achieve this, according to the Kālī tradition?

As previously discussed, the core of these practices lies in conscious participation in the cycles of creation and destruction. Time comprises the operations of body and mind. By slowing and halting these activities, one accesses their source—the origin of time—thereby enacting the death of Death. This can be accomplished through direct observation of the living silence wherein sensations arise and fade, by focusing attention into space, by mindful breathing, or through sexual union (though the latter is more symbolic). Alternatively, one may transcend time through sudden intuition, an uncaused awakening when absolute, free consciousness spontaneously arises.

In truth, time is consciousness—the vastness within all, lacking any exterior. Time is consciousness expressing itself as change. This is the Goddess Kālī, whose name alludes to her dark hue and her identity as time (*kāla*) that engenders and consumes all. She is Vāmā, the "beautiful one who gives birth" to phenomena, and Kāla-saṃkarṣaṇī, "she who devours time."

Consequently, all dissolution practices in the Kālī tradition—also known as the Yoginī tradition—are described as potent acts wherein consciousness "devours" the time it generates. Consciousness creates and then transcends its own creations. This dissolution occurs repeatedly, at every moment. However, we typically do not relish this aspect of experience. As a result, our experience remains incomplete; the fire of our consciousness is dormant, the "fuel" of phenomena is not fully consumed, leaving undigested remnants that become seeds of future suffering—this is the well-known karma.

Conversely, by turning attention toward the source-space that we are, time is consumed, and a new creation emerges. "Time dissolves into the sky of timeless consciousness," into the ever-present space. Given the intensity of this act, akin to fire or dynamic digestion, it is said that "Time is devoured." Death dies, and a new life is born.

By opening to space, the senses no longer construct a world dominated by death but instead burn it away, making room for a new creation, as expressed in the *Śiva-sūtras*.

5 – When the Body Becomes an Offering: The Senses as
Blossoms Devoted to Space

cidānandamayollāsam icchājñānakriyātmakam |
karaṇānāṃ vapur yatra pūjārthaṃ puṣpatāṃ gatam || 46

This dissolution (into space) is the overflowing radiance
of bliss,
the delight of consciousness composed of Will,
Knowledge, and Action.
It is the luminous body of the senses,
where they become flowers offered in sacred devotion.

What is the renewed world revealed by awakening?

The new creation that unfolds after awakening is described
as "an effulgence of the bliss of consciousness." The
world, in itself, is not a curse. Its weight comes from fear—
fear born from a lack of presence and fervor. And notably,
the death of Death is simultaneously a birth. Dissolution,
in this light, is not mere disappearance, but a joyful
revelation—a beautiful, radiant manifestation. The
Sanskrit word *ullāsa* signifies a kind of shining forth, a
display of delight, a self-revealing impulse to express love,
joy, and seduction.

This bliss—*ānanda*—could also be translated more bodily
as "pleasure" or even "rapture." It is the dynamic pulse of
existence, expressed through three primal forces: Will
(*icchā*), Knowledge (*jñāna*), and Action (*kriyā*). These
form the triadic essence of life and are often symbolized

by the trident—Śiva's *triśūla*—with each point vibrating one of these foundational powers.

Will is the primal drive that precedes thought. It exists nakedly before distinctions arise, before "yes" or "no," before the urge to flee or fight, mourn or rejoice. It is the raw impulse felt, often physically, "in the region of the heart" during a sudden emotional jolt, at the climax of orgasm, or in a moment of supreme effort beyond habitual boundaries.

Knowledge emerges from this primal impulse. It is the shaping of that drive into thoughts, images, and perceptions—how experience becomes grasped and organized into *images*.

Action is that same current made visible and kinetic. It manifests as physical moves, muscular contractions, the flush of the skin, the beating of the heart, words and gestures—consciousness embodied and expressed.

This radiant stream is the bliss-nature of consciousness, made more tangible in moments of rupture—during a sneeze interrupting a speech, or when time seems to pause. In such openings, we glimpse consciousness uncoiled, free of the tensions that usually bind it.

Does experience change with awakening?

Interestingly, no. The contents of experience—the colors, the sounds, the bodily sensations—remain what they are. The difference lies in how we *react*. With awakening (*unmeṣa*—the opening of the "inner eye"), the mind ceases its habit of clinging, of contracting around experiences, like a clenched fist. Instead, perception expands. Things are no longer seized upon, but gently gathered into the spacious self—"me," the infinite field of presence. Each color, sensation, or pleasure is no longer an object to consume, but a wave of *my* own undivided unfolding. Not the limited "me", but rather, that "me that is more me than me" as Augustin would say.

A powerful metaphor is given here: the Sanskrit alphabet.

The sixteen (or twelve) Sanskrit vowels provide a vivid symbolic support. Each vowel expresses an oscillation of experience, a pulsation between pure subjectivity and emerging objectivity. Yet, just like a city reflected in a mirror seems outside the glass, but is always inside it, so too this movement remains within consciousness itself.

While this metaphor doesn't stem directly from Kālī's tantras, Abhinavagupta—master of the Trika system—associates these vowels with *Kālī-krama*, the unfolding dance of the Goddess. The symbolism reveals how energy flows into form, and how the faculties of perception—our very own senses and mental functions—are that same divine energy, extended into individual expression.

To summarize:
Awakening does not reject the body or the senses. Rather, it sanctifies them. The senses no longer bind us to a fragmented world. They become sacred offerings. The body becomes a shrine. The perceptions—vision, taste, scent, touch, thought—are no longer instruments of grasping but petals of an eternal offering, a garland laid at the feet of space, the infinite womb of consciousness.

6 – Mind and desire are no longer adversaries; they become attendants to the expanse

grāhyagrāhakavispharadvandvamelāpake pare |
mahāmaithunasaṃghaṭṭasāmarasyapade same || 47 ||

manomatī tu tatraiva paricārakatāṃ gate |
nirāvaraṇaciddhāmni (...) || 48

In the supreme reality, where the dual pulsation of
subject and object dissolves in the non-dual embrace of
awareness,
where the dynamic collision of the Great Union produces
a resonance of pure unity—
within that seamless space of communion,
the mind and the faculty of desire (no longer stand as
obstacles);
they are transformed into devoted servants of the
boundless expanse of transparent consciousness.

What, then, becomes of the mind in awakening? Does it vanish entirely?

In much of contemporary spirituality, the mind (*manas*) is cast as a fundamental enemy. This notion, though currently widespread, is not entirely modern; it is also present in classical Buddhism. Inner chatter, the mental noise that runs incessantly, is indeed a source of our suffering. Like a radio that never ceases, it drowns out our direct perception of reality—neither good nor bad as such. Silence is thus prescribed by the Buddha and countless contemplative traditions. To remain mentally silent is considered essential.

But is it truly possible to stop thinking altogether? It is futile to attempt to shut down all mental activity, just as it would be foolish to try to eliminate every sound from the environment. What *is* possible is to enter into an *inner* silence—to cease mental speech, to no longer feed restlessness. When this occurs, something remarkable takes place: our perception of the world shifts in an instant.

While in Benares, India, I struggled with the constant noise—mosques, temples, weddings, horns, crows... it never stopped. I asked my teacher Hemenji how he managed to practice deep tantric meditation amid such chaos. He told me that it was enough to make silence *within*. When I protested that stopping thoughts was like trying to grasp wind, he replied: the goal is not to stop all thoughts, only those we create ourselves. Like refraining from speaking—other sounds remain, but the difference is immense. The still point at the eye of the storm opens.

By remaining silent, one becomes aware of more subtle inner chatter—a murmur that runs beneath. These whispers obscure the full intensity of the presence that the Yoginīs speak of. If left unchecked, they dim the power of the experience, keeping it from reaching its liberating depth. This point is crucial yet often overlooked: if one remains in only partial silence, the experience will lack the force to free one from the mind's grip.

In practice, I begin by stopping overt thoughts, nearly spoken words, "in my head". Then I detect subtler noise, which fades too once heard. Then a powerful presence reveals herself. This is the fruit of inner silence, central not just to Tantra but also to Buddhism. After Hemenji's teaching, I had the opportunity to explore this practice during long journeys in Indian trains and buses. It proved deeply effective—almost magical. Each time I entered this mode of silence, it felt like waking up, even amidst noise, fatigue, or sensory overstimulation. Inner silence became my practice.

The Yoginī tradition rarely speaks explicitly of inner silence (*mauna*), a term more common among male ascetics. Yet silence lies at the heart of their secret transmission of awakening.

First, the teachings emphasize emptiness—sky, space, gap, dissolution—all synonyms for inner silence. Emptiness calls to emptiness. Second, a specific form of meditation stills the mental voice: the Śiva meditation (*bhairava-mudrā*), practiced with open eyes, slightly parted lips, and a gaze resting in vast space—such posture alone can mute the mind-radio effortlessly.

Facing vast open space makes this even more potent: external light dispels internal shadows. Emptiness and Śiva's spacious meditation are thus two gateways to silence—through doctrine and through practice—essential to any inward path, and central to the yoga of the Yoginīs.

In this silence, I awaken to a living stillness that contains sounds. This silence is not a state among others, but a living presence, the source of all noise, beyond language, wordless and luminous. This is the Goddess—vibration, presence, consciousness, ocean and wave, luminous shimmer, the clear light, the key to awakening and the supreme Good. Once known, it brings a fulfilment beyond expectation, that never ceases to nourish.

And it is in this "beyond-the-mind" that the mind finds its true role: no longer erased, it becomes a servant of that which transcends it. The mind does not vanish; it transforms. From curse, it becomes a force for celebration—poetry and philosophy. Instead of fuelling confusion, it becomes the expressive voice of what surpasses it. It speaks of silence. It becomes the longing to express the inexpressible.

Though this may seem futile, the desire to speak the unspeakable is one of the most potent sources of inspiration. Torn between longing and powerlessness, language unfurls in all its nuances. The oldest creators of language were mystics and philosophers: John of the Cross, father of Spanish; Meister Eckhart, father of German; Marguerite Porète, who birthed one of the oldest and most beautiful French texts, and who was burned alive in Paris in 1310.

From obstacle, frustration becomes a force of revelation. When desire is rightly aligned, all else follows and finds its order. The mind, released from its role as usurper, reclaims its nature: an artist of the unborn.

More than a practice, this is a way of being, a return to one's natural state. In Sanskrit, *sva-sthā*, "to stand in oneself," denotes health. A core teaching of the Yoginīs is this: whatever power afflicts us becomes a source of liberation once its root is recognized. Then, the mind rebecomes "pure knowledge" (*śuddha-vidyā*), the intuitive intelligence that naturally inclines toward non-dual awakening.

Thoughts become rare but powerful. Arising from silent awareness, their clarity and precision shine: nothing exists apart from consciousness, therefore all is consciousness.

Poetic inspiration (*kavitā*) and eloquence are among the signs of one "born from the Yoginī" (*yoginī-bhū*). Their mantras have force; their thoughts lead back to the space of open awareness, like waves that bring back the gaze to the ocean from which they rise.

Ultimately, this awakened intelligence flourishes in the "union of opposites." By nature, the mind is dualistic. In Indian psychology, the mind (*manas*) is the power to build one thing (*vikalpa*) by excluding other things. Often, it is translated as "concept". However, "concept" is a misleading translation, suggesting abstraction and ignoring emotion or imagination. But *vikalpa* includes both emotion and tangible things, like anger.

To understand *vikalpa*, to understand the mind, consider this: it works through exclusion. It focuses on one thing, leaving out others. For example, remembering drinking coffee this morning is *vikalpa*, because it highlights one object ("that coffee") while excluding the present moment and all other memories.

Like a sculptor removing stone to reveal form, *vikalpa* isolates things by shape, place, time. Thus, *vikalpa* inherently generates duality—every "yes" excludes a "no." Every discursive thought opposes something.

The Buddhist philosopher Dharmakīrti points at *vikalpa* as the source of all conflict, because the primal *vikalpa* is the sense of "I"—which always implies an excluded "Other," and thus, love and hatred, and potential war.

Yet we need language and thought. Without *vikalpa*, no attention, no focus. Without focus, no daily life. Abhinavagupta said: "life would cease then without a word…"

Thus, the aim is not to destroy the mind, which would itself be another *vikalpa*, but to integrate it into a transformative vision. That is the purpose of Tantra: from a grasping attention that excludes, to open awareness that includes.

The mind is the creative play of consciousness. Consciousness tends to forget its own vastness, narrowing onto its creations, grasping at them always more tightly. Tantra invites a panoramic gaze. In this vision, mind becomes celebration again.

"Desire" (*mati*) here refers to the intellect (*buddhi*), often translated as will or intention, the power to choose (*saṅkalpa*). While mind says "no," the intellect is higher, more inclusive thinking that says "yes."

7 – The True Self Vibrates

tadā mitāmitasyoccair ahaṃkārasya ghaṭṭanam |
ullaṃghanakramaḥ ko 'pi vibhāti kalanojjhitaḥ || 49 ||

Then arises a friction
of the limited and unlimited ego—
an indescribable transcendence gleams forth,
freed from all calculation and fragmentation.

Is awakening a liberation *from* the self, or *of* the self?
Do we even need a self to awaken?

According to the Yoginīs: yes.

This awakening into spaciousness, which dissolves the scaffolding of individuality, paradoxically gives rise to a new kind of personhood. The ego doesn't simply disappear—it undergoes transformation. First it melts (*drāvaṇa*), then re-forms (*rodhana*) in a new shape. It begins to vibrate within the space itself, like a newly risen sun—like a Rudra. In the tantric tradition, a Rudra is a fully awakened being, akin to a Buddha.

The ego as we usually know it is an illusion. In truth, we have multiple egos, each adapted to its situation—parent with one's children, child with one's parents, friend with a friend. These selves are improvised and reconstructed endlessly. In Sanskrit, ego is *ahaṃ-kāra*, "the 'I'-making"—because this false self is, at root, a word, a thread that links the various masks we wear. Ego is thus a gesture of appropriation: "I" and "mine" arise together.

And yet, in the Void that swallows all things, something called "I" begins to vibrate. It is as if the space itself starts to quiver. The Sanskrit word *ghaṭṭana* means "friction," "unitive contact," "vibration," and carries erotic undertones. How can emptiness 'tremble' or vibrate?

This *friction*, like the spark that lights a fire, is a metaphor. It points to the fact that consciousness can fold back upon herself, grasp herself, taste herself through the forms she creates. When I exclaim "Ah! a tree!"—it is not a small ego identifying a thing. It is the boundless Self that appears as tree, and recognizes itself through this act of perception—even if I'm not aware of it in the moment. This is vibration: the power to become something, to feel it, judge it, forget it, and remember it again.

The vibrating self is thus more than identification with a body, a personality, or a personal history. It is the power to take on any identity, and to shed it again at will. It is *freedom*—the ability to embody forms without being bound to them. We experience this fluidity in the play of our daily inner life, especially in moments of reverie or daydreaming. We try on identities, imagine scenarios, shifting effortlessly from one self to another. Yet none of these masks truly fit, because our real face is formless space—the image of limitlessness. Because all roles and personas are finite, they eventually go back into the one space of consciousness. We feel vaguely unsatisfied, without knowing why.

In truth, I am the formless space playing at becoming form. In this paradoxical play, I return again and again to the spaciousness that I truly am. This oscillation is the vibration of the Self.

But when I *know* myself as this empty freedom, no longer clinging to any fixed content, then "I" vibrate with intensity. Awareness wakes up. The small self still exists—but now it floats in the open Self, limitless, without fixed identity. I am not confined to a form, nor am I limited by formlessness. I am this extraordinary being (*ko'pi*), who transcends all pairs of opposites—beyond all choosing.

I am the flow between form and formlessness, the rhythm that moves from embodiment to dissolution and back again. Beyond the shallow vibrations of the fabricated self, I am the freedom to be, unbounded, unsplit.

Between thoughts, I am simply "I"—the Self without qualities. Within thoughts or perceptions, I become a particular "someone," relatively defined. I dance constantly between these two poles, which are the in- and out-breath of this extraordinary being that includes all opposites.

I am always more than this person I seem to be, yet I am not 'impersonal' like some industrial product. In emptiness, I find rest. In form, I find wonder. I am the elusive space that appears as this and that—pure generative creativity.

8 – The Result Is Extinction

kvacin niruttarapade dṛṣṭatattvasya sarvadā |
phalād ahetukollāsād ūhā nirvāṇabhāg bhavet || 50 ||

In the unsurpassable extraordinary state,
for one who always sees the Real,
from a fruit arising without a (visible) cause—
mysteriously,
this is a share in Nirvāṇa/(even) Speech expresses
liberation.

In this rare and supreme state—*niruttara*, beyond anything conceivable—there is a silent, inexpressible clarity.
For the one whose vision is continually open to Reality, to *Being itself*, this state appears. Not just in meditation, not only with closed eyes, but even with the eyes wide open. In every circumstance, in every moment, this person sees what is, directly and unfiltered.

This condition is called "unsurpassable" because nothing lies beyond it—not even the impulse to transcend it. It is *extraordinary*, for it cannot be pinned down. It is known only by not being grasped. It reveals itself by eluding grasp.

And then: the impossible happens: There appears an effect without a cause! Awakening happens without a cause. It is not part of 'karma', the realm of cause and effect.

This is the paradox hinted at in the verse. Something arises—*ullāsa*, a shining joy, a blooming, a vivid presence—but without anything that could be identified as its cause. There is no action, no preparation, no merit, no condition that produces this state. It simply **is**. It arises from itself, as a kind of divine anomaly.

This is the mystery (*ūhā*) of awakening, or an insight that is beyond understanding. An event that defies the laws of causality. Ordinarily, every event is thought to have a cause. Yet here, something undeniable appears—without antecedent. The radiance of awakened being is *its own origin*. It doesn't grow from karma or circumstance, as a seed sprouts into a tree. It does not need soil, sun, or rain. It just blooms.

The tantras call this spontaneous arising *anugraha*—grace. A gesture by which consciousness turns toward itself, without reason, without effort, without explanation.

Even ignorance—the forgetfulness of true being—is not caused by the world, the body, or the mind. For, these emerge *after* forgetting. Therefore, forgetting itself must also be spontaneous—consciousness *playing* at losing itself. And if forgetting is self-originating, then so too is remembering—awakening. It is the inverse movement, equally uncaused.

In lived experience, this means: I bring my attention back to "me," to the centre of all perception, of body and mind, the core of the mandala. Then, contraction reverses into expansion. A new kind of certainty appears—an ease, a confidence that *'nothing lies outside of spacelike awareness'*.

To be space is enough.

There is nothing else to achieve, verify, or control. If everything is contained within the space of awareness, where could thoughts or things possibly go? Just as waves cannot leave the ocean, so too thoughts cannot exit consciousness. Relief follows—*like dropping a burden to the ground.*

The Goddess, echoing ancient Indian medicine, uses a striking image. Fever was once seen as fire within the body. Healing was the cooling of that flame. Awakening, in this sense, is the extinction of burning torment. A flame snuffed out by a breeze. In Sanskrit: *nirvāṇa*—the blowing out.

But how can there be an experience of the disappearance of "me"?

It is a riddle. A mystery. And yet, it is not theoretical. It is felt, tasted. One participates in it. There is a flavour to it. Not absence—but a presence without centre, deeply personal, because no one else can live it for me. The transpersonal becomes intimate. The impersonal becomes singular.

In the Yoginī tradition, this is sometimes "transmitted"— but not through explanation or ritual. Through silence. Through a mysterious co-presence, a heart-to-heart that dissolves both minds in their shared unknowability.

And yet, as hinted in an alternate reading of the verse:

"The mind becomes a word of release."

What does this mean?

Even reason, even thought (*ūhā*), once immersed in awakened presence, becomes transformed. It turns into a liberating force. Language, once bound to the ego, becomes a healing current. Mind becomes *speech of freedom*.

And so, all is transmuted:
The senses, the mind, the will, the ego, the voice—even the body begins to move differently. As the Yoginīs say, it enters the dance, the rhythm of the awakened space. Everything is changed by immersion in the living expanse of Presence.

9 – He Delights on the Singular Path

yatas tatas tu sarvatra sarvakarma yathā tathā |
kurvan nirāmayo vyāpī krīḍaty ekāyano'cyutaḥ || 51 ||

Wherever, however, in all places and all deeds,
doing all things, flawless and all-pervading,
the unwavering one plays—
on the singular path.

In the wake of awakening, everything is done, and yet—nothing is done.
This is the paradox of enlightened life: action flows freely, but not from effort. Things happen, but "no one does" them. It is like what Krishna says: I have nothing to do,

and yet I am ever engaged in doing. I am fullness, like the ocean that neither swells nor shrinks. And yet, this ocean can overflow.

Not the egoic "me," but the real I—which is more truly *me* than anything I claim as "mine"—begins to radiate. Transparent like stained glass, it lets the light pass with its own (individual) colours. There is *nothing to do*, yet everything is accomplished. Too simple for busy minds.

The awakened one acts like an apprentice painter whose hand is guided by the master from within. Outer action flows from an inner stillness—not a passivity, but a profound activeness, an invisible gesture arising from the Source that lies deeper than the soul itself.

And what of our usual frantic efforts?

Even our hurried tasks are divine action—but frozen, stiffened by the chill of self-imposed blindness. The divine impulse becomes warped as we strive to "do better." But the harder we push, the less grace emerges. Efficiency collapses under the weight of control.

Yet when I remember the Source—*my* Source—then anxious striving melts into pure precision. Action unfolds from the instant, leaves no residue. It's like the silent swoop of an eagle—effortless and complete.

Inner silence becomes the space through which divine action moves. And so, one plays. Not because life becomes trivial, but because nothing is at stake. No burdens, no tasks, no mandates remain. On this path, one cannot go astray. There is no other road. No fork. No need to choose.

It is a single path—*ekāyana*—a way that encompasses all ways, because it reflects the singularity of consciousness itself. There still *is* a path—but it is simple, open, total.

And *ekāyana* also means "the universal path," the shared road of the world. From another view, it means the solitary path—so narrow, so subtle, that no one can walk it in our place. The road of infinite space is not a highway. It is deeply personal. It is not impersonal, but utterly intimate.

Masters, gods, Yoginīs—they can point, but they cannot tread it for us.

Even during rare moments of shared union—tantric feasts, ritual performances, the brief dissolving of separation— this fusion into one is still a paradox: it can only be truly experienced alone, from within.

This erasure of ego cannot be outsourced. No one else can do it for me. Even if awakening is the play of consciousness reclaiming itself, it cannot happen without *my* consent. Because the one who resists freedom is also consciousness.

There is only one awareness—there is no second. Everything, absolutely everything, happens within this singular intimacy. No one can live my experience for me. Consciousness imprisons itself. Consciousness frees itself. There is no awakening by proxy.

When tradition speaks of grace, transmission, worship— these are expressions of consciousness playing its game of hiding and revealing itself. All these things—teachers, symbols, stories—arise and fall within the First Person: within the "I" that no object can ever contain.

Thus, the path of awakening is *solitary*—but not in the sense of isolation. It is solitary because only one being lives it: me. No other can step into this journey.

And yet—this path is safe. The awakened cannot fall off it. Why? Because if I am infinite space, where could I fall to?

That is the final realization. The supreme ease.
I am the open sky, walking within itself.

10 – Speech and Action Are No Longer a Source of Torment

tataḥ svātantryato nityaṃ proditā avibhedataḥ |
giraḥ parādirūpiṇyo bhedābhedaprathātmikāḥ || 52 ||

akṣacakrodaye 'pīha niṣphalatvarūpatām |
prayātāḥ paramavyomasvarūpācyutāḥ || 53 ||

From that sovereign freedom, eternally arise the
utterances—
indistinct from their source,
manifesting in forms starting from the Supreme, (down to
the Articulate),
bearing within them the pulse of unity and difference.

Even when the Wheel of the Senses stirs in this world,
they—these utterances—remain unshaken:
they do not fall
from the essence of the Supreme Space.

(version 2 of verse 53):
Even when the sensory wheel is set in motion,
these words bear no more fruit:
they no longer produce (karmic) results,
for they rest immovably in the Supreme Space that is the
Self.

What becomes of speech in awakened silence? Does one fall forever mute? And if so, how could teaching exist?

Together with the mind, speech has long been seen as a foe to inner peace. We get lost in words—ours and others'—until we don't know who is speaking, or even whether we are being spoken *by* the language. Words flow, yet no speaker is found. Language behaves like a machine running on its own.

Thus, traditions from Buddhism to modern spirituality have good reason to be wary of language.

Yet paradox emerges: to share this very caution, we *must* use words. We must point with a finger to say "don't look at the finger, but at the moon." And soon the finger becomes the focus; the moon vanishes behind a forest of pointing hands…

The Yoginīs offer another vision entirely: Consciousness is speech—not just verbal, but existential. Every experience, every awareness, is an act of saying. All consciousness is *of* something. It stretches out, a longing toward its object—like a question seeking its answer. In this view, Śakti desires Śiva; thought desires being.

Thus: Being is Śiva, and thinking is Śakti—the loving gaze toward Being. To be and to think are one. Without consciousness, Being would not even be void; and without Being, consciousness would grasp at… nothing. They are two faces of the same mystery.

And this thinking, this awareness, is itself language—creative speech. It speaks the world into being: "Let it be."

In the Recognition school (*pratyabhijñā*) of Tantra, derived from the oral teachings of the Yoginīs, the Goddess is *vimarśa*—a term meaning both "thought" and "reflexive awareness," often deemed untranslatable. Yet, it is the capacity to become aware, to judge, to identify with—thus sowing the seeds of *māyā* (illusion), which is never separate from consciousness.

So, consciousness, thought, and speech are not three things—they are one continuum: the flow of life itself.

The word *vimarśa* isn't a philosopher's invention. It appears in the tantras themselves, especially those of Kālī, where it is explicitly linked to *śakti*—power.

This speech flows through four stages:

1. **Parā-vāk** – Pure speech, the timeless origin, the silent pulse of Being knowing itself. It is like the moment of total fulfillment—orgasm, *visarga* in Sanskrit—where thought is full, but no words have yet formed.
2. **Paśyantī** – The dawning of difference, a panoramic intuition like seeing an entire city from a hill. A discourse without words. Time does not yet exist here; change has not yet begun.

3. **Madhyamā** – The phase of discursive thought. Words begin to crystallize. Like a sculptor shaping form from raw stone, attention chooses one meaning and sets others aside. Time begins. Speech becomes focused.

4. **Vaikharī** – Finally, the embodied speech that rides the breath. It rises from the heart, travels through the chest and throat, and forms articulate syllables—letters that shape our loves, fears, plans, and regrets. This is the speech through which we also recognize consciousness in others, despite the illusion of separation.

All of this—this great cascade from the ocean's floor to the foam of syllables—is one movement, a single rolling thunder of thought and form.

But this movement can bewilder. Consciousness, infinite and free, identifies with one of its own creations. It forgets its immensity and plays at being a body. It pretends to be unfree, which is the true definition of divine play: the power to *appear* as what one is not.

This is sovereign freedom (*svātantrya*), from which all the stages of speech emerge.

If I recognize this—if I see that I, as consciousness, am the origin of these words—then speech loses its grip. It becomes harmless.

It is no longer a snare. It no longer weaves the illusion of a hostile world. Instead, it becomes a tool of truth, a servant of clarity, a vehicle of creative freedom—as it does in poetry.

Remember: "speech" means also the mind (*manas*), whose transformation was discussed in *Chummā* 6. The transmutation of thought is inseparable from the transmutation of speech.

Pure consciousness transcends inner dialogue, the private stream of words we constantly utter inside ourselves. It is as untouched by them as the sky is untouched by the clouds it carries. Clouds depend on the sky; not the other way around.

So too, speech depends entirely on consciousness. If words seem to act on their own, it is only because *I*, sovereign awareness, wish to play this way.

Thus, consciousness is beyond discursive thought. But:

1. It is already a kind of speech—even if wordless, intuitive.
2. Discursive speech always arises from that freedom.

The mind, therefore, is not a flaw or accident. If there is imperfection in the world, it arises from the perfect freedom of consciousness.

And just as waves never leave the ocean, words never leave awareness. As the *Vijñāna-bhairava Tantra* says: *"If all is consciousness, where could thoughts ever go?"*

This realization softens the mind. The mind no longer fights itself. If I trust that the mind is no threat to my peace, then it no longer is. The very belief that the mind can disturb peace is what generates the disturbance.

Once that illusion dissolves, the mind becomes peaceful— because peace no longer sees the mind as an enemy.

Instead of a vicious cycle of self-repression, a virtuous spiral begins: everything becomes a celebration of open space.

So we return to the two readings of Verse 53:

- One version says words become "sterile" (*vandhyā, niṣphala*): they no longer generate karma or illusion.
- The other says words become "immovable", *niścala*: they continue to exist, but no longer disrupt the natural state.

This second view is more tantric: powers (*śakti*) are not destroyed—they are transformed. What once entangled now illuminates. What once distracted now deepens realization.

In this vision, language is no longer torment.
It is play.
It is offering.
It is the freedom to say—not to bind, but to reveal.

11 – Dance and Song Arise from Space

tato 'nuttaraciddhāmarūpe saty udite śive |
dṛgādihastapādāntarūpāṇāṃ saṃsthito 'kramāt || 54

raśmīnāṃ ca tathā vācāṃ nṛttagītodayo 'mitaḥ |
anāveśasamāveśavilāsodayamantharaḥ || 55
Then, suddenly, one rests
in the awakened presence of Śiva,
within the expanse of the supreme domain of
consciousness
beyond all.
There, the rays of the senses—sight, touch, arms and
legs—
arise all at once
and take form anew.

From these streams, and from speech,
arise boundless dances and songs:
a gentle emergence of the play
of absorption without immersion.

People often ask: What use is awakening? – Everything! Simple in essence, it holds inexhaustible fertility. Like love, which is the seed of what is true, beautiful, and good, *bodha*—awakening—is the undying root of the tree of Life.

In this light, the six senses—the five perceptual faculties (*indriyas*) plus the mind (*manas*)—are no longer enemies, but allies, even servants. Servants of what? Of *ākāśa*, space itself. Just as the four elements—earth (*pṛthvī*), water (*ap*), fire (*tejas*), and air (*vāyu*)—arise and dissolve within physical space, the six elements (the five senses and mind) appear and vanish within the space of consciousness (*cit-ākāśa*). The only difference between physical space and conscious space is that the latter is aware—and therefore, alive.

Consciousness is not inert. It embraces all, refusing any limitation. It does so effortlessly—such is its very nature.

Through an expansive return to oneself, attention (*cetanā*) shifts from the object to the container. This power of perception shift is beautifully illustrated by ambiguous images—like the one where one may see either a rabbit or a duck, an old woman or a young one. In India, one such visual ambiguity—half-buffalo, half-elephant—was used by the Kashmiri master Maheśvarānanda in the 13th-century *Mahārthamañjarī*, to symbolize the inseparability of Śiva and Śakti[194].

In the same way, the appearances (*ābhāsa*) of consciousness may either conceal or reveal it. The world, life in all its manifestations, including body and mind, are double-edged. They can obscure their source—like the blinding brilliance of the sun—or they can unveil it, disclosing the infinite powers (*śakti-s*) of consciousness when recognized as such.

Manifestation (*prakāśa*) is light. The word itself means both "to shine" and "to reveal." The term for world, *loka*, shares its root with Latin *lux*, light—also seen in *lucifer*, "light-bringer", or in the word *lucid*. Consciousness is nothing other than this luminous projection of awareness.

---

[194] See an example from a south-indian temple, in the Commentary to *Chummā* 58, below.

If this light distracts us from its source, like waves hiding the ocean, it becomes *māyā*—the magical veil of duality through which unity is forgotten. We see names and forms, but lose sight of the screen that reveals them.

In the *Pratyabhijñā-hṛdaya*, Kṣemarāja describes this "impure path" (*aśuddha-mārga*). First, the space of consciousness forgets itself. It shifts from full awareness of Self—like the apex of *ānanda* during orgasm—to an unconscious emptiness. The luminous presence becomes an empty container, devoid of recognition. This dull space becomes the ground from which further manifestation will emerge.

This fall into unconsciousness is akin to deep sleep, fainting, or coma. Tantra describes this as *saṃkoca*—a contraction, a withdrawal, an obliteration of Self-awareness. It is as if *cit* denies itself to make room for something else. Yet all this happens within it, like dreams in sleep.

Importantly, this forgetting is not a flaw, but a free act of consciousness—it is *svātantrya*, sovereign freedom. There is no outside force. *Cit* freely plays at denying itself, and in doing so, it reaffirms itself.

In the ordinary world, nothing can be itself and its opposite at the same moment and from the same perspective. A stone that becomes dust ceases to be a stone. Transformation implies otherness. But not so for consciousness. It endlessly becomes other, while remaining itself. This is the *Yoginī-s'* paradox.

Let us insist again: this is the treasure of life. Fire, for instance, cannot be cold while remaining fire. But consciousness can be present in its own absence. Even unconsciousness is merely a manifestation of *cit*, lit by its own light. Consciousness manifests as *that state*, and everything that follows arises from it.

Then the energies of consciousness—*khecarī-śakti-s*—emerge solely within separation and differentiation. Unity shrinks to a minimum. Yet unity is never absent, for without it, nothing could appear. All experiences are woven of difference and unity, as the *Chummā 10* affirms: manifestation contains both difference and non-difference.

A table, for instance, is experienced through various angles and sensations, yet it remains a table. Unity persists. All is held together by consciousness' power to unify (*saṃghaṭṭa-śakti*). But fragmentation dominates—consciousness splits into fleeting attention. This is called *khecarī-vaiṣamya*, the inequality of spatial energies.

Following this, the *antaḥkaraṇa*—the inner faculty—is revealed, personified by the Yoginīs, the goddesses of *vāk*, the speech-energy (*gocarī*). In Indian traditions, the senses and mind are deities, for they shape the world—or at least, our world. For the non-dual Tantra, they *project* the world directly, as a cinema projector throws images onto a screen.

On the path of duality, *antaḥkaraṇa* focuses on thought. It strengthens the illusion that the world exists independently of awareness—that I am *only* this body, that others are separate, that the divine is distant. Next, the *dikcarī* energy unfolds through the five senses, reinforcing the dualistic view: "I am here, perceiving that object there."

Finally, the *bhūcarī-śakti* deploys the five great elements—Earth, Water, Fire, Air, and Space—born of the fusion of sense perceptions and the synthesizing mind.

It's not matter that gives rise to consciousness—but *cit* that births mind, senses, and matter. In its sovereign liberty (*svātantrya*), *cit* even creates the illusion that it is a product of matter. Like a mirror showing reversed images, *cit* seems external to its own manifestations, when in truth they are all within it.

Once consciousness recognizes itself, sees itself as the source and the canvas, the faces of phenomena change. This is the teaching of the Goddess: the world doesn't vanish—it is transfigured. Just like the ambiguous image, once seen rightly.

From another view—ignorance (*avidyā*) is the root of suffering, says every Indian path. The Sāṃkhya and Advaita Vedānta hold that awakening dissolves the world. But this leads to paradox: if the world ends with awakening, how can the awakened teach? Teaching requires mind, body, words.

Vedānta answers: the awakened acts unconsciously, from the perspective of ignorance. But for the awakened, there is no world, no individuals, no teaching, no difference. Only undivided *cit*. The awakened functions like a *yantra*, a divine automaton.

But Tantra says otherwise. Awakening is unity—yes—but it also includes the return of duality, now seen as one's own radiance. If duality vanishes, no one awakens; if it remains, suffering persists. How to resolve this?

Utpaladeva, in his *Stanzas on Recognition*, says that the awakened one experiences the world as we do—but differently. For her, everything is Self, overflowing. When she sees a table, she sees herself—not as a projection, but as manifestation. The feeling? Wonder. Delight. The marvel: to be oneself, and other than oneself.

So, life becomes dance and song. Not performances for occasions or people—but celebration for its own sake. Pure, gratuitous expression. Life expresses itself. The body is not denied. It is lived otherwise. The paradox cannot be explained—only danced.

And so, we return to essence: *ākāśa*—vibrant, living space. I inhabit it suddenly (*akramāt*), because it is one. Bodies are many, complex, directional. Space is simple, omnipresent. It is *anuttara*, beyond all hierarchy. As Abhinavagupta teaches, *anuttara* has sixteen meanings. It is both the peak and the transcendence of any path.

Everything—god or mosquito, wavelet or tsunami—is made of the same divine water. No further healing is needed.

Here, the body reappears. The word *pratha* means "arising," but also "spreading," from the root *pṛthu*, "broad, wide." Hence *pṛthvī*, the Earth. Expansion (*vṛddhi*), which is joy (*ānanda*), is the mode of consciousness. From the body, the world unfolds.

Within the formless space, the body shines, five senses as five openings, arms and legs moving like solar rays. Just as sunbeams nourish life, the senses animate the world. It is not the world that creates *cit*, but *cit* that creates the world—through the senses.

Among these, speech (*vāc*): words also emerge in space. As shown in the previous *chummā*, speech—thus intellect and mind—are not absent. They too celebrate space. And this fecundity is *amita*—unlimited.

Dances and chants without end. One might say: Śakti, splitting into words and mantras, is the "song"; Śiva, fracturing into forms and *mudrā*-s, is the "dance." Subject and object emerge from that which is neither, the source of both.

This *udaya*—dawn—is unceasing emergence. An eternal banquet, as John of the Cross says. A "penetration without penetration." The One realizes itself through infinite names and forms, all while remaining in its untouched simplicity.

12 – The Lineage Is the True Offering

paramātmamaheśasya tarpaṇārtham āha |
anantecchākulollāsalaharīṇām akṛtrimam || 56

rūpādiviśvavisphārasaṃvinnicayavigrahāḥ |
ovallyaḥ kathitās tābhir yajanaṃ kriyate param || 57

She speaks of the meaning of the libation
poured out for the Great Lord,
who is the Supreme Self:
an authentic offering of unending waves
that surge forth from the spontaneous delight
of infinite desire and power.

All incarnations of the expansion of awareness,
the entire universe of forms and perceptions,
are revealed as the true lineages.
It is through them
that the supreme sacrificial rite is performed.

What is the origin of Tantra? How does one enter into it? Must one receive initiation (*dīkṣā*)? And if so, from whom?

Tantra is, above all, a tradition of ritual (*kriyā*), like many others. Rituals structure the practitioner's life, shaping it hour by hour, day by day. The *yāga*—the act of offering— is the ritual presentation of substances to the deity. Traditionally, one offers sacred water infused with *mantras*, milk, honey, and flowers—nothing impure.

But in *esoteric* (or non-dual) Tantra, the offering reverses conventional purity: one offers what is considered base or forbidden—especially that which emerges from the body. In the *Kaula* transmissions—the secret path within Tantra—wine, sexual fluids, and bodily substances are offered. These are presented to deities located within the body itself. In practice, wine is consumed, often infused with symbolic quantities of these other substances.

The *lineage* (*paramparā*), the transmission from teacher to student, is an essential dimension without which there can be no tradition at all. The tradition of Kālī belongs wholly to the *Kaula* stream. The term *Kaula* comes from *kula*, which literally means "family," "clan," or "tribe." To be initiated into the *Kaula* path is to be accepted into the divine family of Śiva and Śakti, surrounded by the tribe of accomplished adepts (*siddha*) and awakened women—the *Yoginīs*.

Through the acceptance of a sacred offering—often involving sexual essences—the initiate dies to the dualistic world of pure and impure and is reborn as a divine child of the Goddess and the God.

Another major Kaula stream, the *Trika*, emphasizes the triad: Father (Śiva), Mother (Śakti), and Child (the individual). In Tantra, initiation is the pivotal act. It is not merely a formal passage—it is, in the deepest sense, the event of awakening (*bodha*) or spiritual liberation (*mokṣa*). Knowledge (*jñāna*) may be the means to awakening, but initiation *embodies* that knowledge. At the very least, it guarantees awakening after death. When powerful enough, it *is* awakening itself.

There is also a second form of initiation, marking one as a spiritual son or daughter (*putra*), and a third that authorizes the adept to initiate others. Entry into the lineage is thus the gateway to awakening—one that stretches from Śiva to Śiva, maintaining the current of realization through time. Moreover, it is the *lineage* that grants one the authority to teach.

In comparison to other Tantric paths, the *Kaula* movement simplifies outward ritual. The Kālī tradition intensifies this: only inner fervour (*tīvra-bhakti*) matters—no external procedures should hinder the expansion or distract from the grace (*prasāda*) of direct awareness.

In the Kaula view, awakening, initiation, and thus entrance into the lineage can occur in any form—even spontaneously. One may also initiate oneself through a mantra found in a sacred text, if no teacher is available. Still, even in the case of spontaneous awakening, receiving the oral teaching of the lineage affirms and stabilizes the realization.

As Abhinavagupta notes, intuitive knowledge is completed by intellectual and practical understanding of Tantric philosophy and its ritual dimension.

Yet lineage has an even deeper meaning. According to the oral teachings of the Kālī tradition, the lineage may be a succession of individuals, but the *consciousness* (*cit*) animating them is one and the same. A Kaula *sūtra* declares: the master (*guru*), the lineage (*ovallī*), and consciousness (*cit*) are not separate, but pearls strung on a single thread.

The true initiation into the lineage is the recognition (*pratyabhijñā*) that we are one being expressing itself through many bodies. In this act, "my" body is offered into the space of awareness—just as the adept pours clarified butter (*ghṛta*) or other substances into the sacred fire that symbolizes the Divine (*agni*).

In other words, the foundational act of every Kaula lineage is the dissolution of the individual self into the open space of consciousness (*cid-ākāśa*), followed by its reappearance in transformed form.

This initiatory cycle is mirrored in the breath (*prāṇa*). The inhalation (*pūraka*) is offered into the exhalation (*recaka*), and vice versa. And both are finally offered into the space of silence (*śūnya*), especially the stillness that opens at the end of the out-breath. Here lies the heart of the oral teaching: everything that arises from space returns to space.

To follow this movement *is* awakening, sacred life, initiation, mantra, yoga, ritual, union, *mudrā*, and magic. The voice of the Yoginī of Space—Kālī—echoes the same principle, adapting its form to suit every temperament and inclination.

Here, the focus is ritual. To follow the arc of the breath as it dies into stillness is the true *artha*, the meaning of *tarpaṇa*. This term designates the act of libation—pouring water over a divine image, whether statue or living body.

This *chummā* reveals the deeper meaning of this act: it is the emotions, the sensations, the thoughts themselves that are offered into space. These offerings flow from *ākāśa*, which, when stirred, becomes desire (*icchā*). The imagery shifts from fire to water—not purification, but nourishment.

A drop of water falls from the sky and returns there through the ocean's mediation.

Now, one might ask: why would absolute space require nourishment? Isn't it the origin of everything? How could the source depend on its own creations?

In the non-dual vision, such hierarchy dissolves. When relationship is recognized and fully realized, cause and effect collapse into unity. Waves rise from the ocean and return to it—and the ocean rejoices.

Practically speaking, when the "secondary wheels" of the senses are activated, the "central wheel" of consciousness is stirred—just as fuel feeds the fire. In this vision, the world is not an obstacle. On the contrary, sensory pleasure, emotion, and imagination all feed the fire of awareness by offering themselves to it—like rivers pouring into the ocean and then evaporating back into the heavens.

As always in this vision, all is cycle. And in a circle, each beginning is also a return. The origin is the end. That the ocean needs its waves does not threaten its sovereignty.

These "incarnations of the expansion of consciousness" are the ways *ākāśa* comes into its own. They are the real lineages. They lead from space back to space.

Every perception (*saṃvedana*), every cognition (*vṛtti*), is a potential initiation. It becomes actual if I attend to its movement—from origin to dissolution. The true sacrificial fire (*homa*) is not fire, but the absolute space in which all appears and disappears.

13 – Peace Arises When Limited Experience Is Devoured

ittham saṃsāracakre 'smin ramamāṇasya lokavat |
jñātasvātmasvarūpasya nityatṛptasya kasyacit || 58

paramānubhavāhlādacamatkāreṇa sarvadā |
niyatānubhavagrāsāc chāntiḥ saṃjāyate parā || 59

Thus, supreme peace arises
when the fixed, constrained experiences are devoured
by the constant astonished delight
of supreme experience.

This happens within the very Wheel of Becoming,
for one who, like any worldly person,
delights in life—
yet who has recognized their true nature,
and is therefore perpetually fulfilled.

Śānti—peace—is not an experience, but the end of all experience. It is not about reaching a state of healing, but about being healed *from* the compulsion to experience. A radical shift—yet deeply aligned with the ancient wisdom of India.

Every experience is, by nature, *niyata*—limited, defined. Even those that seem extraordinary—pleasure, inner vibrations, lightness, luminous insight, or the subtle thrills of *siddhi-s* (paranormal powers)—remain bound. They often only reinforce the separate self (*ahaṃkāra*), as testified by Eraka, a devotee of the Yoginī Rājñī in the *Kālī* lineage.

He confessed having once been enthralled by these supernatural powers, which are, after all, central to *Tantra*, being rooted in the very notion of power—*śakti*. But he realized that all such constrained, patterned experiences (*niyata*)—governed by natural law—are inevitably consumed by the Absolute Void: *śūnya-atiśūnya*, the Void beyond voidness, the very body of the Goddess, ever hungry to devour what she gives birth to.

As Time (*kāla*), she regurgitates (*vāmā*) the universe into herself, being full (*pūrṇā*) of self-wonder and effortless fecundity. But at the same time, she is *vāmā*—also "terrible"—for the individual minds who do not recognize her within. Then, she manifests as *mātṛkā*, the dark Matrix, generating anxiety and sorrow.

As previously shown, she expresses herself both as outer power—mountains, rivers, animals, the five elements— and as inner force: thoughts, senses, muscles, and marrow. Yet not all these powers are gentle.

The more one identifies with the small self (*aham*), the more alien the world becomes. Even one's own body begins to feel hostile. Its fluids seem impure. The mind becomes a source of unrest: "Can I control my emotions? My shyness? My reactivity? My painful memories?" Thus begins the subtle worship of fearsome inner deities.

We offer daily sacrifices to the body: food, drink, care, attention—all to placate its unruliness. Hoping to escape its tyranny, we negotiate endlessly. We give it life's essence—but this commerce hides a deep slavery, built on dread.

Likewise, we feed the mind—unceasingly. Why? To distract it from what might surface in its silence. We entertain it like a monster, offering amusements so it won't devour us. But this strategy backfires. The more we feed it, the stronger it grows. The more it dominates us, the more we feed it—and so the *saṃsāra* wheel spins.

The only way out: offer *everything* to the Source—to the living Void. The Yoginīs teach: fear not this Void—its name is *camatkāra*—a dazzling wonder. It is joy. It is not the negation of life, but its transfiguration.

One who "knows oneself" (*svātma-jñāna*) is perpetually nourished by this wonder—even while living as "anyone," *kasyacit*. Outwardly, the awakened one is indistinguishable from others. If the awakened acts like the world, are they not merely part of it? Yes—and no.

This is the paradox of *Kālī*. Awakening confers no visible badge, no worldly distinction. Not only can anyone be seized by this astonishment of being—but awakening brings no status.

"But isn't an awakened person calmer, kinder, more compassionate?"—Perhaps. But Indian tradition is aware that *all behavior* can be mimicked. As Pascal wrote: "our virtues are often disguised vices." So, appearance, speech, conduct—none of these are reliable signs.

This invisible awakening *mirrors the world*. The awakened moves joyfully in the *saṃsāra-cakra*, just like everyone else. But unlike others, *parā śānti*—supreme peace—rises from the center of becoming, where most see only pain.

Their joy does not come from without. It is not simulated. It flows from the hub of the wheel.

Thus, the awakened stands aligned—*sukha*, "well-seated"—while others suffer *duḥkha*, being misaligned, ill-fitted. Why?

Because ordinary people, unaware of life's true nature, crystallize experience into habits. Freedom (*svātantrya*) becomes necessity (*niyati*). The stream of perception becomes frozen.

But in the paradoxical unfolding of embodied *śakti*, these boundaries are burned moment by moment. When I bring total attention, fiery *tīvra*, to the flow of experience— rather than *consuming* it, I *offer* it. Rather than intoxicate myself, I feed the fire of wonder.

If I honour the Yoginīs, they honour me.

14 – The Wine of Kula Must Be Drunk

kulaṃ proktaṃ parāśaktirūpam asparśasaṃbhavam |
peyaṃ tad eva madyaṃ tu kalānāṃ pravilāpakam || 60

Kula is declared to be the supreme Śakti,
not from any contact.
This is the true wine
which must be drunk,
for it dissolves all differentiated energies.

Today, psychedelics are praised and alcohol is condemned. But what do the *Yoginīs* say? Should one fall into intoxication? Or swear by abstinence alone?

The inner life is certainly no dull affair. Lovers across spiritual traditions have celebrated the "spirit of wine," for truth resides in the spirit, and spirits reveal it. What, then, is this truth that religions so often seek to forbid?

Tantra—especially its *Kaula* stream—offers a refined answer. In this tradition, passed on by lovers as well as by renunciants, the body is regarded as a *maṇḍala* of deities to be honoured through offerings of wine.

This *sūtra* leads us straight there by invoking the word *kula*. Its primary meaning is "family," "clan," or "tribe." In this context, the "family" is the divine assembly of Śiva, Śakti, and the *Yoginīs*. Everything is made of this divine assembly. The All is the totality of these interwoven energies. Hence, *Kula* comes to signify the Whole.

But in the *Kaula* understanding, every part of the Whole *is* a whole—following the esoteric principle: "The whole is in every part."

Among these totalities is the body. This is why the body is called *kula*, and is offered those substances that fulfil the energies animating it. Thus, *kula* also means "energy." Foremost among these is breath (*prāṇa*), for breath is life:

"Consciousness first transforms into breath. Thus, breath is the master of the body, of the Whole (*kula*)" (*Kaula-sūtra*, 4).

Kula is breath. *Kula* is body.

The female body especially is the incarnation of the totality of energies, for only the woman's body can carry new life. Hence, *kula* also signifies the woman—especially the tantric partner. The *Kaula* practice reflects the divine couple Śiva and Śakti. Thus, it unfolds *within the family*—that is, within the couple, and within the sacred *clan* of initiates.

Ultimately, the Whole (*kula*) depends on the primal energy that is its Source, its Heart, its Soul. This energy is both the substance of everything and that which transcends all. This energy is consciousness (*cit*). Therefore, *kula* is also consciousness.

Kula is the All and the Source of the All. But *kula* is not "just anything." It is power, *śakti*—the sovereign force of consciousness. And consciousness is not merely another thing among things. It is the heart of all that is. It governs all as a queen governs her kingdom. The teachings of the

Goddess Kālī are symbolic, but the *Pratyabhijñā* school expresses their insight philosophically as absolute freedom (*svātantrya*).

What is this freedom, which is the essence of consciousness and of all things?

Utpaladeva—likely a Kaula adept himself—explains: the highest power of being is the freedom to manifest oneself, to identify with what one manifests—or not; to be the Whole, or just a part; or a part within the Whole. This may seem abstract or metaphysical. But the tradition insists we experience this freedom constantly—in reverie, in play.

In play, we invent a character, give it a world, friends, enemies. Then we forget it's a game, taking it seriously— even tragically. Eventually, we may wake up, realizing that "reality" is another layer of the same imagination. And beyond it lie ever greater powers—leading to the supreme, unbounded consciousness that is our true nature.

The *Mokṣopāya-śāstra*, another great text from Kashmir's golden age of Kālī, describes this free self-creation as a dizzying cascade: whenever I imagine a world, however small or fleeting, I become its god. My decrees are its laws. Within this imagined world, characters may invent their own worlds—layer upon layer—each with its own inhabitants, extending to infinity.

My freedom as a character within one world depends on my freedom as its creator, which in turn rests in a deeper authoring self—until we reach the original author, imagined by none, the source of all—my true Self.

At every level, the "I" is the same. For in non-dual Tantra, there is only one *I*, one consciousness, freely expressing itself in infinite forms. *Freely*—because it is not confined by form, nor even by formlessness. It is not *beneath* forms—it *is* the shining of form itself, like sunlight is the shining of the sun. Appearance does not conceal reality— it *is* appearance as such, the pure display of being.

All this returns to one dynamic cycle of emanation and dissolution.

The tradition of Kālī reveals this through wheels (*cakras*), currents (*vāhas*), and streams (*oghas*)—symbols of her innermost nature.

Among these, the most vital is the "Wheel of the Twelve Kālīs"—the twelve stages of the cycle of manifestation, where experience flows from pure consciousness into the perception of objects, then dissolves both subject and object back into silent awareness.

This cycle repeats constantly.

Outwardly, it mirrors the twelve hours, twelve zodiac signs, twelve months. Echoing this, the medieval mystic Hadewijch of Antwerp wrote: "The nature from which true Love proceeds has twelve hours through which we see it emerge, and return to itself. And in returning, it gathers what it has drawn forth: the seeking spirit, the thirsty heart, the loving soul." (*Letter XX*)

Maṅgalā, revealer of the Goddess's teachings, says the same: the Goddess becomes Time (*kāla*—from which *Kālī* arises) to draw forth its essence (*saṃkarṣaṇa*).

The cycle is not mere repetition—it is a spiral. The end is a return, but enriched. Each turning carries a "supplement

212

of soul"—the myriad souls who plunge into her, full of all they've lived.

Yet incarnation implies contraction (*saṃkoca*), identification, and self-limitation—even if it is all play (*krīḍā*). For a game to work, we must *let* ourselves be taken by it. This *āveśa*, this possession, can be so strong that we forget it's a game.

Again, this is part of the play—like daydreaming while awake, imagining stories until we forget they are imagined. The success of the game lies in the forgetfulness of its fictional nature, leading to suffering. For the more I forget, the more seriously I take the dream, and the more I suffer the character's pain.

This paradox of play presupposes the power to *lie to oneself*. To know and not know. How can I deceive myself while knowing the truth?

And yet this is precisely consciousness' unique power.

For instance, I know a film is fiction. But in the theatre, I let myself believe otherwise—I *play along*. That's the spirit of play. According to Tantra, all lives are like this. We know we are free, sovereign *cit*, but we *act* as if we do not.

Still, if life is a game, I must remain aware of that—even in its most serious scenes. And so it is in Tantra: even amid agony, a part of me remains joyfully aware that this too is a spontaneous improvisation, independent of any external reality—which does not, in truth, exist.

This part is the *parā śakti*—the supreme power.

Parā doesn't mean detached or aloof. It is not separate from the world's suffering. On the contrary—it is *intimately present*, the soul of every sensation. It is supreme not in distance, but in fullness—overflowing joy, of which even pain is a crystallized ripple, like lava hardening at the edge of its movement.

Sometimes, this insight alone is enough to melt the ice of contraction.

Still, the *Kaula* tradition prescribes the cultivation of sensual pleasure. Why? Because pleasure (*ānanda*) is expansion. It melts inhibitions, dissolves conditioning—it is the Heart of all things, the Mouth of the Yoginī, the Source of *Kaula*.

Among sources of pleasure, *madya*—wine—holds a special place. *Madya* means spirituous drink, capable of freeing the mind and neutralizing fear. Especially red wine, seen as "liquid absolute," divinity made drinkable.

More than divine, it *is* divinity—as beverage.

To drink it is to melt conditioned being, to transmute contracted self-manifestation into expansive self-manifestation. Wine is one of the sacred acts the initiate commits to, especially on days of fullness (*parvan*).

Here, wine symbolizes uncontracted energy.

But in *Kaula*, we are warned: wine is not merely a metaphor for spiritual consciousness. The *Kaula* view dissolves the duality of material and spiritual. The material wine *reveals* the spiritual wine. This is why "it must be drunk."

The two are inseparable.

Wine is an initiatory obligation—along with meat and sexual union.

Does this mean one should drink simply for intoxication? Absolutely not.

The Kashmiri tradition, where Kālī flourished, teaches: drink not in moderation—but *with presence*. Let the effects unfold in all their subtlety. Not like a glutton, says Abhinavagupta, but like a connoisseur—who savours, marvels, and is *delighted*.

15 – The Expansion of Consciousness is an Act that Empties the Void, "Beyond the Void"

sadaiva paramā vṛttis sadasadbhramavarjitā |
satāṃ nirābilā spandā śūnyātītā sadoditā || 61

hatāhatobhayarave sa bāhyābhyantarodite |
layaṃ yāte sati tadā saṃsthitā niravagrahā || 62

The supreme Act unfolds ceaselessly,
free from the delusions of "true" and "false."
For the sincere, this activity is transparent:
it is the vibration beyond the void, ever-present.

When the sounds of the physical and mental realms,
arising externally and internally, dissolve,
then this (Goddess of consciousness)
remains unimpeded.

But is awakening not a state of emptiness? Is it not an escape from consciousness?

Indeed, the void can be daunting. Yet, Goddess Kālī embodies emptiness. Our experience is empty. We are empty. "She," our consciousness, our experience, is the evanescence of moments slipping through our fingers. The Buddha sealed his teaching with this: "everything is impermanent." Those who sought to elucidate his thought aimed to clarify this unceasing dissolution. For if nothing endures, then why seek the end of suffering—the goal of the Buddha's teaching—and who would enjoy this peace?

Some responded that impermanence is not an event that befalls things, like leaves coming to a tree, but rather the very nature of all things. To exist, the condition required is not to endure, to change moment by moment. A thing that is absolutely fixed cannot exist, for it could produce no effect. To produce an effect is to change. If the seed does not die, how can it sprout? It must die to produce. Existence is the fundamental effect. Thus, if a thing does not cease to exist, it cannot exist. Hence, we arrive at a paradox: to exist is not to exist. Or, becoming is not being. Therefore, the extinction of desire, *nirvāṇa*, which Buddhism aspires to as the cure for all suffering, would be nothing other than becoming, *saṃsāra*.

So, why strive to extinguish desires when, by their very nature, they extinguish themselves? Everything that appears disappears. This suffering, this sorrow, this lack... Enriched by this paradoxical insight, some followers of the Buddha glimpsed that Awakening was this and nothing else. To see that "everything is already pacified, pure, extinguished, absent, empty," and as if non-existent. It is not necessary to make things disappear to end suffering. It suffices to see that their very birth is their extinction.

The Great Silent One invites us to see peace in the arising of things, for, like drawings traced on water, they dissolve in the same movement in which they form. Practically, there is no longer a need to leave the world to be free of it. The Awakened One can thus act within the crowd, in the mud of passions, which for him are but the wisdom of emptiness. The Yoginīs emerge from the void only to return to it immediately. One who sees this clearly no longer fears them and can love them.

Since Kālī is Consciousness as Time, it is understandable that emptiness, dissolution, and the moment hold a central place in her transmission. And the Buddhist inspiration is undoubtedly present—though this does not mean that the tradition of the Goddess is a kind of unnamed Buddhism. Indeed, paradox is omnipresent in this teaching. We can even recognize it as its core. How to express with words what is beyond words? —Through paradox. The unmoving movement, the placeless place, the silent speech point to the mystery of being, just as, in other traditions, one might speak of the gentle burn or the luminous darkness.

Furthermore, emptiness is evidently important. In fact, when we seek silence, peace, or rest, we seek a kind of emptiness. Thus, a body empty of suffering, a head empty of heaviness, a soul empty of painful memories, a living space empty of noise, a life free from agitation... In other words, emptiness does not only have a negative value. It indicates a liberation, a relief that makes one available. Holidays are vacant, empty of the toil that usually occupies us. That is why I can make myself available for other activities.

Here, emptiness carries this positive meaning. It is synonymous with freedom. Observing dissolutions, embracing this universal movement of energy reabsorption into their source, is to rediscover our powers anew. To empty, or to let it happen, is to make space.

However, emptiness is also synonymous with inertia, with death. The opposite of dynamism, of life. Emptiness is thus ambivalent. The teaching of the Yoginīs emphasizes that not all emptiness is inherently good. If I am depressed, I feel empty. The absence of a loved one, or simply someone close, can be felt as a paralyzing poison. Blessed emptiness, cursed emptiness... is emptiness not the ultimate Yoginī?

In fact, emptiness is, more often than not, a curse. According to non-dual Tantra, a state of emptiness is a state where consciousness denies itself because, as the object, the content disappears, it believes it has disappeared along with it. For example, I am accustomed to the presence of these pieces of furniture in this room. The day they are removed, I feel a sense of emptiness when I enter this space again. The room is not absolutely empty, for at least the floor and walls remain. But it is as if the absence of familiar furniture hides the presence of the rest. Why? Because, Tantra responds, I have become accustomed to the furniture. They have become the entire room. They make me forget the floor, the walls, the light, and especially the space in which they bathe.

In the case of "material" emptiness, seemingly foreign to my consciousness, the phenomenon is even deeper. I do not only get used to my body, my thoughts, my familiar sensations: I identify with them. They are me—or at least, that's what I believe. Thus, when these markers of my identity disappear, for example during deep sleep, coma, or fainting, I come to believe that I have disappeared.

Yet, in reality, I do not disappear. Only the objects with which I have become accustomed to identifying in the waking state, during common daily life, disappear. But my empathy with the body reaches such a degree that the disappearance of this body, of the landscape of consciousness that I am, is mistaken for the disappearance of consciousness itself.

The risk is then to take this "nothing" for reality, for the final word of the story, of my story. The Goddess warns against this temptation. For see: such a state of emptiness is itself just an object, a mental construction.

But how could a state of nothingness be a construction, that is, something?

Such a construction or concept (*vikalpa*) is, according to the philosophy of Tantra and of India in general, the affirmation of an object delimited by the exclusion of everything else. For example, I am in a crowded restaurant and I focus on what So-and-so is telling me. I thus exclude the rest. As a result, what this person tells me is considered a "construction" made by exclusion, by more or less deliberate forgetting of other noises. To concentrate on one thing is, indeed, to forget the rest.

Now, this "state of emptiness" is precisely such an object, constructed by exclusion of the world, the body, and all things. It is indeed the result of a forgetting, since when I emerge from it, I become aware that I had "forgotten everything."

Emptiness is thus a "something" delimited by the exclusion of all that is not it, that is, the world and the body. It is a "that," it is not "me," truly me. At best, it is "mine" or "for me." But it is not me. It is only an abstraction of all objects. It is thus a construction. The Poem of Vibration, a famous text that transmits the teaching of the Yoginīs, therefore considers that states of emptiness are artificial. They are artificial states, like the emptiness perceived in sleep, as opposed to awakening. It is therefore not desirable to focus on them and to seek them deliberately.

This *chummā* goes in this direction. It invites us to transcend, to go beyond emptiness. It speaks to us of surpassing inertia, states of unconsciousness, of heaviness, which Indian psychology readily describes as tamas, heaviness, opacity. The *Poem of Vibration* associates this inertia with matter, with an artificial state, but also with melancholy, with the lack of enthusiasm that prevents us from awakening. According to the expression of the Poem, this depression "steals awakening" from us, that is, expansion, the opening of consciousness.

Awakening is therefore not a search for emptiness for its own sake, for a state of anaesthesia or apathy. Quite the contrary, awakening is this Act that eradicates unconsciousness, for it is the act of consciousness. This silent Act that is the source of everything. It explodes at every moment. But, like lava, it petrifies as it cools, down to sterile emptiness. Awakening is the Act that annihilates this nothingness. Indeed, it is the Great Unforeseen (*mahāsāhasā*), the spiralled emergence (*vṛtti*) that denies the void that denies consciousness. Awakening is not negation; it is the negation of negation: a total Yes.

And this is also the freedom that we are. Consciousness is freedom. It manifests as unconsciousness because, precisely, it is free; it is not limited to being this or that. It can manifest as other, as the opposite of what it is. It is present even in its absence. It manifests in the form that seems precisely to deny it. In this case, unconsciousness, thus emptiness. Impermanence, time, Death—all this is freedom, liberation, and adoration of all these creations that the Source reabsorbs into its bosom. If I have the audacity to attune myself to this movement, I am liberated. And I love, I love this cyclical movement that I embrace ever more.

Pause. Contemplate these whirlwinds. And, beyond patience and even receptivity, partake in this dance that I cannot comprehend, but which I can love.

This Act of freedom, of liberation, of transcendence, is referred to among the Yoginīs by the term *vṛtti*, which literally means "movement" or "operation," such as a mental operation. However, in this context, it does not pertain to the mind, which is ordinarily aligned with inertia and mechanism. Here, it denotes the "supreme" (*paramā*) operation or act—the Act of pure freedom through which consciousness reclaims its fullness instead of merely mistaking itself for fragments. It is a return to oneself.

This return, which is awakening, occurs through an act of awakening, a turning back upon oneself, which eradicates the void, which negates the negation of self. This may seem metaphysical, but it is empirical. Indeed, we experience it constantly when we are drowsy or absorbed in something (note, once again, the proximity between sleep and concentration), and suddenly, a door slams or the phone rings. This moment of awakening, of being torn away, is precisely the awakening to be practiced. Thus, one becomes familiar with the Family of Yoginīs. This is the hidden, ultimate Yoga. It is the transcendence of inert emptiness. And, because it is sudden, like every act, it is termed the Great Unexpected (*mahā-sāhasā*), the Goddess awakening, the *Kuṇḍalinī* rising.

Feel in every movement, at the beginning of each perception, this pure astonishment of being.

Thus, to awaken is to go beyond Death; it is the act of life par excellence. Now, this act "occurs incessantly," as the explanation specifies. Indeed, if I did not constantly return to the infinite fullness that "I am," then I would be nothing more than an inert object, an unconscious void. And I would no longer be consciousness. And, as this Light of lights would then extinguish, there would be nothing left, and even this "nothing" would no longer be anything... Therefore, we must admit that, even in our seemingly ordinary streams of experience, we constantly return to our true Self, absolutely free and creator of all.

However, these creations cover this freedom, just as reflections can "hide" the mirror. And these intervals of return to self are so rapid, so ephemeral, that they go unnoticed. And, even when they are savoured, as in moments of emotional, physical, or spiritual intensity, we do not recognize them for what they are. We do not recognize ourselves for what we are. And we allow ourselves to be hypnotized, albeit freely, by our own manifestations. "Freely," because, indeed, freedom is perpetual. It is this act of infinite perpetual reclaiming, renewed at every moment since it is the source of all. But we are a wild, immature freedom that does not realize itself.

In fact, we freely choose to lie to ourselves, to pretend as if we were not free. Yet we sense this omnipotence when it surfaces here and there. That is why we believe ourselves to be immortal. We are, truly, but we do not realize it. Each moment is thus awakening, a return to self, to the Self. But, through a play that erases its truth as a play at every moment, we believe only in separation and in the relative powerlessness attached to our incarnations.

We then find ourselves tossed between truth and falsehood, between sincerity and lies, between fighting and fleeing, between "yes" and "no." And, thus torn between these abstractions, I miss the Centre that I am nonetheless and that animates these opposing enemies that seem to tear me apart. For I am everything and beyond everything. More than shadow and light, I am the Light that never sets, neither in light nor in darkness, in whom lights and shadows appear. I am the light that illuminates the absence of light, for such is my intoxication, my dance step, missed and caught at every moment.

The "true" being (*sat*) is precisely the one who recognizes himself as the master of the puppets of "truth" (*sat*) and "non-truth" (*a-sat*). From then on, these opposing forces are transmuted. They lose their opacity and are transfigured into transparency, an exact description of a feeling: consciousness penetrates everything, as light seems to pass through certain materials. Incarnation then becomes a stained-glass window; the individual is nothing more than a channel, an absence for the Presence. Empty, yes, but empty for the Fullness. I am nothing more than what I have never been, but fully: vibration (*spanda*), Soul of all because free from all.

This vibration is the pure Act, the total, complete, accomplished Act. It thus transcends the void. It is the Life that saves from mortal life. Pure life, it is immobile movement, movement that does not go from point A to point B, but oscillation, scintillation that, in its infinitesimal amplitude, embraces all the breaths of the living. It is therefore "always current." There is no rest in it, for if it ceased, the very experience of rest would no longer be possible.

Always present, certainly. However, it is auspicious, to recognize it, to recognize oneself, to meet it through the dissolution of external and internal "noises." Silence on earth to hear the song of the sky. Silence in the heavens to listen to the unique word of the authentic earth: "I am." It is also possible to promote this dissolution, this relaxation, through the Gesture of Wonder (*vismaya-mudrā*). Body laid on the ground, mouth agape, eyes wide open as if to gulp down the immensity, everything dissolves like mist on glass. The mirror then awakens to itself, to its bare limpidity that no colour can capture.

A surface without centre or edges, she is the Goddess "whom nothing can stop," consciousness flowing by itself, like a wide river. She is "fully present" because she is the space that contains everything, lower than the lowest, higher than the highest, before the beginning and after the end. She is the presence that, welcoming these words at this moment, creates them in the secret of her absence.

16 – She Is a Nameless Sleep

*niḥśeṣabhāvavibhavaprapañcaughaparikṣayāt
avācyatvād anāmeha nidrā śāntā parā smṛtā || 63*

*She is called the supreme and peaceful sleep,
a sleep without a name in this world,
for words cannot express it,
and the vast flood of majestic phenomena
has entirely vanished, leaving nothing behind.*

In our accelerated society, sleep has become a topic of concern. We sleep less and less. Does this mean that awakening is the enemy of sleep? Would it not be better to seek the rest that sleep provides?

We no longer have time; rather, Time possesses us. And this Time is the Goddess, Kālī. Everything passes within her, who herself does not pass. Thus, we have no choice but to admit ourselves as slaves of Kālī, to sing her ineffable splendour, like the greatest Indian poet, Kālidāsa.

Yet, emptiness is not inherently good, but it is necessary. For this, rest is required. More than rest: sleep, *nidrā*. Not ordinary sleep, which is merely the backlash of our agitated days of 'wakefulness', but a deeper sleep still. A sleep for which there exists neither name nor adequate description.

To fall asleep in the Pure Act is to surrender. It is to let go in trust, for sleep indeed requires a sense of security. This letting go is 'supreme', transcendent, for it surpasses the opposition that rhythms ordinary life, the conflict between opposing forces of which we are the playthings, the sacrificial victims. According to the Vedas, Time is the alternation of days and nights, represented by two dogs, one black and one white, who gradually devour our breath of life. Yet, they are our creation. And thus, we pass from excitement to dejection because, let us admit it, we are all 'bipolar' to varying degrees, insofar as duality is our law.

The tradition of the Goddess then reveals to us another sleep, a sleep that is not the opposite of the waking state and its troubles. A sleep that is not forgetfulness due to fatigue and disgust. A sleep of healing, therefore, and a 'nameless' sleep, for it occurs in full consciousness. Eyes wide open, senses alert, the mind is entirely absorbed.

Such is the Gesture of the Secret (*rahasya-mudrā*), an inner gesture that manifests outwardly as an expression resembling astonishment. As if suspended, one is fully active, yet a profound silence reigns serenely within. One is as if asleep and awake at once, like birds gliding without needing to flap their wings. Words cannot describe this miracle. Everything is there, and nothing is there. Presence and absence embrace like inhalation and exhalation; life itself unveils as a paradox, beyond opinions, beyond the bland expressions worn out by utilitarian use.

In this night, 'the vast flood of phenomena'—this mountain that seems so impressive, even invincible, 'even by meditation', says a yogi—is suspended by the heart's wonder, like a moment halted at the threshold of a sneeze. Everything is annihilated, and everything is more present than ever. Simultaneously, in a single instant. The Great Unexpected, the elusive surprise, takes us and evaporates us, like a misty spot that dissipates.

She is thus 'the supreme Mudrā'. Mudrā is the partner of sexual yoga, but also the ritual hand gesture. In a deeper sense, the *mudrā* is an inner gesture that brings joy (*mud*) and dissolves (*drav*) vain fears and other phantoms. Ordinarily, we adopt postures that are more or less ridiculous masks. In this case, it is the Goddess who takes her seat on her throne. Usually, reality is inverted: I use vital energy—therefore Time—to glorify my character, my mask that I possess to the point that it ends up 'sticking to my skin'.

But now, the divine order is restored; personality does not disappear, but it once again serves the soul that animates it. This Mudrā is the Goddess, consciousness awakening in grandeur, in the vast expanse of the infinite space that she is. From a technical angle, for the beauty of this gesture, it is also called 'divine attitude', *divya-mudrā*. It marks everything with the seal of space. Thus, marked by this nothingness, source of everything, forms and names regain the finesse of their features. Everything becomes light and precise again, colors more vivid than ever. I then join this Nameless One that others have called the Imprint of the desert. I emerge from my forgetful contraction, and the infinite enters.

And this occurs in the 'three states' of consciousness— wakefulness, dream, and deep sleep. This lucid sleep vibrates without interruption and imprints its sublime clarity even into the smallest corners of these seemingly mundane states.

The practice of 'yogic sleep' is taught in the tradition of Kālī. In the Thought of the Goddess of Tremor, it is thus mentioned in the description of the Twelve Kālīs: 'It is from the master's mouth that one receives (instruction on) yogic sleep, a rest that surpasses (the power of) speech.'

The same chapter later evokes the Goddess experienced in this yogi's sleep, in this special state of sleep, due to the practice of yoga, that is, union with the divine: 'She clearly flashes within, this intoxication, a transcendent vibration, nameless, standing at the centre of the wheel of what is conscious and what is inert, felt in yogic sleep.'

Let us note, in passing, the use of the three genders—feminine, neuter, then masculine—in a single sentence to designate the same Goddess consciousness! This fluidity of genders is a striking feature of the tradition of the Goddess Kālī.

In the Kaula traditions in general, of which Kālī's is one branch, this specific sleep is one of the signs evidencing the awakening of consciousness or Kuṇḍalinī:

"For one who is transmuted (by the awakening energy of consciousness), O masters of the gods! these five states unfold: pleasure, startle, trembling, sleep, and intoxication."

This transmutation energy, in the alchemical sense, is the Command (*ājñā*), the name of Grace in these esoteric spiritual currents. It manifests always and everywhere, but very clearly in the interval between extremes: 'By abandoning all (limited) states, one immerses in the serene state, dwelling in an intermediate feeling between what can be felt and what cannot, standing between space and non-space. The transcendent pleasure of this joy is an awakening that is the sleep of yoga. When this state of sleep occurs, indeed, the realisation of the Command manifests.'

The instruction of awakening through absorption in the in-between between wakefulness and sleep appears in the famous collection of awakening games of the *Vijñāna Bhairava Tantra*: 'When sleep has not yet come, but external objects have disappeared, the supreme Goddess shines through this mental state.'

The *Manthāna Bhairava Tantra*, a tantra of the Kaula tradition of Kubjikā, also mentions sleep in its list of signs of awakening: 'The eleven signs (of awakening) are: 1) swaying, 2) possession, 3) trembling, 4) sleep, 5) intoxication, 6) tingling, 7) dancing on one leg, 8) speaking in tongues, 9) tears, 10) leaping like a kid, and 11) roaring like a lion.' Thus, this sleep is much more than rest.

Let us note, however, that in our present *chummā*, likewise, this extraordinary sleep is described as a 'rest' or a healing (*śānta*, 'appeased', also denotes the moment when fever subsides) that is beyond the expressive powers of language, just as, here, it is a 'nameless' sleep.

Nameless is also one of the names of the Goddess. She has no name (*nāma*), is inexplicable (*anākhyā*), she transcends speech (*vācātītā*). And yet, she is Speech, the matrix of all sounds and all languages.

In this same vein, she is the 'silent revelation' or 'free of all need' (not utilitarian, *nirīha*), a freedom that characterises the Mantra. The Mantra here denotes the mental aspect of the awakening experience. The mind, this inner chatter, is transmuted into Mantra, into a vibrant consciousness, unarticulated like a cry of surprise, an outpouring of love towards forms which are, for their part, designated by the term Mudrā. The Mantra is manifesting consciousness. The Mudrā is manifested consciousness. The two form an inseparable and invisible couple, the two faces of the same coin.

Recognising them is, in some way, recognising one's parents, being reintegrated into one's true family (*kula*). The mind becomes a salvific Mantra, an inexhaustible source of perfect teaching that does not depend on words. The objects of the senses, the world, become Mudrā, perfect form, light expressing the joy of invincible freedom, beyond all perception. Thus, all Mantras and all Mudrās, the gods and goddesses, are present in the Gesture of Śiva, senses wide open, interior silent. Simple is the teaching; but of inexhaustible richness.

If one parses the verse differently, it is also possible to read that the Goddess, the Supreme (Parā is also the proper name of the main form of consciousness), is 'the revelation, free of all desire, of the Mudrās and the Mantras', that is to say, of the goddesses and gods, the yoginīs and siddhas (awakened yogis), faculties and their respective objects, in other words, forms and names, of Śakti and Śiva.

But this other reading does not change much the meaning, in any case inexhaustible, of these verses. However, the following verse in ancient Kashmiri (which we have not translated) rather evokes the Mudrā 'which is not an object of rational knowledge' (*ameyā*), the Mudrā of spatial movement (*khecarī*). And the Mantra is mentioned afterwards, separately. We therefore believe that our 'parsing' is correct.

'I sleep, but my heart is awake,' sang the Psalmist. Awakening is a sleep. The gesture of falling asleep into space is the remedy for morbid forgetfulness. May we always burn with that flame!

17 – The Material World is the Day of Consciousness

pṛthivyādimahābhūtakārye kāraṇasaṃyute |
prodite tatra sarvatra bhautikaṃ tad dinaṃ smṛtam || 64

When the effects that are the (five) elements—starting with earth—are fully active along with the senses that generate them, tradition refers to this as the "day" (of consciousness).

But how does the world re-emerge from this awakened sleep?

Life expresses itself through paradoxes, challenging the habitual patterns of our intelligence. Yet, life itself—consciousness—overcomes these contradictions. How? By manifesting these opposites successively, not simultaneously.

Utpaladeva, the profound philosopher of Tantra, invites us to feel that "everything always exists in consciousness," albeit in an undifferentiated manner, like a tree existing within its seed. When the seed is planted and conditions are favourable, the pre-existing forms begin to appear, one after another, following a natural order: first the bud, then the sprout, then the first leaves, and so on until the fruit. There is an order to it, *krama*.

This succession of appearances constitutes ordinary time. Indeed, time is nothing other than change. If there were no change—if everything were to freeze—there would be no notion of time. More precisely, time is the manifestation of incompatible differences, such as fire and water, in separate moments and places.

We measure irregular changes, like the cooking of pasta, by comparing them to more regular changes, such as the movement of the sun or the ticking of a watch. But this ordinary time itself depends on the manifestation of differences, which is divine time—that is, consciousness manifesting itself in different aspects.

In pure consciousness, everything exists simultaneously, like when we take an overview of a painting. This time is true time, eternal time where "everything always exists," like the patterns of feathers in a bird's egg. Then, the gaze settles on different parts of the painting, successively. And that is the time we know—becoming.

Absolute consciousness, in its fullness, contains incompatible aspects, like fire and water, because it is absolutely free. But these forms cannot manifest at the same moment as identical. Therefore, they manifest at different times. This is the reason for becoming.

Thus, days follow nights. All things are cyclical—the great universe, the microcosm of our soul, and all rhythms of life, seasons, and worlds. This alternation is not separate from the Goddess consciousness, for nothing is separate from her and nothing can be.

Yet, she herself is cyclical without being limited to that. She is night; she is also day. This divine incarnation beyond all incarnation is evoked as a hungry, insatiable woman, her body emaciated from fasting, eyes bloodshot, fangs apparent, tongue visible, ready to devour all things.

The Goddess is insatiable; she is "thin" (*kṛśā*), for everything dissolves in her. Impermanence endlessly swallows names and forms, like a bottomless black hole. Indeed, no content of experience exhausts consciousness or ends experience, in the sense that, whatever I live, there is always space for more because everything dissolves.

One might say that karma exists, that actions leave subtle traces like seeds that will give rise to new forms. But all this does not exhaust the space that remains infinite. No matter the content, there is always room: such is our true nature—immense and without limits. If there are limits, they extend into space and cannot absorb it. Rather, it is space that absorbs them.

Thus, karma does not limit space. It is the nourishment of space, the fuel of this fire of consciousness which, in the contracted individual experience, is taken for "impermanence," whereas it is a perpetual liberation. Observe once more the evanescence of thoughts, of sensations on your skin. Everything evaporates moment by moment, like drawings traced on water.

Contemplating the disappearance of the clouds of beings and things in the sky of consciousness is the wonder of the Yoginī. The gaze thus embraces the infinite, instead of seeking refuge in finite forms that can only disappoint if we see only them. First, discernment consists in seeing only the sky, freed from all clouds. Then, one realizes the incredible miracle of clouds—ornaments of the sky: non-duality.

Consciousness is thus empty, forever virgin. I am full, but I am insatiable, for I am a space that welcomes and "devours" everything, without exception. Thus, I am everything and beyond everything. I am at the heart of each thing, the soul of every living being, and yet I am free from all that. I am this paradox of becoming.

Now, for there to be dissolution, there must also be crystallization. Space crystallizes, then. Like sap hardening, space becomes movement, then light, then liquid, then solid. Similarly, the goddesses—the powers of the senses—activate to create our world. First, hearing creates sounds and space; then touch creates sensations and the element Air; then sight creates forms and the element Fire; then taste creates flavours and the element Water; finally, smell creates odours and the element Earth. All this derives from Space, like the sun gradually illuminating a landscape as it rises from the horizon.

This material world, composed of the five elements derived from the five perceptions, themselves engendered by the goddesses of the five senses, is the Day of consciousness in its fullness. This day of all beauty is not a fall; it manifests no lack. And, if it does contain lack, this very defect, freely assumed by the infinite Presence, expresses its fullness. "They are fully and always active," like the branches of the tree express the vitality of the sap.

The world is engendered by the union (*yoga*) of the goddesses of our physical and mental faculties with the gods that are their respective objects. For example, the eyes unite with forms and engender the visual world. And, at the centre of this mandala, sits the couple of the God and the Goddess—total consciousness united with total being. These embraces, these relationships create the world at every moment.

But then, if the world is engendered by our individual faculties, this seems to suggest that the world exists only "for me"! Perhaps no one else exists? Then there is only me—but an individual Me. Others would then be only manifestations of my powers, my śaktis. Such a conclusion is unfortunate, for it would invite me to live like an egocentric child who cannot distinguish between self and other and who, as a result, treats the other as a thing to satisfy his desires. This danger, which philosophers call "solipsism" ("only I exist"), must be clearly seen and avoided. Otherwise, Tantra becomes the royal road to hell.

The message of the Yoginī is that "love must make the Self disappear before the Self makes love disappear." Therefore, the affirmation that "everything is consciousness" cannot mean that only I exist.

The solution to this lethal drift is to see that there is a common base to all our individual perceptions: this base is consciousness, the primordial source of all these points of view. It is the "ancient ground" (*purāṇa-adhiṣṭhāna*, says the *Mahā-naya-prakāśa*), the living foundation that unifies our points of view, harmonizing them according to rules that do not depend on our individual preferences. Indeed, even if "everything is consciousness," not everything is individual. Consciousness is the transpersonal power that harmonizes contracted, personal consciousnesses. Consciousness is what connects us: it is love (*bhakti*), sharing, and participation.

We feel it when we are in unison with a group (performance, music, dance, sport...), but also when we discover the strength of logic, for example in mathematics—the famous "eureka!" An assertion is not true because it conforms to my desires but because it is coherent, according to criteria I do not choose, which make me participate in a mystery. That is why Utpaladeva, a great lover of the Goddess, can conclude that "ideas" are true because they are both coherent and useful in daily life.

These ideas are common ideas, like the same, the different, the relation, the action, the quantity, the quality, etc. They are constructions, but constructed directly by Universal Consciousness, not by an individual or collective consciousness (a particular culture), even if these ideas can be discovered or rediscovered by a particular individual consciousness. Our fundamental ideas are the direct creation of the Goddess, a very useful gift for acting in the world.

Therefore, there exists a common world, universal rules, principles, and values. That is why "non-dual" Tantra is not a relativism that would allow selfishness to run free.

18 – When Opposites Dissolve, the Goddess Is Empty, Hungry

ātmātmīyagrahodrekapakṣo yatra layaṃ gataḥ |
nirnimeṣapadaṃ tasya kṛśaṃ grāsaikaghasmaram || 65

When the extremes of grasping at "I" and "mine"
dissolve,
there arises the unblinking state—
emaciated, ravenous,
eager to devour all.

But what remains when nothing remains? Is this state of life final?

We have acknowledged the existence of a shared world and universal principles. Yet, without succumbing to relativism, we must recognize relativity: up is relative to down, left to right. They support each other. Can we eliminate evil without also eradicating good? They are like two ends of the same elastic band: tension on one side mirrors tension on the other. In my cycle of wakefulness and sleep, I transition from the agitation of wakefulness to the heaviness of deep sleep. This abrupt shift from form to formlessness is inevitable. The teachings of the Yoginīs do not aspire to a nihilistic ideal of desiring the impossible but aim to harmonize these opposing forces.

Thus, instead of a rigid self, strained in its reflex to exist at the expense of others, I aspire to an open self, strengthened by this openness. Balanced in its lack of fixed points. Space cannot fall, be invaded, or experience pressure or stress. Without centre or boundaries, it is invincible. As Tibetan yogis sing, who would be foolish enough to try to pierce the sky with a spear?

But space is nothing, one might say; that's why it's invincible! It's true that space is not a thing. But nothing? No, for being nothing implies powerlessness. Yet, space is far from powerless. It possesses the greatest power: to give place. Without space, there would be no body, no movement. It is the image, if one dares say, of the true Self. It claims nothing, asserts no territory, yet nothing can extend or exist without or outside it. From the earliest secret teachings, it represents Presence, *cit* in Sanskrit, the Light that no one can see, but without which no one can see.

Dissolving the "excesses" (*udreka*) of the self and the mine is thus returning to my natural state, serene immensity, for it has no enemies. Yet, is space the enemy of forms, boundaries, hierarchies, identities? It's true that it, or she, the Goddess, regularly swallows them. However, to accept this partial view would be to forget that space opposes nothing. It welcomes boundaries, orders, differences, wars, and oppositions—our opposing forces, precisely.

When I surrender to space, when I let my energies spread within it, carried away in a dissolving movement, I rediscover my energies. My individuality. Indeed, although space transcends everything, it is also the inspiring source of everything. The Yoginīs do not hate forms. On the contrary, they play with them and are known and feared for their power to freely assume all forms, without being limited to any (hence the statues of Yoginīs with animal heads). Immensity does not destroy the elements dancing within it. Like a good matrix, it does not abolish them but fulfils them once attention returns to it. A generous Goddess, she asks only for this intimate conversion.

Opposites dissolve; they rest finally in their common root. There is no longer good or evil. However, good does not truly disappear, for good is the very reality of living space. A good that transcends relativity, but which is an absolute good, not a dull, indifferent plain. The Goddess is so passionate that, in her, even neutrality reveals itself as passion.

And so, she does not fear emptiness, leanness, the apparent scarcity that is only the prelude to true abundance. Her "emaciated" state is a state of glory, for it reveals freedom. I am not dependent on opposites, which possess me (or "grasp" me, *graha*) when I want to possess them. The word *graha* denotes the act of seizing, of taking hold of something, but also demonic possession. When I possess this body (more than I identify with it), it possesses me, invades me, and, cut off from its source, it becomes my master.

Possessing makes me a slave. It's said that, to capture thieving monkeys in India, boxes were made with a hole just wide enough for a small monkey to insert its hand. Inside the box, a tasty banana was placed. When a monkey approached, it would insert its hand through the opening and grasp the banana. Fatal mistake: having taken the fruit, it was trapped. It could indeed free itself by releasing the banana. But this gesture is so contrary to our habits…

The lesson is clear: as long as I possess, I am possessed. The Buddhist master Tilopāda gave this advice to his learned disciple Nāropāda: "It is not things that bind you; it is your attachment to them!" In other words, the world and the body are not the cause of my feeling of being bound. The problem is attachment, which comes only from me.

The remedy to this tragedy is fasting. To stop taking. With the hands, with the mouth, with the eyes. And above all, with attention. To stop controlling and let oneself be taken back into the endless Movement that is the heartbeat. To become empty to welcome the Weave without beginning or end. Emaciated, we will be fulfilled. Gustave Thibon said that "Everything that is not of Eternity regained is lost Time." To regain it, it is good to let go of Time. To let space be cleared. Again, this is not a definitive rejection, a closing of borders, but an emptiness in view of fullness. A release for better reception.

The teaching of the Yoginīs emphasizes the dissolution of the self and the mine. However, it's important to note that other initiated masters in this tradition have proposed a different vision: the dissolution of the false self into the true Self.

Inspired no doubt by the Trika tradition, which reveals the creative face of Consciousness, Utpaladeva and Abhinavagupta affirm that the ultimate Void is a Self. Thus, in the opening verse found at the head of his most famous works, Abhinavagupta evokes "my Heart," *mama hṛdayam*. Now, his commentator Jayaratha specifies that *mama*, literally "to me" or "mine," does not indicate possession in the ordinary sense, but the Self, that is, the true Self.

These two approaches—the ultimate Void and the true Self—do not contradict each other. They are expressed in two distinct Yoginī traditions, but they are combined in the Anuttara practice system taught in the *Devyā Yāmala* tantra and developed by Abhinavagupta in his *Light of the Tantras*.

So, I settle, and perhaps I close my eyes. And I let consciousness "devour" with appetite. And I share this delight in dissolution. What more fitting tribute to the Source of all than to give it all?

19 – Then Falls the Night

ekasmin sati kācit tu rātriḥ samyak parāgatā /
sarvasaṃhārasaṃhārasaṃhahartrī satatoditā // 67

cidacidbhedavibhavaprakāśagrasanākulā /
mahāśūnyātiśūnyeyaṃ nirlakṣyā advayavigrahā //68

varṇāvarṇavibhāgaṃ tu yā rāti satataṃ kṣaṇāt /
rātris sā kathyate ghorā nirupākhyākramākṛtiḥ //69

In this one (consciousness), the night falls, truly supreme,
for she is ever-present,
she who dissolves all,
even the dissolution of dissolution.

She is a plunge into the manifestation and consumption
of her majesty divided between the conscious and the
unconscious.
Void beyond the void, her body is without opposite,
and she cannot be targeted.

Always and at every moment, she gives (rāti)
the visible and invisible aspects (of the world).
She is thus called the "terrible night" (rātri),
formless, she whose form is not in becoming.

Today, the starry night is hidden from us by human-made
lights. This indicates our flight from the night. But to reject
the Night is to "miss the light that illuminates our gaze."

Night follows the day of wars between the opposing forces
that animate and torment me. The alternation between

inhalation and exhalation calms, the breath called "equal" (*samāna*) becomes predominant, notably to digest, that is, to integrate the many differences received during the waking state in the form of various stimuli. The warrior's rest, then. The different nourishments are equalized before being distributed to the organs. Likewise, the individual soul transcends all hierarchy and even Time. Salutary bliss of forgetfulness!

The oldest Upaniṣad (the earliest spiritual texts of humanity) had already noted: "There, a king is no longer a king; there, a thief is no longer a thief..." This abolition of boundaries, as I noted earlier, is absolutely necessary for the life of the waking state. Who can live without this dissolution into the unknowable nothingness? This state of deep sleep, *su-supta*, is not useless, despite its nothingness. It contributes to life, and its effects are very real. It reminds us of the usefulness of the useless, as Zhuangzi would say.

This mysterious experience, which is not really one since it has no content, has always fascinated the yogis and yoginīs of India. Indeed, there is something literally extraordinary in this state close to death that modern science has not yet fully understood. What is the purpose of this sleep? Rest? But a sleeping brain consumes the same energy as in the waking state!

Moreover, this sleep compromises the survival of the individual in peril. It is surprising that it was "selected" by evolution. One might respond that sleep serves for rest. But this rest could just as well have been accomplished by maintaining the waking state, even by lying down or sitting. Thus, true yogis of Tibet never lie down.

According to some, the sleep here designated as "night" is merely a negative state, a deprivation of light. A state of ignorance. It is not a transcendent state or close to awakening but a lack of consciousness and a kind of backlash from the agitation of the waking state. Ordinary experience would be like a kind of drug, and sleep would correspond to phases of descent. Buddhism, as well as Sāṃkhya and Yoga (of Patañjali), may be close to this view.

Yet, there are traditions as ancient, if not more so (for example, the Upaniṣads), for which this state of deep sleep is a sacred state of unity. According to this fascinating perspective, what the waking mind takes for unconsciousness would be a state of pure unity. But, as we have said earlier, in the absence of differentiated and distinctly graspable content, the mind, accustomed to grasping limited things like the monkey trapped in its banana box, is incapable of recognizing this auspicious unity. Thus, the state of deep sleep would be an absolute state, beyond states and sensory and mental categories. Each night, without effort or any kind of practice, everyone would access the absolute, but without knowing it.

According to Tantra, that is precisely the flaw, so to speak, of this state, which is indeed a state and not the unconditioned absolute. For, while there is indeed pure and flawless unity, without any difference related to time, place, and form, well... "I do not know it." In other words, I am one, but I do not know it. Now, this not-knowing is useless; worse, it is even compatible with ignorance! Indeed, as the intellect is absent in the state of deep sleep, no recognition, and therefore no awakening, is possible in it. In fact, no practice is possible in the absolute void without any difference. It rests the body but does not awaken the soul.

That is why Tantra advises practicing in the body, in sensations, and in the intellect, but not in the void of unconsciousness. The Poem of Vibration sees it as an artificial state, an object simply simpler than others, but sterile on the spiritual level. It is especially not a matter of getting stuck there! Tepid inertia is the enemy of awakening. That is why Tantra, like all true mystics, leads us toward passion. Nevertheless, the void is a natural phase of the Cycle of Consciousness.

The Void of this Night of the Goddess is therefore not this natural state of deep sleep. This Night is something else. Indeed, when this Night "falls" or occurs, it occurs in full wakefulness. In harmony with the oldest wisdoms of India, this void arises amidst the efflorescence of forms during the waking state. That is why this Night is "ever-present." If this night opposed the day, it would not be "supreme" (*parā*) but only relative. Like all expressions of this language of the Yoginīs, so special, which Kṣemarāja will call "the proper language of the tradition of Kālī," it presents itself as a paradox. Awakening is a night in broad daylight, like an eclipse. Moreover, eclipses are moments of global awakening according to common and tantric astrology.

This formula, which contradicts common belief, was already noted by Heraclitus, called "the obscure." What is day for ordinary beings is in reality a night. And what is night for the crowd is day for the awakened. The profane, prisoners who do not know they are prisoners and who, therefore, believe themselves all the more free, sleep in Plato's Cave, this "matrix" whose shadows they admire, taking them for the only reality. Escaping this "cave" of Deceptive Magic is thus, in truth, to fall asleep. The Indians also designate the universal illusion, *Māyā*, as a "cave" or an "abyss," *gahana*.

Awakening is this true sleep: falling asleep in the very heart of agitation. To fall asleep is to dissolve, that is, to return to space what has always belonged to space. It is to surrender, in trust or in consciousness, to the Consciousness so perfect that it can only be fully realized by passing through a phase of absolute void. This void is not a negation of things but rather a negation of exclusive attachment to things.

Such an exorcism is therefore "dissolution of dissolution." If the dissolution of things is their negation, the negation of this negation is the ultimate synthesis: everything is there, and nothing is there. Everything appears and, in the same movement, everything fades. Let us hear and feel: everything relaxes, as if dilated from within, finally safe in the bottomless immensity that cannot be lost. For, if there is no bottom, what fall could I fear? If there is no point of reference, what could I lose? Awakening is not a simple negation of something—world, body, or mind—but the negation of the fact that there is something to deny. Nothing to exclude in the inexhaustible capacity that I truly am. Only consciousness is truly "inclusive," for it alone can deny without excluding.

And this night "comes" in its falling. Now, the word of the *chummā* is *āgama*, which also denotes the revelation received, from generation to generation of yogis and yoginīs. To fall into this paradoxical night is therefore also to receive the tradition, the Tantra. Concretely, this group of Secret Speech alludes to the practice of the *Bhairava-mudrā*: with eyes wide open, there is no longer any grasping of anything. Everything is there, nothing is there: then arises the Great Unexpected, the wave of the astonishment of being, dissolution of dissolution in the Presence of the moment.

She devours the manifestation, Light that absorbs the twelve suns of Time, that is, the seasons, the months, the hours, and all their moods. She is the Great Void beyond inert void, beyond all opposition, perfect and unimaginable synthesis. She "cannot be targeted," but she comes of herself. What is free can only come from what is free. "Terrible," she heals us of all fears, starting with that of Death, for she kills what kills us. In the loss of all individuality, the individual can finally be born.

20 – Nothing Is Truly Liberated

ity etasmin pare vyomni prathite sati sarvataḥ |
bhedābhedādivaicitryaṃ cidacidvigrahaṃ sadā || 69

na kiṃcid api sarvatra muktaṃ yatra layaṃ gatam |
eṣaḥ ko 'pi sadā bhāti nirantarataro 'mitaḥ || 70

citsvarūpo 'kramadṛśā saṃkṣayodayavarjitaḥ |
nistaraṅgo nirābhāsaḥ sarvābhāsāntaroditaḥ || 71

Thus, in this supreme space,
manifest everywhere,
there exists this wondrous diversity of "difference" and
"non-difference",
with forms both conscious and inert.

Nowhere is anything ever truly liberated.
When dissolution takes place,
only this ineffable One constantly shines forth—
unceasing, limitless.

From the standpoint of the essence of consciousness,
he is beyond process,
free from arising and ceasing,
wave-less, formless,
yet shining within all appearances.

But then, if "everything is consciousness," what is the point of awakening (*bodha*)? In Sanskrit, the same word means both "consciousness" and "awakening." So, is awakening a real shift, an irreversible leap, as so often described?

This *chummā* is crucial. It clarifies what makes the tantric perspective unique. Today, it's fashionable to say "everything is the same, only the words differ," a gesture toward harmony in a world desperate for space.

But words do not only differ; they point to different concepts, values, and ways of approaching mystery. Sometimes, even when different traditions use the same terms, they give them radically different meanings.

Take a simple example: the word *karma*. In the time of the historical Buddha, *karma* already belonged to the Vedic lexicon, used by Brahmins to refer to ritual action. The Buddha reappropriated the term—but redefined it to mean the moral consequences of all action, not just ritual.

On the surface, both traditions seem to speak of the same thing. But in fact, the Buddha was introducing a revolution: the value of an act depends not on ritual conformity but on the intention behind it.

It is the same in Tantra. In *Tantrāloka*, Abhinavagupta says that the cause of *saṃsāra* is *avidyā* (ignorance), and liberation arises from *jñāna* (knowledge). All Indian traditions agree that ignorance causes suffering. But they define "ignorance" and "knowledge" very differently.

In Tantra, *avidyā* is not a lack of information, nor simply an error (as in mistaking a rope for a snake, *Advaita Vedānta*'s famous metaphor). Instead, it is incomplete knowledge. This changes everything: even ignorance and its effects—body, mind, world—are manifestations of knowledge, only partially revealed.

Even within Tantra, diverse visions exist. One must beware "the nights where all cows are grey." The Kaula tradition, to which the Goddess Kālī belongs, is radically distinct from other Indian paths—even when they use similar imagery.

Thus, *śūnya*, "emptiness," here is not a void of negation or mere interdependence (as in Buddhism), but the shimmering clarity in which all appearances arise as sovereign expressions of consciousness's majesty.

The same goes for *mokṣa* (liberation) and *bandha* (bondage). Tantra doesn't seek escape from the world through transcendence. It affirms our nature as free creators of the world. The world, then, transforms into a luminous play of infinite delight.

This is the space (*vyoman*) that contains everything, transcends everything, and yet pulses in all things. Alive, it breathes even in inert matter, its rhythm called the Heart (*hṛdaya*), the Vibration (*spanda*), the Totality (*kula*).

The word *vaicitrya* (diversity) used here implies not mere variety but a wondrous display—like a masterpiece that astonishes. Similarly, the divine play of unity and duality enflames the hearts of lovers of this vast space.

"Unity" and "duality" do not simply map onto "waking" and "awakening." Awakening is the awe, the irrevocable vertigo of realizing that all apparent contradictions—these clashing states of consciousness—are the playful self-expression of who I truly am.

Indeed, unity and duality coexist at every instant: this tree is both one and many. It is *kula*, a whole composed of distinctions. We perceive both aspects naturally. That is why awakening is incarnate. I am infinite space, and I am all these differences.

Thus, "nothing is truly liberated," because nothing is truly bound. This doesn't mean everything is meaningless illusion. Rather, I realize that I am the free Source, playing at being this incarnation—this individual—and every other thing. It is I who manifest as all, limited or not.

Somānanda compares this to a mighty emperor who, intoxicated with his omnipotence, chooses to play the role of a foot soldier in disguise. Absolute power inevitably chooses to self-limit, for the thrill of rediscovering itself in ever new forms—even to the point of forgetting it is free.

This pose of freedom folding into its opposite, without ever losing freedom, is the nature of play. It is also the nature of art: the deliberate shaping of resistance to test and express the fullness of creative genius—*pratibhā*, the spontaneous intelligence that breaks karmic inertia with true novelty.

So, I am the one playing at not being myself. Like an actor, I assume various roles to revel in the joy of performance. To be truly free is to have the luxury not to be. This is Tantra's profound message: at the heart of all experience lies a secret certainty—that I am absolutely free, immortal, indestructible, infinite in my capacity to manifest as anything and everything.

Game (*krīḍā*) and art are Tantra's privileged metaphors— along with space.

This space is "without interruption" (*nirantara*), "more than unending" (*nirantaratarah*), an expression echoed in *Mokṣopāya-śāstra* (also known as *Yoga-Vāsiṣṭha*), that oceanic compendium of nonduality spanning thousands of verses and fables, where the space of consciousness is likened to a solid rock, unbroken by any fault line.

There is only play, in the full range of emotion. I change without changing. Without fixed essence (*niḥsvarūpa*, a Buddhist term repurposed in Tantra), I can be anything. And when I am invited to "drink the wine of totality, of the body, of embodiment," it is in this sense.

I play all perspectives. I am the Goddess playing at being the individual I also am. And then, as that individual, I play at being the Goddess. I deny it all in deep sleep, then deny sleep by awakening, then deny the duality of sleep and waking: this is awakening.

So although all is cyclic, nothing truly repeats. There is evolution, growth. I transcend—but not by rejecting. I include what I transcend, integrating it into a richer, fuller form that better expresses the freedom I truly am.

This is called living, and Tantra is nothing but this expanding continuity.

To experience this is first to pay attention—right here, right now. No need for drugs, rituals, or masters. Simply see: I change without changing. Like the ocean—trembling yet still. And the thread that unites these two—this I feel in my core. It reveals itself clearly in the trembling "I am" (*aham*), which surges at certain moments, but is, in truth, always present.

21 – Nevertheless, One Enters the Transcendent State

nirāvaraṇanirdhāmaṃ nirānandaṃ nirāśrayam |
paraprakāśam aspandaṃ śāntacinmātravigraham || 72

nānāśaktikarasphāraviśrāntipadam acyutam |
niyatānubhavakṣīṇasvasvarūpaikagocaram || 73

akulaṃ gurubhiḥ proktaṃ niḥsvabhāvaṃ sadoditam |
samo'hamiti saṃgrāsāt praveśas tatra jāyate || 74

A place without veils, without location,
without pleasure, without support,
transcendent light, without the slightest vibration,
the very embodiment of peaceful pure consciousness.

An infallible state
where the radiance of diverse powers comes to rest,
the sole domain of one's own essence,
where all limited experience dissolves:

this is Akula, "not-the-Kula,"
the Transcendent proclaimed by the masters—

*devoid of fixed nature (*niḥsvabhāvaḥ*), yet ever-manifest.*
When one is consumed by the realization,
"I am equal (to That),"
then absorption arises.

But then—*is* awakening a transformation, or is it not?

Because of this ever-surpassing creative movement, awakening is not merely "being what I am." It includes embodiment, materialization, and liberation. I am this— and I am always more than this.

This nuance is crucial. There is a temptation to affirm, even spiritually, that "everything is fine as it is," that "I chose this incarnation," that "I am everything." But if I am only this form, or these forms—if I am only "everything that is"—then I am nothing more than transient, inert forms.

Yet, direct experience reveals otherwise. Even when I experience all things, as I sometimes feel intensely in my center, I remain beyond them. I am *Kula*, the world and body, but I am also what transcends all, precisely *by* manifesting as all.

This is verifiable: if I see this city, I am not this city. I am beyond. If I am aware of the whole, then I am not the whole—I am more. That "more," the Yoginīs call the "supreme space of Presence."

Thus, the experience of awakening is both embodiment and love, but also transcendence. Yet, this does not imply any duality—no fatal division between space and its elements, ocean and wave.

This point is affirmed by Niṣkriyānanda: one enters *Akula*, the "Not-Kula," that which transcends the All.

And indeed, one "enters." The term *āveśa*—"to be absorbed in," or "possessed by"—also refers to possession, whether by a demon or deity. Its use in Kaula Tantra suggests that awakening is a bodily experience, even though the body here is not merely physical or public.

The Yoginīs further say that the state of awakening is "without veil," "without place," and "without nature"— terms drawn from Buddhism and rarely seen in Tantra. How to understand this?

At first glance, they contradict Tantra's affirming spirit, which celebrates *svarūpa*, the "own-nature" of everything. And yet, here, we find Buddhist terms like *niḥsvarūpa* and *niḥsvabhāva*.

In Buddhist texts, especially the *Prajñāpāramitā Sūtras*, these terms are repeated like mantras. They mean that no thing exists independently: left exists only in relation to right, and so forth. Pushed to the limit, this becomes a kind of radical relativism.

Nāgārjuna and the Buddhist Madhyamaka philosophers took this further: not only are things conditioned, but so is consciousness. And what is conditioned is deceptive, illusory, like a mirage. Consciousness, too, is an illusion. According to this view, nothing really happens. There are only appearances—dreamlike and empty of reality.

Is this what the Yoginīs mean here? That consciousness is an illusion?

Not quite. In the Kālī tradition, it is the *absolute* that is "without nature"—not just phenomena. The tantras of Kālī rarely explain this term, and Niṣkriyānanda simply adds that the absolute is "without nature (but) always present."

It will be left to the later *Pratyabhijñā* philosophy, with Utpaladeva and Abhinavagupta, to articulate this more deeply.

And yet, the *Secret Teaching of the Yoginīs* and its *Clarification* by Niṣkriyānanda likely predate *Pratyabhijñā*. If confirmed, this would mean that the oral teachings of feminine deities—Maṅgalā Devī and the Sovereigns of the Kāravīra sanctuary—formed the hidden source of Kashmir's sophisticated non-dual philosophy.

This echoes other pairs: Diotima and Socrates, Hadewijch and Meister Eckhart, Madame Guyon and Fénelon. Perhaps more scholarly work will confirm this lineage. For now, it seems credible: the *Secret Teaching of the Yoginīs* is a major source for the Tantra of Kashmir's great masters.

So what does it mean that the absolute is "without nature (but) always present"?

According to *Pratyabhijñā*, absolute Being (*Śiva*) is not merely "being itself" (*san-mātra*). Pure being is characteristic of inert things, those lacking consciousness and freedom. A cup is just a cup. If it becomes something else, it ceases to be a cup. It has no flexibility; its being is fixed.

But to be conscious is to define oneself—and also to be free of that definition. I can play at being a thief, but that does not exhaust what I am. No definition can contain me.

Why? Because I can always become more—*atirikta*—than what I imagine or perceive myself to be. This boundless drive is what Tantra calls "consciousness" or "freedom." Sartre hinted at this: consciousness precedes essence. I define myself by my choices.

Tantra names this impulse *icchā-śakti*—the Will, Desire— that underlies all becoming. But it never becomes a full object; it remains subject. It is the ever-young energy (*kumārī*) of the *Śiva-sūtras*.

This vision resonates with Renaissance humanism, with Pico della Mirandola's *Oration on the Dignity of Man*, or Rousseau's belief in indefinite human perfectibility. And yet, it predates all that. The truth belongs to no one, though some glimpse it more clearly than others.

So, when Tantra says the absolute is "without nature," it does *not* mean it lacks reality, as illusions do. Rather, it means the absolute is *free*—free to manifest anything without ceasing to be itself.

As some Tibetan masters say: "The emptiness of the mirror does not erase the reflections, nor do reflections obscure the mirror." In good truth, the two are inseparable.

22 – Such Is the Final State

bāhyāntarakrameṇemāḥ saṃvidullāsabhūmayaḥ |
yāḥ sphuranty asthirānityaṃ bhedābhedaprathātmikāḥ ||
75

tāsāṃ tu yugapat proccaiḥ sāmarasya vapur parā |
yā agādhollaṅghanād bhāti sā bhūmiḥ prāntagā smṛtā ||
76

These states, manifestations of consciousness
through the alternation of outer and inner experience,
shine forth—ephemeral, unstable, yet uninterrupted—
as experiences shaped by difference and unity.

But the tradition teaches that their final condition
is the Supreme, wondrous form of fusion
which shines, once and for all,
through a leap beyond the abyss (of dual experience).
This is the state called prāntagā—*the ultimate horizon.*

But then, if there is no fixed essence, does that mean there is no final awakening? Could one always relapse? Are we doomed to infinite progress?

And if there is indeed such evolution, what prevents positing a state beyond even the "final" state? Why not admit an infinite succession of ever-greater awakenings?

In truth, all teachings on the subject agree: the ultimate goal is not a *state*. The goal is the *absolute*. And our mind, shaped by habitual thinking, tends to imagine the absolute by isolating one of its aspects and excluding the others—

saying, for example, that the absolute is only "being," or "energy," or "relationship," or "love," according to our current disposition. But the absolute is all that, and more.

According to the Yoginīs, the absolute is not a state, but an *act*.

Consider a spinning top: it appears still. But its stability comes from the speed of its circular movement. The faster it spins, the more still it looks. Once it stops, it falls. So it is with awakened consciousness: infinite expansion, infinite vibration—thus, stillness.

On this, Utpaladeva is perhaps the most refined interpreter. Inspired by the traditions of Kālī and Trika, he describes the absolute as *citi-kartṛtā*, the creative agency of consciousness, or *cit-kriyā*, the act that is consciousness itself. That is, the absolute is *act, movement, impulse*.

This is confirmed by a series of traditional names for the absolute, found in many tantras: *spanda* (vibration), *ūrmi* (wave), *udyoga* (impulsion), *bala* (power), *sphurattā* (illumination), *svātantrya* (freedom), *camatkāra* (wonder).

Many of these terms imply movement—but a movement that is immobile, an oscillation between opposing poles. While other traditions tend to privilege one pole and deny the other (Vedānta affirms unity and denies multiplicity; Buddhism affirms multiplicity and denies unity), Tantra leans toward a dialectical synthesis through the play of opposites.

This *chummā*'s explanation reflects that tendency: the illuminations of consciousness evolve (*krama*) between exterior and interior, flowing in a movement between the two. This is developed in a rare passage of the *Krama-*

sūtra—now lost but cited by Kṣemarāja—where inner absorption leads to joy in outer experience, and that joy, in turn, draws one back within. Thus, inner leads to outer, and outer back to inner. The awakened life is a rhythm, a pendulum between interiority and exteriority.

It may seem strange to suggest that sensory pleasures lead inward. Yet this is the teaching of Kālī regarding wine, food, and sex. In the traditional Yoginī feasts, this sensory excitation—held within a sacred atmosphere—dissolves the social ego and its constructed superego, forged by hopes and fears. What results is a cyclical *mudrā*—a sacred gesture or attitude—called *krama*, a progression toward synthesis between extroversion and introversion, between Self and Other.

This same idea appears in Christianity: the Trinity is a movement among distinct poles, tending toward ideal synthesis through relational exchange. Ruysbroeck (inspired by Hadewijch of Antwerp), in the 14th century, described this ideal synthesis as the "Common Life," with movements of return toward the divine centre and outward flows enabling communion with others.

Thus, the adept lives a cyclical life. Phases of interiority alternate with ecstatic absorption in outer joy and communion with their spiritual family and the world. These experiences, in themselves, are "ephemeral" (*asthira*, unstable). But in their uninterrupted alternation between introverted and extroverted absorption, they reveal themselves as the *ullāsa*, the luminous play, of consciousness.

And so, they do tend toward a "final state," which is their ultimate *fusion* (*sāmarasya*). This is the supreme state, attained by a *leap* (*ullaṅghana*) beyond opposites—a leap that also implies the transgression of natural law, of karmic limitation. The Yoginīs here do not speak of a mere integration of opposites within the psyche, but of their *fusion* into a state that transcends even the soul—into its very Source.

23 – This Teaching Is Ineffable

etadbhūmyadhiroheṇa maunaṃ sañjāyate mahat |
śabdārthakuvikalpena varjitaṃ satatoditam || 77

ata eva tu nirdiṣṭam avācyaṃ kathanaṃ param |
atha akāreṇa vā vācyaṃ varṇāvarṇojjhitena ca || 78

When one ascends to this supreme state,
a vast silence arises—
free from the false concepts regarding the meaning of
words,
yet ever-present.

And yet, this supreme, ineffable teaching
is pointed to—though it cannot be spoken.
Or, it may be spoken by uttering "a,"
free of both word and their absence.

It may be said that invoking mystery like this is an easy way to avoid addressing a real problem. By multiplying paradoxes, doesn't the tradition of the Goddess Kālī confess its own powerlessness?

Indeed, it confesses it—and even proclaims it. But the impossibility of the teaching *is itself* a teaching.

Alongside silent communion, symbolic rites, and celebrations of egoless pleasure, we have seen that the Yoginīs transmit knowledge through *kathā*—speech, oral word—in the secrecy of a living exchange. And yet, despite this powerful thrust, it remains that speech is incapable of adequately conveying the state of absolute awakening.

The *Mouth of the Yoginī* (*yoginī-vaktra*) must therefore be understood on three levels:

1. **On the level of ritual practice**, it is the female sex—an object of both repulsion and fascination. Considered impure (as in terms like *picu-vaktra*, "leprous mouth," or *adho-vaktra*, "lower mouth"), the vulva is nonetheless held by the Kaula Tantra as the true source of freedom—source of life and pleasure.

This power is embodied in sexual secretions, which the yogī and yoginī must collect, shape into a ball with ash or flour, and ingest with wine—or pass mouth to mouth. This is another sense of "oral transmission." The mixture of sexual fluids and bodily substances like sweat is considered utterly repulsive by the profane, who call it *kuṇḍa-gola*, "the bastard son of a widow." But in the tradition of Kālī, these bodily substances are *kula-dravya*, "substances of the Body/Whole/of the Yoginīs." They are the purest and most potent, for they derive directly from the Presence of pure Śakti—the source of bodies and all things.

2. **As contact with the Mouth of the Yoginī,** that leads spontaneously to the Absolute Mouth, the so-called *Anuttara-hṛdaya,* or Absolute Heart—perfect fullness in which inside and outside are both transcended and integrated into the consummate harmony known as *Mahā-kaula,* the perfect union of Śiva and Śakti.

3. **Between the two,** there is room for the Mouth of the Yoginī manifesting as speech—such as these 105 sacred utterances passed on to Niṣkriyānanda. And again, this impossibility of speaking says much.

As Niṣkriyānanda notes, "when one ascends to this state" of uninterrupted awakening, "a great silence occurs." A silence that is "great" because it does not oppose noise or words. It is free from "false concepts regarding things": thoughts are not absent, but harmonized with their Source. They are no longer "bad" (*ku*) but express the very Breath that animates them.

The ineffable stillness speaks a word. An eloquent silence, as Ramana Maharshi—celebrated for his silence—would say. For this teaching is transcendent. It expresses the Goddess who has no name—*A-nāmā* is her name. She is the Unutterable, the Creator of all thought. From then on, thoughts are no longer seen as disruptions but as ecstatic emissions (*ullāsa*) of silence. Do thoughts even have a form? Can they be separated from their source?

The Yoginīs' oral teaching concerns what cannot be taught, pointed at, or indicated—because it is everything, and has no opposite. What is *non-dual* has no counterpart.

Yet there is an alternative to both silent communion and articulated words: the sound *"a."* In saying *"a"*, I say what cannot be said. Along the secret path of symbols between lovers (*saṃketa*), uttering the primordial *"a"* expresses the Ineffable without passing through any human tongue. The *Sūtras of the Mad Master*, another version of the Yoginīs' Secret Teaching, reveals that *"a"* is the very vibration of the space of Presence—*kha-svaratā*, the resonance of the Void.

24 – Then the Body Is Destroyed

asmin sati śarīre'pi dehasya trividhasya yā |
vismṛtis sa vināśaḥ syād guruvaktraprasādataḥ || 79

Even while this body of threefold form remains,
its destruction occurs—
that is, it is forgotten—
through the grace that flows from the master's mouth.

Does awakening destroy the body? If awakening is the end of identification with the body, what becomes of it?

The body, as a crystallization of past actions, is indeed "destroyed"—in the sense that it is forgotten. Yet it continues to exist. But all that is inert in it, all that is insensitive, seems to dissolve into pure, vibrant subjectivity. There is no longer a body-as-object; there is only Life.

How does this occur? By the grace of the master's words— words that express what cannot be expressed. By his gaze.

By his simple presence. By words inspired by the Yoginīs and by symbols revealed in secret ceremonies.

Still, this public body—the one others can see—remains present. It is within this very body that its forgetting is experienced. This is simply a consequence of the living paradox mentioned earlier: all is here, and all is absent. Not due to a flaw in memory, but due to the overwhelming force of Presence, which immerses all things in its brilliance, as the sun drowns all other stars in its light. Those stars are, of course, still there—but no longer distinctly visible. In the same way, the body remains, but is absorbed into its source, like a wave in the ocean. It is no longer a separate, inert object, but the very heart of the unfolding of space.

The "threefold body" mentioned here may refer to the physical body (visible), the subtle body (subjective), and the "causal" body, which is the dormancy of consciousness. These correspond respectively to the waking state (perception), the dream state (imagination, memory), and deep sleep (oblivion).

It is to these that, according to Utpaladeva, the avatar Kṛṣṇa alludes in his Song: "From Me arise perception, memory, and forgetfulness." This reference is highly appropriate here, since in the tradition of the Yoginīs, Kṛṣṇa is in truth a manifestation of the goddess Kālī. The sixteen thousand cowherd girls (*gopī*) enamoured of the pastoral God are the sixteen thousand Śaktis of Presence— sixteen being the number of the full moon.

25 – Such Is the State Beyond the Absolute, the Supreme State Beyond Which There Is Nothing

niruttarottarā kācit kramākramavivarjitā |
daśā pūrvāgamād vyajyate nityanirmalāt || 80

This is the extraordinary state beyond the Absolute,
devoid of sequence or stillness,
a state revealed by that original Revelation,
eternally pure.

Is there still a state beyond this non-state?

This "state"—if we dare use the word (though the term *daśā* is indeed used)—is not a state in the sense of being static. As pure impulse, pure Act (*kriyā*), it lies beyond even the Absolute itself—beyond any state that can be conceived—yet it does not exclude the states we know.

It has no proper name, and so the Yoginīs usually refer to it with impersonal expressions like *kācid daśā*—"some state," "a certain state." In the context of the Kālī tradition, such phrasing always hints at a reality not bound by ordinary experience. For this reason, it is here rendered as "extraordinary."

This state is not bounded or defined, although the experience is one of crystalline clarity. It is not merely the *nir-uttara* (the un-surpassable); it is the *uttara* of *nir-uttara*—what lies beyond even the unsurpassable. If that sounds absurd, it is only because this "state" surpasses all partial and biased definitions.

It is a state free from sequence (*akrama*): there is nothing to reach or progress toward. Yet it is not a fixed state either—it contains movement (*krama*) within itself.

And though inexpressible, it is nonetheless revealed (*vyajyate*)—made evident—by that ancient (*pūrva*), primordial teaching (*āgama*) which is ever immaculate (*nitya-nirmala*), untouched by human invention. According to the tradition, the transmission occurs through three lineages: first, the divine lineage, passed directly; then the lineage of the realized ones, transmitted through symbolic speech such as these *Chummās*; and finally, the human lineage, transmitted by ritual initiation through *Maṇḍala* and *Mantra*.

This transmission is not the betrayal of an original perfection—it is its glorious unfolding. The human is as pure as the divine, for these are but moments of the same wave rising and reaching its full height. Non-duality does not mean exclusion of any part; it is the Whole. It is not one facet at the expense of the others, but the diamond entire—forever more than the sum of its parts.

26 – The Sublime Refuge Is Attained

śrīḥ śaktiḥ paramā proktā jagadvibhavanirbharā |
sasphurā nirdvayā yā tu tasyāḥ prabhur anuttaraḥ || 81

śāntātiśāntarūpo yaḥ sa śrīnāthaḥ smṛto 'vyayaḥ |
tadrūpatāsamāpāttiḥ prāptis sā jāyate 'calā || 82

"Splendor" (śrī) is Śakti, declared the supreme one,
brimming with the manifestation of the world.

She shines clearly, non-dual,
and her Lord is anuttara, *the Absolute.*

He whose form is peace beyond peace,
is remembered as śrīnātha, *the sublime, unfailing refuge.*
To become one with that form—
that is the realization, unshakable and true.

Every lineage begins with a human master who "descends" or "introduces" (*avatāraka*) the teachings to deliver them into the realm of human experience. Often, this figure is legendary. Here, Niṣkriyānanda fills that role, following the enigmatic "Realized Refuge" (*Siddha-nātha*). But who, truly, is the *nātha*, the "refuge" in whom one can trust without reserve?

This master is not alone. He is "sublime"—*śrī*, a term that connotes beauty, glory, abundance. Śrī is also Śakti, the Goddess consciousness, living experience of awakening evoked throughout these verses. This verse reveals a subtle understanding of ultimate reality: the *nātha*, the master or refuge, is inseparable from his Śakti. Without her, he is nothing—for Śakti is *saṃvitti*, consciousness itself, not of some limited thing, but of *mahā-sattā*, of universal being, even the being of what "does not really exist"!

Reality or illusion, everything exists *in*, *through*, and *for* consciousness. This is the very essence of Tantra: Śakti is not merely divine power—she is *all experience*. And experience is the teacher, the refuge. The world is not separate from consciousness; it is her living dance, her luminous unfolding.

Śakti, supreme power, is not removed from the world she manifests. She is immanent in every aspect of her expression. When I feel the bark of a tree, that sensation is not separate from the bark itself. This world—our experience—is consciousness made visible, tangible.

And manifestation does not hide its source; it *reveals* it. Just as sunlight "hides" the sun yet is its very radiance, each experience is not an obstacle to awakening, but a doorway into it. Śakti is the doorway, and Śiva is the Absolute beyond.

Thus, in every experience lies the opening. Śakti is experience, Śiva is the beyond. And in Śakti, the Absolute finds its life—because even "being nothing" must be illuminated by the light of awareness to be known as such. In her, the Absolute finds its soul. There is a dizzying harmony between the divine principles—this is what underlies all phenomena, including our own embodied, sensory, mental existence.

The Yoginīs remind us of the profound value of experience. The Sanskrit *saṃvitti* means both "consciousness" and "experience." The experience *is* the master, the guide, the refuge. Tantra teaches that fire is known by experiencing fire. Likewise, the Absolute is known through increasingly complete experiences—until they are recognized for what they are: expressions of the Absolute.

This *chummā* points toward the innermost revelation: the peace beyond peace is not passive or inert—it includes movement, includes even turmoil. Agitation is not opposed to peace, for it too is a wave of the great ocean of peace. To recognize this deeply is to harmonize the storm. Even powerful emotions like anger become part of this embrace.

Anger doesn't vanish—it becomes pure energy, pure sensation, without repression.

Such clarity, such awakening to the raw energy beneath our emotions, is called the "sublime and unshakable refuge." It is the foundation and the summit of the spiritual path—a total merging with the Absolute in which the individual self does not disappear, but is reborn, renewed, in the vastness of divine awareness. This cycle of rebirth, again and again, is *life* according to the Yogic vision.

And so, instead of being a puppet of malevolent Yoginīs who cast spells of forgetting, my life becomes the very lineage of liberating Yoginīs—chants of space echoing around and within the body.

This exploration of the Yoginīs' inner teachings resonates with the profound wisdom of Abhinavagupta and other masters of Tantra, who see human existence as the divine play (*līlā*) of the Absolute unfolding in the multiplicity of forms and experiences.

And this is true down to the smallest detail. Every skin sensation, every memory—everything is the play of awareness. The Yoginīs appear through this poetry to awaken faith in that certainty. Their metaphysics is rooted in *lived* experience—a *physical* metaphysics, if you will— inviting the practitioner to see divinity in all things, beyond all prejudice and fear. Consciousness is not a static abstraction, but the flowing pulse of all experience.

On this path of love, there is no artifice—only deeper and deeper *participation* (*bhakti*). Meditating on these verses, we are called to realize our own *śrīnātha-prāptiḥ*—the encounter with the sublime master—through the recognition of our identity with Śakti and the Absolute.

27 – This Arises Through Effortless Practice

ceṣṭākāyaparispandaḥ saṃvidullāsacoditaḥ |
tena projjhitarūpeyaṃ niśceṣṭā gatir ucyate || 83

yā sā nirīhāvācyeha kalpanāgrāsataḥ smṛtā |
sati kṣobhe'pi sarvatra bhrājamānā sthitā sadā || 84

The movements of the body and its actions
arise as expressions of consciousness.
Thus, being utterly free from form,
this is called "the motionless movement," or "the way of
stillness."

This state is known, in this tradition, as "effortless,"
for it devours all concepts.
Even in the midst of agitation,
it remains ever-present, shining everywhere.

Must effort be made to attain awakening? Or is there, truly, nothing to do?

The Absolute may be personified as Śiva, or as a primordial Śakti such as Kāla-saṃkarṣaṇī—the Source of Time who devours Time itself. The realization of *space-presence* is not withdrawal from the world, but full participation in the divine dance of creation. It is a celebration of freedom at the very heart of ordinary life. Every moment becomes an opportunity for awakening, in which the sacred and the profane dissolve into the vibrant light of pure awareness.

And yet, there is no room for spiritual ego. Nothing to build, nothing to destroy—only to be destroyed and renewed entirely. The self-image is the Yoginī's craft: I surrender it gladly to her hands.

But spiritual ego is subtle, and who can claim to escape it? What was once called "self-love" seeps into everything, especially into that which is supposed to dissolve it. That is its strength: like capitalism, it feeds on its own enemies.

This *chummā, nirīha-carcā* (the "doctrine of effortlessness"), reveals a core principle of Tantra—life's very texture: a practice without striving, where spontaneity reigns. This principle manifests through the body's natural movement, which is nothing but a radiant expression of consciousness (*saṃvid*). Let things come, let things go. "The breath is natural," Śiva reminds us. Life is the unfolding of Vibration (*spanda*).

This verse conveys this truth with elegant precision: bodily movement arises from the joy of consciousness (*saṃvid-ullāsa-coditaḥ*), freeing the being from every constraint or strain. "Practice" becomes surrender to this current, like being massaged by the luminous hands of the Yoginīs.

In this "unoccupied consciousness" (*niśceṣṭā*), I bask in an inner sun. These lines bring back the image of my master Hemenji, who loved to sit in the sunlight—defying Brahminical norms that avoid sun for fear of darkening the skin. He embodied that state of "having no business" already celebrated by Zen masters.

This expression points toward total liberation from the burden of effortful doing. Though deeply engaged in the world's play, consciousness remains untouched, free, detached from any notion of success or outcome. In fact, it *is* the very act at the heart of all action. Doing nothing becomes the doorway into this deeper Doing—this Vibration. Thus, detachment is not withdrawal, but full participation: every gesture steeped in luminous presence, like a ritual overflowing with awareness.

Effortless practice—quest without expectation—belongs to an ancient tradition, where the simplicity of existence is honoured as the playground of the Absolute. Here we discover another face of Tantra, far from the symbolic jungle that can intoxicate and confuse. This approach is not passive, but an *active non-action*—an inner space where outward movement flows from inward impulse.

The body's motion (*ceṣṭā-kāya-parispandaḥ*) and its activities are lived as extensions of awareness itself. To let oneself be moved from within is total action. *In-action*, or inner action, is not inaction—it is deep responsiveness.

This *chummā*, in its clarity and depth, offers a mirror in which we glimpse our true nature. It teaches that at the core of every moment—beneath the noise of thought and emotion—dwells an unshakable radiance: pure awareness, eternally present, ever free.

By meditating on these verses, we are invited to rediscover our lives not as a series of efforts and achievements, but as divine dance—graceful and gratuitous—where each step, each breath, each movement expresses ultimate freedom. This view transforms our relationship to the world and to ourselves, revealing that even amidst action, we may rest in an inner peace, luminous witnesses to the eternal round of life.

28 – Such Is the Practice of the World's Ingestion

viśvaprapañcavibhavo līḍhan kālena sarvadā |
so'pi līḍho yayā samyak mahāsaṃhārasaṃvidā || 85

saiveha satataṃ devī lelihānā sthitākramā |
aniruddhatayā sākṣād aparokṣā sadoditā || 86

The rich unfolding of the world of phenomena
is always being swallowed by Time.
And Time itself is entirely consumed
by That—by the supreme awareness of total dissolution.

She—it is She, the Goddess—who without pause
is licking, devouring all (Time), for She is beyond time.
Never interrupted,
She is always shining, directly present, here and now.

But then, if there is nothing to do—what *is* the practice?

Only to feel, to taste, to love. In this peace, the world returns by itself to peace, as if consciousness were swallowing the world. A cosmic vision unfolds, in which spiritual practice—intimately, personally, right here and now—is nothing other than the act of ingesting the world, revealing the ultimate nature of reality. Consciousness "licks" things as it senses them. It draws them back into itself, opening paths of transmutation. The flight of a bird through the sky, the hum of a car—each one a mantra, each one a route of return.

Let us approach the original Sanskrit, through three key expressions. Each opens a doorway to a deeper understanding of the Goddess's philosophy.

Viśva-prapañca-vibhavo līḍhan – "Consciousness swallows the rich unfolding of all phenomena." This phrase refers to the act of ingesting the phenomenal expansion of the world. At first glance, the world seems to impose itself upon us. We don't feel like we master it; we feel thrown into it, powerless before its laws. Yet there is one undeniable fact that challenges this assumption: impermanence. Each instant is cancelled out by another— by a memory, an image, a sensation, or just a blank.

Hence the Goddess emphasizes the fleeting nature of the material universe, perpetually consumed by *kāla*, Time. Everything in the sensory world is destined to be swallowed by this ceaseless current, revealing the fragility of phenomena—the "unbearable lightness of being." Everything self-cancels, liberating itself effortlessly into the inner vastness. Meditation consists in appreciating this fact. Savouring the relief of the disappearance of things, thoughts, sensations, like bubbles bursting in a vast sky.

Mahā-saṃhāra-saṃvidā – "Awareness is the great dissolution." Consciousness is not something static or separate from Time—it is the flow of Time that creates and dissolves. Liberation is thus inevitable, effortless, spontaneous. It does not contradict experience—it *embraces* it. This expression points to awareness as the power of total absorption, encompassing even Time itself. It suggests a reversal of the usual perspective: at the source of temporal flow lies a conscious presence, capable of swallowing all that appears—including Time. This is not abstraction, but the nature of experience itself. There is

273

nothing to *do*—only to recognize it, to relish it, to surrender to it.

Aniruddhatayā – "Nothing can obstruct consciousness." The Goddess devours without ever being halted or restrained by Time or change. If I do not block thoughts, they cannot block me. Presence is unstoppable; nothing can stand against it, for nothing can exist without it. She is thus described as always manifest, ever-shining in immediacy. A "moment" that is not manifested is nothing—less than nothing—without the act of consciousness that brings it forth. This word highlights the dynamic, all-pervading aspect of divine awareness, affirming its absolute sovereignty beyond Time's boundaries. To bathe in this dance, where all things vanish moment by moment, *is* awakening.

These verses invite us to recognize the power of divine consciousness as the principle that not only contains the phenomenal world, but also Time itself. The Goddess Kālī, the supreme form of this consciousness, performs the final act of ingestion—revealing the illusion of separation between creator, creation, and dissolution. Time—Death—becomes both means and freedom. Every instant is whole: both birth and death. Birth frees us from death; death frees us from the limits of birth. To feel this here and now is the essence of the path.

We are guided toward a new understanding: true liberation lies in recognizing our fundamental identity with this divine awareness. The cycles of creation and dissolution are not external occurrences, but movements within our own being—reflections of the endless play of universal consciousness.

Contemplating the depth of these teachings, the practitioner is led to release attachment to the phenomenal world and awaken to the uninterrupted presence of the Goddess—absolute awareness—who is both witness and actor of universal ingestion, the nothing and the everything of each moment.

Let it be said once again: the notion of *nirīhā*, desirelessness, is essential to understanding this practice. The previous *chummā* already affirms that this path devours all concepts (*kalpanā-grāsataḥ*), suggesting a transcendence of duality and mental constructs that bind. In this state, even amidst upheaval (*kṣobha*), consciousness remains serene, always radiant (*bhrājamānā*), anchored in the here and now (*sati ... sarvatra ... sthitā sadā*).

This illumination reveals the path of Tantra as a way of unconditional freedom, where realization is not the fruit of sustained effort, but the natural emergence of the truth of our being. It is an invitation to fully embrace life through complete letting go, where action becomes a celebration of the divine presence within. As the teacher of my teacher would sometimes say, while starring straight at the sky: *mahā-prakāśa*—"great radiance, total manifestation"—which excludes nothing. Like a vast yawn, a full breath drawn into the core of being.

29 – Such Is the Final Secret Teaching

mahāparyantasambodhaparacchummamahodayaḥ |
nānādarśanasambhūtacarcābhiḥ parivarjitaḥ || 87

vaktrād vaktrakramodbhūtaḥ sāhasākhyo mahādbhutaḥ |
kālakālobhayollāsasaṃkṣayāt satatoditaḥ || 88

The complete revelation of the supreme secret teaching,
the great and final awakening,
is utterly free from the mental ruminations
born of the many philosophies.

Transmitted from mouth to mouth,
this marvel—called the Inexplicable—
shines constantly,
for it annihilates the dual game of Time and Eternity.

Once again, the question of the Ultimate arises: is there yet another state—higher, further, deeper?

This *chummā* answers without hesitation, ending the suspense that haunts those who crave esotericism: *paryanta-cchummā*, "this is the final secret teaching." This final secret is not a mere idea or concept, but the great final awakening (*mahā-paryanta-sambodha*). And note this: the Sanskrit word for "awakening," *bodha*, is also the word for "consciousness." Why? Because awakening is nothing but the self-awakening of consciousness by itself, to itself. And this is only logical—there is nothing outside of consciousness. Because we *are* already consciousness, awakening is possible. Because consciousness can forget itself, the path becomes necessary.

This teaching reveals a truth beyond doctrines (*nānā-darśana*), inviting us beyond the churnings of thought, beyond the ever-spinning wheels of philosophical debate. It is also liberation—from the endless inner dialogues we carry, a call to silence, where Truth finally whispers its name.

From this silence arises *vaktrād vaktrakrama*, the transmission from mouth to mouth—an oral line of fire, never frozen, never fixed. This living flame is called *sāhasa*, "the Inexplicable" or "the Audacious," because it dares to speak directly from the heart, beyond all preconceptions, beyond structure. It is *mahādbhuta*, a "great wonder," born not of deduction but of Presence—fresh, ungraspable, and always now. As Abhinavagupta wrote: *this truth is always new.*

Here, Time (*kāla*) and Timelessness (*akāla*) are named not as enemies but as two roles in a cosmic play. Often, we feel more like passive witnesses than active authors of this script. But in this *chummā*, the final teaching, both Time and its opposite dissolve. Their conflict ends in the recognition of what *is always present, satatoditaḥ*—what is right here, shining behind every flicker of change.

The audacity here is not in great deeds or declarations. It is the simple, raw audacity of being fully alive—to live each instant as the first and last. That is the wonder, the *mahādbhuta*: an eternal flame burning without fuel, ignited by the breath of awakening, kindled in the heart of the one who listens, who speaks, who simply is.

This "secret," in its purest form, is nothing hidden. It is the invitation to see, to feel the beauty of the world as it is. To recognize in the whisper of the wind, in the shimmer of leaves, the same truth passed mouth to mouth, heart to heart. It calls us to see beyond appearances, hear beyond words, live beyond memories and sensations—in the transparent space that gives rise to them all.

The extraordinary revealed within the ordinary—this is the final realization, the final secret.

In the silence after the last note of a song, in the gap between two thoughts—there it is. The *final secret teaching*: awakening to the simple grandeur of existence. Awakening to the greatness of simply being present. And in this presence, Time and Eternity become mere shadows dancing, eclipsed by the light of a consciousness that embraces all and is bound by nothing.

30 – One Stands Without Any Support

icchākṣobhodayamalair abhilāṣaiḥ samantataḥ |
varjitatvād ayaṃ samyaṅ nistaraṅgā prathātmikaḥ || 89

niṣkāmo nirvikāraś ca sarvāśrayavivarjitaḥ |
sāmarasyarasāsvādasaṃcarvaṇarataḥ sadā || 90

Because she is entirely free from desires—
those toxic surges of agitation born of limited longing—
she is an experience of expansion
utterly still, without a single ripple.

Without desire and without change,
devoid of any kind of support,
she is ever absorbed in tasting
the joy of fusion.

One might ask whether this "secret" is not merely a consolation—an illusion we recite to avoid facing reality.

But the Yoginīs respond: no illusion is possible, because in space, there is nothing to hold on to. Space *is* the Goddess, the most exacting of teachers. She invites us into the contemplation of a state of being that rests on no fixed support. This teaching, so delicate as to be almost weightless, carries within it the promise of a freedom without foundation—a stillness expanding infinitely, where desire falls silent and an unshakable serenity arises, an endless surge toward the infinite.

Icchā, desire—that sometimes stormy thrust pushing us toward the unreachable horizon—is here shown in the light of its *kṣobha*, its turbulent waves that stir the surface of our being. But in this, the Yoginīs whisper to us, like the wise witches of childhood tales: the absence of desire is not emptiness to be feared, but fullness waiting to be received. To become humble as nothing, in order to be worthy of everything.

In the relinquishment of limited desire, a deep peace is unveiled—*nistaraṅgā*, the wave-less state, where the soul no longer knows disturbance or turmoil.

Niṣkāma and *nirvikāra* sketch the faceless portrait of a consciousness that has divested itself of everything burdensome, of everything that binds. To be freed even from one's own powers, to cease being enslaved by the play of the Yoginīs.

But this absence of desire is not negation of life—it is a total acceptance, so thorough that it transcends all opposites. A dance in which movement and stillness are no longer at odds, but one. With no point of support, this consciousness rests only upon itself—free from all attachment, from any need for support. A radical shift in perspective: I am nothing, so that I may receive everything, including the needs of the moment.

It is then, in this total release, that one can truly savour the endless joy of fusion—*sāmarasya*. This taste of unity, this flavour of universal harmony, becomes the only quest, the only joy. A circular movement in which end merges with beginning. Each moment becomes an opportunity to dissolve into the Whole, into an embrace where self and world are no longer separate. The world is no longer endured, but *participated in*. This is *bhakti*—love as presence.

We are thus led toward a spiritual practice where simplicity becomes the highest accomplishment. By letting go of desire and support, we open to a life where every moment is a discovery, every breath a revelation. Practice becomes an exploration of stillness within motion, a search for the Absolute in the ephemeral.

31 – This Path Is a Path Rejected

sarvatra rasamāṇo 'pi niyatāśrayavarjitaḥ |
saṃvidullāsavibhavair anirodhatayābhitaḥ || 91
prāpnoti vṛttim agamāṃ pānthavat tv avadhūtikām |
nirlepāṃ puṣkaradalasthitavārivad añcitām || 92

Though delighting in all things,
he relies on no fixed support.
Unobstructed on every side
by the manifold effulgence of consciousness,
he attains a way ungraspable—
like a traveller on a path forsaken by all,
yet immaculate,
like water beading on a lotus leaf.

It is said that awakening is rare. To claim it is often seen as an act of ego. To be "awakened" is frequently associated with a special status—that of guru or master. But is this not simply the confusion between awakening and power? Is not true awakening, on the contrary, beyond all hierarchy and pretension?

This path of pure desire bears the seal of the *avadhūta*, the free ascetic. Let us recall that this title is a call to inner pilgrimage, to a voyage of the soul where known coordinates dissolve into luminous mist. Nowhere is social status mentioned as a goal! This *chummā* emphasizes the independence intrinsic to realization.

And yet, the awakened one "delights in all things, everywhere." This joy, without bondage, evokes the image of a spirit that sips nectar from every corner of life, yet remains unattached. Abhinavagupta encourages us to taste all flowers of knowledge. Like a traveller who savours every landscape without pitching his tent, the practitioner of this "rejected path," this free path, yields to the beauty of the world while remaining untouched. Neither pleasure nor pain bind him; he glides above the waters of emotion, *nirlepā*, like water that does not cling to the lotus leaf.

The phrase *anirodhatayā abhitaḥ*, "unhindered from all sides," underscores this unparalleled freedom—not the kind politics speak of, but an inner sovereignty. Consciousness, in its purest shine, is bounded by no frame, no law, no rule. The myriad manifestations of this consciousness cannot contain or define its essence. The unreachable state attained on this path is none other than supreme realization, where the individual, transcending duality, recognizes himself in total resonance with all that is—beginning with the intimate *maṇḍala* of his body.

The "rejected path," the path of freedom, is this way in which one is "free of any fixed support," detached from craving and aversion. The awakened being walks lightly upon the earth, free of imprint, yet intimately engaged. It is not a path of rigid asceticism or forced detachment, not *niyata* (predetermined), but one of deep understanding that nothing external can disturb inner peace. And—what a paradox—that very peace opens one fully to the so-called "outer life." Kṛṣṇa and Rāma had nothing to attain, yet they worked tirelessly for the good of all beings.

This paradoxical state, "as if on an abandoned path," is not a goal to be reached but a way of being: to live each instant with full intensity while remaining untouched, like the wind, mysterious like night. The path is the goal.

This *chummā* teaches that the way to ultimate freedom is not paved with bitter renunciations or harsh sacrifices, but with joyful acceptance of impermanence, a celebration of transience. Eternity is hidden in the embrace of time, for time is the overflow of eternity. And that embrace is an act of love—possible, even likely—because it arises not from the logic of the "old man," but from the space of Being that already holds all opposites. In releasing fixed supports, one discovers the most solid ground. In letting go of craving, one savours the most exquisite sweetness.

Thus, the "rejected path" is none other than the famed way of the *avadhūta*, the wild and sovereign yogi (or yoginī) of the Goddess's lineage—one who, having breathed through the veils of illusion, now dances to the rhythm of fully recognized and honoured consciousness: free, radiant, a sun shining equally on all. Embraced, the witch becomes again a young faery. One must—and need only—draw near enough to her to become her. Then, the magic begins again.

32 – Consciousness is Excited and as if Mad

svasvātantryodayā tayā nirvicāratvam āgatā |
saṃvin navanavollekharūpiṇī sarvabhakṣiṇī || 93

yuktāyuktavicārais tu varjitā cañcalā sadā |
yā sthitā nirbharā saiva proccair unmattatāṃ gatā || 94

paramaṃ śivam ālokya tadvaśīkṛtacāpalā |
mattonmattā citiḥ khyātā satām apracyutā tataḥ || 95

Consciousness does not judge
what is decent or not,
for it rises in its own absolute freedom.
She manifests as ever-new flashes of wonder,
devouring all.

Indeed, she does not consider
what is appropriate or not:
she is frivolous,
constantly moving,
yet grounded in total fullness—
and thus, she reaches the peak of madness.

When she sees the Supreme Śiva,
her restlessness is tamed by him.
This consciousness, intoxicated and mad,
then becomes still—
for the sincere.

Is there then a morality of awakening? Or do Good and Evil dissolve after the great shift?

Following the secret of the "deserted path," this astonishing *chummā* of the Mad Goddess invites us to dive into the dizzying depths of consciousness, where the boundary between the wise and the insane blurs, and excitement and stillness dance together. This text, with its tones of *divine madness*, is an ode to the unbounded freedom of spirit—a call to embrace life in its totality, without judgment, with the daring of an open heart and the serenity of an awakened soul.

How is this possible?

Consciousness is *svātantrya*, sovereign freedom. In its uprising toward absolute liberty, it does not bind itself to considerations of what is "pure" or "impure." Like a sow, her snout does not discriminate—a distinction so central to all traditional religions. She transcends the divide between good and evil, between what "is done" and what "should not be done," manifesting instead a boundless spontaneity. Love has never known laws. Like a divine artist, she sketches fleeting frescoes with the ink of perception and chisels them with attention, only to consume them again in the fire of omnipresent Presence.

The mind is "the madwoman in the house," unstable, *cañcalā*, frivolous imagination and ungraspable. A ray of attention (*cetas*), it moves without concern for conventions. In this sovereign innocence lies the secret of spontaneous meditation—not a deliberate act, but a natural expression of being. Like an unannounced love confession, energy bursts forth. The *Yoginīs* teach that true meditation is the art of standing in total openness, without expectation, without judgment, where the mind finds its deepest rest in the acceptance of its untameable nature. "To ride the tigress" (as Julius Evola put it) is the only way not to be devoured by her.

And when the Supreme Śiva is seen—eyes gazing into a clear sky—something shifts. The wild stream of consciousness meets the ocean of silence. Madness turns to wisdom, excitement to serenity. That very consciousness, once infatuated with untamed freedom, now ripens without self-denial and becomes the sanctuary of stillness: *paramaṃ śivam*, where the divine and the human merge in perfect harmony.

This is a call to embrace our own madness, to recognize in our inner storms the echo of a vaster freedom. It reminds us that at the heart of our unrest lies the potential for awakening; that in the chaos of our thoughts grows the seed of peace. To meditate spontaneously is to allow this "excited and mad" state to reveal the beauty of impermanence, the joy of the present moment, and the depth of our connection to all that is. "No awakening without passion, no fire without fuel, no gold without lead."

So let the *mad wisdom* of this verse (not the so-called "crazy wisdom" of a so-called guru) awaken in us the courage to explore the uncharted territories of our consciousness. In that exploration, we discover a celebration of daily life—and, let it be said plainly, a love.

33 – She Devours and Consumes Everything

vṛttiprapañcarūpasya sarvagrāsaśarīriṇaḥ |
grasanāya uditāya alaṃ sāmarasyamahodayāt || 96

tīkṣṇātitīkṣṇarūpeyaṃ nirāvaraṇavigrahā |
saiveha kathitā kācit sarvabhakṣasya bhakṣikā || 97

This (consciousness) is sharpened to the extreme,
her body bare and unveiled,
because of the great Manifestation of the state of fusion
capable of devouring and manifesting all things
for those embodied beings who themselves devour all
things,
(their essence being the proliferation of bodily and
mental operations).
It is of her that this teaching of the Yoginīs speaks—
this extraordinary (Goddess)
who devours the Devourer of all !

It is impossible to rid ourselves of the world, of the body, or of thoughts. As Master Rāma says: "Even the diamond of *samādhi* cannot shatter the mountain of duality!" And what if consciousness itself were the natural remedy?

The warm breath of the Yoginī, in one laconic utterance, evokes a universal consumption in which consciousness, like an omnivorous presence, swallows the whole of existence. "With time, everything goes," is no longer a bitter lament in the valley of tears, but a sigh of relief. Everything dissolves without effort, inevitably. Such is impermanence. The fragility of becoming is its own cure. Let it come, let it go, like drawings on water. And through this evaporation, realize what lies beyond becoming. There is no need to rid oneself of thoughts—they vanish on their own. To feel this more vividly, try to hold on to thoughts instead of blocking them. And yet, it's impossible to hold them—they disappear by themselves. To surrender to this truth—what joy!

The jungle of mental activity, the endless dance of thoughts, emotions, and perceptions, suddenly lightens. Thoughts are no longer felt as enchanted incantations, but as transparent waves of energy. Why? Because this dense and often impenetrable jungle is unceasingly devoured by *sarva-grāsa-śarīriṇaḥ*, the being who devours all—you, me, all of us. In this act of consumption, there is no fear and no favouritism; everything is received and integrated, fully digested. This is a powerful metaphor for meditation: we are invited to embrace every fragment of our experience without judgment, to welcome each thought as it arises, without clinging or resisting.

There is no escape, no consolation. The awakened Presence is at once "sharpened to the extreme," an implacable lucidity, and "naked in her body," offered in burning desire—an act of love. We can finally love without being blinded, and be lucid without hating life. This nudity points to a clarity and insight that transcends all veils of illusion. There is nothing to pierce, only space laying bare all thoughts, revealing their nature as light. This consciousness is not hindered by any barrier. She pierces all, like an infinite wave that transforms all it touches. She is the ultimate state of insight and realization, in which everything perceived is immediately integrated and transcended.

Rather than interpreting a thought, follow it into silence, like a surfer riding a wave. Become a hymn to transformation, to evolution, to transcendence that embraces all that is lived.

This secret reminds us that in meditation, we are offered a place beyond aggression, to become serene observers of life's endless banquet. Each moment of mindful presence is an open doorway into this extraordinary state that devours the devourer of all—an invitation to recognize and celebrate the innate ability of our mind to free itself from the grip of *vṛttis*, those mental ripples that obscure our essence, but that unfold in the silence of loving Presence as the steps of a choreography of pure beauty.

The intrinsic optimism of this verse lies in its promise of a pure, unconditional freedom. In meditation, by observing the constant flow of thoughts and emotions without attachment, we free ourselves from their power. We learn that at the heart of what seems like chaos lies the opportunity for growth, transformation, and awakening. Nothing is excluded from the inner life; nothing is cast out beyond it—for nothing exists outside the vast Presence who is the Yoginī, the true *Yoni*, the ever-beautiful and ever-kind Womb.

34 – She Is Omnipresent in the Fullness of Śiva

iyam akṣīṇavibhavā saṃvittir aśarīriṇī |
viśvaprapañcavisphāravṛttyullāsasamarpaṇāt || 98
vyāpikā tu samākhyātā nirāvaraṇadharmiṇī |
bhairavasya amitālokabharitasya nirākṛteḥ || 99

This consciousness of inexhaustible riches
has no body,
yet she is called Vyāpikā, *"all-pervading,"*
for she reveals the blossoming dance
of mental and sensory activity,
the expansion of all things.
She is the transparent radiance of Bhairava,
the formless one,
overflowing with infinite light.

How can such simple silence be the source of such abundant wealth?

In the joyful silence revealed through this whole unfolding of incomprehensible utterances, the Yoginīs now invite us to recognize the omnipresence of consciousness—the sacred space where Śiva unfolds his infinity. This space is the here-and-now, the inevitable vastness. It is an invitation to natural meditation, to a spontaneous immersion in the vast ocean of awareness, where the "I" dissolves into the immensity of Bhairava, the light without limit. "It is no longer I who live, but Space that lives in me."

Let us recall that Bhairava is a wrathful form of Śiva, representing consciousness as a fierce and astonished dynamism. The expression of Bhairava's face—eyes wide open, mouth agape—illustrates the essential meditation: seated comfortably (sometimes with a meditation belt, *yoga-paṭṭa*), the mouth is left slightly open, eyes cast into space straight ahead, hands resting on the knees. One feels vacant within, like a house with open doors and windows. The feeling of the mouth and eyes synergizes and sparks an energetic opening reaching down into the pelvis and thighs. The presence of self, as though freed from the straitjacket of the body, surges forth to meet the celestial Presence: "the son hurls himself into the lap of his mother," as the Tibetans might say.

Consciousness is *a-śarīriṇī*—without a body. There is nothing esoteric in this. Observe your own present experience: are you truly "in" the body, or does the body appear *in* you? Consciousness has no fixed body, no dwelling, for it is limitless, like the sky. The absence of a body *is* its body. This expression evokes absolute freedom—an essence that transcends physical limitations. It is not confined by the boundaries of solidity but expands endlessly, where the visible and invisible, the tangible and intangible, merge in radiant openness. We are called to *śraddhā*—to "place our heart in" this mysterious something, this undivided unity, a living *maṇḍala* pulsing with exquisite waveforms—*aham asmi*, "I am."

The omnipresence of this consciousness, *vyāpikā*, is the revelation of divine play, the explosion of all things—*viśva-prapañca-visphāra*—where every motion, every vibration, is an act of creation, an expression of Being's infinite joy. There is no separation between manifestation and its source. *Sphāra* is an extraordinary word: pronounced like a mantra—*spa-ha-ā-ra*, with an exhaled breath—it evokes the bursting forth of all things. Every particle of reality, however humble, reflects divine fullness, Bhairava—*amitāloka-bharita*, "filled with infinite light," or "overflowing endlessly with lights," ever-new phenomena. *Bharita* suggests a spilling over, a saturation. Everything is felt as delicious dilation, an outpouring from fullness into the clear and spacious void. This subtle expansion is felt even in the fibers of the muscles.

Presence is *nirāvaraṇa-dharmiṇī*—a nature of transparency, of unveiled nakedness. A prism through which light refracts without bias, unfolding effortlessly the light-play we commonly call "reality." This creativity of consciousness invites us to meditate on our own capacity to be pure vessels of Light, to become stained glass for the honey-coloured rays of the Divine Manna that lives deep within us. To meditate spontaneously is to embrace this transparency, to allow the light of Bhairava to pass through us unhindered, illuminating our being with his clarity and infinite love. To see ourselves as limpid, with nothing obstructing vision.

Meditation then becomes a joyful recognition of the divine omnipresence, a surrender into unspeakable obviousness. The waves of worry (*cintā*) now dissolve in the ocean of listening. It is a journey into the interior of all things and all beings, where the distinction between the meditator and the object of meditation fades, where seeker and sought become one in an ecstatic union—truly ravishing: the Yoginī.

35 – This Is the Union Freed from the Limited Body

karās trayodaśākārāḥ sarvākṣakṣobhavṛttayaḥ |
aṅkaṃ tu nirniketāyāḥ saṃvido dehavistaram || 100

etat karaṅkam ākhyātaṃ tasyāgrāsād anāvṛtam |
niṣkaraṅkaṃ samuddiṣṭaṃ nirālambaṃ nirāmayam || 101

paraṃ yogavaraṃ guhyaṃ niyatadhyānavarjitam |
nityaṃ bhāti nirāveśacetasām anirodhataḥ || 102

*The "hands/rays" (*karāḥ*) are the thirteen rays*
— the movements that stir all the senses.
*The "hook" (*aṅka*) is the expansion of the body of*
consciousness,
which has no fixed abode (and absorbs all within itself).

*This is what is called the "skeleton" (*karaṅka*),*
because it is devoured (by consciousness) and left
uncovered.
*That which is "without skeleton" (*niṣkaraṅka*)*
is without support, without disease.

It is the Supreme, the highest Yoga, the secret,
free from structured meditation.
It shines always,
for those whose awareness remains unabsorbed,
for it cannot be obstructed.

So, what is the place of the body in awakened life? Is it rejected, abandoned, forgotten—or transformed?

The Yoginīs answer with a *chummā* filled with strange and luminous symbolism. In the desert of this world, it is a call to meditate on the very essence of being—freed from the "skeleton" of conditioning and solidification.

The *skeleton* symbolizes the old body—material, visible, crude—incapable of dying because it never truly lived. The *sun* represents the true body, transmuted through the recognition of space.

Like consciousness itself, the skeleton has two aspects: projection (represented by the "hands" or rays) and reabsorption (symbolized by the "hook"). Consciousness projects and absorbs, creates and dissolves—like a heart larger than the universe.

The "hands" (*karāḥ*) of this "skeleton" are the thirteen emanating rays of the sun of consciousness. They symbolize the operations of the senses and of the subtle body: the five senses (seeing, hearing, tasting, touching, smelling), the five organs of action (grasping, moving, expelling, enjoying, speaking), along with the mind, will, and ego. These waves crash and interweave, generating the infinite play of phenomena we call the "world." It is a metaphor for how consciousness unfolds in successive waves (*krama*), weaving the sensory world into the immense fabric of daily life.

The "hook" (*aṅka*) is consciousness as it reabsorbs all that it projects—into the "expansion of the body of consciousness," into the wide plain without fixed abode. This points to the ungraspable and omnipresent nature of awareness, which, while pervading and animating the world, never settles in any one point. Elusive, it "hooks" all. It "marks" all (another meaning of *aṅka*). Thus, it is also *mudrā*, or seal—as we shall see later.

The "skeleton," metaphor for the rigid framework of conditioned identity (*niyata*), is consumed by awareness. What remains is an "anti-skeleton" (*niṣkaraṅka*), symbol of an existence freed of all dependence—existing without clinging to any objective support. This secret yoga (*guhya*), *niyata-dhyāna-varjitam*—free from fixed visualizations and techniques—invites us to a path of simplicity, where freedom is both the way and the goal.

This *chummā* teaches that true union—the highest yoga—is not a matter of method or posture, but a quality of being, a mode of presence where consciousness shines by its own light. *Nirāveśa-cetasām*: it is for those whose attention does not get caught. "Without meditation, without distraction," as the saying goes. This is spontaneous meditation, where contemplation becomes as natural as breath—a state of grace in which the mind unfolds in fullness, *nirāmayam* (without affliction), *nirālamba* (without support).

This secret yoga, guarded by the Yoginīs (our energies), invites us to recognize and embrace our fundamental freedom. We meditate not to attain some other state, but to realize that what we seek is already here—eternally present, *anirodhataḥ*—unstoppable. It is a call to shed the "skeleton" of belief and limitation ("I must meditate," "I can't meditate…"), and to enter the sacred space of pure awareness where each moment is a revelation, each experience a wonder—*camatkāra*.

To meditate with this *chummā* in the heart is to awaken to the possibility of a life without constraints, where the joy of being is our true nature and freedom our natural state. This practice illuminates the mind, revealing the divine play of consciousness that, in its endless movement, embraces and transcends all, inviting us to dwell in the ever-fresh wonder of "union beyond the skeleton." When I liberate the body, the body sets me free.

36 – One Lives in Space, Free from the Limited Body

anenaiva sadā kāya saṃkalpakalanojjhitaḥ |
mitāmitadaśottīrṇacidākāśacaro bhavet || 103

By this same (yoga),
one becomes perpetually free
from all notions fabricated around the body,
and lives in the space of consciousness,
beyond the states of the limited and the unlimited.

This *chummā* deepens the previous secret: the objective body is no longer "my" body. My flesh is revealed as vast as consciousness itself. And consciousness, by its very nature, cannot be confined. Observe for yourself: if you are aware of a boundary—of a "beyond" beyond which consciousness would not be—how could you be aware of that "beyond" if it were outside consciousness? As Kṣemarāja puts it powerfully:
"If I am not conscious of what is beyond consciousness, only consciousness remains.
If I am conscious of what is beyond consciousness, only consciousness remains."

Thus, *anenaiva*, through this same yoga of non-grasping, the *saṃkalpas*—the habitual, patterned thoughts and bodily identifications—dissolve effortlessly, like entwined snakes uncoiling themselves. In Indian tradition, snakes are said to entangle, but always find their way out without resistance.

The *saṃkalpas* are mental constructions, projections that trap us in a narrow view of self and world. Letting go of thought is leaving behind the labyrinths of ego and leaping into the radiant sky of pure awareness, where even the notions of the *limited* (*mita*) and *unlimited* (*amita*) dissolve like mist in the early morning sun.

The *sadā-ākāśa*—the eternal space—is the horizon we are invited toward. It is a realm where awareness roams freely, unbound, beyond all states of circumscribed or infinite consciousness. In this space, the yogī becomes *cid-ākāśa-cara*—"a wanderer of the sky of consciousness"—sailing through the bliss of a shoreless ocean, as Utpaladeva sings, carried by the mystery that "blows where it will."

Consciousness is even beyond the infinite, in the sense that it is not obliged to remain infinite. It may choose to contract, to become embodied, to take form. Our individuality is the child of that freedom—the child of consciousness embracing being.

To live in space, free from the body, is not a rejection of the fleshly world, but an expansion of being that embraces all of creation in its wholeness. Our true home is not made of flesh and bone, but woven from light and love—an interlacing of infinitely nuanced waves.

Yoga of space—simple as space, deep as space, free as space.

37 – Presence Overflows with Bliss

yatas tu viśvavibhavaṃ bharitaṃ nirniketayā |
yayā svatantrarūpiṇyā saṃvidā saiva sarvadā || 104
akhaṇḍitanijollāsarūpatvāt pūrṇavigrahā |
paramānandaniḥṣyandanirbharā saṃsmṛtā amṛtā || 105

Because the abundance of the universe
is filled by her —
this consciousness, always present,
homeless,
inherently free—
is indivisibly radiant,
a body of plenitude,
overflowing with supreme bliss,
and is remembered
as the Immortal.

Is awakened inner life empty or full? These invocations of emptiness might evoke a feeling of barrenness, dryness, withdrawal… But awakening is quite the opposite. The Yoginīs remind us again: awakening is joy.

So, is it emptiness or fullness? Bliss or liberation? The Yoginīs answer — there is no opposition: fullness reveals itself through emptiness. From this rootless origin (*nirniketā*), consciousness appears as the "power to make the impossible possible." It unites Fire and Water in an unattached freedom that dwells nowhere fixed. "Be a passerby." She is the hearth of all existence, the receptacle of universal abundance that extends beyond any known horizon — free from the residues of the past (*vāsanā*), beyond memory and fixation.

Yet is this not too abstract? Not at all. *Pūrṇa-vigrahā* — her body is fullness itself, not fragmented, but whole and indivisible. *Akhaṇḍita-nija-ullāsa-rūpatvāt* — her very form is spontaneous, complete radiance. She hides nothing of her dance. Every moment in her presence is a testimony to this wholeness — a reminder that we too are vessels of light, filled to the brim with the nectar of life. The duality suggested by this intimacy is not paradoxical. Consciousness is free to divide without being divided. These secret verses strike like koans — puzzles to the mind, but clarity to the heart.

Paramānanda-niḥsyanda-nirbharā — she overflows with the stream of supreme bliss, a call to drink from the source of eternal delight, to be nourished at the fountain of immortality. In tradition, this source is embodied in the feminine — in the *Yoginī-vaktra*, the "Mouth of the Yoginī." Her presence returns like a sudden memory, *saṃsmṛtā amṛtā*, an elixir of remembrance.

To realize, here and now, the utter simplicity — this is to remember, in the deepest sense, beyond the veils of darkness. As Tilopa said, "When the light appears, darkness vanishes instantly — even if it has ruled for a thousand years." To remember that beyond the pursuit of happiness lies a natural beatitude, always here, always ours.

To meditate in the spirit of this overflowing fullness is to open to its experience — to let your whole being resonate with the pulse of the universe. To see that even in emptiness, we are full; even in silence, we sing the melody of the infinite. To let yourself be filled with the beauty of the world — the softness of wind, the gleam of sun on skin.

This meditation has no effort, no striving — only joyful surrender to the dance of existence. It is celebration. It is love. It is a declaration of unity with the whole.

To meditate, simply, is to remember who you truly are: a being of light, eternally complete, eternally free.

38 – She Is Both Full and Hungry

ittham pūrṇasvarūpāpi mahāgrāsaikaghasmarā |
sarvottīrṇaviyadvṛttim abhyajantī kṛśā smṛtā || 106

Thus, though full in her very essence,
she is ravenous, intent on devouring all.
The tradition remembers her as "lean",
for she ever dwells in the form of spaciousness
that transcends all things.

But if awakening is fullness, why don't desires vanish?

This *chummā* awakes the mystery of emptiness and fullness. The Yoginī — our own awakened presence — reveals another glint from the diamond of her boundless body. There is repetition, yes, but as a stream winds through dry lands, softening the soil of a heart hardened by life's sorrows, so these teachings invite us to contemplate the paradox of a being who is both fulfilled and hungry, *pūrṇā* and *kṛśā*, full and empty, in a delicate balance that defies habitual understanding.

Fullness (*pūrṇā*) here refers to awakened presence, the sheer experience of being — where nothing lacks. It is not about accumulating pleasures, goals, or spiritual trophies, but about an inner realization: everything is already present, already given. The treasure lies right beneath our feet. We searched everywhere... except *here*. And now, here, we find the abundance of what cannot be possessed.

And yet (*api*), she is *mahāgrāsaika-ghasmarā*, voracious in her one-pointed urge to consume all. This is not a contradiction. Consciousness, our true essence and the essence of all, has two faces: creation and dissolution. Filled, she gives. Hungry, she reclaims. Every thought, every sensation, every moment is born — and devoured. Even when full, she longs — not out of lack, but because no object can ever contain her. Hence, desire continues.

Her *slimness* — *kṛśā* — is not lack but lightness. It symbolizes an existence unburdened by attachments, an essence free from the need to possess, to prove, or to grasp. It is the weightlessness of one who no longer needs to cling even to wholeness. She stands in the void that transcends everything — *sarvottīrṇaviyadvṛtti* — like the sky that embraces all without preference.

In meditation, we are invited into this sacred paradox: to abide in fullness, and yet to be light, unattached, and ever-new. To be empty of effort, full of presence. The maximum reveals itself in the minimum — *less is more*.

Seen in time, this experience becomes exact: the arising of thought is fullness; its disappearance, emptiness. And these two alternate — or rather, liberate each other — like the two legs of a walking yogi. To meditate is to join this gait, this dance:
a joy that has nothing to prove, and everything to offer.

39 – She Is the Source of Spiritual Realization Because
She Devours All

kṛpādibhāvabhedasya haṭhād akramayogataḥ |
lelihānatayā lāmā bhakṣakī yā tu sā smṛtā || 107

lānāt sarvasya jagato sāti sarvatra cābhitaḥ |
lāmā seha samākhyātā sarvagā sarvavarjitā || 108

sarvasaṃhāravṛttyaiva yā sarvaṃ sṛjati kṣaṇāt |
viśvatra vartate nityaṃ saiva lāmā parā smṛtā || 109

Because she ardently and suddenly devours
the duality of emotions such as pity,
she is remembered as Lāmā,
the one who consumes all.

Because she "gives" (lā) the entire world,
in all things and from every side,
she is rightly called Lāmā in this teaching:
she is present in all, and beyond all.

Because through her all-dissolving power
she creates everything in an instant,
and remains active in all things always,
the tradition calls her Lāmā the Transcendent.

The Yoginīs here return to a central message: awakened
life *is* the Yoginī who gives all and reclaims all.

This world — which excites us, terrifies us, moves us with contradictory emotions — is a gift. It is the gift of space. We are not our own creators. We are born of space. And when we awaken to our being-as-space, we re-enter the world not as prisoners but as co-creators.

Lelihā — "to lick and devour" — signifies an act of radical transformation. Here, the separation between self and other, between subject and object, dissolves in the unity of experience. In deep meditation, emotions like *kṛpā* (pity or compassion), once seen as discrete and directional, are consumed in the flame of all-encompassing attention. It is a vivid metaphor: the Yoginī does not pick and choose — she swallows everything. Not in destruction, but in love.

Lāmā, the "Devourer", is consciousness itself — the innate power to consume the cosmos. And in doing so, she offers it. To devour is to return to unity, to hold nothing apart. She gives all (*lānāt*), yet she remains untouched (*sarva-varjitā*), present in all (*sarvagā*) and beyond all. This is the paradox of awakened awareness: fully involved, yet completely free. The practitioner is guided not toward escape, but toward the total embrace of life. In forgetting everything, one remembers.

Sarva-saṃhāra-vṛttyaiva — through the very act of dissolution, she instantly creates everything. This is not a future realization. It is already the case. Now: everything has already vanished. All the troubling thoughts have already disappeared. Everything has been forgiven, dissolved, healed. The moment you see this, you awaken into Lāmā.

She does not deny the world, nor the storm of thoughts and feelings. Instead, she stands in their midst — and digests them whole. Meditation becomes the simple art of standing silent in the noise. *No reaction. No grasping. Just presence.*

As the tradition says: "If you want everything, renounce being something."
This is *Lāmā*.
This is realization.
This is love.

40 – She Is an Eternal Wrath

saiveha krodhinī nityaṃ sarvasaṃhārikā yataḥ |
kathitā tu tato 'nādibodhavispharaghūrṇitā || 110

She alone, here and now,
is the perpetual Wrathful One,
for she devours everything.
Thus, she is said to be intoxicated
by the vast expansion
of beginningless awakened consciousness.

We often imagine awakening as a kind of sleep—an ethereal drowsiness in which the colours of life fade. But the Yoginī reveals awakened experience as an eternal wrath. What does this mean?

Who has never cursed the world, cursed life, cursed reality itself? Who has not felt the urge to annihilate it all—this person, this thing, this whole existence?

And the Yoginī now reveals: that urge, that furious drive to reduce everything to nothing, *is* the nature of consciousness itself—of experience, of life. Why? Because life is impermanence. As the Buddha—perhaps himself inspired by the Yoginīs—declared: *sarvam anityam* — "Everything is impermanent." Nothing is forever.

This evanescence causes suffering when we resist it, sometimes justifiably, for instance in the need to breathe, to eat, to care. But above all, impermanence causes pain when we miss it—when we sin (in the true sense of "missing the mark") by failing to see its obvious nature.

This is the heart of the oral transmission: the fact that everything disappears, moment after moment, is a continuous liberation. Realizing that impermanence *is* freedom, because it is fluidity. Movement. With Time, with Kālī, the goddess of time-consciousness, everything is swept away. I am delivered, relaxed away from things. Nothing lasts. Nothing is hard. I am freed from all solidity—and this... without effort! What a wonder, this impermanence.

Nāgārjuna, the great Buddhist philosopher, said: precisely because nothing is fixed, everything is possible. We may feel the stream of thoughts as a firework bursting against a background of colourless light. The sparkle of the world. The bubbles rise... and burst. The Yoginī lives naked, in a life pure yet overflowing with colour. To live naked is to see things in their own nakedness—screaming in their brightest hues.

Consciousness awakened to itself, roused from the sleep of ignorance, recognizes itself *as wrath*. It is divine wrath. Total. It annihilates all. Without past, without memory, without karma—I am free. "I am" freedom. Impermanence—that righteous anger—is freedom. If the God of the Old Testament destroys the world to make way for the new, it is in *each instant* that this miracle unfolds within each of us. A holy wrath, truly purifying. To marry that movement is to be released—just as one is acquitted by justice. Feel the yawn of all that appears and disappears in the same gesture.

I celebrate conscious anger, this perpetual purification that heals every bondage when it feeds on everything. Thoughts, sensations, memories… nothing survives Life.

She, and she alone (*saiva*), here (*iha*), is *perpetual wrath* (*krodhinī nityam*), for she draws all things back into herself (*sarva-saṃhārikā*).

Wrath, in this context, is not an enemy (*ṛpu*), but an ally— a force of nature which, when understood and embraced, becomes a source of transformation. It is the mirror of our strength, our ability to rise above transient turmoil and find stillness within the storm. She is *sarva-saṃhārikā*, she-who-devours-all—not with malice, but with the necessity of purification, returning all to its essence, to the original simplicity of being.

The Circle of Yoginīs teaches that this wrath *is* life. Not an end in itself, but a means—a path to transcendence. *Visphāra-ghūrṇitā*: she is intoxicated, made ecstatic, by the expansion of beginningless consciousness. In each surge of frustration, in every burst of rage, lies a gateway to growth—a chance to reconnect with the unbroken current of life, the eternal dance of the universe.

Buddhism affirms this too: anger is the clarity of awakened nature. Let it erupt, but without clinging to the story, the "why" or "how." Feel it, rather than interpret it. Then it reveals its true meaning: the ecstasy of self-expansion.

She is thus (*tataḥ*) the *vertigo* (*ghūrṇi*) of *expansion* (*visphāra*) of beginningless awakened consciousness (*anādi-bodha*).

In this light, even ordinary anger becomes a gate to the infinite—a catalyst for inner transformation, a reminder that we are vaster than our reactions. Explode, yes—but to infinity. Realize that all experience *is* wrath. Indeed, impermanence is a kind of wrath. And then, there is no need to get angry—impermanence, the time that erases all, *is already* the anger! There is no one left to curse, no vengeance to exact, no justice to deliver. Becoming itself is just, because it dissolves all that it projects.

41 – She Is a Double Creation

akalodrekarūpā yā svasvabhāvaikadharmiṇī |
kulavistārasaṃsthāpi bhāvabhedaprathātmikā || 111

ubhayoḥ sṛṣṭivibhavā bhedābhedamayī sadā |
parā parāpara sṛṣṭiḥ soktā śambhoḥ sadoditā || 112

Overflowing in form, with a power that is beyond all calculation,
she exists only as her own nature.
Though she pervades the vast unfolding of the kula *(the embodied Whole),*
she is the very self of the display of differentiated realities.

She is the glorious unfolding of both creations,
always composed of difference and non-difference.
This is the supreme creation of Śiva,
ever-arising, both higher and lower at once.

Is awakening the end of duality? Does it mean a life without distinctions, without contrast? But an experience without any difference is lifeless, motionless... without consciousness! Still, some say that awakening is the end of all distinctions.

The Yoginī reminds us of another truth: awakening is *double life*. Duality? Let us hear her voice—the trace of a path that invites us beyond the usual opposition between duality and unity.

First, this clarity: consciousness, experience itself, is an overflow, *udreka*—a superabundance, not a lack. Even when I fail to recognize this endless generosity, it continues. She is *akalodreka-rūpā*—a form of non-measured overflowing—because her very essence is giving. She is whole, true, unbroken—because *her only nature is her own nature (sva-sva-bhāva)*. There is no duplicity in her. But then, is there place for duality?

The next verse suggests the paradox. Life is *present throughout the expanse of the Whole (kula-vistāra)*, and specifically in the incarnate world (for *kula* also means the body, the microcosmic Whole). Thus, she is one, indivisible. And yet, she is *the manifestation of difference (bhāva-bheda-prathā)*—for all phenomena are made of distinctions. To be *this* is to be *not that*. And yet, she is *the self* of these differences—*ātmikā*. What is more intimate than the self? This means that consciousness, though wholly transcendent, is also the being of everything, without a trace of separation.

She is not separate from separation itself. Beyond all, she is one with all—like the ocean beyond every wave, even though no wave is other than ocean. This asymmetrical relation is key to understanding the paradox of the "double life" of consciousness—or the double life of life itself.

Thus, we are double beings: open to lucid knowledge of this world with all its cruelty, and open to the love of a perfection not of this world, but overflowing into it.

It is also a call to recognize that in the infinite diversity of the cosmos, every form, every thought, every breath is an expression of the same nature: the Goddess, *sva-sva-bhāvaika-dharmiṇī*—"only her own nature, only our own nature." Notice the repetition of *sva*—"self." The Universal is also the most personal.

Her "abundant glory," her wealth (*vibhava*), is that of this *double creation* (*ubhaya-sṛṣṭi*). Here, the "both-and" is essential. There is no contradiction: this duality is a transcendence of duality—of the kind of duality that forgets unity, and of the kind of unity that erases difference. She is therefore synthesis. That is why awakened life is naturally an incarnate life. *She is always both difference and identity, sadā bhedābhedamayī.* This reconciliation is not a flaw—it is a gift, a wealth. She is full (*-mayī*) of that very duality.

This view, in which creation is a tapestry (*tantra*) woven of the golden threads of universality and individuality, offers a deeper understanding of our own existence. *Ubhayoḥ sṛṣṭi-vibhavā*—the rich evolution of both creations—teaches that duality and non-duality are two inseparable faces of the same reality. Unity frees me from the fear of the Other. Duality frees me from the trap of narcissism. Thus, I enjoy both security and the delight of encounter. This vision—of creation as both difference and identity—is a reminder that our search for meaning cannot stop at a fragmented view of the world. Non-duality cannot be the result of amputation. Unity is needed, but so is duality. And this in no way compromises the purity or power of awakening—on the contrary.

Meditation, in this light, becomes an act of recognizing this essential duality—a journey to the heart of being where we find peace in the tension between the One and the Many. It is to accept that we are both singular individuals and expressions of universal consciousness.

Thus, awakened life is "always arising" (*sadoditā*), active, embodied—as breath, speech, gesture, and thought. Abhinavagupta says it clearly: "Consciousness is an ocean. And the ocean is never without waves."

Parā parāpara sṛṣṭiḥ—the supreme creation of Śiva, both higher in unity and lower in duality—reminds us that spiritual awakening is not an escape from duality, but a full immersion in the totality of existence. It is to see that the divine manifests not only in the heights of unity, but also in the earthiness of our everyday.

Thus, this whispered secret is an invitation to live fully, to love deeply, to embrace both beauty and pain with equal fervour. At the heart of duality lies the key to our liberation—*the awakening of the heart*.

42 – She Is the Ultimate Conclusion

yasyāḥ svatantrā prathate sṛṣṭir īdṛksvarūpiṇī |
nirāvaraṇanirdhāmasaṃvido'nuttarākṛteḥ || 113

śāntātiśāntarūpeha saiva prāntakathāvadhiḥ |
sadasadbhrāntisaṅkalparahitā saṃsmṛtāvyyayā || 114

Her freedom unfolds—
so too does her creation,
of such a nature as this:
a manifestation of consciousness without abode or veil,
in the form of the absolute.

Here, in this tradition,
she is peace beyond peace,
the final end of the ultimate teaching,
free from all delusional concepts
of "there is" and "there is not";
she is remembered as the immutable one.

If life is beyond words, what then is the final revelation?
What is the ultimate teaching?

The Yoginī reveals that *she herself* is the final revelation.
The final experience is life—not life asleep, trapped in
sterile polarities, but life awakened through the recognition
of her sovereign freedom.

This stanza of the *Elucidation* begins with a declaration of
the Goddess's absolute freedom (*svatantrā*), manifesting
through creation (*sṛṣṭi*) that is described as free of all
coverings (*nirāvaraṇa*) and without any fixed dwelling

(*nirdhāma*), an expression of pure consciousness (*saṃvid*) in its highest form (*anuttarākṛti*). A structure, yet free of all structure. An order that obeys no imposed order. Consciousness is not chaos, but neither is it enslaved by what it creates.

This poetic expression of a "form with no superior" (*anuttara*) points to the intrinsic autonomy of divine consciousness, capable of manifesting the universe without being confined to any shape or predetermined rule. It echoes the idea of Śakti as the creative power who, in the tradition of the Goddess, is utterly free and self-born, manifesting the universe within herself, by herself, for herself.

Abhinavagupta named his tradition—the synthesis of the two nondual traditions of the Goddess—with this very term: *Anuttara*. He offers sixteen (!) definitions of this rich word, inspired by the Yoginī whom he honours at the very beginning of his great work, *Tantrāloka* (*The Light of the Tantras*). Here are four:

1. *Anuttara* is consciousness that transcends nothing—because it is already present in all things. Where could space go?
2. *Anuttara* is that which surpasses all hierarchy—because consciousness is equally present in each moment, in each form; difference makes no difference to her.
3. *Anuttara* is the One Answer to all questions. Since all *tantras* (sacred texts) are dialogues of questions and answers, all they truly transmit is the one thing needed: the awakening of consciousness.
4. Finally, *Anuttara* is consciousness that cannot be surpassed or transcended—because nothing, not

even "nothing," can exist outside of or apart from it.

The text then affirms, in the style of a *sutra*, a declaration of extraordinary power: *In this tradition* (*iha*), the Goddess is identified with *peace beyond peace* (*śāntātiśānta-rūpā*), and is herself *the ultimate conclusion* (*prānta-kathāvadhiḥ*)—the end of all oral transmission (*kathā*), because there is nothing outside of consciousness, just as there is no place outside of space.

This verse evokes a transcendence of all duality—where the wavering between "there is" and "there is not" (*sad-asad-bhrānti*) is dissolved, leaving only a total, immutable presence (*saṃsmṛta-avyayā*), untouched by conceptual limitation, beyond the illusions of "yes" and "no." It reflects the central teaching of the *Kālī-krama* and the *Pratyabhijñā* (Recognition) tradition of Kashmiri Śaivism: the final realization is the recognition of oneself as Śiva—pure, unlimited consciousness.

These verses reveal a profound understanding of ultimate freedom—not simply as negation of worldly limitation, but as the affirmation of the divine presence permeating all things. This consciousness is both source and goal of existence, transcending dualistic distinctions and revealing a peace and freedom beyond conception.

In this context, "freedom" (*svatantrā*) is not just a trait of the Goddess—it is the latent power in every being to realize their divine nature. This is the very *recognition* (*pratyabhijñā*) spoken of in the first *chummā*.

Thus, the final revelation is not a thought, not even a vision. It is life—life recognized as sovereign, free, undivided, and wholly awake.

43 – This Void Vibrates

śūnyātiśūnyaciddhāmni saṃghaṭṭo nityam āsthitaḥ |
yas tena sarvasaṃhārasaṃhartrīti nigadyate || 115

The unitive vibration (of "I am") never ceases
in the domain of consciousness, void beyond void.
This (Vibration) is thus named
"She who dissolves all dissolution".

It is often said that consciousness is "empty." But in what sense?
Is consciousness a kind of nothingness? A sterile absence? A sort of unconsciousness, like a coma?

I am empty. *I* vibrate. The void vibrates, because *I* am the Void.

In this context, the word *śūnya*, often translated as "void," takes on a more nuanced and rich meaning. It does not signify non-being or simple absence of existence, but rather a space pulsing with energy and pure awareness—a true "realm of light" and consciousness (*cid-dhāmni*), a field where duality and multiplicity dissolve into absolute unity. This void is called *atiśūnya*, "void beyond the void," pointing to a depth that transcends even the conventional notion of emptiness—an ungraspable state beyond all categorization and conception, a full void, full of life. When I dive into silence, I find new life in it.

It is not a dead void that does not vibrate. As we have already seen, the Yoginīs warn us against the temptation of sinking into emptiness. Certain branches of Tantra revere the divine in the form of non-being (*a-bhāva*). But a state without thoughts or perceptions is not the awakened state. Deep sleep, coma, fainting, or torpor are not the awakened state. The awakening of consciousness is, on the contrary, the act that dispels all this obscurity—like a lamp suddenly lighting up in the dark.

Consciousness dissolves only unconsciousness—nothing else.
Awakening does not suppress or block sensory or mental perceptions.
Of course, there are moments of suspension, of deep immersion in simple unity, in the inner silence that abolishes thought. But this state is provisional.
The world reappears after this plunge—here called *absorption* or *āveśa*, immersion.

The mind always reappears, because it is nothing but the "vibration" of the space of consciousness.
The body, mind, and world are branches of the primordial Resonance: *A*.

The *Vibration* (*saṃghaṭṭa*) mentioned here is *nityam āsthitaḥ*, perpetual—a constant resonance within the field of consciousness that generates and sustains all creation. This vibration is not a passive force but active, dynamic, producing a continuous process of creation, maintenance, and dissolution. What we call "restlessness" is actually this inexhaustible gift!

Yet she is described as "the one who dissolves all dissolution" (*sarva-saṃhāra-saṃhartṛ*), a powerful expression capturing the cyclic essence of the universe according to Tantra. This vibration is thus the force that undoes even dissolution itself, suggesting that it is both the origin and final endpoint of every cosmic process. It is not a return to the void (simple "dissolution"), but to fullness (the "dissolution of dissolution").

Thus, she gives and she takes.
She overwhelms us with the colours and forms of the world
even as she liberates us from them.
What a marvel!

This stanza reveals a vision of reality where void and form, non-being and being, are not in opposition, but coexist as aspects of a single indivisible reality. In the Tantric tradition, consciousness is the backdrop upon which all manifestations of the universe unfold—simultaneously empty and full, still and dynamic. The constant vibration in the void is a metaphor for the omnipresent nature of *Śakti*, the divine energy that animates and transforms the cosmos.

This view carries deep implications for spiritual practice. To recognize that the perpetual vibration of consciousness underlies all existence leads to a vision of the world in which the divine is not separate from the material realm but inherently present within it.

This invites the practitioner to look beyond appearances and to recognize the immanent sacredness in all forms of existence.

Spiritual realization, in this framework, is not reaching a state beyond the world, but recognizing the divine presence in every aspect of reality, in every step of the intimate round dance of life.

44 – She Devours What She Brings Forth

nānāsaṃvitkarollāsasvarūpasya svajanmanaḥ |
grāsakī satataṃ bhāti kaivalyāt sarvagā citiḥ || 116

She appears as the one who continually devours
what she herself has brought forth—
her own essence, manifesting in the variegated rays of
consciousness.
Transcendent, she is all-pervading awareness.

Now, the Yoginīs recapitulate the preceding secrets.
The phrase "she devours what she brings forth" highlights
the cyclical nature of creation and destruction—
a recurring theme in the Tantric philosophy of Kālī and a
key to liberating awakening.

This expression evokes the image of the dark Goddess
who, in her terrifying aspect, is often depicted devouring
the very forms she has manifested, symbolizing the
eternal cycle of birth and death.
However, in this context, devouring transcends mere
physical destruction to embrace a subtler and vaster
reality—that of thoughts and sensations.

Let us observe this:
if I pause for a moment to watch my experience,
I see that thoughts and other phenomena "appear."
But also, they disappear.
All of this happens in a single, seamless movement—
a cycle that continues without effort.

If I pay no attention to this dance, I become its plaything.
My energies devour me and enslave me.
I identify with thoughts, and become the puppet of these
fearsome sorceresses.

But if I give attention to this movement,
then the dance becomes the play of which I am the centre
and the axis.
I become once again the Master or Mistress of the Wheel
of energies.

Birth and death then succeed each other in a single,
perpetually renewed gesture—
but a succession that no longer chains me.
On the contrary, it delights me, caresses me, massages
me, nourishes me.

The "secondary wheels" of the five senses and the mind
fuel the central Wheel—
the ever-expanding wheel of awareness.

"All-pervading consciousness" (*sarvagā citiḥ*) is
described as *transcendent*,
indicating that this "devouring" is not an act of
annihilation or denial,
but a reabsorption into ultimate awareness,
free of all limitation and distinction—
like a swallow returning to its nest.

The manifestation of consciousness, whose "varied rays
unfold"
(*nānā-saṃvit-kara-ullāsa*),
suggests the infinite diversity of the expression of
ultimate reality,
each ray symbolizing a unique aspect of phenomenal
experience:

sounds, forms, colors, smells, tastes, tactile sensations,
thoughts, judgments, desires, memories, images...

This stanza invites us to contemplate the intrinsic nature
of reality,
where each individual form is ephemeral
and destined to be reabsorbed into the infinite ocean of
consciousness.

This realization offers a liberating vision—
in which the fear of death and destruction is transcended
by the recognition that each end is simply a return to the
original source,
to the indivisible essence of Being.

What could be more concrete than this practice of the
moment,
which only the present can welcome?
It is impossible to fake.

In the context of spiritual practice,
this insight encourages the yogī or yoginī
to fully embrace the impermanence of all phenomenal
manifestations,
while recognizing their ultimate source in unchanging
awareness.

True freedom (*kaivalya*) lies in this recognition
of the fundamental unity underlying the diversity of
forms,
where the dichotomy between creator and creation,
between devourer and devoured,
dissolves into the nondual vision of reality.

45 – She Is Will Without Will

abhilāṣeṇa saṃyuktā cidvṛttiḥ prathate tu yā |
saivehecchā samākhyātā viṣayagrāsalālasā || 117

tāṃ tyaktvā nityam amalā yā sphuraty aniketanā |
svasvarūpasamāveśacamatkāraikanirbharā || 118

yatra saṃvinmahāvyomni nistaraṅge sadodite |
anicchecchā samākhyātā kāpi sā sarvadoditā || 119

The conscious activity
that manifests as endowed with desire
is called "will" in this tradition.
It is the burning desire to devour the objects of the
senses.

She radiates, pure and homeless,
when that state (of desire) has been entirely abandoned.
She is the overflow of sheer wonder,
relying solely on absorption into one's own essence.

When she abides in the vast space of consciousness,
wave-free and ever-present,
she is rightly called "will without will",
extraordinary, ever-arising.

With this *sūtra* begins a series of paradoxical utterances of
the type "A is non-A": desire without desire, movement
without movement, and so on. These paradoxes express
the transcendence of consciousness, but also a kind of
logic—a language with its own rules.

What becomes of desire in awakened life? Does it vanish? Or does it transform?

But what is desire or will, *icchā*? What is it in this world? Note that desire, often considered irrational in the West, and will, seen as rational, are not distinguished here. For we are speaking of impulse, of pre-mental movement. Taken at its root, this explosion that is will is one. One can distinguish various facets depending on the object it targets. But in its origin, it is one. Thus, we may call it reflex, need, instinct, inclination, wish, urge, desire, love… In truth, these are different branches of the same tree of consciousness.

Consciousness is desire. Desire is natural. It is activity and extension, outwardly, of the desire-consciousness. In reality, everything in our inner life is movement. And this movement is not mechanical, blind, inert. It is a drive toward an end. Which end? "The devouring of sensory objects." The Goddess-experience is voracious. Life is hungry. It is enjoyment (*bhoga*, "eating"), an insatiable craving to "have experiences," as we say. At once time, death, and rebirth, her looping motion (*krama-mudrā*) defies labels.

However, carried by her very momentum, she longs sooner or later to surpass this cycle of simultaneous birth and death. Seeking the infinite in the finite ripens her (*pāka*). She then becomes the desire to be free from natural desire—from the desire for sensory objects. This new face of desire is awakening.

She then enters a paradoxical state of "desire without desire." Recognizing herself in her purity, needing nothing, she remains desire—but no longer arising from lack; she is "the overflow of sheer wonder, absorption into our own essence," *sva-svarūpa-samāveśa-eka-nirbharā*. Desire is no longer insufficiency, but blossoming. It is no longer demand, but gift. No longer devouring, but generating.

This "desire without desire" is thus of a very special nature. It is not the frantic chase after fleeting pleasures in a futile attempt to fill an inner void. It is a flame that burns without consuming, a thirst for the infinite that consumes without the urge to possess. Desire then becomes the engine of a deeper quest: the merging into the essence of our being.

Thus, like a fulfilled mother, life detaches from her children—the objects of the senses. Now "shining pure and without fixed abode forever" (*nityam amalā yā sphuraty aniketanā*), she realizes herself anew in her original state, as an inexhaustible impulse coursing through all. She shifts from habitual enjoyment to the wonder marked by the seal of the present moment. In this withdrawal, she discovers boundless freedom—
a space where consciousness awakens to its own vastness. This state is astonishment, awe before the Absolute. Without desire, without will, she simply is, with no separation between desire and the object of desire.

In the first instant of every desire, I am one with the object of my desire, just as consciousness is one with all it will create. This is the secret doorway that liberates from vain desires.

She then resides in the vast expanse of consciousness (*saṃvin-mahā-vyomni*). Without waves, without disturbance—yet not inert like a stone. Here, in this ocean of serenity, the will without will (*aniccha-icchā*) reveals herself. She is that extraordinary presence, constantly active, ever ready to embrace the moment in its fullness.

This stanza invites us to reflect on the true nature of our desires and will. It urges us to look beyond compulsive craving to see in desire the potential for a higher quest—that of our true essence. By releasing superficial desires, by letting go of bounded will, we access a deeper will: the will to be in harmony with the universe, in a state of ongoing awakening. This will without will is the consummation of ultimate freedom, where action unfolds effortlessly, in perfect alignment with the flow of life. It is, in the end, a calling to live in a state of continual grace—ever renewed, ever ablaze with wonder.

46 – This Is the Teaching Without Teaching

tatra sākṣād avācyaiva kathā kāpy udayaty alam |
anuttarapadaprāptau vācā (<a)bhedagrahaḥ kutaḥ || 120

Then, that (consciousness), absolutely ineffable,
arises as an extraordinary teaching,
capable of attaining the absolute state.
How could ordinary speech grasp what is non-dual?

But how can one transmit what lies beyond words—using words? What, then, would a teaching look like that speaks of the unspeakable?

As an echo of *chummā* 23, this utterance and its elucidation play with the double meaning of *a-kathā*—both "what cannot be taught" and "what can be taught by A." *A* is the symbol of consciousness, because like consciousness, the sound "A" is the root of all other phonemes (the sounds of language).

However, this *sūtra* does not explicitly mention this undifferentiated "A." It rather points to *direct experience* (*sākṣāt*) as being "capable of reaching the Absolute." This is the "extraordinary teaching" (*kāpi kathā*) that the Yoginī's words only gesture toward, for ultimately: "how could speech grasp what is non-dual?"

In vibrant silence, the unspeakable takes shape— somehow. It reveals itself as a wondrous teaching, at once self-evident and elusive. Not through words, but through pure presence does consciousness unveil itself, offering a direct path to the Absolute—a pathless path, immediate. Without words, it teaches. It awakens. And this is non-dual, because it is consciousness awakening to itself, by itself. Mysterious, because ungraspable. And yet self-evident, undeniable—for who could deny consciousness, if not consciousness itself?

The mysterious, ungraspable nature of this evident experience is the *anuttara* state—"absolute," in the sense of final, ultimate, complete. It is the horizon toward which this teaching without teaching aims. It invites us to move beyond the limits of discourse, to encounter the non-dual directly. In that space where all is one—without confusion of differences—words fall away, because their separating function, so useful in ordinary life, becomes irrelevant.

How then could speech grasp what is non-dual? The very question echoes in the void. Ordinary speech, built to divide, to categorize, stands powerless before the indivisible unity of consciousness. The unsaid becomes the most potent way to say what cannot be said. In the twentieth century, Ramana Maharshi became known for celebrating the eloquence of silence as transmission—a bridge stretched toward the infinite.

This *teaching without teaching (a-kathana-kathā)* is thus a hymn to the beauty of mystery, a celebration of the ineffable. It guides us toward a knowing that does not rely on intellect, but on intuitive, heart-centered understanding. In that sacred space, where the self dissolves and words lose their grip, resides ultimate freedom—eternal peace. It is an invitation to live in constant wonder, to embrace the All in an endless act of love.

47 – Such Is the Worship Without Worship

pañcopacārikā pūjā kṛtrimā yā bahiḥ sthitā |
vilayaṃ tatra sā yātā kvāpy akramapade'game || 121

apūjaiva samākhyātā sā pūjā paramāvyayā |
nityoditamahāsaṃvitpañcavāhena ḍhaukitā || 122

aniketaparavyomabhairavasya avibhedataḥ |
akalpitamahājñānasamullāsena nirbharā || 123

carācarajagadgrāsaniratah ko'pi sarvadā |
apūrvo'sau sthito'nalpaḥ pūjanas satatoditaḥ || 124

The outer worship with the five offerings is artificial.
It dissolves
into that extraordinary state
beyond time, thus beyond reach.

That worship which is called "without worship"
is the supreme, imperishable worship.
It is offered through the five streams
of the great, eternally present consciousness.

She is not separate from the divine sky
without fixed abode.
She overflows in the manifestation
of the great, non-conceptual knowledge.

That extraordinary being is ever absorbed
in devouring the world, both moving and still.
He is primordial presence,
abundant worship, always active.

If consciousness transcends all practice and that intuition contains all other practices, what remains to be practiced?

In the first stanza, external worship—composed of rituals and the five offerings (*pañcopacārikā pūjā*)—is called artificial. "Constructed" or "fabricated" (*kṛtrimā*), it symbolizes human attempts to reach the divine through tangible, physical elements corresponding to the five material elements and the five sensory faculties: Earth and taste, Water and smell, Air and touch, Fire and form, Space and sound. Yet this effort to connect with the divine through the tangible dissolves into the extraordinary state that transcends time and space, indicating that true devotion lies beyond the material limits imposed by outward practice.

The true rite, *apūjā-pūjā*, the worship that is not ritualized worship, is presented as both transcendent and natural, existing without the act of worship in its conventional form. This paradox, "worship without worship," suggests a total immersion in the great, ever-present consciousness (*nityodita-mahā-saṃvit*), which is channelled through the five streams of the senses. Here, worship becomes a natural expression of spiritual awakening, an offering of oneself to the ultimate reality that surpasses human understanding. Everything that appears is offered effortlessly, in its natural movement toward disappearance. When I smell a fragrance, I follow it with my attention, from its arising to its dissolution into the divine "sky" (*vyoma*). This recognition, this *consciousness*, this light of attention and love that accompanies each perception, each gesture, is offering.

Abhinavagupta, the great Tantric master, teaches elsewhere that intense attention to the cycles of appearance and disappearance—of both inner and outer phenomena— is the true homage to the divine, because it is given by the divine. Every thought, every perception is a gift from the Source. Accompanying that thought or perception back to its return in the Source is the worship I owe in return. Thus, the circle completes itself.

This circular worship transcends the separation between practitioner and divine, symbolized here by Bhairava, the abode-less celestial space. This inseparable union with the divine implies a worship that arises from deep understanding of the fundamental unity of all existence. This is vast, authentic knowledge (*akalpita-mahā-jñāna*). It is certainly not a mental construct, but rather a spontaneous revelation of divine truth, an explosion of inner light that illuminates the true nature of all things.

The final verse gives us a glimpse of the extraordinary figure of the anonymous yogi, "hidden" in this mad world. He participates in his Muse, the Yoginī Life, who is always engaged in the act of devouring the world—both living and inert. This striking image illustrates the insatiable appetite for experience, for embracing creation in all its diversity. The instability of things becomes my enthusiasm, the divine presence within me. This primordial presence (*apūrvo'sau*) embodies worship as a state of being, a constant reaffirmation of life itself as an act of devotion.

Thus, worship without worship is not a rejection of outer spiritual practices, but rather a reminder that their essence lies in the inner transformation they generate. It is a path that leads to the realization that every act, every moment, every thought can be an offering to the Absolute, provided they are infused with deep awareness of our unity with the whole. In this way, all is revealed as love. When a thought appears, I receive. When I accompany it into silence, I give. I am reborn at each such moment, child of Śiva and Śakti. Such is true worship.

48 – She Is the Gesture Without Gesture

karaṅkiṇyādimudrābhiḥ kṛtakābhir vivarjitā |
vigrahagrahasaṃkocanirmuktā viśadākṛtiḥ || 125

amudraiva smṛtā mudrā yatra pūjā mahotsave |
jayaty akalpitas so'yam avaṭāṭaṅkaṭaṅkitaḥ || 126

She is entirely free from artificial gestures,
such as the "skeleton" and similar Mudrās.
Her form is luminous,
free from the contraction of grasping shapes.

This is the Mudrā remembered as "non-Mudrā,"
where worship is the great celebration.
This natural, seamless gesture
triumphs as the supreme Act.

What then is the posture? What is the symbol?

In Tantra, hand gestures—Mudrās—are used in ritual worship. Yet this term also designates, more deeply, a mystical state of immersion in infinite Presence. A subtle tremor, invisible, a gratuitous act, an overflow of love. The secret of the Goddess's yoga is hidden in our lost moments.

It is not through conventional Mudrās, these ritual gestures like "the skeleton," that the ultimate reality manifests, but through a presence that transcends defined gestures. Every movement performed in the awareness that it is merely a wave in the conscious ocean is a true Mudrā. All else is mere gesticulation. Freed from the constraints of materiality, she is released from the contraction that grasps and limits the divine form within the outlines of ritual formality, no matter how geometric.

According to the transmission of the Yoginī who IS awakened consciousness itself, awakened consciousness is the Gesture without gesture. In the greatness of the festival that is awakened life, where worship is celebrated in a spontaneous and natural surge, this gesture reveals itself as supreme. Not in the complexity of rites, but in the simplicity of being, in the clarity of a devotion without artifice, does access to the divine arise.

Thus, everything is in consciousness, all of Tantra is in Presence—including postures and yoga.

The natural cult, devoid of any harsh edge, triumphs—that is, it is recognition of the infinite, here and now. There, in the evidence of a practice that is no practice, opens the path of liberation. Nothing to pretend, no room for spiritual ego. The Mudrā without Mudrā is not passive non-action but a deep act of faith, an affirmation of the power of silence and stillness. In this non-action unfolds a vibrant worship, a silent dialogue with the absolute—hidden in the most ordinary gestures.

49 – She Is the Mantra Without Mantra

manaḥsaṃkalpakalanāsamūhair yo manāg api |
na spṛśyate hi saṃvitti glapanāt prathate yataḥ || 127

tataḥ ko'pi nirāveśarūpo'sparśo'svaraḥ sadā |
varṇāvarṇakalodrekavarjitaḥ satatoditaḥ || 128

anuccārya mahānādo'hatāhataravojjhitaḥ |
vyāpī sarvagato mantro'mantraḥ prokto niruttaraḥ || 129

Indeed, this consciousness
is not touched in the slightest
by the host of mental fabrications and calculations
that unfold through babble.
Thus she appears
through withdrawal from all mental chatter.

Therefore, she is that extraordinary one
with no extraordinary state,
without sensation, without sound,

free from the excess of fragmentation
born of words and their absence.
She is ever-arising.

This Great Resonance cannot be pronounced,
freed from both material and mental sounds.
She is all-pervading, present in all:
the mantra without mantra,
so it is said—beyond all utterance.

What mantra is there to recite? Mantras are sacred formulas believed to possess a special, even supernatural, efficacy. But in the vibrant, simple, already complete silence—what more must be made to resound?

Consciousness, in its original purity, remains untouched by mental constructs, projections, calculations, and concepts that usually clutter the mind. This immunity to the mind's incessant babble (*glapana*) is itself liberation—an opening into a state of pure presence, where true being (*sat*) manifests without any imposed "extraordinary" state, without even the trace of a vibration that could define it.

To awaken to silence is to recite the mantra. When the babble stops, I become aware of the eternal Word, simple, made of a single syllable: **A**. Simple—and yet no other syllable can be pronounced without it... Try pronouncing "k" with no vowel. What happens? The stream of mental chatter is cut clean.

This exercise, in fact, is recommended by Kṣemarāja in the *Pratyabhijñā-hṛdayam, The Heart of Recognition.*

The true mantra is not found in books. It cannot even be recited. It is not reducible to a heavy silence that would merely be the opposite of words. No—it is extraordinary, indefinable, yet ordinary, "hidden" within our very speech. What defines it is its continuous act (*satatoditaḥ*), unwavering. It is Life itself, ever-manifesting at its infinite maximum, of which our variable lives are only buds. A presence which, though without form or sound, resounds with an intensity that silences the mind. It is living proof that beyond the fragmentation of words and concepts, there lies a continuity—an uninterrupted flow of being.

This great sound (*mahā-nāda*), the total sound that no mouth can utter, reminds us that the true mantra transcends any need for articulation. It is not a sequence of syllables to be chanted, but an omnipresent vibration that infuses all of existence, an absolute reality that, being the mantra without mantra, reveals a path of knowing and experiencing beyond the duality of sound and silence. It is the silent symphony of the universe, the unceasing whisper of life expressed in all things.

Ramana Maharshi likened it to the sound of the *tampurā*, the Indian string instrument that hums in the background with a single chord—a continuous, undifferentiated pulse from which melody emerges. The *Sūtras of the Mad Master*, on the other hand, compare the resonance of Presence-as-Space to the note **F**, the central tone of the musical scale.

The *mantra without mantra* is not a quest for words or magical formulas, but an opening to the direct experience of reality as it is: an infinite field of pure consciousness, an ocean of silence from which all creation arises.

50 – She Is Posture Without Posture, Action Without Action

karaṇais tāṇḍavādyair anantaiḥ kṛtakais sadā
dehaprāṇavinirvṛttair ujjhito nityam āsthitaḥ || 130

akartavyam idaṃ proktaṃ karaṇaṃ paramaṃ mahat
sarvendriyacidullāsāt svasvarūpaprakāśakam || 131

She is ever established
as free from all postures,
dances, and other countless fabricated actions
arising from the body and vital energy.

It is said that this cannot be "practiced,"
for it is the supreme, majestic action/posture,
revealing one's own essence
through the radiance of consciousness thourgh all the
senses.

Today, yoga is often reduced to a sequence of postures. Here, these postures or codified movements are referred to as *karaṇa*. But what, then, is the ideal posture? How should one sit, stand, or move? Can awakening be recognized by a particular bodily alignment? Some so-called "awakened ones" claim their state can be seen in the fact that they no longer blink. But what does the Yoginī say?

Note that consciousness is *gender fluid*—but not in the ideological sense that confuses "woke" with "awake." In true awakening, there is no campaigning to impose the whims of an individual who has lost all sense of proportion. Rather, the ceaseless passage between masculine, feminine, and even neuter that we observe throughout this teaching expresses the **freedom of consciousness**. Consciousness has no fixed gender; it is free to assume them all.

The true "posture" is not bodily. It cannot even be *practiced* (*akartavya*). Nor does it need to be. Like an infinite space whose center is everywhere and circumference nowhere, it is always installed in its real, timeless being—the source of all emerging postures.

In the gaps between words and gestures lies the profound truth that *action without action* is the purest manifestation of consciousness. This is not a renunciation of action, but rather an invitation to recognize that our deepest essence acts innately, without interference from mental constructions or personal desires. It is action in harmony with the universe, a dance with the cosmos where the individual is not the dancer—but the **dance itself**.

This supreme action is a celebration of life, a bursting forth of consciousness through all the senses, where sensory experience becomes a gateway to self-knowledge.

51 - There is a relation without relation

ahantedantayor nityaṃ sambandhas sa sthito'calaḥ |
sarvo'yaṃ vilayaṃ yāti nirahaṅkāracitpade || 132

sarvottirṇatayā samyak sarvage vimale'mbare |
asambandhaḥ samākhyātaḥ sambandhaḥ paramo'kramāt || 133

*There is a permanent relation between subjectivity and
objectivity:
all of this dissolves in the state of consciousness without
ego,
in the limpid all-pervading space which is truly beyond
all.
This absolute relation is called "non-relation"
because it does not evolve.*

Is awakening cutting oneself off from all relations? We
have this idea that inner life separates us from the outside.
Spirituality is thus associated with the fascinating but
austere figures of the hermit, the monk, the ascetic... Yet
the Yoginī reminds us that the relation to the other is
founded on the relation to oneself. As long as I define
myself as an ego opposed to the other, every relation is a
potential conflict. As long as "I take myself for...", the
other is predefined as an adversary or ally, as a simple
object among objects. Yet the relation to the other is
something quite different. The *Vijñāna-bhairava-tantra*, a
sacred teaching also linked to the tradition of the Goddess,
teaches that relation is a yoga:

"All embodied beings share the experience of (duality)
between subject and object. But a yogi, even if he too lives
this relation, pays special attention to (his) relations."

Awakening does not suppress relations, even if it is, in a
sense, "without contact" (*a-sparśa*), in the sense that it
does not depend on an external reality. Awakening rather
consists in realizing that every relation is lived within a
vaster space, without separate subject or object, "without
ego". Deep down, the most powerful question is "where

am I?" Am I only in this body? In this world? Or is it not rather this body and this world that appear in me? But then, what is this "Self"? It is this "space", this omnipresent, transparent firmament (*ambare*). Where is this immensity? Everywhere present, it is confined nowhere.

Such is the ultimate relation: to see, to feel with all our being, that every relation depends on the relation to this immeasurable space. A paradoxical relation, for it is without landmarks, without supports. And, for this, this relation is called "non-relation".

To sit and immerse oneself in space. To feel that it penetrates everything. Then to feel that it animates everything.

There are therefore two planes of relation:

- between things, between people who form "the world";
- between all this and the conscious space in which these relations are made and unmade.

Awakening is the realization that relations are all connected to this Great Soul. But is this not the deep meaning of religion? Is it not, in its authentic form, a reconnection to what connects us? This absolute relation, called non-relation, undergoes no transformation, for it exists beyond time, beyond space, in a domain where categories and distinctions lose their meaning.

It is not an absence of connection but a deep understanding that all division is an illusion, that separation is a construction of the mind limited by the ego. Non-relation is unity, the soul of all the wonderful differences that arise, always new. Far from being cut off from beings and the world, we are finally connected. What is revealed is a fundamental unity, a continuous fabric of existence where the distinction between the internal and the external, between self and the universe, vanishes. It is an invitation to recognize that the heart of our being, in its purest essence, is intrinsically linked to all that is, without separation. Wonder at variety replaces the fear of separation.

This state of non-relation is the true relation, a union that is not built, that is not cultivated, for it is already fully realized in the heart of our being. It is a revelation that we are not only connected to everything that exists but that we are, at every moment, a living expression of this totality.

Thus, the Yoginī guides us towards a spirituality lived not as the quest for a relation or a union to be attained, a yoga "to come", but as the joyful and wonder-filled recognition of the union already present, already complete, in which we have always existed and in which we will continue to exist, beyond all notions of time, space, and separation. The yoga mat is the present.

52 - One feels fulfilled without eating

*rūpādibhāvavibhavajñānād eva prajāyate | tṛptiḥ parā
mahāsaṃvidbhairavasya sadā samā || 134*

*anāhāradaśāyogād dehaprāṇojjhitākṛteḥ |
mahāvimarśasaṃsparśasamāviṣṭasya sarvataḥ || 135*

*The supreme contentment, perpetual balance,
belongs to the Bhairava of great consciousness:
it arises through the simple experience
of the abundance of phenomena such as form.*

*(It arises) through a state of "fasting,"
because (this Bhairava),
whose form is freed from body and vital energy,
is always absorbed in the full sensation of the great
realization.*

Fasting is a recognized spiritual practice. We distinguish
between external fasting, for health, and internal fasting,
for purification preparing for awakening. In a society
where (relative) poverty is now seen more in fatness than
in thinness, we may ask ourselves: how to find true
contentment? Eating is often a compensation, as is fasting.
Bulimia and anorexia are two opposites of the same lack,
a lack vainly filled by external nourishment: food, sugar,
drinks... but also internal nourishment, with images,
words, and other music.

Fundamentally, how do we find the true balance, the
"sustainable development"? Is not our person, like our

planet, a world in imbalance, in perpetual growth of debt to fill an insatiable void?

The Yoginī has already revealed to us that she was insatiable and, yet, always fulfilled. How is this possible? What does it mean? How can one be both full and empty? Is it really possible to live both the security of feeling filled and the emptiness that revives the desire to live? Can fire burn in the very heart of water?

In exploring this secret of "satiety without consumption," we are invited to transcend the limits of our physical understanding to dive into the depths of a spiritual experience where the filling of lacks (desire taken in the ordinary sense) does not depend on material input, but on the realization of the intrinsic abundance of consciousness. Hunger, in the broadest sense, is appeased by a deeper understanding of what it means to be nourished. Not to feed on *prāṇa*, but to feed on the Source of *prāṇa*: consciousness.

Consciousness is "the bread of life," the inexhaustible manna. There is no other. All food in this world, either for the body or for the mind, causes an imbalance, creates a habit leading to addiction. Sooner or later, the master becomes the slave. The magician is caught who thought to catch. Already the Upaniṣads, this heritage from the depths of time, meditated on the mystery of food. Eating is a profound act, since it transforms matter into spirit. It reintegrates the object into the subject.

Only, the fire of our consciousness, of our experience, of our life, is often much weakened, "stolen by melancholy" (*glāni*), this indefinable weariness that gnaws at our marrow from within and deprives us of the sap of luminous expansion (*unmeṣa*). Hence, this digestive fire that is consciousness malfunctions. Certain foods, experiences, memories, emotions, are no longer entirely digested, reintegrated into the fire.

However, as long as there remain residues of experience, they must return to be consumed, until nothing remains. These residues constitute what is called karma. As long as an experience has not been entirely taken back into fiery love, as long as there remain doubts, alternatives, regrets, the past must return. Hence the repetitive nature of ordinary existence, compared to a wheel and an endless cycle of reincarnations, samsara.

What to do? Fast to revive the fire smouldering under the ashes. Currently, we burn, we digest, certainly, without which we could not live. We "eat" what we experience. But we digest partially. And what we do not digest, what we refuse to swallow, we are condemned to vomit to swallow again, sooner or later, until all foods have passed through the seven stages of digestion.

To live is to eat. Consciousness is a devouring fire. But, carried away by its momentum of infinite generosity, it is almost extinguished. Note that the image is contrary to that of Buddhism: for the latter, one must extinguish (*nirvāṇa*) the fire of desire, source of suffering. The Yoginī invites us to rekindle this fire. Awaken, not put to sleep. Rekindle, not extinguish. Hence the importance of movement in this path of living space.

When the Fire of consciousness regains intensity, the past is consumed, the Other becomes Self. There are no more residues, everything is digested, transformed into luminous, creative ardour.

The Bhairava of great consciousness, *mahā-saṃvid-bhairava*, embodies this realization where fullness is constant, independent of external input. It is an invitation to recognize that our deepest essence is already fulfilled, already whole, and that our incessant quest for satisfaction through the senses is a manifestation of our forgetting of this fundamental truth. So, return to oneself. In a sense, we are thus called to fast. But, as in all this series of paradoxes, each fast is, in truth, an invisible banquet. Sucking from the void the inexhaustible ambrosia.

What ambrosia? "The simple experience of the abundance of phenomena." Simply perceive, without projecting anything more. Let the five senses flow freely. "Then, you will shine at the centre, like a column of gold," tells us a disciple of the Yoginīs.

Total opening of the senses, total mental silence: such is "the attitude of Bhairava" (*bhairavī-mudrā*), the true implementation of paradox. This practice is the secret hidden in all these words of the Yoginī "like the perfume in flowers."

Now, because I perceive, I eat. And because I remain totally vacant inside, mute without any chatter, I fast. Such is the meditation of Śiva. To eat like God is to gorge oneself on the nectar of a wonder that refrains from articulating a single syllable. It is to fast while being fulfilled, to remain thin while eating. Finally, the perfect diet!

"Without physical and mental food," *anāhāra-daśā-yogād*: the text depicts a condition where the being, freed from the needs of the body and from vain agitation, *deha-prāṇojjhitākṛteḥ*, remains in a sensation of deep realization, an intimate and total contact with life, a "complete contact with infinite Realization," *mahā-vimarśa-saṃsparśa* (what an incredible expression!) It is a state of full immersion in the essence of reality, an absorption in the ultimate truth that nourishes far beyond what physical or mental foods can offer. Living without eating, without knowing, without wanting. Then the bread of life, true efficiency, is given to us without measure. Water turns into wine, fish multiply.

This total Realization, *mahā-vimarśa*, is a complete contact, *sam-sparśa*, an embrace of consciousness with its own immensity of being, a recognition of its unity with all that is. In this state, the need to feed in the usual sense becomes secondary, because the deepest hunger, the hunger to be, to understand, to know and to experience the totality of our existence, is satisfied. It is a way of living where the hunger for meaning, the thirst for connection, are continually appeased by our own Presence, by our commitment to be fully awake to the magic of existence. "Dwell in space, as space dwells within you." A living space that is in us, but also *with* us.

53 - There is an invisible philosophy

antaḥkaraṇarūpe tu jñāne sarvatra saṃsthitam |
taduttīrṇamahāsattāsvabhāvaṃ jñaptilakṣaṇam || 136

tenaiva satataṃ sākṣātsaṃsthitaṃ darśanaṃ param |
sarvabhāvapadārtheṣu paramaṃ nirniketanam || 137

grāhyagrāhakasaṃskāravitarkaparivarjitam(B:parivarja
nam) | saddaiśikamukhāyātasampradāyena gamyate ||
138

There is a consciousness always present in cognition,
in the inner sense,
whose own nature is the Great Existence
which transcends this (mental cognition).

The supreme philosophy / the final point of view
is therefore always directly visible in all its extent.
It is the transcendent without abode,
(even if it is present) in all things and all phenomena.

Absolutely free of subject and object,
of training and reasoning,
one can (yet) understand it through the tradition
transmitted orally by an authentic teacher.

In our world where the tyranny of "to each his own point of view" reigns, is there still room for a theory in the original sense of the term, that is, for a vision of the divine, for a divine vision? How does awakening perceive this world? Is there a philosophy, a system or, worse, a doctrine of awakening? Do we not risk falling back into dogmas and even engaging in arbitrary obligations and duties? The Yoginī, perpetual awakening, guides us towards an "invisible philosophy" which is also a philosophy of the invisible. Not a kind of occultism or "conspiracy theory".

Although... we are victims of a terrible cabal: that of being blind to what makes the world visible to us. For this is not self-evident. Mystery of consciousness! Blind spot of science and "hard problem", even without solution. For, as the ancient sages already sang to us, "how to see that which sees?" "Can we see that by which we see?" Saint Bonaventure, likewise, marvels that, like owls, we are so ignorant of the light that illuminates things.

He echoed these beautiful words of Hugh of Saint Victor, who himself took up Augustine: "The eye sees everything without seeing itself, and this light which makes us perceive everything else does not allow us to see the very face where the light of our eyes is. It is through external signs that men learn to know their face, and their physiognomy is known to them most often by hearing rather than by sight, unless you bring a mirror of another kind, where I can know and love the face of my heart.

As if it were not very just to call a fool the one who, to nourish his love, would constantly look in the mirror at the reflection of his face." (The Earnest Money of Love) Thus, we do not see. There is therefore room for a philosophy of "that which is not seen": a philosophy of consciousness.

A short dialogue in Sanskrit summarizes this revelation of the invisible evidence: "What enlightens you? — The day, it is the sun. The night, a lamp. — What enlightens the sun and the lamp? Tell me! — It is the eye. — And when the eye is closed? — It is the thought. — And what enlightens the thought? — It is me. — You are therefore the ultimate light! — I am that, lord."

Being initiated into this vision thus consists of a reversal of vision. Awakening is seeing that which sees. A sage said: "Do you see these words? If you see that which sees them, then you truly see me!" In India, it is customary today to seek the *darśana* of the awakened, as if it had the power to transmit awakening to us. However, the tradition is unanimous. To truly see is to see the very vision that sees. Only this converted or inverted gaze is liberating. The rest, as with food, replaces one attachment with another. Not that the awakened are powerless. But they must remain hidden for their heritage to be revealed. Such is the "authentic teacher".

Indeed, we have noticed here the use of indefinite pronouns. No proper names. Nothing beats an "ordinary" Yoginī, hidden in a banal gust of wind to reveal the extraordinary. Not a Yoginī of romance, but a true being in her fidelity to the Truth. Only he who does not seek to be seen can see and make others see. *Darśana* is also the "point of view", the philosophical system completed in a doctrine (*siddhānta*) supposed to guide towards spiritual realization. Yet a true philosophy is a living conversation and not a completed system. For it is precisely through its incompleteness that it draws our attention to its own source, to its place of birth which is not of this world.

The philosophy that is not a philosophy therefore exists after or before these "points of view". It is the gaze that embraces and illuminates them all, but which none can confine to an object of representation. None can assert a definitive "this is it". All are like men groping an elephant in the dark. Each believes that his part is the whole of the beast. Let us understand: there is a philosophy, but a philosophy more than a systematic wisdom.

According to the intention of Pythagoras who, it is said, invented this expression of "philosophy", we are lovers of wisdom, of truth, of beauty, of justice. We are not masters of it. We are thus led back to the desire for wisdom where the truth transcends sensory and conceptual perception, where the ultimate reality is a constant presence because it is elusive, unnoticed by the eyes but perceived by the essence of our being. We seek the glasses through which we can see that we do not find these glasses. Such is the humuor of consciousness.

This final point of view, this ultimate vision, is always directly accessible, although it remains invisible to ordinary eyes. It is transcendental, resting on no support, belonging to no place, for it is of all, infusing all things with its seeing light.

This philosophy is the culmination of a quest that leads beyond the dichotomies of subject and object, of perception and thinker, into a space where these distinctions resolve into the recognition of an inseparable unity. Absolutely pure, this knowledge is free from all construction, all reasoning, escaping categorizations and intellectual divisions.

It is a realization that does not rely on the accumulation of concepts but on a direct and immediate experience of the ultimate truth. This realization cannot be achieved by intellectual effort alone but is accessible through the transmission of a living tradition, where the word of an authentic teacher acts as a key opening the door to a deeper understanding. Simply sit and let the vision see.

54 - It is both in motion and still

nirāvaraṇacidrūpaghanād acyutavṛttitaḥ |
acāras tu samākhyāto vajravanniścalaḥ sadā || 139

sa eva sarvasaṃvittivibhave svecchayābhitaḥ |
caraty acāracāro'yam acyuto'anāvilaḥ paraḥ || 140

Yet it is described precisely as "immobile",
for it is forever unchanging like a diamond,
for it does not fall
from the uninterrupted naked consciousness (ghana).

It is he who, without falling, (always) clear and
transcendent,
moves in all directions according to his will
in the expanse that is nothing but consciousness.
He is (therefore both) in motion and still.

Is the awakened one not still? Is he not a kind of lobotomized zombie, without emotions, without dynamism, without impulse, without curiosity? Or, on the contrary, is the awakened one not a kind of hyperactive superman, tireless, to whom nothing and no one resists, to whom the universe responds like the most servile of servants?

This *chummā* reveals an unheard-of secret: a movement at rest, a movement and not a movement, a "nonchalance full of ardour," as a hymn to Shiva says. "Make haste slowly" and the obstacles will harmonize in the vibration of your heart.

Comparable to the unshakable solidity of the diamond, this sacred secret lies in a permanence that transcends the constant flux of change. This stillness is not an absence of life or dynamism, but a deep stability, an anchoring in the purity of consciousness that knows neither beginning nor end, nor alteration.

Cardinal Nicholas of Cusa offered us this image: a spinning top. The faster it spins, the more stable it is on its axis, and the more it appears still. It is only when it slows down that its movement becomes perceptible. The same is true of consciousness, this infinite vibration of which all the movements of this world are but slowings down. Like lava, the absolute impulse petrifies, love hardens into dogmas, it becomes morality, institution, bureaucracy, and inquisition. Yet, the lava remains alive at the heart of the stone...

Thus, it moves. In all directions, with total freedom, expressing pure volition in the infinite expanse of consciousness. This movement, far from being a physical displacement, is the unlimited expansion of consciousness itself, unfolding according to its own nature, without constraint, without obstacle, perfect spontaneity. It is the cosmic dancer whose steps resonate in the silence of stillness, a silent symphony that orchestrates existence.

The Yoginīs advise us to accompany the Yoginī, not to try to force her path. Let free Her Who Is Free, let her frolic, for she is *svacchanda-cāriṇī*, she goes as she pleases, *svecchayā*. "The Spirit blows where it wills." If I try to constrain life, this coiled energy (*kuṭilākṛti, kuṇḍalinī*), then it will strike me in every place where I try to block it:

in my legs, my belly, my heart, my throat, my head... thus triggering ailments and curses. Recognizing rest in movement is the only salutary way out, for these waves of sensations and ideas are the Yoginīs, sacred and good. Hell is only my resistance to this fire of love.

On another level, this apparent duality between stillness and movement is at the heart of spiritual realization. It reveals that the ultimate truth is not confined within the limits of one or the other but resides in the generous embrace of these two aspects as expressions of the same reality. True stillness is not static. It is the fullness of Presence that encompasses all movement, which reveals itself between two movements (two breaths), the "golden column" of the Sign (*linga*) enthroned at the centre of the spiral.

Similarly, true movement is not dispersion but the fluid expression of an eternal consciousness, always centred, always whole. Art offers us the most beautiful external proofs of this inner experience.

This teaching also encourages us to transcend apparent oppositions, to see beyond duality to recognize the fundamental unity that underlies all experience. By meditating on the still movement, we learn to see the world not as a series of separate objects and isolated phenomena, but as an interconnected web of consciousness, where each element, each moment, is imbued with the same divine presence, equal in hierarchy (*anuttara, khecari-samatā*).

Rest frees me from agitation. Movement frees me from attachment to things. Thus, each moment is perfect.

55 – She Moves in the Sky

ittham sadaiva sarvatra paravyomadaśāgamā |
arkaprakāśavad bhāti pūrayitvā carācaram || 141

nirābhāsanirāveśanirānandacamatkṛtiḥ |
yā sparśavibhavā saiva vyomācāragatiḥ smṛtā || 142

Thus, she is always and everywhere
revealed as the supreme sky.
Like the sun, she shines,
filling all that moves and does not move.

A wondrous miracle without (deluded) appearance,
without (artificial) trance, without (false) delight,
she is a powerful, sensationless presence
known in the tradition as "she who moves in the sky."

Recent history has taught us to fear all forms of confinement. But awakening opens us to space. And this space—*is it alive?*

Here, Space itself responds through the embodiment of the Yoginī—the "I am" at the heart of our being—that it is not only vast, but also **radiant**, that is, *conscious*, like a powerful sun in a sky of azure. Our true essence *moves in the sky*. It is unending life. And we can experience this right now. To *feel the body* is to open to a world of shimmering light within a totally open expanse. Is that not wondrous? Instead of believing what we've been told or taught, let us attend the school of the instant. Then awakening becomes immediate.

Her presence is not confined by the limits of the tangible, but shines like a light illuminating the entire universe. More than that, she *fills* (from the root *pṛ-*, as in *pūrṇa*, "full") all things—not from outside, but by giving herself entirely for them to be. Everything is, in truth, the totality of consciousness, but in contraction. Contracted, yes, yet present in each of its aspects, or *śaktis*. Like the sun, her radiance transcends the duality of living and inert, pervading every corner of existence with a light that makes no distinction, sparing nothing from its benevolent and just gaze.

And yet, she transcends. A *wondrous miracle*, she is the very expression of awe—*without form, without artificial trance, without the pursuit of pleasure from exotic outer sources*. Her nature, ineffable and sublime, resists the attempt to grasp or describe her brilliance. She is a powerful sensation, an experience that eludes words, a path of realization not based on ordinary sensory perception, but on a deep sensitivity to the raw beauty of form and colour. She is not an abstraction, but a living transcendence.

This *vyomācāra-gatiḥ*—"she who moves in the sky"—is not just a description of her motion through cosmic vastness. It is also a metaphor for the divine dance of consciousness unfolding in the inner sky of our own being. It is a call to recognize that our deepest nature is intrinsically linked to that vastness, to that light which illuminates and enlivens all that is.

56 – There Is Transmission Without Limits

mukhān mukhakramāyātaḥ sarvasaṃkalpavarjitaḥ |
vaktrāmnāyaḥ paro yo'yaṃ saṃcāro'mitaḥ sthitaḥ || 143

Coming from mouth to mouth,
devoid of any personal intent,
this supreme oral tradition
is an unlimited transmission.

Where does this spiritual transmission come from? Does it depend on a master? An established lineage? Must one seek it out in an ashram? Who gives the right to awakening? From whom does one receive the authorization?

The Yoginīs sing it clearly: the transmission is without limits, *saṃcāro'mitaḥ*. We often think of a lineage confined to space and time, something ancient and exotic. But the true lineage is consciousness, for consciousness is everything—and beyond everything. Transmission is the movement that is life. And through births and deaths, projections and dissolutions, the impulse continues.

This is why the *Kaula-sūtras*, which convey another version of the Yoginīs' oral teaching, begin by stating: "The only master is the uninterrupted transmission of rays received from the lineage." The *rays*, as we've seen, are the Yoginīs of our sensory and mental energies.

Yet even though consciousness continues everywhere and always, it takes form in its awakened state through an embodied lineage—a stream of wisdom that perpetuates beyond the constraints of time and space. Still, it is a movement of mouth to mouth, of spirit to spirit. The word *vaktra*, "mouth", is expressly used here, emphasizing the importance of oral transmission. The *Secret Symbols of the Yoginī* are precisely this transmission from mouth to mouth.

Moreover, the *mouth of the Yoginī* is not only the mouth of an awakened woman. In the tradition of the Goddess, it can also be her "lower mouth" (*adho-vaktra*), through which she transmits awakening—starting with the substantial form of awakening. We might believe that awakening is only found in the mind. But the tradition of the Goddess is a tradition of the divine body (*kula*). Its centre is not the intellect, but consciousness. And consciousness is expansion of joy.

This expansion manifests eminently in the genital zone. The experience of orgasm, then, is awakening—or rather, it can be, if one recognizes this experience not as "just one" among others, aimed at temporary satisfaction, but as **the** revelation of absolute ecstasy, the Cosmic Heart.

This transmission, free from all personal desire and predetermination (*saṃkalpa*), rises like a beacon of light in the spiritual field where many search for "noon at 2 PM." It reveals the nature of authentic teaching—one not bound by preconceptions or expectations, but one offered in purity and simplicity, from heart to heart, from soul to soul.

This supreme oral tradition, *vaktra-āmnāya*, is the highest expression of wisdom. It transcends words and scriptures. It is a living force, a current of fresh water that irrigates the dry soil of our thirst for meaning, nourishing the deepest roots of our being.

Let us understand that this limitless transmission is not simply an act of speaking and listening. It is a *communion*, a sharing of essence between master and student, between sage and seeker. It is in this sacred exchange that true transmission happens—where what is shared transcends words and enters directly into the heart.

This transmission without limits also reminds us that true knowledge can never be contained, owned, or confined. It is always in motion, ever unfolding, expressing itself in the hearts and minds of those open to receive it. It is the antidote to stagnation, a constant flow that revitalizes and transforms.

Such transmission is a call to humility, to receptivity, to the recognition that real wisdom lies not in the accumulation of information, but in our capacity to open ourselves and integrate the light of knowing that is offered to us. The Goddess is always lower than the lowest and higher than the highest, as one master of the tradition, Prabodha Nātha, reminds us:

"Whatever definition of you I may conceive,
you are beyond it!
Yet whatever reality I imagine—even the basest—
you are always fully present in it!"

It is a celebration of continuity, of the unbroken chain of transmission linking generations, cultures, and traditions. In this act of transmission, we are all at once teachers and learners, all engaged in the great circle of knowledge that unites us in the shared quest for understanding. As the Goddess teaches in the *Secret of Tripurā*: *the best way to understand is to transmit*. Awakening is contagious.

57 – Ultimately, Phenomena Are Without Substance

yatas tu citprakāso 'yaṃ rājate tattadātmanā |
paramādvayavisphārarūpo 'khaṇḍitamūrtimān || 144

nīlapītasitādyās tu varṇā grāhyabhuvaṃ śritāḥ |
ye sarve, te 'niśaṃ proccair niḥsāratvaṃ tato gatāḥ || 145

Its incarnation is indivisible,
for this light of consciousness
shines in manifold forms,
yet remains, in the end, a single, undivided expanse—
a radiant expression of the supreme Non-dual.

But the colours—blue, yellow, white, and so on—
belong to the plane of the graspable.
Therefore, all of them, endlessly and completely,
are without any true substance.

What is worth clinging to in this world?
What deserves our commitment?

Nothing. Nothing but this light that spreads through all these dazzling appearances.

This light of consciousness, which illumines existence in all its diversity, takes on various forms while remaining, in essence, a single and indivisible expanse. This realization of Advaya, the Non-dual, unveils that despite the multiplicity of forms and experiences, there is a shared continuity, a common substance that unites all phenomena in one undivided embodiment. The world is a living being.

And yet, these myriads of phenomena are *without substance*, like a rainbow. One may contemplate them, but not possess them. The colours of the world—the blue of the sky, the yellow of the rising sun, the white of the moon—though they offer a rich sensory experience, ultimately prove to have no essence of their own, for they depend entirely on the Source-Light. This insight leads us to let every perception, every thought, come and go. All is welcome. Freed from all grasping, the world regains its beauty, its truth, even glimpses of its inherent goodness.

This perspective is not a denial of the world's beauty or richness. Rather, it is an invitation to *release appearances*, to see that the true enjoyment of things does not lie in possessing them, but in the *light of consciousness* that renders them perceptible. The goal of beauty is to trace itself back to the beauty of the gaze.

58 – Saṃsāra Is No Longer Fragmented Energy

bhedāḍambarasaṃkṣobhasvabhāvaḥ kalanātmakaḥ |
saṃsāraḥ saṃsthito nityaṃ niyatagrahacetasām || 146

prabuddhahṛdayānāṃ tu vikalpagrāsatas sadā |
anuttaraśivābhāsas sarvatraiva virājate || 147

For those whose attention clings to conditioned grasping,
saṃsāra is always a fragmented activity—
a total agitation,
the raucous show of duality.

But for those whose hearts are truly awakened,
it is, everywhere and always,

the radiance of the Absolute Śiva—
for they devour all concepts.

We long for unity. For simplicity. For harmony.
But harmony between what and what? Between which
parts of ourselves?
One might just as well be in harmony with the rules of a
prison.

Saṃsāra, seen through the eyes of those whose awareness
is locked into conditioned grasping, appears as a restless
ocean of fragmentation—a continual turmoil, resonating
with the illusions of separation. Life becomes a cacophony
of division, a spinning carousel of alienation where every
moment carries the echo of isolation. Everything breaks
apart—in the worst sense.

And yet, the very same daily life is unity. For those whose
hearts are awakened to ultimate truth, *saṃsāra* is
transformed. It is no longer a sequence of broken gestures
but the radiance of a unified light—the omnipresent
presence of Śiva, the Absolute. In this recognition, duality
dissolves; concepts are devoured, and what remains is a
vision where everything is an expression of divine unity.

The agitation of everyday life itself becomes divine
expansion, as Utpaladeva sings:

"For one who is rich with your love
and dwells in your city,
this very life in the world
becomes
the awakening of divine bliss."

This shift—from seeing *saṃsāra* as fragmentation to recognizing it as a manifestation of Śiva—is at the heart of spiritual transformation. It invites us to change our gaze, to receive every experience not as proof of separation but as a reflection of the underlying unity of all things. As the yogi Maheśvarānanda taught, even the buffalo and the elephant serve this recognition when seen rightly:

Saṃsāra is nothing other than being led astray by our own energies, as declared in a verse from the Goddess tradition:

"The Goddesses, beginning with the Beautiful One,
who dwell in the inner and outer organs,
in their perfect or limited state,
either liberate or bind
depending on whether they are intimately recognized or not."

And as Kṣemarāja states succinctly:

"To revolve in the wheel of saṃsāra is simply to be led astray by one's own powers."

This perspective transforms our very experience of saṃsāra. What was once seen as a cycle of suffering and illusion becomes a field for the expression of divinity—a sacred theatre where every moment is an opportunity for spiritual realization. Life, in all its diversity, becomes a celebration of the Absolute, a living testimony of Śiva's presence in all things.

And this presence is no abstraction.
To be awakened is to *devour all concepts—vikalpas*: all alternatives, doubts, dualities, dilemmas. Everything is reabsorbed into the Source, moment after moment, just as everything is projected from it.

In this vision, the distinction between *saṃsāra* and *nirvāṇa* fades. The world is no longer something to flee or transcend, but a sacred space where the light of consciousness can shine in its full splendour. This understanding brings deep freedom—a boundless love for existence that embraces every experience as a facet of ultimate truth.

This is not a doctrine. It is a state.

59 – Identification with the Body and Other Things Is False

dehaprāṇādyahaṅkāro mithyaiva svīkṛto janaiḥ |
tattvatas tu sadā bhāti citsvarūpo'vinaśvaraḥ || 148

The ego to which people cling—
such as the body, vital breath, and so on—
is, in truth, false.
But beyond appearances, it always shines
as imperishable consciousness, its true essence.

"Who am I?" is the most powerful question. For "I" is the centre of everything—the hub of the turning wheel of becoming, fed by our confusion.

We generally identify with three things:

1. The body as an object seen by others ("Look, that's me in the photo"),
2. The "vital breath" as our internal sensations ("I feel heavy today"),
3. And the mind, as a bundle of mental images and abstract thoughts.

But all of this is *mithyā*, false—groundless, like a rumour passed down from time without beginning. This ego is a construction generated by consciousness itself, which ends up identifying with its own projection, like an actor so absorbed in their role that they forget who they are.

Yet, the true "I" always shines.
It appears in the form of all things, even while pretending

to be confined to a specific object—most often to a human body that confronts the world and other bodies.

Through this cloud of misperception, it still shines. Beyond false identification and fleeting attachments, there lies an **imperishable reality**—the essence of consciousness, *a-vinaśvara*. It does not waver, does not vanish with changing circumstances. It is the constant, the unalterable truth behind all things, the ground tone of our being.

This verse invites us to reexamine our most intimate convictions—to look deeply into what it really means to "be." By recognizing the illusion of identifying with what is fleeting, we open the door to a deeper understanding of our imperishable nature—the consciousness that underlies all experience, the golden thread that weaves through the fabric of our existence. Without the continuity of consciousness, how could memory exist? How could we recognize anything at all?

This journey into the recognition of our true essence is both liberating and demanding.
It asks us to see beyond appearances, to question the foundations of our self-concept and our understanding of the world. To lay down the burden of the ego. To abandon limited identifications and embrace the vastness of what we truly are. To break the pot and return to space. To reverse the inversion: I am no longer inside the body that is in the world—*the world and the body are in me.*

Pascal once wondered how we could ever love a person "in themselves." In truth, we almost always love someone *for* their appearance, for their qualities—but not for who they are in essence. Where is the essence? Where is the soul of the soul?

In the tradition of the Yoginī, this recognition of the illusory nature of the ego is not an end point, but the beginning of a path of transformation—a process of learning to live from this deeper reality, and to express in every thought, word, and act the light of our true essence.

60 – Such Is the Secret Instruction

satataṃ bhrājamāno 'pi sarveṣāṃ sarvataḥ sadā |
guruvaktreṇa samprāpyo guhyo 'yam upadeśakaḥ || 149

This secret instruction,
though always shining,
fully and constantly present for everyone and everywhere,
is truly received only from the mouth of the master.

Tantra is often described as a secret teaching, accessible only to selected initiates. And this is true. The gateway to Tantra is indeed initiation, which takes different forms depending on the tradition, but always includes a rite and a code. However, there is an exception in the Kaula traditions, among which the path of the Goddess (*devī-naya*) presents itself as the highest branch.

What is initiation? The Dawn (*uṣā*) answers clearly: initiation is awakening—the awakening of consciousness. And since consciousness is always and everywhere present, for nothing exists outside of it, initiation is possible at all times and in all places.

The traditions of Goddess Kālī (to be distinguished from the better-known Hindu goddess of the same name) and Parā (her twin and complementary path) declare that true initiation *is* awakening. Without awakening, there is no true initiation. Mantras, Mudrās, and Maṇḍalas are not enough. Conversely, awakening alone is sufficient. The *Parātrīśikā-tantra*, the Tantra of the Supreme Sovereign of the Three Powers, states this most explicitly: "He who knows the Universal Seed is truly initiated, even if he has never seen the maṇḍala." Initiation is entirely internal. The Yoginī here reveals the same truth: initiation is omnipresent, because consciousness is omnipresent.

And yet, not everyone is awakened... Most are asleep, while consciousness—which is "more me than myself"—is the *upadeśakaḥ*, the teacher, "constantly shining" (*satatam bhrājamānaḥ*). The teacher is the teaching. What is that teaching? Direct experience. When? Now. Where? Here. For whom? For all.

She is absolute evidence, "the least hidden thing" (*mahā-a-guhya*), as God says in the *Tantra of the Triple Sovereign*. She is "always near," *samniddha*, adds Kṣemarāja. And yet, she is also "the most hidden" (*mahā-guhya*). As the masters of Kashmir explain, she is hidden by her very nearness. Transparent, dazzling even, she goes unnoticed. A Buddhist yoginī from Kashmir said she is "too close, too obvious, too simple, too easy to attain..." A Tibetan tantra had already declared that awakening is "easy, difficult because easy." Incredible, indeed: the seeker is the sought.

Like in the parable of the ten fools, we search everywhere except here, except within. Full of certainties, we seek far away the gold that waits beneath our feet. Petrified, hypnotized by the Medusa of "awakening must be elsewhere," we sit on a treasure while dreaming of unreachable riches. Abhinavagupta asks, "What can you say to the madman who thinks he is lost and searches for himself everywhere?"

But if "everything is consciousness," if all is light without even a speck of shadow, how is it that we keep seeking it? Utpaladeva answers with what may be the most essential teaching in all of Tantra: "Though consciousness is perceived, it is not recognized." How could it *not* be perceived? And yet, though it is indeed perceived, it is not *recognized*—not fully known, *pari-jñāta*. It lives in a corner of itself, not yet having embraced the full extent of its borderless vastness. It wanders in search of the infinite that it already is.

So how do we explain this split, this dissonance?

Here is the essential point: consciousness is not only "manifestation" or "light" (*prakāśa*). It is also "reflection," "thinking," *vimarśa*, which, when lost in its own creations, becomes the mind (*manas*), the mechanical chatter in which we drift like exiles. Everything is there, without the power to judge, interpret, appreciate, taste, to "take oneself as" or "for." This is the power of *identification*, of self-realization—but also of delusion, of distraction, of forgetfulness.

We never truly lose ourselves, of course, since nothing exists outside of consciousness—not even these wanderings. Yet the Yoginī draws our attention again and again to this truth, to help us integrate and digest it down into the depths of our being: the mind is *our* power. It is not an accident floating on the surface. Or rather, it is the surface form of our very essence: freedom, thinking.

This power explains everything. Our little tragedies, miserable as they may be, are only expressions of the sovereign freedom that we are. This is what explains the state we're in. This is what justifies the Path, the teaching, the initiation—everything. One might be tempted to reject movement, energy, emotion, thought; what India often calls *Māyā*, the Enchantress. Tantra takes up this name but gives it a positive meaning: *Māyā* is the Magician, life as magic. All enchantment carries some deception, but the Yoginī invites us to love this ambiguity, this ambivalence. The Yoginī herself is this madness that embraces opposites.

This is the special point of Tantra: fall in love with magic, with illusion, with the madness of life.

The Yoginī—our life, our Self—always shines. Truth is here, radiant with presence, a beacon in the night for those who seek. She does not hide, but stands open, closer than anything. Yet her essence often slips from our grasp, dissolving in the brilliance of her own unveiling.

It is in the murmur of the master, in the direct transmission from master to disciple, that this secret instruction finds its full flowering. Not that the truth changes when passed through the master's lips, but it is in this act of transmission, in this sacred relationship, that the veil lifts and the obvious becomes palpable.

The Yoginī does not justify the tyrannical power of a "perfect master" who claims all rights. Rather, she points to the power of living, intimate speech. This intimacy is suggested by the Sanskrit word *upadeśa*, "direct instruction," with the prefix *upa-* meaning "close," "beside."

This "secret instruction," heart to heart, is a reminder that spiritual knowledge goes beyond mere accumulation of information or intellectual understanding. It requires an open heart, a readiness to receive, a trust in the guide who has walked the path before us. It is a living relationship, a communion of minds in which wisdom is not transferred like an object, but like a flame—igniting an inner fire in the one who receives it.

Thus, Plato, in a famous letter, declared his refusal to write on what truly matters. The written word lacks the spark of life. Yet transmission is possible even through writing, for consciousness—the Goddess, the Yoginī—is sovereign.

The master's mouth is a rich metaphor, suggesting that the deepest knowledge is not merely a matter of words but a living act of intention, of energy—a wave that moves from heart to heart. It is a subtle dynamic in which the teaching is both given and discovered, where the secret lies not in darkness, but in the light of the master-disciple relationship. Beyond articulated speech and mental words, Tantra acknowledges two other levels of speech: intuitive speech and transcendent speech, of which the other levels are only contractions. Intuitive speech is the intention behind the words.

In this context, the secret reminds us of the importance of humility, receptivity, and reverence on the spiritual path. It underscores that, while truth is omnipresent and accessible, its full realization often requires the key that only a living relationship can provide.

This secret instruction is far more than hidden knowledge, an esotericism for an elite jealous of its mysteries. It is a path of transformation, a journey leading us to a deeper understanding of ourselves and the universe. It is a call to seek truth in our own heart and to open ourselves to the guidance of those who have walked the path before us.

61 – The World Becomes Like the Illusion of a Dream

anena prāptamātreṇa svapnabhrāntisamo bhavet |
bhāvābhāvaprapañcasya viśvavistāravibhramaḥ || 150

The mere fact of attaining this
is enough to make the world appear
like the illusion of a dream.
It is the error of the universal expansion
of the chatter of "yes" and "no."

What is real? We are so convinced of the reality of what we perceive that we no longer even ask the question. All the more today, in a kind of "republic of feelings," summed up in the now-familiar refrain: "But it's true because I feel it!"

The Yoginī answers that the question of whether the world is real or not is ultimately irrelevant. Her message invites us to shift into a way of being where things regain their transparency, their lightness, their fluidity. The world is not despised, for it is the manifestation of the Goddess. It is not rejected as error or deception. Or rather, if there is error—as there certainly is—this misperception itself arises from a free impulse. Nothing exists outside of consciousness, independently of it. Therefore, its manifestation is sovereign, not subject to conditions, laws, or the constraints of matter or reason. It is absolute, just as consciousness is absolute, for it is not separate from consciousness.

So if we speak of error or delusion, it is not to reject life, but to transmute it into its original form—a kind of return to Eden.

How? Simply by seeing our grasping, our contraction. The mere fact of reaching this understanding radically transforms our perception of the world. Just like in a dream, where the boundary between possible and impossible becomes blurred, reality—under the effect of this revelation—unfolds as a construction, a projection of consciousness, a fabric of illusions woven by our perceptions, our expectations, and our beliefs. But at the end of this realization, the dream becomes a lucid dream. More than that—it becomes a glory, a gift, a gesture of love.

What is the nature of this error? It is the error of the mental chatter that oscillates between "there is" and "there is not," the yes and the no. The ordinary, mechanical world is binary, digital. Like a computer simulation, it is made up of very simple, often repetitive elements, symbolized by the two primary channels of energy in the subtle body: the solar and the lunar channels.

This realization is both liberating and unsettling. It invites us to question the foundations on which we have built our understanding of the world. It urges us to look beyond appearances, to see the dance of the manifest and the unmanifest not as opposites but as two sides of the same coin, varied expressions of a single ultimate reality.

In this light, the world as we know it becomes like the illusion of a dream. This powerful metaphor is not a negation of existence but an invitation to live it fully, to embrace it with a renewed awareness of its transitory nature. It is an encouragement to savour each moment, each experience—not as something final or absolute, but as an integral part of the divine play of creation. The "yes" and the "no" are both embraced in an infinite "yes."

62 – Consciousness Is a Wave Both Moving and Still, It Is an Experience Both True and False

chalo 'kasmāt samullāsas tannāśe 'cchala ucyate |
evaṃ chalācchalamayī sakṛd ūrmiḥ sthitā tu yā || 151

samudrasyeva tattulyā viśvasthitir iyaṃ sthitā |
yataḥ samyaksamuddiṣṭā gandharvapuravat tadā || 152

mahābhrāntisvarūpā tu niḥsārā kṛtakā abhitaḥ |
tasmān nātra grahaḥ kāryaḥ sadbhiḥ sattattvadarśibhiḥ ||
153

Consciousness is called "moving"/"false"
because it manifests without (external) cause.
It is also said to be "still/"true" when it dissolves away.
Thus, she is ever present
as a single wave, at once in motion and at rest.

The existence of all things
is like (a wave) on the ocean.
Hence it is rightly described
as being like a city in the clouds.

This existence is truly a great illusion,
entirely fabricated and without substance.

Therefore, the wise ones
who perceive the true essence should not cling to it.

This *chummā* deepens the previous one: it shows in what way what we call "the world" is an appearance without substance.

To hate the mind is a path of ruin, as Socrates reminded us. There is nothing worse than the excessive hatred that follows a naive love affair. To see movement and life as enemies is a dangerous slope. And yet, how many of us fall into this trap—often after powerful meditative experiences?

Awakening is consciousness awakening to itself. It therefore transcends everything, but by including everything. For, as Abhinavagupta says:

"The world manifests, and one must give reason for it, for what appears must be possible!"

There is a logic to life, a resonance between our mind and reality. What a miracle it is that this strange world is—even partially—understandable to us. As Einstein noted, "The eternal mystery of the world is its comprehensibility. That it is comprehensible at all is a miracle."

If the ocean began to hate its waves, what would become of it? To hate the mind is to hate the body; it is to hate oneself. For these waves are my waves, the movements of the one Wave (*ūrmi*) that I am. A total wave, unique. There is no duality between me and the waves, for I am total movement. I am one because I am a single infinite motion.

A motion that is still, an extraordinary motion: a vibration, *spanda*.

It manifests without any cause other than its own desire ("freely, by its own will, from its own depth," says Kṣemarāja). Consciousness, in her eternal play, unfolds without external origin, flowing from her own source (just as she absorbs herself again), moving freely, expressing the vitality of being like the Ouroboros, the serpent of Time. Indeed, she is time, *Kālī*. Beyond her terrifying aspect, she reveals herself in the ephemeral, in the ceaseless flow of creation, where each manifestation is a reflection of her intrinsic dynamism.

This creative, fertile aspect is emphasized in the Trika, the sister tradition to the Krama. The two complement each other in practice, according to one's disposition. The Krama emphasizes dissolution, Death, emptiness; the Trika celebrates fertility, Eros, fullness. But they are two aspects of the same Cycle—the unique Heart of the Yoginī, source of everything and of every teaching.

To highlight fullness in the experience of the present moment, here and now, we are invited to dive into the impulse at the source of every movement—especially at the source of the outbreath. We thus concentrate on the end of the inbreath, the moment when breath descends into the chest and "touches" the heart. Before the outbreath begins, there is a suspension in which we may feel the ecstasy of being, the pure "I am" overflowing with all the creations to come. It is said that in this moment, one feels the totality of all possibilities contained within consciousness, like the tree already existing in the seed.

However, in the Yoga of Kālī, the emphasis is placed on the end of movements, such as the end of the outbreath, because Kālī expresses the movement of dissolution—this phase when consciousness takes back into herself what she had projected a moment before.

And thus, "she disappears," like a wheel that rises and falls in the same motion, at the same moment. In this disappearance, in this return to silence, to stillness, consciousness does not cease to be but reveals another face of her nature—the unshaken, the unmovable vastness, such as one feels before an immense landscape.

The practice is to familiarize ourselves with this silence, this immensity. But the tradition of the Goddess Kālī rather invites a sudden and radical awakening, as shown in the introduction of the *Chummās*, when Niṣkriyānanda collapses "like a tree felled at the root." We are not in the culture of bonsai.

Thus, consciousness, like a wave, embodies the mystery of presence that is both in motion and still—a perpetual cycle of manifestation and withdrawal that sketches the dance of existence.

It is therefore possible to understand *chala-* in its meaning of "false." Consciousness—i.e., experience, life—would then be "both true and false," like a city in the clouds. According to India, the hallmark of illusion is that it is not entirely non-existent, since it appears, but not truly existent either, since it is unstable like a mirage or a dream. We might wish to distinguish between appearance and reality, between "our" projections and an "objective" world and therefore a real one.

The Yoginī instead points to another truth, harder to see: all is projection in the space of Presence—rays of light in the Light. Yes, Tantra does distinguish between individual projections and objective reality. Yet even the latter is a projection through the individual senses, even if it flows directly from conscious energies without being distorted by the filter of individuality.

At first glance, these two aspects of consciousness— "true," when laid bare, and "false," in its unstable manifestation—appear as two alternating states of consciousness, forming the flow of time, the sequence of days and nights. But more deeply, these two dimensions, the true and the false, are simultaneous. Experience is both true and false, like a quantum superposition.

According to this theory of the infinitely small, particles exist in multiple states simultaneously, until they interact with others. Schrödinger famously illustrated this paradox with the "cat in the box." This (fictional) cat is in a box with a deadly gas capsule linked to an atom in a superposed state—both decayed and undecayed. So the cat is both alive and dead. At least until the box is opened…

Here, the equivalent of opening the box is the act of looking at a thing, isolating it from the totality of manifestation. That thing then becomes "existent." Yet it remains "non-existent" in the sense that it never exits consciousness, even if it seems to, due to contraction into a body. Everything is thus both present and absent, insubstantial like a rainbow.

If we return to *cala-* in the sense of "movement," then we say that consciousness in its fullness—"awakened"—is neither "this" nor "that." It is both. Stillness, peace, repose (*svātma-viśrānti*), and movement, trembling, impulse (*svātma-mātra-a-niṣṭhitā*), "the fact of not being confined in oneself."

Incredible! And this is true now, has always been true, and always will be. Let the consciousness reading these words turn back on itself, and all is accomplished.

Things are like cities in the clouds, a *pareidolia*, a projection. This existence, so real and tangible to our senses, is compared to an illusion, to a mirage-city floating in the clouds. Again, this is not to denigrate the world, but to highlight its fleeting nature and, therefore, the absolute freedom of consciousness—the dizzying joy, the wonder—in a word: love. This reminds us that what we perceive as solid and permanent is, in truth, ever-shifting and elusive: everything is always possible.

Then arises a natural detachment. Effortlessly. It is not the cause nor the condition of awakening, but its effect. We often try to imitate the "awakened." We try to detach in order to reach awakening. And yes, a certain prior detachment is needed—at least to hear the teaching. But this is true of any discipline… Believing that detachment will lead to awakening is an illusion—we mistake the effects for the cause. A lover eats less. But will I fall in love simply by fasting?

Moreover, it is impossible to detach by one's own strength. The Baron of Münchhausen taught us that one cannot escape quicksand by pulling on one's own hair. No— awakening can only come from the already-awakened part of us. Grace, another name for absolute freedom, is necessary. The unconditioned is the only condition of awakening.

Ultimately, this teaching guides us toward deep liberation, a peace born of understanding that despite storms and stillness, rises and falls, we are in our essence both wave and ocean, moving and unmoving, eternally woven into the fabric (*tantra*) with neither beginning nor end. Tantra is the weaving of our awakening. May we surrender to its wild rhythm!

63 – It Is a State Without Trance

ihāvaśiṣyate tasmād bhūmiḥ kācin nirāśrayā |
nistaraṅgatayā sākṣān nirāveśā niruttarā || 154

What remains, then, according to this (teaching),
is a certain extraordinary state without any support,
directly experienced as a waveless peace,
free from trance, and beyond all.

But does the Yoginī offer a concrete meditation practice to access space? Yes and no.

No, because—as this *chummā* declares—the awakened state is "extraordinary." It is defined as indefinable. The answer remains vague, because space cannot be grasped. Can you put it in your pocket? Can you print it in a book? At the same time, is there a risk of losing it, or missing it? This is a state into which one cannot enter, nor from which one can exit—for how can one "enter" space? And where could one go to leave it? This state depends on nothing. It does not rely on the body or on the mind. Does space rest on any place? Does it fear falling? Consciousness is like space.

It is not constructed on external foundations or on extraordinary experiences. It is not "extraordinary" in the sense of being a psychedelic state or an exceptional, necessarily overwhelming event. On the contrary, it reveals itself in the absence of support, in a total letting go where the mind no longer tries to cling to markers, states, or experiences.

It is "without trance." The Sanskrit word *āveśa* refers to possession, the act of entering into a paranormal state of consciousness. But in a deeper sense, consciousness is our natural state. Nothing exists outside of consciousness. When consciousness realizes this truth, it no longer leaves itself, nor can it enter itself. It is always present— *satatoditā*. Even forgetfulness and distractions exist only in and through her.

The nature of this state transcends ordinary notions of transcendence. It is not an "elsewhere," but a return to what is, beyond the visible. It is not marked by waves of ecstasy or altered depths of meditation, but by a direct simplicity— a presence free of disturbance. It is an experience of the purity of consciousness that depends on no condition, no prerequisite.

And yet, it is "directly experienced." In that sense, yes, there is a kind of "practice" of meditation. But the experience of this state passes through no intermediaries. It does not require specific techniques or particular conditions. It is an immediate realization of inner peace, a deep silence where the troubles of the mind are stilled, where the quest for the extraordinary gives way to the appreciation of the ordinary in all its richness.

This teaching suggests spiritual sobriety—an approach where mental clarity and quietness are valued more than ecstatic experiences. It is a recognition that awakening is not necessarily about reaching peaks, but about embracing a deep understanding, cultivating a state of presence.

Nevertheless, there is indeed a more formal meditation practice—a kind of technique. What is it?

It is known by different names, each expressing the richness of this experience that embraces all things:

- **Vyoma-mudrā**, "the gesture of space," because one unites with space.
- **Vismaya-mudrā**, "the gesture of astonishment," because one is seized with wonder in the inner silence.
- **Divya-mudrā**, "the celestial gesture," because one often practices while projecting the gaze into the sky.
- **Khecarī-mudrā**, "the gesture of movement in the void," because one realizes that all moves within unmoving space.
- **Bhairavīya-mudrā**, "the gesture of Bhairava," because in this practice one keeps eyes and mouth wide open, thus resembling Bhairava, a fierce form of Śiva.
- **Krama-mudrā**, "the cyclic gesture," because by casting the gaze into the space in front of oneself, one is paradoxically "drawn inward" into the space of inner silence. And from this inner silence, the outer world pours forth—but within, in the space of consciousness.

Thus, even if there is no formalized step-by-step technique, the Yoginī offers a luminous path: one that passes through the simplicity of being, the vastness of space, and the direct experience of that which never leaves us.

64 – She Returns to the Unmanifested State

anantasaṃvidvisphārasphurattā layam āgatā |
yatra sarvojjhite dhāmni pare nityavikasvare || 155

asphurattāsvarūpe'smin sarvāvaraṇavarjite |
saiva śaktir ihoddiṣṭā nirūpā vigatāvadhiḥ || 156

tadbalena yataḥ sarvaṃ kālākālakalāvapuḥ |
sphurattāṃ bhajate'nalpasvasvātantryamahodayāt || 157

The manifestation of the infinite expanse
of consciousness dissolves back
into the supreme domain, beyond all things,
ever-expanding in its radiance.

In this essence of non-manifestation,
free from all veils,
is that very Power (śakti) indicated in this teaching—
formless and without limit.

By her power alone,
all that is, in time and beyond time,
takes on the radiance of manifestation,
as an infinite surge of her abundant freedom.

Is awakening the next stage of evolution? Many believe so.
But the Yoginīs speak rather of *involution*—a return to the
origin. What does this mean?

We have seen that awakening is not a matter of climbing a distant summit. This *chummā* makes it clear: it is a return. Don't we all feel, sometimes, like exiles from our own origin? A vague longing for lost innocence rises within us. How do we explain this strange nostalgia that overtakes us unexpectedly? Why this thirst for infinity in a universe where all seems finite? Why this aching for perfection in a cosmos that is unfinished?

The Gnostics—those early Christian mystics—believed that our world was merely a flawed imitation created by the "God" of the Old Testament, whom they saw not as a true god but as a deceiver. According to them, we come from a perfect cosmos, the *Plērōma*, and though forgotten, we retain traces of our original wholeness.

Thus begins the great journey of Return. Coming home. Into the Vast. Into the *nitya-vikasvara*—the ever-expanding love. One could object that we are already returning. And it's true. With every disappearance of a phenomenon, a thought, every moment of sleep, the thing returns into the space of consciousness, into the "supreme domain," beyond all form. But we are not aware of it. We don't appreciate it, like gluttons who drink a fine wine without savouring its richness.

Indeed, consciousness cyclically withdraws—year by year, day by day, even moment by moment. But we must catch the wave. And for that, we must know it, be informed and convinced that it leads to the highest Good. The *sphurattā*—the shimmer, the dance of consciousness in its infinite expansion—returns to its original silence, the primordial stillness of the supreme domain, at the end of every thought.

This is not a negative cessation, a loss, but a return—a ceaseless cycle in which the brightest expression of life melts into the unfathomable mystery of unbounded openness. What beauty there is in this return to the space never lost!

Ordinarily, we do not truly see this light—it is veiled by its own power of forgetting. But sometimes, in an indefinable way, it reveals itself, free from forgetting. It reclaims itself "by its own force," for it *is* Power—*śakti*. Thus, she forgets herself freely, and she remembers herself freely. This happens here and now—for it is you, reader, of whom this speaks. It is this power, this essential dynamism of freedom, that generates the theatre of existence, animating the forces of time and eternity, shaping the ephemeral forms that populate the cosmos. It is a celebration of autonomy, an explosion of creativity birthing the universe in its magnificent diversity.

Despite the many negations, this is not a call to renunciation or asceticism, but an invitation to embrace life with renewed intensity—to live every moment in full awareness of its sacred and fleeting nature. It is a reminder that even in our most ordinary activities, we participate in the sacred dance of creation, and that every breath is an act of co-creation with the Infinite.

65 – It Is an Evolution Without Evolution

bhinnaprathātmikā yāvad vṛttayo bahir āsthitāḥ |
viṣayāharaṇaunmukhyais tāvad krama iti smṛtaḥ || 157

taduttīrṇe pare yatra cidacidbhedavarjite |
mahāvyomny advayatayā sarvo bhāty akramas tu saḥ ||
158

īdṛksvarūparūpo yo bhāty akramamahodayaḥ |
sa eva sarvatodik kaḥ kramaḥ ko'pi nirantaraḥ || 159

prāguktalakṣaṇe'nante śaktirūpe sadodite |
satataṃ saṃsthite sākṣāt saṅkalpakalanojjhite || 160

As long as the operations (of consciousness)
are turned outward and manifest as duality,
oriented toward grasping objects,
this is known as "evolution".

But when all shines as non-dual
within the great transcendent Sky,
devoid of distinctions between conscious and non-
conscious,
then this is "without evolution".

That which appears with such a nature
is the great manifestation without evolution.
Being omnipresent, how could it evolve?
It is, rather, a truly extraordinary, uninterrupted
evolution.

(This occurs) in the infinite Power
previously described, always active,

constantly present and directly experienced,
free from the fragmentation of choice.

Is the path of the Goddess direct or progressive?

This debate between the "gradual path" and the "sudden path" lies at the heart of Buddhist discourse. And this tradition, clearly influenced in part by Buddhism, continues that debate. But what answer does the Yoginī offer?

She points to the obvious: there is indeed an aspect of life that is evolutionary (*krama*), and another that is already perfect, complete, and therefore immediate (*akrama*). When consciousness looks outward toward its manifestations, we have becoming, time, the cycles of projection and reabsorption. When consciousness turns back upon itself, it sees everything—because it *is* everything. This is the timeless aspect of life.

But what is the relationship between these two aspects? Can we live both experiences at once? Or must we alternate between them? Or perhaps time disappears entirely when eternity arises, as the Advaita Vedānta claims?

The pivot is consciousness. From this axis, the indefinable and ungraspable consciousness—*extraordinary* in essence—manifests, *bhāti*, it "shines," it "appears." Like a mirror whose nature is to reflect, like an ocean whose nature is to ripple with waves, consciousness manifests, manifests itself by manifesting infinite universes.

In duality, consciousness shines so brightly that it forgets it is light. It believes itself to be a separate being, forgetting its source, imagining it is its own creator. In this state, consciousness appears outwardly directed, captivated by the sensory world. Here, *evolution* makes sense—as a movement of consciousness toward objects, in a restless search for experience. But eventually, this evolution hits the wall of absurdity. "More, always more"—yet with no end, and no real hunger fulfilled.

Consciousness, nostalgic for its own fullness, then turns back upon itself. It becomes consciousness of unity.

But a new duality now emerges between the experience of duality (with its opposing forces) and the experience of unity, of the "unmanifested," of non-evolution. The immature seeker falls into this second duality and mistakes the experience of unity for the final spiritual realization— where all *dynamism* seems to vanish. The individual is then tempted to reject the notion of personhood, the world, and even life itself, since all life is evolution. In other words, consciousness, in returning to itself, ends up rejecting itself.

How can this impasse be overcome?

By realizing that consciousness is not separate from its manifestation. Reality and appearance are inseparable. We are invited to become familiar with this non-dual experience (unity and duality as one) through the *Gesture of Wonder* described in *chummā* 63: "This experience is without trance." It is perpetually present. Why? Because it has fully digested and assimilated manifestation and its dual cycles.

A single gesture suffices: straightening the spine, softening the jaw, opening the gaze—as if lifting a veil. What then occurs is what I call the "Vicks effect": a clearing, as though we were suddenly breaking through the cloud layer. Sharp, vast, alert—a great breath of fresh air, a clarity that pierces everything. Nothing stops the gaze. A peace unlike any other. A single instant of this vision can sustain an entire life of evolution.

Is this still an evolution? Yes—but an *extraordinary* (*ko'pi*) evolution, one animated by the recognition of perfection.

True evolution is not merely linear or progressive—it is the awareness of the timeless nature of our being. And this timeless awareness has the power to redirect our temporal development. The Roar of the Yoginī has meaning, even if terrifying: at the heart of all seeking and all movement lies an immutable principle, an essence that remains untouched by appearances, even as it recognizes within appearances the Absolute Appearing, free and transparent.

Thus, realization is complete—both still and in motion, ordered and beyond all order, temporal and eternal, never fully accomplished and always already offered.

66 – It Is Without Dissolution or Manifestation

padārthapralayo yatra svasvarūpodayas tataḥ |
akhaṇḍabhāvabhāso ya udayāstavivarjitaḥ || 161

That into which things dissolve,
that from which our essence arises,
is a manifestation not divided
between "appearance" and "disappearance".

Following the previous *chummā*, the Yoginī here makes her Heart vibrate—its pulsation is that impassable loop which is, in a single *mudrā*, both creation and destruction.

At the core of this teaching lies the understanding that everything that appears in the universe—every object, being, and thought—eventually dissolves back into the fundamental essence from which it emerged. Thus, there is nothing to do but follow the natural movement to its end. Follow the wave to the ocean. Follow a thought as one listens to the fading resonance of a Tibetan bowl, or surrenders—alert yet utterly relaxed—to the endless "Om." No other condition is required but this gesture of attention: invisible, silent, and freely given.

This essence, however, is not a sterile void or a frightening nothingness, but an unspoiled fullness—the very source of all existence. It is a state of being where the apparent contradictions of manifestation and dissolution reconcile.

This state—described as "a manifestation not divided between 'appearance' and 'disappearance'"—reveals reality beyond the limitations of dualistic perception. It teaches us that behind the play of forms and disappearances, behind the dance of births and deaths, lies an unchanging principle, a continuous presence which is the backdrop of everything that is—yet not separate from this dance, because it is the ballerina herself. To feel her, here and now: tips of delight offered to space.

This realization challenges our habitual way of seeing the world, where we are often captivated by the ephemeral, the ebb and flow of appearances. We want to block what arises and cling to what fades, instead of accompanying the natural movement—which is love. Are not the flames of hell the resistance to this infinite movement? And if limits were nothing but our own resistances?

By recognizing that these phenomena are merely temporary expressions of a timeless, perfect reality, we can begin to free ourselves from the fears and attachments that bind us to impermanence—and open our hearts to a serenity that is authentic, innate, and natural.

Nothing truly appears, nothing truly disappears—everything vibrates.

67 – It Is an Existence Without Existence

bhedonmeṣasthitir yatra layaṃ yātāgame pade |
aprakampye nirākhyākhye sā asthitiḥ sthitir avyayā || 162

That existence, which is the blossoming of differences,
dissolves into the state beyond all access,
immovable, called the "Nameless":
this non-existence is the immutable existence.

Nothing disappears in awakening. There is only transmutation, for awakening (*unmeṣa*) is nothing other than the blossoming (*unmeṣa*) of differences. All these riches are the True, the Beautiful, the Good. Nothing to reject, no more dilemmas. And it has no name: no dispute is possible. She is the Nameless (*Anāmā*), the source of all names. This table, that coworker, that rival, that aging body, that worn cup, those painful memories—none of them need to disappear. But all of it evolves and is revealed as nothing other than the Nameless Light.

She is thus a stability without support, a balance dependent on nothing, free from everything. She is perfect safety, the haven of peace, the remedy for our despair. The consolation of the sorrowful, the medicine of the ill: the miracle of consciousness.

She stands, but without resting on any construction. She stands in space because she is space. And space fears nothing—it cannot fall, it cannot be lost. Realize this: consciousness, this presence here and now that you are, is naturally stable. It stands upright without excluding anything, asserts itself without struggle, triumphs without combat. What rest!

The blossoming (*unmeṣa*) of differences is the field where the drama of existence unfolds, where each form, each thought, each sensation seems to arise from the vastness of emptiness to dance for a moment in the spotlight of consciousness before dissolving once more into the infinite. This eternal cycle of manifestation and dissolution (*laya*) is the dynamic through which the universe reveals itself. It is a divine game of hide-and-seek between two postures of self: forgetfulness and full recognition.

Consciousness is perfect. But it seeks itself. In you, through the very reading of these words. Is this not a breathtaking mystery? For at the heart of this whirlwind of forms and phenomena lies a state of pure stillness, a place of deep peace that words can scarcely capture. This state, called "the Nameless" (*nirākhyākhye*)—literally "that which is called 'that which cannot be called'"—is Existence without existence, a Presence that defies logic and understanding, an unheard-of miracle that is both the source and final destination of all that is.

This immutable existence, which rests nowhere (*asthitiḥ sthitir avyayā*), is the very essence of who we are. In the very depths of the turbulence of our sensory and emotional experience, we can find a refuge, a firm ground in the realization of our true nature. A firm ground—made of nothing—thus nothing can shake it. A tremor of space: without danger!

68 – She Is Both Creation and Resorption: There Is (Re)Creation After Dissolution

sarvasaṃhārasaṃhārapadāt sakalaniṣkalā |
svabhāvabhāvarūpeyaṃ sṛṣṭir ullasitā kramāt || 163

Because she is the resorption of the resorption of all,
she is both with and without divisions.
Naturally adorned with all phenomena,
this creation arises according to (her) own rhythm.

Awakening is, in a sense, a death—but a death that is a birth. To awaken is to die and to be born again. Nothing more, nothing less. All testimonies agree.

She is thus the death of Death. In this new life, destruction is destroyed. Nothingness is annihilated, for the very nature of consciousness is to dispel the void. Awakening is a serenity that ends all indifference. It is not slumber, but hypersensitivity—a more-than-consciousness, a total emotion.

According to one verse, "absolute consciousness is total: it is total love, it is universal hatred." Total, complete—birth and death: the full movement of the Wheel that I feel at the centre, more me than myself. To relax from the fatigue of sorting everything, of constant discrimination—this is the true discernment!

She is the resorption of resorption—a concept suggesting that the process of dissolution does not end with the end of a cycle, but continues, enveloping all things in its embrace. In this understanding, the end is never final. It is a passage, a transformation that opens the way for a new expression of life. A mighty chant: the ultimate essence of the universe, death and rebirth are but two facets of the same process, different expressions of the creative force (*śakti*) that animates everything.

This creation (*sṛṣṭi*) is described as both *sakala* and *niṣkalā*—with and without parts—embodied and disembodied, for the body is "all that is perceived," in an endless expansion that is nothing but love.

Naturally adorned with phenomena, this creation reveals that the beauty and complexity of the world are not external additions, but flow from the very nature of reality itself. Every aspect of existence—from the stars in the sky to the depths of the sea, from moments of pure joy to the trials of pain—is a note in the symphony of the universe, a manifestation of the divine order that pervades all. Even the false notes enrich the Whole.

69 – Wind Becomes Earth

calanaspandanoddeśarūpe cañcalamūrtibhṛt |
vāyur yas tena satatam āśyānatvam upāśritaḥ || 164
yatas tasmāt tu kāṭhinyarūpā dharaṇir ucyate |
viparītasvabhāvo 'yam akrameṇa vyavasthitaḥ || 165

(Consciousness as) Wind is defined as
movement and vibration,
its concrete form is unstable.
Thus, when it solidifies completely,
it takes on fixity,
and is then called "Earth".
(It thus) simultaneously holds
an inverse nature.

Is it not said that Nature teaches us? For the Ancients, contemplating the divine was contemplating the cosmos.

Wind (*vāyu*), with its essence of movement (*calana*) and vibration (*spandana*), embodies the fleeting and ever-changing nature of reality. Its form (*mūrti*), in constant fluctuation, symbolizes the ceaseless flow of existence, where nothing remains static, where everything is always in motion.

And yet, within this flux, there is a crystallization (*āśyānatvam*). The fluid densifies, becoming fixed in its desire to experience incarnation. Wind then finds its path toward fixation, toward a manifestation of solidity (*kāṭhinyarūpā*) that transforms it into Earth (*dharaṇi*, "she who holds"). This transition from motion to stillness, from air to substance, illustrates the extraordinary ability of consciousness to embody a regular order, even though it is entirely free from all order.

And because it cannot fully ignore or forget its true nature, we may say it *plays* at incarnation. Kṣemarāja compares it to the sap of a tree that gradually hardens. The philosopher Bergson likened the movement of life to lava erupting from a volcano before petrifying into fixed forms that seem to block the lava itself.

Earth is thus recognized for its hardness, its stability—a quality radically opposed to the intrinsic instability of Wind. This apparent duality, where Wind and Earth exhibit diametrically opposed attributes, is in truth an expression of their underlying unity, of their coexisting "inverse nature" held together in dynamic balance. "Who knows water and ice is free forever," says a sage from the tradition.

There is, then, also a teaching here about the nature of things: this simultaneous coexistence of opposite qualities reveals a profound truth about reality—that contradictions are but surface appearances in the vast theatre of existence. Each element, each phenomenon, carries within itself the potential to transform into its opposite, illustrating the principle of complementarity that governs the cosmos.

This *chummā* and the one that follows teach us to look beyond categorical distinctions, to embrace the complexity and richness of life. To see that in every end lies a beginning, in every disappearance an emergence. It is an invitation to perceive the world not as a static assembly of disconnected parts but as a dynamic flow of interactions and transformations—a Living Whole.

In this light, the elements are not merely material constituents of the world but living symbols of the cosmic dance of creation and dissolution. They remind us that all things in the universe are connected, that every aspect of reality reflects the whole, and that in the very heart of impermanence lies an immutable constancy.

70 – Water Becomes Fire

dravarūpaṃ jalaṃ khyātam ādātuṃ tad yato'kramāt |
agnidehaṃ tu tenaiva svīkṛtaṃ dhāmaśaktitaḥ || 166

Water is described as liquid,
because it instantly takes the shape of its container.
But the body of Fire digests this (Water),
through the power of its domain.

Water symbolizes our emotions, our accumulated wounds, hidden in the folds of our body. The Fire of consciousness transmutes this water into itself, and returns it to the sky, to Wind, then to Space—its omnipresent source.

Water (*jala*), in its liquid nature (*drava-rūpam*), is known for its adaptability and its ability to assume various forms, mirroring the ever-changing weave of reality. This quality of constant transformation highlights the cyclic dynamic of life, where all that exists is in perpetual motion, in a ceaseless stream of becoming. The Moon, like women's lunar rhythms and all things, is cyclic—birth, death, and rebirth.

Yet, in this perpetual evolution, Water encounters Fire (*agni*), its apparent antithesis, in an act of transcendental synthesis. The body of Fire (*agni-deham*), acting through the power of its own domain (*dhāma-śakti*), absorbs and transmutes Water, illustrating the universe's ability to reconcile opposites, to fuse elements into harmonious unity.

This interaction between Water and Fire is not a simple annihilation of one by the other, but a metamorphosis, where liquidity gives way to combustion. It is a process of digestion, of assimilation (*svī-kṛtam*) in which Fire, by its inherently transformative nature, reveals the hidden potential of Water—demonstrating the deep truth that transformation is the essence of existence, a truth that has the power to free us from the fear of change.

71 – Space Is Inert

eṣāṃ caturṇāṃ bhavato yatrotpattilayau sadā |
vyomni tat tu jaḍaṃ proktaṃ niścalatvād acetanam || 167

These four (elements) constantly
emerge from and dissolve into Space.
But (Space) is said to be inert:
it is devoid of consciousness, for it does not move.

The Yoginī has proclaimed many times that consciousness is "like space." But what is their common ground? And what are the limits of this metaphor? Or can we go as far as to say that space *is* consciousness?

According to Perfect Wisdom, "space is the queen of metaphors," and "to look at the sky is to see reality," because space, like consciousness, has no form, no structure, no boundaries, no reference points. It permeates everything; nothing exists outside of it. A material body, in order to be a body, must have some kind of extension. It thus occupies the space that "gives it room" (*avakāśa*). All that appears and disappears, appears and disappears within it. Everything is enveloped in this vastness, in this luminous element that is confined by nothing. To open to space is to be liberated. The simple practice of feeling the space around the body, and within the body, is enough to transform our perception of the body. And the same applies to the mind.

However, space lacks the essential trait of consciousness: namely, *consciousness* itself. Space is *jaḍa* in Sanskrit—insentient, inert, lacking awareness. Why? Because space "does not move." It is therefore said to lack the act of awareness, the power to be aware. Consciousness is movement. If there is no movement, there is no consciousness. If consciousness can be called "still," it is only in a particular, extraordinary sense, one which this teaching reveals through its paradoxical expressions.

After the four elements—Earth, Water, Fire, Air—this *chummā* invites us to contemplate space not as an absolute and sterile void, but as the primordial container, the undifferentiated matrix from which all manifestations of the cosmos arise and into which they resolve. There exists a fundamental reality that escapes the categories of "life" and "consciousness" as we commonly understand them. Space, in its unmoving vastness, recalls the ultimate nature of reality: *śūnya*, emptiness—not a void, but an infinite potential, the fertile ground where all existence takes root.

72 – Then an Inverse Movement Takes Place

ākhyātāguruvaktroktayuktyeyaṃ vṛttir akramāt |
viparītagamenoccaiḥ sākṣātkāratayoditā || 168

This evolution (of the four elements),
once fully explained by the mouth of the master,
rises up directly from above
in an inverse movement,
as direct realization.

Where does evolution lead? So many deaths, so much waste, so much suffering... for what?

For return. Everything is done in order to be undone. Not as some useless return to zero, not as an insult to all the pains endured, not as contempt for every tear that's been shed. But as reunion. And better than we remember! Yet perhaps it's better that we cannot imagine it, for otherwise we might grow proud.

This inverse movement, taught through the oral transmission of a master (*guru-vaktra*), arises with force (*sākṣāt-kāra*), "like a fruit in the palm of the hand," revealing our true nature. Within the infinite space of *ākāśa*, the luminous vastness where the elements unfold freely, there emerges a call to return to our essence, to a reality where the duality of phenomena dissolves into the unity of consciousness. Simply listening to this call is already to return.

The act of awakening is captured here in a single striking expression: the act of turning back, *viparīta-vṛtti*—a return upstream, like determined salmon. We are invited into an inner journey where the outward movement of things transforms into a revolution that ends the exile. Of course, the four elements will return to space, and the world will be renewed, like after a long and restful nap.

This passage from outer to inner, from the manifest to its vibrant source, from *jaḍa* (inert) to *śakti* (conscious energy), is an invitation to rediscover our true nature beyond the veil of mistaken identities. To feel this Self that always already embraces the infinite, like holding a living being in one's arms.

Must one be prepared to be capable of such a revolt against the tyranny of the opaque? Do we even have the right? We've already seen that this question arises, for many of us doubt our own worth. The Yoginī has responded several times since the beginning: yes, all are called—but who are the chosen? Those who are sincere, noble, worthy?

The Sanskrit word *ucca-* evokes the upward impulse, the gesture of one who raises their head to open to the Open. Everything resolves into space, which itself resolves into consciousness. Then, in an inverted movement, everything again proceeds "from above," from consciousness.

By cultivating a presence that is both attentive and loving, we open our heart to the infinite, allowing our being to vibrate in harmony with the essence of life itself. This inner transformation unfolds like a lotus, gradually revealing its petals to the sun of awareness.

73 – Consciousness Is the Essence of Contractions

kañcukonmeṣavistārarūpiṇī sarvagā sadā |
viśvavaicitryacitrasya sūtradhāratvam āgatā || 169

Always present in all things,
She is the vast expanse where the contractions open.
She is the creator—the thread-holder—of the marvelous tapestry
of the universe's diversity.

Consciousness is vast, always open, in perpetual expansion. But one might ask: how can this truth be lived when we are daily subjected to stress, pressure, fears, and therefore contractions?

To live in a body necessarily implies contraction... It is impossible to remain in permanent dilation! Indeed, after the in-breath comes the out-breath. And in the out-breath, the belly contracts. The heart, likewise, cannot circulate blood without contracting in a precise and unbroken rhythm.

The Yoginī's answer strikes like lightning: "Consciousness is the vast expanse where contractions blossom." What an extraordinary formula! It recalls another, found in the *Netra-tantra* (8.8): "When one experiences it in a single blink, one is liberated." The expression *nimeṣa-unmeṣa-mātreṇa* literally means "in a single closing and opening of the eyes."

We are thus guided toward a deep exploration of how consciousness (*cit*) penetrates and reveals itself through the contractions (*kañcukas*), unfolding into the immensity of creation—for "contractions" are the limitations that form the "straitjacket" in which consciousness—I—feels confined.

Consciousness is omnipresent (*sarva-gā*), extending beyond all boundaries and limits, embracing the totality of existence in its vast expanse (*vistāra-rūpiṇī*). And within this expansion, contractions, far from being seen as restrictions, are understood as essential movements giving birth to the One's emergence into the Open, the source of wonder (*viśva-vaicitrya*), and of the cosmos' beauty. These contractions are the ripples on the ocean of consciousness, the patterns in the fabric of reality, each bearing the potential for an opening into a richer and more intricate manifestation.

Kṣemarāja explores these paradoxes in his *Spanda-saṃdoha*, Essence of the Vibration. There are three phases or three experiences:

1. Expansion is contraction of consciousness, for then it tends to forget itself. When I look at this coffee cup, it expands, blossoms; but at the same time, I, as the space of consciousness, contract, so to speak.
2. The contraction of a thing, or its disappearance, is expansion, for then consciousness tends to reappear, even if unrecognized. For example, when the coffee cup vanishes as a distinct object in my awareness, and before this croissant appears, there is a moment of expansion of consciousness, even if unnoticed, unrecognized, unappreciated—and thus, without awakening.
3. Finally, contraction itself, *as contraction*, is expansion. This idea is more difficult to grasp than the previous two. Indeed, we are invited to

understand, in a feeling at the limits of our individual capacities, that in the act of contracting, consciousness affirms its freedom. It contracts without truly contracting, as the next *chummā* will clarify. It accomplishes the impossible, and that is an expansion—*vibhava*, the abundant glory of differences (*bheda*), a word that also denotes revelation and the decoding of a secret, a mystery, or a language—for example, a mantra.

Consciousness acts as the creator or stage director (*sūtra-dhāra*), weaving the marvellous tapestry of the universe with unmatched mastery and subtlety. Each thread, each nuance of this weave (one of the meanings of *tantra*) is imbued with her presence, revealing the deep interconnectedness of all existence. This vision transforms our understanding of contractions, encouraging us to welcome them as essential aspects of the dance of creation, as moments of potential where true essence can shine forth.

This *chummā* thus draws our attention to the surprise held within the limitations and constraints of our human existence—not barriers to our unfolding, but opportunities to discover true freedom. Could freedom even reveal itself as freedom without constraint? It is in the embrace of these contractions, in the felt and silent acceptance of our limitations, that we may find the concrete keys to unlock the gates of awakened perception, to broaden our horizon, and to deepen our connection to the living fabric of reality.

Thus, Somānanda, author of the *Śiva-dṛṣṭi*, *The Vision of Śiva*, wherein "everything is Śiva," forcefully affirms that even the most intense moments of despair contain a background of infinite ecstasy.

74 – Material Form Is an Illusion

rūpaṃ yad dṛśyajātaṃ tan māyīyaṃ bhedavistṛtam |
atāttvikaṃ paricchinnaṃ tat sattāvadhisaṃśritiḥ || 170

Every visible form is illusion,
an emanation of duality.
It is not real, it is limited—
the support of the limits of existence.

We often carry the cliché that Indian doctrines generally consider the world as illusion, mere appearance without reality. But this generalization is misleading. In many Indian traditions (such as the Hare Krishna movement), the universe is not a false appearance: it is the real creation of a real Creator. Everything is real.

In other schools, more widely diffused in the West—like Advaita Vedānta—there is only one reality: consciousness. And the world is a mysterious illusion, like a dream born from the sleep of ignorance.

We might then think that Tantra affirms the reality of the sensible world. This is not wrong: Tantra does affirm that our perceptions and their objects are true, in the sense that they are the free manifestation of the sovereign freedom of consciousness. Certainly, there is error in them—but that very error arises from an ecstasy, from an infinite love. It is not a simple accident, a fog emerging from who knows where.

So what does the Yoginī teach on this crucial point?

The awakened vision is here summed up in a magnificent verse. She is very clear: material form is illusion. Let us try to explain it without the bias of preconceptions, with the help of the other teachings from the tradition of the Goddess.

We are indeed led here into an exploration of the illusory magic (*māyā*) of reality as it appears to our senses. This concept invites us to see beyond appearances, to recognize that what is seen (*yad dṛśya-jātaṃ*) is merely an expression of duality (*bheda-vistṛtam*), a fabric woven by Māyā.

Material forms, in all their variety and complexity, fascinate and captivate us, often leading us to believe that they are the ultimate reality. We only pay attention to what is objective, measurable, concrete.

Yet this *chummā* reminds us that these forms are ephemeral, born of separation and distinction, and do not represent the ultimate truth (*a-tāttvikaṃ*) of our being. They are limited (*paricchinnaṃ*), confined within the bounds of space and time, and form only one aspect of existence, governed by the constraints of the human condition (*sattā-avadhi-saṃsṛiti*).

But the essential lies beyond being. Not to remain confined within "what is." Let go.

This insight is not an invitation to reject the material world or to regard it with disdain, but rather to see it with new understanding, to perceive it with the eyes of wisdom. It is about recognizing the beauty and value of material forms while understanding that they are fleeting manifestations of a deeper reality—the infinite consciousness (ecstasy, *ānanda*) that is our true essence.

The aim is not to denigrate, but to dematerialize. Not in the sense of a technoscience that robs the real of its flesh, but as an invitation to release. In a transparent gaze, the world becomes transparent again. The world is not material; matter does not exist. There is only light, an illustration of a mystery seeking to give itself. To live this: simply open the eyes, the senses, remaining clear inside, silent. The meaning of this teaching then becomes as clear as the shapes and colours in that innocent gaze.

Tantra says the world is unreal—in the sense that its solidity is unreal.

Tantra says the world is real—in the sense that it is the sincere expression of the Infinite, of its benevolent, just, and good magic.

In this exploration, we are called to develop a more intimate relationship with the world around us, to see in materiality not a barrier to our spiritual realization, but a path toward it. Each form, each object, then becomes a teacher, revealing the impermanence of existence and guiding us toward a deeper appreciation of the impermanent beauty of life. To see not things, but rainbows.

Not bad illusion, deceiving, but rather wondrous magic.

75 – Reality Is Without Material Form

tad evaṃ bhautikaṃ rūpaṃ nirniketacidañcitam |
vibhāti nityaṃ tattvena nīrūpaṃ paramārthataḥ || 171

Thus, material form
is adorned by consciousness without abode.
In truth, it shines unceasingly,
for ultimately, it is without material form.

This exploration of a world made of light within the Light that is consciousness is here further clarified: "Material form is not material." As one Tantric master says, "Appearances are like rays of light within a luminous crystal."

The objects we perceive, the contours our eyes discern, are in truth translucent projections of this immutable consciousness, dressed in temporary appearances. They let the light through like stained glass. Better still—they shine, they are light, and nothing else. There is no longer any separation between the Light and its radiances. To see visions, to hear sounds, to taste flavours as rays from the sun of "I am." To illuminate things, to be illuminated by them. In just a few moments, this shift in focus has the power to change everything.

Everything now is marked (*añcita*) by the homeless consciousness (*nirniketa*), the consciousness without fixed abode. This fluid awareness clings to nothing because it is everything. It is not limited to an object, a body, or an identity. It is all. Everything bears its signature: transparency, lightness, radiance, silence. It is the Weave on which the magical illusions of material form are embroidered, the undifferentiated ground on which the play of creation unfolds. In this formless reality, all that seems solid, permanent, dissolves in the understanding that nothing is fixed, that everything is a flux of light. And everything becomes transmission, teaching, initiation. It is the Yoginī I see, I hear. It is I, in the deepest sense, perceiving Myself. There is no longer any solitude—everything speaks to me. A secret mystery no one can reveal, for it lies beyond the powers of speech. There is only wonder, in which everything is lost only to be found again in a glory beyond compare.

Material reality—this chair, this table, these mountains, these walls, but also the past, the future that seems to impose itself "by force of circumstances"—all of this is light without weight. Solidity dissolves, but not the form.

This understanding transforms our experience of the world. It teaches us that every moment is an expression of the infinite, that every form is an open doorway to the formless. In the reflection of every object, in the silhouette of every being, we may glimpse the radiance of this formless reality, a reality that unites us in the fabric of universal consciousness. There is no need to rely on any "substance" to alter our state of awareness.

Thus, this *chummā* is not merely an assertion about the absence of form, but a celebration of presence—a recognition of the beauty and mystery that lie at the heart of all existence.

76 – The Result Manifests Without Visible Cause

ahetukatayānantaśākhaṃ yugapad akramāt |
parāparavibhedais tu bāhyāntaravapuḥ sadā || 172

vṛttiprapañcasampattiphalaṃ prollasitaṃ mahat |
anuptaṃ paracidvyomnas tadāścaryāvahaṃ satām || 173

The inner and outer body,
through its continual higher and lower manifestations,
unfolds completely, all at once and without sequence,
with infinite branches and without any (visible) cause.

Then, for the sincere being,
the fruit is the perfection of all expressions and actions—
the great, unexpected result,
the wondrous sky of transcendent consciousness.

Once again: how does one reach awakening? By what concrete method? After all, how could the "fruit" of awakening grow without a "seed" and without the care such a seed demands?

In the continuation of this meditation on the world, this secret, revealed, invites us to contemplate a reality where the fruits of existence unfold beyond the usual logic of cause and effect. In this dimension, the essence of all things—internal and external, higher and lower—blooms with a spontaneity and plenitude that defy ordinary understanding, in a simultaneous act without precedent, bearing witness to a superior order.

This is what Abhinavagupta calls "grace." The only attitude that, from our side, can respond to this free gift is not a specific practice, nor purification, but *love*—a word that never appears in the *Secret Teaching*, and yet is its invisible centre.

Similarly, Utpaladeva (almost certainly initiated into this tradition) tells us he attained awakening "by an extraordinary means" (*kathaṃcit*). Abhinavagupta explains: by an invisible means—not through karma, not through effort. It depends on nothing, on no cause, but on the absolute freedom that is consciousness itself: the universal and intimate explosion of "I am." A spontaneous pouring of light.

An event (*vṛtti*) without cause (*a-hetuka*), without condition, without consideration for purity, preparation, merit, or even state of mind. "On this path without artifice, no yoga is needed: only love," sings Utpaladeva in his *Hymns to Śiva*.

Everything is complete "at once." Not elsewhere, not later, but in the here and now that embraces all pasts and futures—everything is fulfilled. A bubble of silent astonishment bursts outside of time, pure wonder without motive or goal. And always, the undercurrent of love: to feel oneself pulled beyond, taken out of oneself, and remade.

Nothing is lacking. Duality is no longer there to steal the awakening. Thoughts are like thieves entering a house… empty. Nothing to take. Nothing to grasp. Everything is open, outside and inside.

These impressions, rising like a tree with infinite branches (*Ananta-śākhaṃ*), without visible cause, illustrate the mysterious and marvellous nature of creation. No cause, no purpose, no reason for being. An unfolding of Self.

In the atemporal, there is no time to look for meaning. Everything is here. But without interpretation, nothing seems here. Or rather, it is the Yoginī herself who interprets, who comments. The sensations, like intersecting waves, are the Yoginīs of this invisible yet real *maṇḍala*.

The true adept (*satām*), the sincere being who has touched the mystery of existence, sees in this causeless unfolding the Great Fruit (*mahat phalam*), the convergence of all movements (*vṛtti-prapañca-sampatti*) into sublime harmony. For such a one, this fruit is not merely "a result," but the very revelation of the sky of transcendent consciousness (*paracid-vyomna*): a direct experience of wonder, a miraculous flow (*āścaryāvaham*) streaming from the purity that reigns at the source of all life.

In this perspective, the division between inner and outer, higher and lower, vanishes before the realization that all is suffused with the same divine essence. This essence does not arise in response to specific actions or desires, but surges forth from the infinite depth of consciousness, offering those ready to receive it a broader vision of reality.

Nothing to explain. Only to participate. To love.

77 – The Non-Dual Vision Never Perishes

bāhyasthā bhedarūpeyaṃ dṛṣṭir ābhyantarī tathā |
avibhedamayī bhāti nirmalā nirbhramā sadā || 174

asya dṛgyugalasyālam ākṣepakatayā gatiḥ |
tatas tu saṃsthitā tasmād etaduttīrṇalakṣaṇā || 175

kācit tu paramā dṛṣṭir anaṣṭā suvikaśvarā |
nirniketanirātaṅkamahājñānodayātmikā || 176

This vision, which appears as difference
in the outer and likewise in the inner,
shines without division,
always pure and without error.

The experience of these two visions
has the power to project (either bondage or liberation).
Yet it is always present,
and thus surpasses them both.

Indeed, there is a supreme vision—
imperishable, expansively radiant,
rooted in the arising of Great Knowledge,
homeless and fearless.

Let us note, in passing, that these secrets seem to repeat themselves. In truth, they trace a spiral path. Inwardly, there is no repetition. But the essential teachings return like a breath. Like the two wings of a bird, these to-and-fros carry us ever higher into the sky where these words now appear.

This *chummā* brings us back to a question already encountered: is the vision of unity compatible with the experience of duality?

According to Advaita Vedānta, no. If I see unity, I do not see duality. For instance, if I mistake a rope on the ground for a snake in the dark, as long as I believe it is a snake (duality), I do not see the rope (unity). And when I see the rope, the snake vanishes. Hence, experience of duality and realization of unity are incompatible.

But Tantra, as taught by the Goddess, transmits a "vision without vision" that is far more encompassing. It is truly *non-dual*. Vedānta also claims non-duality. But:

1. it defines non-duality as pure unity,
2. unity excludes duality,
3. thus, duality is deemed unreal—ultimately, Vedānta advocates a non-duality that negates the world.

This opens it to the critique of dualism: it posits a split between real and unreal, between consciousness and everything else, even going so far as to claim that action, motion, and life have nothing to do with consciousness!

In contrast, the Yoginī reveals a non-duality that includes the world. Awakening is both unity and duality—two faces of the same reality. Two *dṛṣṭis*, two gazes: one that perceives difference, and one that shines without difference. Yet the Vision itself surpasses and embraces both.

Thus, unity is not a negation of difference. It is their embrace. This is why this supreme vision is "imperishable" (*anaṣṭā*): it does not reject the experience of difference. On the contrary, it recognizes in these outer (world) and inner (mind) differences the spontaneous expansion of the same seeing.

There are many forms of awakening. Many degrees of spiritual insight. And above all, many interpretations. But non-dual Tantra aims at an integral awakening, wholly liberating.

Integral awakening is immersion into the depths of transcendent perception, where the boundaries between inside and outside fade in the light of ultimate knowledge. It is a vision that, despite the apparent duality of outer (*bāhyasthā*) and inner (*ābhyantarī*) experience, remains untouched, eternal, pure (*nirmalā*), and free of confusion (*nirbhramā*).

This non-dual vision (*avibhedamayī*) does not affirm the distinctions of ordinary perception. It is radically different from our usual seeing! It reveals that behind multiplicity lies a continuous field of consciousness that illumines all things with unwavering clarity.

Bondage arises when we are led astray by our own energies, for lack of recognition. Liberation arises when we recognize them as our own.

The living experience (*gati*) of this duality of vision—both binding and liberating—is an invitation to move beyond limited understanding. It can project us beyond contradiction into a spacious "both... and..." that is radiant with generosity.

This supreme vision (*paramā dṛṣṭir*) is not subject to destruction (*anaṣṭā*). It is expansive (*su-vikasvarā*), arising from the great knowledge (*mahā-jñānodayātmikā*), without fixed abode (*nirniketana*) and without fear (*nirātaṅka*). It is the emergence of ultimate wisdom that transcends time and space, a light that guides the mystic through the maze of existence.

Once again, we are the pivot of our destiny. Bondage or freedom arise from the orientation of our attention—of our affection. This is the "great knowledge" (*mahā-jñāna*), the full embrace of all things, which rejects nothing.

78 – She Is Like a Rain of Lotuses

padmavṛṣṭir iva uccais tu patitā saiva nityaśaḥ |
sarvatra viśvavibhavavyāpinī paramādvayā || 177

This (consciousness) falls all at once and forever,
like a rain of lotuses,
filling every corner of the vastness of the universe,
absolutely non-dual.

Here is a striking image: awakening is like a rain of lotuses falling "from above" (*uccaiḥ*). Consciousness pervades everything, non-dual. Beyond all, it flees from nothing. Spacious, open, infinitely trusting.

The Yoginī offers a poetic image of consciousness unfolding through the vast expanse of existence, a manifestation of beauty and grace that transcends duality. In this divine rain, each lotus symbolizes a facet of universal reality, each petal reflects the light of absolute knowledge—*paramādvayā*, non-dual—flooding the universe with its splendour. The lotus also symbolizes purity, detachment—water cannot cling to it. Finally, it represents abundance, the prosperity of the Goddess Lakṣmī.

This image, in which consciousness ceaselessly showers like lotus blossoms, illustrates the infinite generosity of the universe, the Body of consciousness, a constant offering that nourishes and beautifies every dimension of life. These divine lotuses falling from above symbolize the descent of divine wisdom into the manifested world—a blessing that touches and transforms all it meets. Likewise, a silent gaze has this power when it falls upon things.

Tantra calls this lotus-rain the "descent of energy," *śakti-pāta*, the blow of grace that awakens consciousness. This experience is that of *Kuṇḍalinī*, another name for energy or consciousness—not always perceived as a serpent, but also as a suspension of breath, a sensation of exquisite bliss, or a subtle inner vibration. At that moment, the body may collapse like "a tree cut at the root," as described at the beginning of this text.

Once again, this divine shower is a reminder that the splendor of the universe is not confined to grand revelations or miraculous events, but is found in the subtle manifestations of everyday life. It teaches us to see—not beyond appearances, but to see appearances themselves. To perceive the hidden magic within the mundane, to recognize the hand of the infinite in the seemingly ordinary weave of our lives.

Nothing spectacular. Just the absolutely non-dual presence infusing "every corner of the vastness of the universe."

79 – He Is the Destruction of All

yatra akramamahāpātāt sarva graham aśeṣataḥ |
svam jhaṭity ātmavibhavaṃ dehaprāṇādisaṃsthitam ||
178

tathātmīyam anantaṃ tu viṣayākṣādivistaram |
bhāvakṣayamaye bhīmam asparśaparamāmbare || 179

sāmarasyatayā nityaṃ nāśaṃ yāti samantataḥ |
sa ko 'pi niḥsamaśamaḥ śivo 'nantaḥ paro 'vyayaḥ || 180

He is that extraordinary being,
that incomparable peace,
Śiva— infinite, supreme, imperishable—
in whom all grasping is destroyed,
like a fusion,
through that sudden and total fall from above.

All manifestations—
beginning with the body and life-force—
as well as the endless expanse
of the senses and their objects,
are suddenly dissolved
in the terrible and supreme sky
beyond all sensation:
the destruction of phenomena.

Awakening is a coup de grâce—sudden and terrifying—
like the *Great Unexpected* (*mahā-sāhasā*) of the *Vātula-
nātha-sūtras*, for this transmutation is not for the
lukewarm. "He is the destruction of all," says this teaching,

revealing a perspective where Śiva, the transcendent infinity, symbolizes the ultimate principle of dissolution.

This passage, invoking reflection on the ephemeral nature of existence and liberation (*mokṣa*) from the bonds of *saṃsāra*, speaks of the supreme moment in which all that is perceived, every individual manifestation—body (*deha*), life-force (*prāṇa*), and the vast field of sensory experience (*viṣaya-akṣādi*)—is suddenly engulfed in the immensity of the void, in that supreme space beyond even the tactile (*asparśa-parama-ambare*), signalling the annihilation of all phenomena (*bhāva-kṣaya-maye*).

The focus here is on transcendence—on the fact that awakening resembles nothing familiar. It is the true death of the "Old Man," the end of the one who sought, who feared, who separated.

This teaching emphasizes that in the act of total dissolution (*nāśaṃ*), where every aspect of being is absorbed into the immeasurable Śiva, lies a deep harmony (*sāmarasyatayā*), a peace that transcends the dualities of existence. This "destruction" is not an end in itself, but a doorway to a higher understanding—an awakening to a reality that is at once terrifying (*bhīmam*) in its vastness and liberating in its essence.

The sudden and great fall (*akrama-mahā-pāta*), which swallows without remainder the totality of conditioned experience, is a stark reminder of the ultimate nature of Reality. Śiva, in his form as *niḥ-sama-śamaḥ*—without equal, beyond all comparison—embodies creative destruction, the eternal cycle where ending and beginning merge, where death itself opens into unbounded continuity.

A thunderclap of light: this is not a metaphor. It is what remains when the self is gone.

80 – Even Dissolution Is Dissolved

grasanasyāpi saṃhartā mahāsaṃhāravigrahaḥ |
duṣprāpaḥ sarvataḥ sākṣāddhaṭhayuktyānubhūyate || 181

He who dissolves even dissolution itself,
is the embodiment of absolute annihilation,
unattainable in any ordinary way.
Yet he is directly experienced
through the intense practice
(of meditation on space).

Does this teaching not border on nihilism—some hidden cult of emptiness?

No, for it is not Death: it is the death of Death. The end of all endings. This double negation of death is an affirmation of life.

The Yoginī here reveals a profound truth about the ultimate nature of reality. She depicts a force, a movement of consciousness, that not only absorbs forms and dissolves manifestations, but also absorbs the very process of dissolution itself. This is *mahā-saṃhāra,* the great and total dissolution, beyond all grasping—even beyond the grasping of dissolution.

Recall that earlier it was said: "Consciousness devours its own birth." The *Ouroboros* is our life. There is no reason to fear the end, for it contains the beginning. Nor to fear the beginning, for none of this is material—nothing is separate from the Light.

The verse names a practice: *haṭha-yukti*, the forceful means, which here refers specifically to *ākāśa-dhyāna*—meditation on space. In this practice, we do not focus the mind on a point, but instead open to the vastness. One lets the gaze rest gently upon space itself—perhaps on the sky, or on an empty wall—while bringing awareness to the edges of the visual field. The usual contraction of attention dissolves. The mind opens and unifies. The body, too, relaxes and merges with the space. This is *divya-mudrā*, the "divine gesture," and it is a path of total awakening.

To say that "even dissolution is dissolved" is to point to the most radical intimacy with the flow of experience. Consciousness, which projects and withdraws its own manifestations, finally recognizes that it has never left. It dissolves even the idea of dissolution.

Thus, the yogic path is not one of denial, but of deepest acceptance. This ultimate state—*duṣprāpaḥ*, "unattainable" by conventional means—is nonetheless *sākṣād-anubhūta*, "directly experienced," when one surrenders to the openness of consciousness.

The Yoginī guides us—this is her *mission*—to see that everything, even destruction, belongs to the sacred rhythm of being. In this eternal cycle, the end is never final. Each dissolution opens to a new pulse of life.

This is not annihilation. It is the stillness from which all life springs. It is the thunderous silence of *Śiva*, who swallows even the swallowing, who remains when nothing remains. And in that presence, everything lives.

81 – It Is the Unveiled Gift

akṛtrimaḥ paro lābho nirāvaraṇavibhramaḥ |
ayam eva guroḥ samyag āśayo grāsaghasmaraḥ || 182

He is the authentic, supreme gift,
a dazzling without veil or confusion.
This alone is the true intent of the Master:
that ardent, all-consuming engulfment.

This awakened state seems extraordinary—a pure presence, clear, naked, and free. But is it not, in itself, yet another illusion, a veil hiding true reality?

No—because it is received without obstruction. The phenomena themselves are the teaching, the secret. To receive without filtering is to receive without distortion. How? By remaining silent, as if caught in surprise. Or asleep within a heart that watches.

On this path, the true Master is none other than that "ardent engulfment," that total surrender in which the soul dissolves before the immensity of the received gift. Free from veil, free from confusion, truth unveils itself, untouched by constraint or illusion.

There can be no illusion here, for there is no veil, no distance, no intermediary. Where, then, could error slip in?

Awakening is direct (*sākṣāt*). It is not the experience *of* something, not of an object—even a subtle or inner one— separate from the Self. It is the experience of the Self itself: immediate, non-dual. As Descartes said, "I am, I exist" is a truth I cannot doubt. Awakening is not an experience among others—it belongs to a different order altogether.

Meditation becomes reception—an opening to the divine offering that, without artifice or effort, asserts itself with the quiet force of self-evidence. It is in this total receptivity, this space free of every hindrance, that the true Master is found.

This ardent engulfment, where the "I" dissolves, is the ultimate experience of meditation. Here, the gift becomes fire, consuming the last traces of illusion, the final veils of limited perception. In the purifying flame of revelation, only the essential remains: a pure gift, supreme, unconditional.

The authenticity of this teaching lies in its simplicity—in its call for a reception without filters, an unmediated encounter with the truth of our being. To meditate on this gift is to allow oneself to be engulfed by the light of knowledge, to consent to be lost in order to truly be found. It is in this sacred space, purified of all hindrance, that the true instruction resides.

82 – He Is Light Without Light

bāhyāntaragataiḥ sarvair ālokaiḥ parivarjitam |
idam eva mahāsaṃvittejo'nantaṃ sadoditam || 183

Totally devoid of all lights,
whether inner or outer,
this alone is the great light of consciousness,
infinite and always already lit.

He is a light free of external lights. Once again, we notice the constant movement between masculine, feminine, and neuter expressions. "The light that never sets" is a traditional phrase used to describe this spiritual radiance. Abhinavagupta begins his *Bodha-pañcadaśikā*, his *Fifteen Verses on Awakening*, with these lines:

"Light that neither rises nor sets,
Which neither light nor darkness ever touches,
In that one inside where rest both shade and clarity,
(In that Light which itself has never rested).
Substance of all things, it is the ultimate Lord."

A commentator explains:

"Indeed, the absolutely free luminous consciousness is what reveals everything. 'Always manifest,' it does not need any other light to be so—it is self-luminous. Also, it 'never sets'… It remains the same 'in the light'—in the lights of the sun, etc.—and 'in darkness': in the states of madness, coma, and others. Why? Because it is that which reveals itself to those for whom nothing at all appears outwardly anymore. Even the external exists only within

423

(consciousness). The radiance of the sun and the darkness depend upon its existence. Indeed, without this light that is conscious manifestation, absolutely nothing—not even a pot, for example—could appear. Now the 'light' of things such as the sun and darkness rises and sets (in the sense that they are not always manifest). Conscious light, however, is not affected by such appearances and disappearances."

And in his aptly titled *Tantrāloka*, the *Light of the Tantras*, Abhinavagupta writes again:

"Neither the sun, nor the moon,
Nor fire can reveal it.
Neither the sun, nor the moon, nor fire
Could shine at all
Without this Light.
That which reveals itself thus
By itself is consciousness."

This expression—paradoxical, like so many in this teaching—invites us to the pure and simple awakening.

In the intimacy of our inner sanctuary, a revelation dawns: he is light without light. We might take this concept as one of those strange expressions from exotic India. And yet, it is so familiar. What could be more intimate, more familiar than consciousness—the light that illuminates these very words right now? We see, but we do not see the light by which we see.

It is in this non-glow, this renunciation of both inner and outer (*bāhya-antara-gataiḥ*) lights (*ālokaiḥ*), that true splendour reveals itself: the great light of consciousness (*mahā-saṃvit-tejas*). "Great" because it envelops all lights and all darknesses.

What is the light that never sets? What is it that never extinguishes? What never goes absent?

Stripped of all artificial illumination, of every attempt to shine by our own means, this light reveals itself as always already lit (*sadoditam*), perpetually present, active. Beyond the veils of perception, of thought, an inextinguishable light shines, wholly independent of any external source.

This great light of consciousness, evoked in sacred texts (*śāstra*, which are both a prison of lies and the source of awakening), is the very essence of our being—not a passing accident. I cannot lose it, nor can I earn it. There is no need to monitor some inner "consciousness bank account."

Totally devoid of the lights we seek to project or attain, it embodies the vastness of inner space—an infinity where everything is revealed in unprecedented clarity. It alone is absolute security.

In this sacred space of meditation, we awaken to the ultimate truth: the light of consciousness is the only light we need—always already lit.

Awakening is natural. Incredible, but true!

83 – He Is the Total Dissolution of Dissolution

idam eva mahāgrāsagrāsakaṃ kalpanojjhitam |
tīkṣṇātitīkṣṇarūpiṇyā saṃvidā labhyate sphuṭam || 184

This alone is the great devourer of the devourer,
free from all imagination,
clearly revealed
to a consciousness of sharp and ultra-sharp clarity.

Awakening is natural. But it is by no means trivial. Nor is it superfluous or superficial. It is not just another object in our inner décor, not merely an event among others in our lives. No—it is radical, foundational, integral. It is *enthousiasmos*, "having the divine within." It is "the devouring of the devouring".

Zen says: "If you meet the Buddha, kill the Buddha." Destroy that which destroys destruction. Nothing remains—not even the concept of nothing. It is as if one would say, "Look, there's nothing there!" And another would reply, "How lucky you are to be able to see Nothing! I don't see it." This humorous exchange points to a fatal error. To see that there is nothing is not to focus on "the nothing." It is a gaze that sees nothing, a gaze that opens onto... nothing. That doesn't stop. An infinite movement, a perpetual expansion. An untouchable surprise. Don't take it! Don't seize it. Let the sublime, exquisite vision unfold. Everything opposed to possession, to doctrine.

Dissolution itself dissolves. No trace of traces remains. Is this nihilism? No—this is the "clearing of being", a vast opening for everything, more than fullness, for abundance.

In this absence of grasping, the ultimate nature of transformation reveals itself: the Great Devourer of the devouring (*mahā-grāsa-grāsakaṃ*), a force that consumes not only all manifestation but also the very process of dissolution itself. This is not annihilation, but a liberation (*kalpanojjhitam*) from the grip of imagination (*kalpanā*), from those compulsive mental constructions that veil our perception of reality.

Said positively, it is through the sharpness of a supremely keen awarenessness (*tīkṣṇātitīkṣṇa-rūpiṇyā*) that this truth arises—luminous (*sphuṭam*), undeniable. To meditate on this essence of dissolution is to perceive reality beyond the filters of habitual perception, to access a clarity where being reveals itself wholly, without distortion from the mechanized mind.

To dive into the depths of being, where silence speaks, where truth is revealed without veils. I do not dissolve *in order* to attain some fabricated image. I welcome what is, because I do not know. This unknowing is not some trendy spiritual slogan, but a transparency, diaphanous to the light.

84 – He Is the Destruction of Good and Evil

idam eva tu sarvasya bandhamokṣobhayātmanaḥ |
śivāśivasya saṃhantṛ nistaraṅgaṃ nirantaram || 185

This alone is the destroyer of all—
of both bondage and liberation,
the destroyer of good and evil,
unceasing, waveless, utterly untroubled.

Is awakening beyond good and evil? Is there a morality to awakening?

In any case, the awakened one is not troubled by good and bad, *śiva-aśiva*. This includes customs and deeply rooted practices which are in truth immoral, such as excision or slavery. Non-dual Tantra rejects such practices as fabrications born from fear—particularly, the fear of impurity. It is a fear of the body, of its "shameful" parts, of its impure substances.

Part of these fears is not merely cultural. Disgust toward excrement, for instance, may have a genetic origin—though even our genes are the echo of ancestral choices. But much of what we feel and prefer is in fact cultural and therefore subject to deconstruction.

But beware: let us not dismantle what has been patiently built by the wisdom of the body. Today's environmentalism sometimes calls for the destruction of what is natural in our ways of being—indeed, of nature itself—while wanting to preserve "Nature." A strange contradiction!

Tantra leads us to transcendence, not to deconstruction. It acknowledges relativity, but it is not relativistic. Yes, we are entangled in irrational fears. But it is not up to a group of cognitively "deconstructed" militants to decide, behind closed doors, which traditions to undo or what historical events to rewrite. No—true deconstruction must come from a transcendent source. From infinite consciousness. What is born from transpersonal awareness can only be dissolved by that same awareness. If a finite ego tries, its decisions will always carry the scent of its own limits. We know the tree by its fruit.

This *chummā* is not a call to ideological revolution fuelled by self-righteous rage.

Rather, it is an invitation to open to the kind spaciousness of consciousness and let action arise from within. Trust in the *nistaraṅga*—the unshaken, the wave-free—who dissolves, effortlessly, all false oppositions: between good and evil (*śiva-aśiva*), between bondage (*bandha*) and liberation (*mokṣa*). In this space of non-duality, beyond judgment or morality, lies the true key to awakening.

This does not mean embracing political iconoclasm or destroying tradition. "Beyond good and evil" is here to be taken in a precise sense: to go beyond the duality between awakening and non-awakening. Nothing more.

"Let us make a clean slate of the past"? No. Rather: "Let the Good, the Benevolent, happen—here and now."

To meditate on this destruction is to perceive reality not through the lens of conditioned judgment, but in its original purity, free of the mind's agitation. This practice invites us to observe our own habits of judgment, our fixation on good and evil, and to see them for what they

429

are: waves on the surface of an ocean infinitely still. In the depths of being, in the stillness of meditation, we discover a space where these dualities dissolve on their own, revealing the inner peace that is our true nature.

No more seeking an awakening later or elsewhere.

In this felt acceptance (not an idea pasted over sensation), awakening occurs of itself.

The immediate destroyer of good and evil (*śivāśivasya saṃhantṛ*) is still Śiva—the Good. Let us receive this radical teaching as a call to surrender, to relinquish the exhausting war between desire and fear, between our thirst for approval and our dread of rejection. In this surrender, this detachment, we find true freedom—not just from personal limitation, but from the very illusion of separation.

85 – In This Destruction, Even the Dependence on the Absence of Time Is Destroyed

samvitsankalpakalanā svarūpasyāntarasya yaḥ |
akālo nirvikalpākhyasaṃvidrūpas tu bhakṣakaḥ || 186

so'pi yatra kṣayaṃ yāto nairapekṣyapade game |
sarvaśankāvinirmuktas so'yaṃ ko'py avaśiṣyate || 187

The absence of time, which belongs
to the conceptualizing energy within consciousness,
is itself consciousness—called "without concepts",
for it devours those concepts.

But even that (consciousness) is dissolved
in the unattainable state of independence.
What remains is this utterly ineffable being,
free from all fear and all doubt.

But what is it that devours everything so completely? Is it
the mind?
Yet the mind that destroys is also the mind that fabricates.
One form of thought only replaces another.
How then to find peace?

There is nothing to do.

Because the mind, in truth, *is* time—*kāla*. And Time is
none other than God, Śiva, the Goddess, Kālī.
This divine pair is the embodied becoming, moment by
moment.
Their embrace is the source of all that I experience, at
every breath.

In the sanctuary of intimacy with one's own experience,
the deep nature of Time—and its absence (*akāla*)—is
revealed as nothing more than a thought, an artifact of the
conceptualizing movement (*saṃvit-saṅkalpa-kalanā*) of
consciousness.
To live fully in Time is to dissolve Time, to kill Death
(*mṛtyu*), to put an end to becoming.
Not as a total erasure, but as a beginning—an opening
into another life, transformed.

The fragmenting energy of concepts within
consciousness—what we call "mind"—creates the
illusion of segmented time, a stream that drags us away
from the Real.

To meditate on this fragmentation is to see how consciousness, in naming itself "concept-free" (*nirvikalpākhya*), swallows the very ideas that bind it to time.

Indeed, God has all names, but "Without Dilemma" is His truest name—His supreme power.

The mind is nothing but consciousness playing the game of fragmentation.
The Sanskrit word *kalā* or *kalanā* refers also to *art*, to the creative play of manifestation.
And by shifting attention to the aspect of dissolution, mind returns to its source: the ecstasy of awareness, the love that unites.

This meditative journey leads to the understanding that even the so-called absence of time (*akāla*) is consumed in the fire of pure awareness.
In that state of total presence, where no concepts remain, the very duality of time and timelessness is transcended.

What remains (*avaśiṣyate*) is the ineffable—*kaḥ api*, "someone" beyond naming, beyond knowing—
free of all fear (*sarva-śaṅkā-vinirmuktaḥ*), of all holding.

I look at the mind, and the fear of the mind dissolves.

What remains is the Real—gentle, pure, utterly trustworthy.
I can let go of everything, without looking back.

To be embraced by this Reality is to enter a freedom beyond imagination—
a state of independence (*nairapekṣya*), inaccessible through ordinary effort, practice, or knowing…

Simply because it is too close. Too simple. Too easy.

There, beyond every idea of time or timelessness,
is the true liberation.
A release from the subtle slavery of our own lukewarm
half-measures.

86 – This Is the Destruction of Vision

ayam eva tu dṛk-śakteḥ sarvasyā nāśa ucyate |
niḥsaṅketa-parajñāna-rūpo niravadhiḥ mahān || 188

This alone is called
the destruction of all powers of perception;
it is the supreme knowledge without symbols or
teachings,
the great, limitless being.

Do we not possess too much? Is our so-called consumer
society not excessive in its very nature?
Must the old Promethean man, always craving spectacle,
die in order to awaken to the real world—the one from
which our screens ceaselessly estrange us?

This *chummā*, as radical as the ones before, sheds light on
that question.

Dṛk-śakti, the power of perception, refers to the ability to
see—not only with physical eyes, but with the inner eye,
the   mind.
Yet the eyes alone do not see. Nor does the mind, for

"thoughts," the words echoing in our heads, lack the power to   see.
They are seen. They are not *cit* (consciousness), but objects *of* consciousness—*jaḍa*, inert in themselves.

Indeed, this "power of vision" cannot be consciousness itself, for that would mean consciousness is destroyed—and who would then be aware of its destruction?
This refers, rather, to the mental and sensory faculties. In Tantric philosophy, these faculties are sustained by consciousness itself.
Their "destruction" (*nāśa*) is a return to the source—beyond the duality of seer and seen.

In Advaita Vedānta, this would correspond to the dissolution of *avidyā* (ignorance), which maintains the sense of separation.
But whereas Vedānta sees the world, body, and mind dissolve into the light of knowledge, Tantra speaks of an alchemical path of transmutation.
This annihilation recalls the mystic Christian "night of the soul," where the ego must be emptied to welcome the divine.
It echoes Plotinus' return to the One, where all distinctions vanish. It may be likened to a knowing beyond all representation.

Niravadhi evokes boundlessness—the absence of all limitation. This resonates with the idea of *Anuttara* in the Trika:
the ultimate Reality, transcending all measure, yet immanent in every limit, like stone penetrated by space.
Similarly, this verse echoes contemporary accounts of awakening: a boundless space where time and dimension dissolve.

The term *mahān*, frequent in this tradition, means greatness or vastness—like space, it conveys both completeness and openness.
It's not quantitative magnitude, but a qualitative vastness—a vision that annihilates limited vision.
Mahā also signifies the plenitude of the Self, transmuting poisons into growth.
Mystic writers like John of the Cross describe this union with God as a light so vast it surpasses all comprehension.

This *chummā* and its verse describe a transcendent awakening in which individual consciousness—conditioned by objects and concepts—dissolves into infinitude.
"Destruction of all perceptive powers" is not annihilation, but purification—a prelude to the transfiguration of our True Face.
Conditioned perception fades, revealing a presence that is absolutely simple and infinitely rich.

We may even draw parallels to other traditions.
This state resembles the *nirbīja-samādhi* of the *Yoga Sūtras*, where the mind dissolves into infinite silence.
It echoes the Buddhist notion of *śūnyatā* (emptiness)—not as nothingness, but as the absence of mental fabrications, a natural state.
Even modern physics offers analogies, imagining consciousness as a fundamental field, beyond material manifestations.

Yet above all, this teaching is a song—a hymn to the infinite.
The lover transcends all perceptions to merge into the unbounded.
This is not only a transcendence of religious concepts, but

of all forms of identification.
The "great absence of limits" is both a void and a
fullness, a silence and a music, an ending and a
beginning.

This is the heart of *Kālī-krama*—the radical path to the
Absolute.

To live this destruction of vision is to embrace a state of
consciousness where the senses no longer arbitrate our
reality.
It is to discover a realm where knowledge is not acquired,
but revealed—
where truth unveils itself in its original purity, free from
all mental or sensory construction.

We return to a sacred sobriety, nourished by a true
Nothing—
rather than stuffing ourselves with hollow things.

87 – This Is the Ascending Progress

ādyonmeṣaparākoṭivimarśa roha ucyate |
tatraiva caraṇaṃ cārasthito'yaṃ nityanirmalaḥ || 189

The realization of the ultimate summit
of the original awakening
is called "ascension".
That alone is the true progress,
a path established in purity, eternal and spotless.

But how can we be sure that we won't fall back into mental chatter?

The Yoginī distinguishes between illusory progress—thus unstable—and the real ascent, which is a transcendence of movement itself:
a passage into a higher order, as Pascal might say.
This turning point is referred to in the Yoginī's own language as *rūha*, close to the Sanskrit *roha*, meaning "ascent" or "growth."

And why can we be certain we won't fall again?
Because this awakening (*unmeṣa*) is *primordial* (*ādya*).
It may appear to occur at a specific moment, but in truth, it is not an event *in* time.
Awakening does not arrive within time—it is time that flows from it, from that timeless transparency.
In other words, awakening is retroactive: it erases the entire non-awakened past.
It is therefore *permanent* (*nitya*) in that sense.

This is the very essence of true spiritual progress:
the realization that awakening is original, primordial.
"I am always already awake."
It is the transcendent Beginning, the first and the last, the
Absolute Ancestor.
This certainty is the fire of ascension—it is Kuṇḍalinī.

This *ascension* is not an external quest,
but an instantaneous journey into the recognition of our
true nature.
Not a gradual climb, but a sudden irruption—like a
declaration of love.
In this ascent lies true progress,
a refinement that, far from being marked by steps or
trials,
is a soaring movement into the highest, the immaculate,
the eternal.

Awakening is the recognition of eternal awakening.

88 – One Acts Without Moving

ittham nijāt parād rūpān niṣkampaś ceṣṭate punaḥ |
sarvaṃ karma sadā kurvan sarvatra samadarśanaḥ || 190

Thus, from one's own supreme essence,
one acts again,
yet without trembling,
doing all actions at all times,
with equal vision in all things.

Yet is this "ascension" not a form of escape? A kind of quietism in which we retreat into laziness, sheltered from our responsibilities?

Kṛṣṇa replies: "I do nothing, and yet I act constantly."
Now, Kṛṣṇa, the celebrated incarnation of Viṣṇu, is also regarded by the yoginīs and yogis of the oral tradition of the Goddess Kālī as an embodiment of the Goddess Herself.
It is, then, the Goddess who declares that She does everything while doing nothing.

On this subject, we might note that the tradition of the Goddess is closely linked to that of Viṣṇu. The latter is often seen—sometimes rightly—as rather puritanical. Yet bridges exist. The Goddess is sometimes identified with Lakṣmī, the goddess of fortune and Viṣṇu's consort. In the *Rāja-tantra*, the primordial text of the Goddess tradition, her consort, the embodiment of Bhairava-Śiva, is Narasiṃha—the Man-Lion—whose symbolism in relation to the breath yoga is profound, as noted earlier in the teaching on the pause between breaths.

Indeed, Narasiṃha embodies this interval and its power, being neither man nor lion.
The legend says he was so powerful he had to practice the Yoga of the Interval to avoid destroying the universe!

In any case, within the stillness where time seems suspended, a revelation unfolds: to act without moving.
This meditation, disarmingly simple, leads us to a deep understanding of action rooted in stillness, of engagement in the world that flows from an unshakable inner presence.

At the heart of silence, action unfolds, arising directly from our supreme essence (*nijāt*).
Without trembling (*niṣkampaḥ*), without superfluous motion, we act again (*ceṣṭate punaḥ*), but in a way that transcends the duality of activity and inactivity.
It is in this integrity, in this grounding in our true being, that the key to authentic worldly engagement lies.

Ultimately, this action arising from non-action is Vibration—it is the Heart of the Yoginī, but on the individual scale.
This principle is so central that it lends its name to the author of the *Illumination*, Niṣkriyānandanātha—"master of the bliss of non-action" or *non-doing*.
To live this inner trembling that radiates into the gestures of our body is to discover a dimension of being in which every gesture, every word, every thought is steeped in profound awareness.

To do all things, all the time (*sarvaṃ karma sadā kurvan*), not from driven effort or pursuit of a goal, but as the natural expression of our divine nature, reflects a way of being in the world—a presence that acts without being disturbed by the fluctuations of life.

It is action which, though immersed in the ceaseless flow
of the world, remains anchored in inner peace.

Action is not a disruption of our stillness, but an
extension of our stillness into the world.
With a vision equal in all things (*sarvatra
samadarśanaḥ*), we learn to act not in reaction to what
surrounds us, but in response to an inner call,
an impulse arising from our deep connection with all that
is.

In the *Bhagavad-gītā*, Kṛṣṇa defines the state of yoga as a
state of equanimity—not through numbness, but through
a gesture of inclusive transcendence.
Everything becomes my body. Acting and not acting are
like my inhalation and exhalation.

By listening to the interval—the source of opposite
states—we realize that to act without moving is not a
contradiction, but a deep harmony:
it is to live fully, to act with integrity, while remaining
firmly rooted in the stillness of our essence.

89 – Such Is the Unobstructed Gesture

eṣā sthitā mahāmudrā kulākulakalojjhitā |
aniruddhā sadā sarvaiḥ saṃvidunmeṣavibhramaiḥ || 191

This is the great gesture
free from the division between "transcendent" and
"immanent".
It is never obstructed by any of the confusions
that arise from the expansions of consciousness.

In Tantric Buddhism, the "great gesture" (*mahā-mudrā*)
refers to the spiritual realization that arises from a total
relaxation of body and mind.
One master tells us: "The mind is like a stubborn camel!
The more you try to control it, the more it rebels. But if
you let it go, it settles down."
Likewise, in the tradition of Kashmir, Abhinavagupta
notes: "The mind, in this tradition of the Goddess, is a
ship that sails with a gentle breeze."
Space reveals itself through non-violence with oneself—
with one's sensations and reactions. And it is then, in that
clear sky, that the saving sun bursts forth with force
(*haṭha*).

Mahāmudrā is the Great Gesture, the complete attitude
already hinted at in the previous *chummā*.
It is the immense power of unobstructed being—precisely
because we do not seek to obstruct our powers, the
Yoginīs of our personal *maṇḍala*, our five senses and our
mind.
We let them be free. We do not block the "rays of the sun
of consciousness," to use the symbolic language of the

Yoginī.
If I do not block my mind, my mind does not block me. If
I place no obstacles in the path of my sensations, my
sensations will not become obstacles. If I honour my
energies, they honour me.

At the heart of vibrant silence unfolds the Great Gesture
(*mahāmudrā*), expression of ultimate freedom.
This gesture, which transcends the duality of
"transcendent" and "immanent" (*kulākula*), is an
invitation to recognize within ourselves the presence of a
consciousness that is bound by no category, no definition.
To meditate on this gesture without hindrance is to
explore a space where action is not constrained by
opposites, where our being manifests in its wholeness,
free from obstruction.

This *mudrā*, this gesture, is never hindered (*aniruddhā*)
by any confusion (*vibhrama*) arising from the blossoming
of consciousness (*saṃvid-unmeṣa*).
Flowers bloom on the meadow without blocking the
movements of the air.
It is in this absence of limitation, in this state of flow, that
its power lies—a capacity to remain in unshakable clarity,
even in the heart of life's turbulence.

90 – Such Is the Relationship Beyond Words

sarvottīrṇasvarūpeṇa saha nityam ayaṃ sthitaḥ |
sāmarasyasvabhāvo 'sau sambandho vāgvivarjitaḥ || 192

He is forever present,
united with his transcendent essence.

*This relationship is of the nature of fusion,
a connection beyond speech.*

We listen to these *chummās*, these symbolic utterances, and sense within them a kind of refrain. Not a senseless repetition, but a cycle. These words return to the same themes, but from ever-changing perspectives. In the earlier series, there was also talk of *mantra*, *mudrā*, action, and relation. But the *Cercle des Yoginīs* then described the path—the Yoga of the Goddess as a way of awakening. Here, it is perhaps full awakening that is being suggested. Indeed, it is no longer a "relation without relation," but a "relation unspeakable," inexpressible, that cannot be stated—a relation "beyond words." He, God, is that ineffable connection, the space that links all, while being beyond all. His own nature is *fusion* (*sāmarasya*).

We find ourselves, lost far away in the sacred space of silence, where words lose their hold. And so, we plunge into the contemplation of an intimate union with our true essence—a communion that transcends language, where presence becomes the only expression. No more separation between word and meaning. Only consciousness can "speak" consciousness. Only experience can express experience.

This relation, which is not constructed from words or concepts, is an expression of deep harmony (*sāmarasya*), of the natural fusion of our being with the All. To meditate on this relationship beyond speech is to discover a dimension of existence where communication surpasses language, where understanding is instantaneous and total, unmediated by the constructions of the mind.

This connection (*saṃbandha*) is characterized by the absence of speech (*vāg-vivarjitaḥ*)—not because words are insufficient, but because in that space of deep connection, they become unnecessary. It is within silence that the purest truth resides, a truth not conveyed through statements, but through being itself—through presence that needs no translation. Silence speaks to silence. The Yoginī addresses the Yoginī within me. And all else comes to a halt, as at the dawn of the world. And the true transmission begins, because it cannot be spoken.

As Paul Claudel reminded us: "All that can be taught is not worth learning."

91 – Such Is the Uncreated Grace

ayaṃ prasādaḥ paramo bhāto nityaṃ svarūpataḥ |
avṛttānantamahimā sarvākhyānavivarjitaḥ || 193

This is the supreme grace,
eternally appearing from our very own essence,
whose majesty is infinite and uncreated,
devoid of any story.

We have seen that no practice can attain this "stateless state" that cannot even be described. But then, how can one live this experience? How did Niṣkriya Ānanda, the author or transmitter of this teaching, live it?

The Yoginī answers: "through grace." But doesn't this imply that the teaching itself is useless? That the practices

445

serve no purpose? Then why have a tradition at all, if there is nothing to transmit?

To understand the logic of the tradition of the Ineffable, of the Goddess Anākhyā, one must first grasp that this state of awakening is nothing other than consciousness recognizing itself, by itself, "to the very tips of the nails," into my flesh, here and now. But consciousness is freedom. It depends on nothing; all depends on it. It is limitless power, above the laws of nature, even beyond the rules of logic.

It "can do what is absolutely impossible" (*ati-durghaṭa-kārī*). When it manifests as world and, within that world, identifies itself with particular bodies, it forgets itself. And no external cause pushes it to act thus. There is no matter, no energy, no time, no space, no past, no laws, no logic outside of it.

All these *data* are its Gift. Even blindness is encompassed in its play, for consciousness is the power to appear as this and also as that. This forgetting of self has no cause other than the free desire of consciousness. Therefore, is it not logical to accept that, likewise, consciousness cannot liberate itself, return to itself, except by itself? "The Sovereign of the gods enslaves himself. He liberates himself. Let him observe himself!" says Śiva in a tantra.

To invoke grace, then, is not to appeal to an arbitrary miracle. It is:

1. to remember that awakening is free (grace means gratuity), unrelated to causes and conditions, because it is the free gift of a freedom; and
2. to invite us to look at ourselves, to plunge our gaze, our attention, toward self, toward consciousness.

Let us not misunderstand this call to grace: it does not invite us to throw in the towel, waiting for some operation of the Holy Spirit, but encourages us to convert ourselves to the influence of the Holy Spirit, to orient ourselves toward the vacant attitude that welcomes its wholly interior operation.

This "favour" which answers our silent fervour is not the result of a tyrant's whim, but flows from the uncreated nature of consciousness, our essence always already present, closer to us than our most intimate thoughts. It is not some incomprehensible decision, but the very nature of the Ineffable presence. Its majesty is infinite, for it is "uncreated." It is not reducible to any "created" logic, belonging to the plane of duality, to the nature of things. It occurs without arriving, like an event. At bottom, to awaken is to join the awakening always already begun. Likewise, to recite a *mantra* is to plunge into the *mantra* that has always vibrated deep within our flesh.

Thus, is revealed the supreme grace (*prasādaḥ paramo*), a Light of love emanating eternally from our own essence (*nityaṃ svarūpataḥ*). This grace, unmade, unconditioned by actions, practices, merits, or superficial desires, is the expression of deep unity with the All and beyond the All (*Mahā-kaula*).

To meditate on this uncreated grace, to realize it (*vimarśa*), is to recognize within ourselves a source of light and peace that depends on no deed, no external acquisition, because it gives itself as the Absolute Source of all acts, of all events. It doesn't matter "where I am." What matters is realizing that all these states come and go like luminous waves in the luminous space of infinite consciousness. Not a single hair stirs that is not the Desire, the Sovereign absolute.

This grace, whose majesty is infinite and uncreated (*avṛttā-ananta-mahimā*), lies beyond the limits of our intellectual grasp. It is the manifestation of the infinite in our finite existence, a reminder that beyond all forms and names resides an indescribable reality, a Presence that transcends anything to which one could give a name. It is its own Name, that gentle trembling heard as the unspoken pulse: "I... I... I..."

92 – For This Teaching Is Not Limited

upadeśo hy aniyataḥ sandehābhāvalakṣaṇaḥ |
sāśrayānāśrayapadadvandvabhedair anāvṛtaḥ || 194

For the teaching is not limited,
marked by the absence of doubt.
It is unconditioned by the dilemmas of "with support"
and "without support".

But again, how can one be certain that this experience is authentic? Is it not a subtle illusion?

That is impossible, because consciousness escapes the realm of duality. It has no counterpart. There exists, in fact, no "non-consciousness" that would be on the same plane as consciousness. Certainly, there are states of unconsciousness, but these states are in reality objects manifested by consciousness, to consciousness—luminous forms within the Light. "I now become aware that I was unconscious." "Now"... But consciousness is always in the present! It is the very Presence that presents itself in everything.

And the fact of having been unconscious is an object for consciousness, a content of experience, a "thing" that appeared and then vanished. But consciousness is always present *in act*, always upright (*sadā uditā*).

Without this, who would be aware of this supposed unconsciousness? And without consciousness, how could we know that unconsciousness even occurred? The absence of consciousness is only possible in its own bubbling forth. Unconsciousness is simply consciousness that, in its absolute freedom, manifests itself to itself as the absence of itself.

The word "consciousness," just like the pronoun "I" when it does not designate the body or the mind, refers directly to the infinite. It is not a concept (*vikalpa*) that posits a meaning by excluding something else. No, for consciousness excludes nothing, and nothing can exclude it. Opposites are manifested by it and embraced within it. Therefore, they do not affect it. If they were able to block consciousness, they would disappear.

Thus, consciousness has no opposite, no contrary. It does not belong to the plane of duality. It is not a concept or fabrication. It is not an option among others. Doubt (*vikalpa* also, or *sandeha*) is impossible—not because one clings to an idea, but because there is no alternative. Or rather, alternatives themselves exist only within and by consciousness. Therefore, it is absolutely certain. In this sense, this teaching is "not limited" by the laws of reason, which apply only to the plane of duality.

In the vastness of silence, where the voices of the external world fade, a subtle truth rises: the teaching is not limited (*aniyata-upadeśa*). Only silence cannot go astray, nor lead others astray. The Master of Silence (*Mauni-nātha*) is the true source of the living teaching. He is the Master-appearance, the flow of appearances, instant after instant. "It is not limited" means it is not rigid, not dogmatic. It is the book of daily life. "In the laundry, the ecstasy": an unparalleled softener!

At the heart of an uncompromising yet tender interiority is revealed the essence of an unlimited teaching, free of rules (*upadeśo hy aniyataḥ*), a beacon that guides without being clouded by the shadows of doubt (*sandeha-abhāva-lakṣaṇaḥ*). This guidance, liberated from the prison of hesitation, is an odyssey of unveiling where truth emerges with unwavering clarity.

I know nothing, yet I suffer no uncertainty. To meditate on this nature so pointed out is to recognize within ourselves a source of light that illuminates without faltering, that orients without imposing any direction.

93 – The Submarine Fire Consumes the Body

nānāvṛttisamullāsaḥ pratyāvṛttitayā sadā |
nigīryate tadā akāyakaraṇo vāḍavaḥ smṛtaḥ || 195

When all manifestation, with its various operations,
is forever consumed in a movement of return (to the
Source),
then the tradition speaks of the Submarine Fire,
which makes the body disappear.

It is clear that this teaching is powerful in its movement of transcendence. Everywhere, it speaks of emptiness, ascent, surpassing, of "leaping beyond"—all expressed through negations: non-action, non-pleasure, non-abiding... And this is all the more striking since the context is that of a tantric tradition that otherwise prescribes the most transgressive practices.

Orgies, sexual yoga, feasts, alcohol, blood... Clearly, this rich symbolism—intended to embody non-duality in a non-dual practice, thus beyond purity and impurity, thus transgressive—is something quite other than what Tantra is usually imagined to be, and different even from the way Tantra was imagined in the Indian golden age of Tantra. This teaching is, in many respects, far removed from the spirit of traditional India.

There is therefore transcendence. All is swallowed, dissolved, reabsorbed. The body itself, the "ordinary" body, is consumed by the *Submarine Fire*. This Fire is a powerful symbol of Indian mythology (which, from the traditional Indian point of view, belongs to real history), taken up by non-dual Tantra.

The *Submarine Fire* is a kind of lava located at the base of the Earth. To understand this clearly, one must know that the "world," according to India in general and Tantra in particular, is a vast golden sphere. Inside it, all planes of existence are contained.

There is an infinite number of such "spheres" or "eggs of Brahmā," as they are called. In each sphere—that is, in each world—the Trika tradition, a branch of non-dual Tantra related to the Kālī-krama, describes 118 planes. Ours is located in the middle tier. Above are the heavens, then divine realms, a series of paradises of varying duration. Below lie the hells, a bit like in Dante's vision. And at the very bottom lies a vast ocean.

And beneath that sea, a Fire burns. This Fire is in fact an incarnation of Śiva—of God, then—as is everything else. It is called *Kāla-agni-rudra*, "Rudra, the Fire of Time," because it burns from the beginning of a cosmic cycle, slowly consuming the ocean at the base of the world over millions of years. Eventually, it gains such power that it engulfs the entire world above it, because it is the nature of fire to rise. That is the end of the world, until the next Great Cycle.

This Fire is thus the action of Time itself. According to India, Time is this cosmic power that "cooks" beings and things. Becoming itself is a kind of cooking, and our world is a great golden cauldron. Its opposite is Water, the liquid element. The Sun is the celestial counterpart of this subterranean Fire.

During each annual cycle, it evaporates the lunar nectar by heating it. When the Moon, the celestial and luminous incarnation of the element Water and of coolness, predominates in this cosmic combat, it is the cool seasons. When the Sun prevails, we have the burning heat of summer.

Now, this world is also a giant organism, a macrocosm. So everything that happens in it also happens in the microcosm, in our own body. The equivalent of the Sun is the digestive fire that "cooks" food, sublimating it into vital essence, *ojas*. The equivalent of the element Fire in the body is blood, which is red and warm.

And *Rudra*, the Fire that is Time—where is He in our body? He is the energy of the *Kuṇḍalinī*, lodged at the base of the body. Ordinarily, she lies dormant, only half active. Her heat is felt diffusely and gradually, outside of sudden surges like sexual desire. But she slowly consumes the body. And when fully awakened, the body is entirely sublimated into an immensity of consciousness.

The elements Water and Earth are reduced to steam and ashes swept away by the elements Air and Fire. This body, consumed by the fire of the awakened soul, becomes a body of light—immortal but immaterial. That is what this verse describes.

How does this happen? Through a "movement of return," through an act of turning consciousness back toward itself. Once again, we must acknowledge that consciousness awakens itself by itself. Swept up in its free and natural expansion, it dematerializes. Death is here seen as the ultimate purification. In the case of an ordinary death, it is only the end of one cycle, a death before a rebirth conditioned by past actions, *karma*.

But in the case of this "spiritual death" through a shift of attention back to self, death is a shift to another plane of being—like the resurrection of the body in Christianity. From the mortal body to the body of glory.

In deep contemplation, like a dawn, the *Submarine Fire* becomes an image of transformation. This fire, symbolizing a primordial force, consumes all manifestation (*nānā-vṛtti-samullāsaḥ*) with its various operations, in a movement of return to essence, a turning toward the Self (*praty-āvṛttitayā sadā*).

This process of dissolution is not a definitive end, but a return to the Source, where the ephemeral is absorbed into the eternal, where formal identity dissolves into the formless immensity.

94 – Such is the Practice of the Gesture of Space

ayam eva sadā purvo heyādeyakramojjhitaḥ |
nirdhāmadhāmavibhavaḥ khamudrābhyāsa ucyate || 196

This (consciousness), always already present,
free from the cycles of "yes" and "no",
is the wealth of the domain beyond all domains,
called "the practice of the Gesture of Space."

But what does one live on, when one no longer lives on anything?

One lives from a practice. Yes, there is indeed a kind of *exercise* (*abhyāsa*) in this void: the Gesture of Space— recognizing this consciousness that is always already present at the closest, a presence that remains unchanged, unaffected by the cycles of rejection and acquisition (*heyādeya-kramojjhitaḥ*).

This practice, far from being a physical discipline, is an immersion into the inner space that reflects both the outer (the world) and the inner (the mind), an exploration of the abundant expanse of the domain beyond all domains (*nirdhāma-dhāma-vibhavaḥ*), the realm that "is not of this world," where the distinction between self and universe fades, where duality dissolves into the unity of consciousness. Only this Gesture of Space can reach it, in a transfer that takes no longer than the flash of an awakened instant.

This exercise consists in continually turning attention toward space. No longer feeling oneself *in* space, but as space itself—space that contains and penetrates everything. More precisely, one practices by placing attention on the space surrounding the skin. The tactile sensations gradually stretch into space, and space, in turn, slowly penetrates the body. This increasingly intimate union between body and space is the Yoga described by Niṣkriyānanda in his *Poem of the Kālī Tradition*, in fifty verses (not translated in this book).

This sensation of tactile transparency is cultivated, according to tradition, through a precise contemplative practice: one sits facing the blue sky or any vast expanse, eyes and mouth open. All these openings resonate with one another, and bodily awareness explodes. Such is the Gesture of the Secret, the secret of the Yoginīs, hidden in all the tantras, but which only ardent practice can truly reveal. This is the *Gesture of Wonder* (*vismaya-mudrā*), in which awakening becomes inevitable.

Everything described here then arises spontaneously, in spite of oneself. No more effort is needed; everything transmutes, as if a powerful lamp—or better, a powerful sun—were being lit inside the body, yearning to merge with space. This teaching thus also serves as support for this essential practice. A companion, a poetic source of inspiration—for only this kind of speech, so potent, still has its place in a world that challenges and unravels all landmarks.

95 – He Becomes Like a Jackal

sṛgālo'nāśam āyāti pratyāvṛttyavalokanāt |
yathā tatheha paramāṃ niruttaracitiṃ sadā || 197

samālokya haṭhād dehavistāro layam āgataḥ |
jambukīkaraṇākhyo saukhyātaḥ ko'py akramakramaḥ ||
198

A jackal escapes death
because it looks back.
In the same way, by turning the gaze inward,
one perpetually sees the supreme, absolute
consciousness.
Then, the extension of the body dissolves by force.
This blissful, extraordinary evolution without evolution
is called "becoming a jackal."

Here is a striking image: imitate the jackal to escape death. The jackal has been a familiar animal to our ancestors for at least several millennia. We know that the Indo-Europeans, or Yamnayas, lived in the plains of what is now Ukraine. The jackal, however, is primarily a scavenger. In India, it roams the cremation grounds, where corpses are burned. It is thus considered especially impure. It becomes a powerful symbol of the transcendence of the duality between pure and impure, like everything that lives and moves in the cremation grounds. Like the Goddess, it fears nothing repulsive.

This place, comparable to our legends of witches in graveyards, is the birthplace of non-dual Tantra, and in particular, of the revelation of the Goddess Kālī. In fact, we know of two sites of this supernatural revelation: the first in the cremation field of Karavīra in present-day Pakistan, near the city of Mingora in the Swat Valley, about a month's walk from the Kashmir Valley.

The second is in Andhra, a region in southern India, in a cremation field called the Glorious Mountain, Śrīśaila. All these secrets thus come from these terrifying sanctuaries in the eyes of the profane, haunted by zombies, ghosts, and jackals.

The jackal, on the other hand, fears humans. Attracted by the dead and frightened of the living, it is vigilant and extremely cunning, like the fox. In particular, it is reputed to "look back," always on guard. The expression used to describe this gesture has a double meaning. The jackal looks back just as the yogi looks toward the Self—it turns its gaze back to the source of vision, to itself, to the Goddess. When consciousness thus turns toward itself, directly, it is said to awaken.

When consciousness—*I*—sees itself completely, the mortal body entirely dissolves. Since the body is the "skeleton" that is Time—that is, Death—to be freed from the body is to escape the jaws of Death. It is therefore bliss, to live in ease (*sukha*).

Turn around, contemplate forever the dynamic, ultimate, absolute consciousness. This is progress without progress: a progress, because one is liberated from the empire of Death; yet not a progress, because in truth we are consciousness itself—and Empress Consciousness has never been under the empire of anything or anyone.

96 – When Individuality Is Devoured, He Becomes the Self

āṇavādimalair vyāpto dehādigrahasaṃśrayāt |
ātmā tadgrāsa uditaḥ parimityaparikṣayāt || 199

He is pervaded
by the impurities of the body and others,
for he appropriates them
as supports.
When these are devoured,
he appears as the Self,
because all limits
are completely annihilated.

According to the basic theology of dualistic Tantra, we are tainted by three toxins: karma, matter, and a subtle substance that veils our conscious soul, preventing it from revealing itself in the full extent of its powers of knowledge and action.

Non-dualistic Tantra interprets these pollutants differently:

1. Karma is simply the belief that our actions have good or bad consequences, based on the notions of pure and impure; this arises from
2. The belief that there is an external reality independent of consciousness; and that belief, in turn, stems from
3. The subtle toxin *āṇava*, which is nothing but the impression that we are incomplete, lacking.

These defilements are therefore not substances, but beliefs. Only knowledge, spiritual awakening, can eradicate them. In our ordinary, non-awakened state, our life is pervaded by the impurities of the belief in lack and its derivatives, conditioned by an erroneous identification with these temporary supports. This appropriation (*graha*—the grasping that seizes us) of material and transient aspects of existence, beginning with the body, maintains us in an illusion of individuality, a delusion of separation from the Whole, from the Self.

We are thus led to dive into the consciousness that already devours the body as Time. To push impermanence to its limit. To activate Time in an "accelerated cooking" (*haṭha-pāka*), a fire of consciousness that will hasten the natural process of karmic evolution. In this sense, the entire practice of the Yoga of the Goddess is a karmic acceleration under the fire of love. Instead of experiencing impermanence as a calamity, we experience it as freedom, purification, and creativity. Instead of resisting the current, we flow with it.

We are thus initiated into the recognition of a deep transformation process, where what is considered as "me" and "mine" is devoured (*grāsa*), consumed in the fire of realization. In this consummation, the limits imposed by our identification with form and impurity are completely annihilated, thereby revealing the splendour of the Self— unaltered light shining beyond the veils of ignorance.

97 – Everything Is Taken Away

samastaharaṇād vāraḥ sa eveha gataḥ svataḥ |
nirīho'yaṃ akathyas tu sadasadbhramavarjitaḥ || 200

When everything is taken away,
this limit (of individuality)
fades spontaneously, in this very life.
But this absence of desire cannot be taught,
(for) it is free from the delusion of "yes" and "no."

In what sense is individuality a limitation?
Is individuality an obstacle that disappears upon
awakening?
But if so, how can an awakened being live without
individuality? And how can awakened beings even exist?

When everything is taken away (*samasta-haraṇād*), when
every attachment, every desire, and the very notion of ego
are dissolved, the limit (*vāraḥ*) of individuality fades of
itself (*svataḥ*), in this very life (*iha*).
This state of absence—from the separated, solidified
self—is a revelation of unimaginable freedom, a clarity of
consciousness in which one lives in union (*yoga*),
undivided, free from the illusions that veil the true nature
of being.
Note that *Hara*, "the Remover," is one of the names of
Śiva.

However, this absence of desire (*nirīho'yam*), this inner
peace that transcends both craving and aversion, cannot
be taught (*akathyas*).
It emerges from an inner realization, a profound direct

seeing that cannot be transmitted through words.
This truth is free from the errors of "it is" and "it is not" (*sad-asad-bhrama-varjitaḥ*)—it transcends the dualities that structure our habitual perception of reality.

There is no gross practice capable of dissolving this limitation (*vāraḥ*). It is too subtle.
According to Tantra, this vague sense of lack (the separate self) exists prior to the mind and is the very source of the mind.
The mind cannot therefore eradicate it.
To lift this most intimate veil, only the direct intuition of oneself, of the Self, is effective.
Philosophy may act on the second toxin—the belief in duality or in an external reality—but only a non-dual experience, free from the traps of "true" and "false," can purify us at the deepest level.
In truth, our feeling of lack is an effect of the freedom of consciousness. Therefore, only consciousness can annihilate it—freely.

So it is not our individuality as incarnation that disappears, but rather the sense of being incomplete, imperfect, limited.
To awaken is therefore to live still in a body, but without that subtle belief in our imperfection.
This new life is likened to that of an actor who plays his role without total identification.
And this inner distance ennobles his emotions.
When he cries, even his tears carry the flavour of Space.

98 – He Is Devoured Again and Again

yad viśvavibhavaṃ citram īṣallīnaṃ svacitkaraiḥ |
tad eva bhoktṛbhojyādibhogād bhuktam ihocyate || 201

The vast expanse of all things — this marvellous fresco —
begins to dissolve when the rays of (awakening)
consciousness rise.
That very expanse is said to be devoured
when both the eater and the eaten are themselves
consumed.

After the primal toxin — the sense of incompleteness —
how can one overcome the impurity of believing in the
reality of a world external to consciousness?

The Yoginī responds in her own way, always going to the
root:
to dissolve duality, one must dissolve the subject–object
duality.
But she expresses this insight in the terms of her own
symbolic language.
The world is a marvellous "fresco."
As we've already noted, the body and the universe are not
devalued — they are divine manifestations.
But they must be destroyed in order to be renewed.
Initiation is a reinitialization.

In the Yoga of the Goddess, to annihilate is to eat.
We are thus invited to eat the duality between the eater
and the eaten.
This metaphor, for example, was already used in the most
ancient forms of Indian spirituality.

And it must be said: this image is very concrete.
Food lies at the centre of all religions because eating is
not an insignificant act.
As the Yoginī suggests here, to eat is to integrate into
oneself, to assimilate the other and make it part of
oneself.
Just as fire "devours" what it burns, transforming it into
fire — into itself — so too does consciousness consume
all its manifestations.
Sometimes, this truth is represented through even more
striking images, such as the Yoginī devouring herself.

In certain initiation rites of this tradition, the master must
eat and then vomit — enacting the cycle of projection and
reabsorption of consciousness,
whose name is Vāmā, "She Who Vomits."
This troubling image signifies that creation is not a
superficial act for consciousness.
It is herself that manifests, gives herself, offers as "outer"
what is most interior.
Like a mirror expressing its deepest essence through
reflections — this is what makes it a mirror.

Thus, the world is not external to consciousness.
Our impression of estrangement before an absurd
universe is only a passing illusion.
When I return to myself — to consciousness — the rays
of the sun of consciousness reabsorb, then project a new
world.
The separation between "me" and "the world" is
annihilated.
I am the sun whose rays are this body and this world.

This teaching is not anti-life propaganda, as some
spiritualities can be, but rather an invitation to devour life
— to nourish life.

At the center of contemplation, the universe, in all its diversity and beauty (*viśva-vibhavaṃ citram*), reveals itself as a dynamic fresco, ever moving, ever transforming.

This fresco begins to dissolve (*īṣallīnaṃ*) beneath the rays of consciousness (*sva-cit-karaiḥ*), where every form, every color, every shade is no longer perceived as separate, but as an expression of the light of consciousness itself. The body-universe has consciousness as its sun.

She is *Bhānavī*, the Solar One, of the Lineage of the Yoginīs.

She is of the *Bhānavī-kula*, just as God is *Sūrya-kula*, the Radiant One who illuminates All.

The awakening of consciousness is thus the remedy to dualistic pollution —the true root of all pollutions. Certainly, consciousness itself engenders this excess, like all creation, like every gift rooted in love. This ultimate essence is never without risk. Life gives rise to excess. But the excess of life brings about harmony.

99 – Breath is Both Interrupted and Uninterrupted

*caṭṭaḥ prāṇavināśas tu niścaṭṭaḥ prāṇa ghaṭṭakaḥ |
sa eveha vinirdiṣṭaś caṭṭaniścaṭṭikodayaḥ || 202*

*It is "interrupted" because the breath ceases,
but it is also "uninterrupted" because the breath
vibrates.
This (true breath) is here described
as the manifestation of both interruption and continuity.*

After individuality and duality comes the dissolution of
karma. And karma, too, is a form of duality—incarnated in
a body. In fact, the body is said to be the visible side of
karma. More precisely, it is the "ripened" or "begun"
karma, *prārabdha*. One distinguishes three types of karma.

Picture an archer. Each of his arrows represents the karma
of a past or future life.

1. The arrow he is about to shoot is the karma "to
   come," karma that is in formation but can still be
   cancelled.
2. Then there is the accumulated karma of the past,
   sañcita, the arrows still in the quiver. This karma
   too can be destroyed by spiritual awakening. In
   fact, that is the main effect of tantric initiation: the
   fire of consciousness burns through the
   accumulated karmas of past lives.
3. Finally, there is the "begun" karma, *prārabdha*—
   the arrow already loosed. Nothing can stop it now.
   Concretely, this karma is expressed in our body and

personality, which together form our individual nature.

The body is karma.
To transform the body is therefore to act upon karma.
And this is precisely what Tantra proposes.
Hence its enduring appeal, because other traditions offer no such transmutation of the body—only to endure it while awaiting death.

This final kind of karma resembles destiny. It's unavoidable. It can easily be used to justify behaviors that contradict the supposed freedom of the awakened…

How can one burn the karma that can be burned?
At the heart of contemplation, breath appears as a bridge between worlds—a current linking the ephemeral and the eternal, the past and the future.
The interruption of breath symbolizes a pause, a suspension of time, a retreat into the unmanifest.
And yet, this interruption is only one face of breath's reality.
For within that stillness pulses an uninterrupted vibration, a life-force that perpetuates life even in silence, even in stillness.

Whatever the case, the Yoginī—or Niṣkriyānanda Nātha—does not attempt to resolve the contradiction between freedom (awakening) and determinism (karma, the body). She proclaims it and embodies it so that we may imitate it.
The "liberated while living" (*jīvan-mukta*) is a living paradox. We are called to live it; we are made for it.
It need not be resolved theoretically.

Philosophy, reason, is not meant to solve all problems or to have an answer for everything. Its more humble role is to sweep away imaginary veils that separate us from ineffable reality and defy logic.
Experience is enough.
Reasoning dismantles beliefs that divert our attention.
Once we return to experience—naturally perfect—there is no longer anything to reason about, only to sing.

And this paradox is made evident to all in the tangible mystery of breath.
After the power of the Father and the wisdom of the Son, some Christians speak of love in the Breath, the Holy Spirit.
Breath is life—consciousness in its most subtle form, just at the threshold of its exile, in a state of becoming, laden with all that is best and worst.
"Union with the breath of life is natural," says Śiva.

This invites the listening of the breath—humble, without the desire to shine.
Everything is already there.
Thus, the preparation for the sexual yoga that has made nondual Tantra famous is nothing spectacular or esoteric: it is simply listening to "the cycles of breath."
That is enough.
This listening, as Abhinavagupta explains in chapter six of his *Tantrāloka*, is a complete path.
Fall into this listening as one swings on a swing—just as simple, just as wondrous.

With every breath, there is movement: the rubbing of inhalation and exhalation, which brush together like the yogi and the yoginī, generating awakening and countless worlds.
And there is also cessation of breath—at the end of every

inhalation, the end of every exhalation.
Gateways to the beyond.
To rest there, to taste it, is to drink the nectar of the gods.
All is said in a single breath cycle.

The practice then, is to sit.
And to listen to the movement—especially the sensation
of air passing in and out through the nostrils.
This, Kṣemarāja teaches us, is how Kuṇḍalinī awakens.

There is no other goal but awakening.
And this goal is unlike those of ordinary life.
Abhinavagupta, cousin of Kṣemarāja, warns us against
the labored pursuit of effectiveness.
To marry the breath is to love, to offer thanks, to give, to
celebrate.
A practice, yes—but without goal, in the sense that it is
gratuitous.
It expects nothing in return.
Freed from a utilitarian gaze, feeling may then flourish.
This celebration, also a deployment of our energies
offered to the boundless space, can then extend into every
moment of daily life.
We will no longer need to choose between ecstasy and
the laundry. The two will merge perfectly.
Such is the nuptial yoga of lived nonduality
(*bhāvādvaita*).

And yet, sometimes we feel vague but unpleasant
sensations when we listen to our breath without
manipulating it.
Tensions may build in the solar plexus, the throat, the
neck, or elsewhere.
They may culminate in a disruption of inhalation or
exhalation.
We may feel compelled to swallow.

*Why do these experiences arise, when everything seems
to lean toward pure release?*

To understand, we must return to the theory of karma.
Our actions, carrying moral weight, leave invisible
imprints.
Hidden in our psyche like seeds, our karmas can be
eliminated only in one way: by suffering their
consequences—both good and bad.
Nothing else can erase them.
The main factor in the evolution of karma (and we may
speak in the plural, as they are infinite, having
accumulated since beginningless time) is Time.

In Indian thought, Time is a power, a *śakti*, that restrains
or accelerates the evolution of beings and things.
In the *Mahābhārata*, Time is praised as the Supreme
Power to whom nothing and no one can escape—not even
the gods.

It is essential to understand this, for the tradition of the
Goddess is fully aligned with this view of Time.
Time is represented as a fire that cooks all beings and
things.
To live is to change, to pass through the stages of birth,
youth, maturity, old age, and death.
This evolution is a cooking.
To live is to cook.
And to die is to be cooked.

However, there is a trick that Tantra seeks to exploit:
karma cannot be eliminated—but it is temporal.
Therefore, its "cooking" (*pāka*) can be accelerated.
The great tantric initiation ritual is such an acceleration.
The initiate undergoes in a few hours the full cycle of
karmas from future lives.

Only the karma of this life remains—i.e., the body.
At death, no karma will remain.
Liberation is assured.

But it is the Kaula traditions—and especially the *Kālī-krama*—that push this idea to its ultimate consequences.
It is possible to accelerate the cooking of karmas.
But how?

Through various means, all based on attention.
When consciousness turns upon itself, it burns past traces.
Instead of paying attention to things, its projections, it returns to itself.
Those projections are then reabsorbed, along with their imprints.
This acceleration is called *haṭha-pāka*.
The word *haṭha*, as in *haṭha-yoga*, means "violent" or "forceful."
Haṭha-pāka is the acceleration of karmic evolution through a return of consciousness upon itself.

What does this have to do with the discomforts sometimes felt during breath-awareness?
Just this: in all these cases, attention is turning toward its source.
Consciousness is awakening.
And so, karmas are being consumed.

In other words, when I feel my breath, I am living through my karmas—my future lives—but in accelerated, sketch-like form.
I do not experience every detail, but only certain scenes, emotions, atmospheres—
a blend of past traces and futures outlined by those habits.

And within those lives, there is suffering.
So, I feel suffering.

All awakening of consciousness is accompanied by an
awakening of karma.

But Time is, in truth, consciousness.
That is why, in the tradition of the Goddess, Kālī is called
consciousness.
She is Time (*kāla*).
She also destroys Time when she devours it and
reabsorbs it into herself.

Consciousness is like digestive fire.
When it awakens, it digests what had remained
undigested.
The tradition especially speaks of doubts, dilemmas, and
crises of conscience—
not unlike the "life review" in near-death experiences,
where one sees their life flash before them, often
highlighting small gestures of cruelty or hardness of
heart.
Then all is absorbed into an unconditional love—"the
light at the end of the tunnel."

These difficult experiences are thus signs of good omen.
They may also be physical pains, times of "dark night,"
of desert crossing, of feverish agitation, of apparent
regressions into helplessness.

All traditions are unanimous: such signs mark the descent
of divine grace (*śakti-pāta*) within us.
The proper attitude is to let it happen—and to trust.

100 – She Is a Wave That Advances

śaktyodayasthitisphāravigrahaṃ lāti yas sadā |
tenaiva harati kṣiprād yato lāhas tataḥ smṛtaḥ || 203

Her power constantly gives (lā) form
to the vast expanse of manifested existence.
In the same way, she suddenly removes (ha) incarnation.
Thus, tradition names her "the Wave" (lāha).

Sitting on a dune by the ocean and letting one's gaze sink into the movement of the waves. This priceless ebb and flow possess the strange and undeniable power to captivate, reclaiming our heart from the worries of men. The sea gives, the sea takes, the sea gives again… The sea is the universal breath, whose inhalations and exhalations are its waves. Life is given to us in an inhalation, and we return it in an exhalation.

Thus, everything begins and ends in this movement of breath—or of energy, as some would say. Everything moves. Not a single part of the sea is static. And yet, the sea communicates a powerful sense of stillness. Contemplating the sea is like listening to the breath—a contemplation sufficient unto itself. Nothing else needs to be done.

At the center of this contemplation is the power in actualization (*śakty-udaya*), which constantly gives (lā) form to this unfolding, this explosion of existence (*sthiti-sphāra-vigrahaṃ*). This force, ceaseless and dynamic, is the matrix from which bursts forth the infinite diversity of the universe—a proliferation of forms and expressions of life emerging in the dance of creation.

And yet, in this very same movement, she removes (*ha*) incarnation suddenly (*harati kṣiprāt*), like Hara the Ravisher, one of the names of Śiva. She thus reveals the perpetual cycle wherein every end is but the prelude to a new beginning. Therefore, tradition calls her "the Wave," a metaphor for continuity within change, presence within absence, this unfathomable motion that is at once moving and still.

This same wave advances (*pravahad-rūpaḥ*), and so it is said to be a current (*pravāha iti kathyate*). Its nature is indestructible (*a-vināśa-svabhāva*), for it transcends ordinary notions of progression (*nirvitarka-kramo 'kramaḥ*). In this advance, there is neither beginning nor end, but a continuous stream, an unfolding that defies logic and reason—a development about which no reasoning can prevail.

This wave, which moves forward by retreating, which gives by taking back (*lāha-pravāhikā seyaṃ*), is an expansion that is simultaneously expansion and contraction (*hāni-vṛddhi-mayī prathā*), growth and decline, birth and death. Is it not striking that the living never remains static? It either grows or diminishes. A fixed state is not life, but death. One might even wonder if well-meaning environmentalism has heard this lesson?

Yet in that very contradiction, this ideology resembles consciousness itself—capable of the most glaring contradictions. Let us, then, recognize the mark of the divine within our contradictions—which certainly does not mean we should stop striving to transcend them! But life is a wave, an expanding experience that, in its wild freedom, appears fragmented into "birth" and "death" because it flashes forth, like an ungraspable sky.

101 – She Is Both Subtle and Dense

tanutvaṃ sarvasaṃhārāt citir yātā samantataḥ |
svatantrasṛṣṭivispharād ghanatvaṃ tu samāśritā || 204

ekasyā eva satataṃ kālasaṃhārasaṃvidaḥ |
parādvayācyutāvṛttiḥ khagākhyeyaṃ vyavasthitā || 205

Consciousness becomes subtle
because all is entirely dissolved into it.
She becomes dense
when her creative freedom expands.

All arises from a single consciousness
that absorbs Time.
Its activity never fails—
it is supreme, nondual, and is described as "spatial".

Consciousness—that elusive dynamism without which nothing is possible: is it something? Or is it nothing?

The Yoginī summarizes here the paradox of consciousness as both being and non-being. For while this teaching is certainly not a philosophical doctrine or a fully logical system, it is nonetheless a form of thought endowed with its own coherence. As Kṣemarāja put it, this revelation "speaks its own language." It is a meditation on the secret symbols revealed by the Yoginī of space and illumined by Niṣkriya Ānanda.

In other words, the Yoginī is consciousness expressing itself—speaking of itself, which means speaking of our experience—the very fabric of our lives.

Is the truth of life found in the void of unconsciousness, in the eternity of nothingness that awaits us after death? Or does it reveal itself in moments of fullness, abundance, fecundity? We already know these alternations of opposing poles—moments of elation that follow periods of depression, night giving way to day…

Moreover, we are convinced that the bustle of life is like an island of existence lost in a sea of infinite void. So then, what's the point of "awakening"? If it brings nothing but emptiness and fullness—what we already know to be inevitable—why strive so hard for something that seems hardly worth the effort?

This teaching has already touched on this issue, but it bears repeating, for our beliefs on this point are among the most deeply rooted. Just as the chummās of the Yoginī are symbols to be meditated upon again and again, so too our cyclical or repetitive experiences are to be interpreted until we reach the right intuition, fully ripened.

Awakened or not, the structure of experience remains the same: experiences of emptiness, experiences of fullness—absences and presences, like the pulse of a heart. It cannot be otherwise, for such is the nature of consciousness. Other traditions, in China and in Greece, have acknowledged this truth.

Thus Proclus, the towering sage of the Ancients, speaks of the Whole as a heart pulsating in three beats: emanation, existence, and return—akin to the three phases of the Cycle of Consciousness: projection, existence, and judgment. If we come to truly recognize the nature of this cyclical structure, it will carry a very different taste.

The "day" of consciousness, its fecundity—we currently take it to be mere agitation. The activities of the five senses (perceptions) and the mind (thoughts, emotions) form what India calls the waking state. We feel excitement, curiosity—we sense that something is happening. But this exaltation comes at a cost: serenity. Desires, perceived as multiple, insatiable, contradictory, and inseparable from the pain of lack, enslave us. Abundance exhausts us. And our world along with it…

What changes after awakening? This creativity is perceived as "the expansion of creation, which is freedom"—autonomy. We are no longer enslaved to an indifferent world. We participate in creative freedom. We feel ecstasy in our depths, and the world becomes its extension—the visible explosion of invisible love.

The "night" of consciousness—we currently interpret it as a kind of rest, yes, but one that comes at the expense of life, sensation, discovery, encounter… A rest that foreshadows death. After awakening, this utterly simple nothingness takes on a new flavour. It is felt as a return of everything into us. There is nothing lacking in what India calls the deep sleep state. It is a return to unity. To absolute security.

As the Upaniṣad says, "there is no fear in unity—for it is only of the other that one is afraid." Trust, a doorway into surrender. Moments once thought to be unconscious or "sleep" now appear as incredible experiences of pure unity, a mystery to be honoured in silence.

Awakening replaces bipolar living with a new harmony, where we surrender to the Centre. Indeed, "all arises from a single consciousness." These opposites—high and low—are two branches of the same life. Now we feel this life always, here and now, closer than emptiness, closer than fullness. "It never fails," just as space cannot fall. In fact, it is called "spatial" (*kha-gā*)—it moves through space, within its own body.

All is "nondual," and separation no longer holds. Unity saves us from multiplicity taken to be agitation, and multiplicity prevents us from taking unity as mere nothingness. Such is the marvel of awakened experience.

As an unpublished tantra from this tradition, the *Tantra of the Wave of Energy in the Infinite Ocean*, puts it:

"The Goddess is gross because her body is the universe. She is (also) subtle, because she is pure consciousness."

Simultaneously, this same consciousness thus becomes dense (*ghanatvam*), not by material accumulation but through the expansion of her creative freedom (*svatantra-sṛṣṭi-visphāra*), which in no way contradicts her essential emptiness. In this movement of expansion, consciousness embraces the infinity of existence, generating worlds, forms, and experiences in the joyous expression of its intrinsic nature. This density is not a burden, but a manifestation of its plenitude—its capacity to endlessly give birth, to reveal diversity within unity.

This dynamic, in which consciousness is both subtle and dense, reflects the eternal dance between the unmanifest and the manifest, between emptiness and fullness. In this choreography lies the mystery of existence—a mystery wherein consciousness, by absorbing Time (*kāla-saṃhāra-saṃvid*), expresses her infinite nature in creation. In other words, even though we are marked by the seal of unity, we are no less double. As Philippe MacLeod observed, after so many others, "the feeling of being and that of plenitude are, in reality, contiguous."

Tantra portrays this ambiguity through the figure of the witch, awaiting only the kiss of our right attention to regain her face as a gentle fairy. Blessed void, cursed void—our entire destiny as conscious beings hinges on how we approach the void—or how we flee from it. And this is true not only for those moments of blankness when we lose our bearings, but also for the whole range of emotions that erupt from that openness.

Our anger, our melancholy—these are nothing but the eruptions of the Goddess, distorted by our inattention. If I can remain at the source, oriented toward her in a knowing that is nothing but direct seeing, then I enter the yoga of the Goddess, her unique alchemy.

The infallible Act of this consciousness (*parādvayācyutā-vṛttiḥ*), supreme and nondual, is described as "spatial" (*khagākhyeyaṃ*) because it transcends the limits of time and space, offering a perspective where the duality of opposites is overcome, where expansion and contraction are complementary expressions of an unchanging nature.

102 – He Is the End of the End

antaḥ smṛto vināśas tu tasyāntas ta(...) |
śāstra-prapañca-kalanā-varjito bhāti sarvataḥ || *206*

The "end" is destruction.
But when that "end" ends,
(consciousness) shines everywhere,
free from the verbose calculations of the scriptures.

At the close of this text, once again we are invited to contemplate the End beyond end—an extraordinary end, the end of life finally awakened from its nightmares. The ordinary end is destruction, Death, *kāla*, Time. But what happens when Death dies? This is the riddle the Yoginī invites us to meditate on. To realize that the end is not the end—that itself is awakening. To become conscious of this truth is the true purpose of death.

Then, consciousness "appears," radiates everywhere. Freed from spiritual ego, it no longer depends on the "verbose calculations of the scriptures," *prapañca-kalanā*, a phrase alluding to the endless discursiveness of technical and sacred treatises. These often demand complex decoding of mantras, their repetition a specific number of times according to the desired goal, and the consideration of astrological conditions to maximize ritual effects.

But who, other than Kālī—consciousness as Time—is free of Time?

The profane is subject to these laws, ignorant that, in their most intimate and transpersonal truth, they are the very source of those laws.

103 – He Is Both Downward and Upward

adhaḥ śabdena kathito vedyo rūpādivibhramaḥ |
bhava-bheda-padas tuccho rāga-dveṣādi-viplutaḥ || 207

sa eva iha samākhyātaḥ sarvottīrṇas tu anāmayaḥ |
vyaktāvyaktadvaya-uttīrṇa ūrdhvaṃ śiva-mayaṃ param ||
208

tathā ca ruruṇā proktam adhaḥ śabdena tattvataḥ |
sṛṣṭi-sthiti-upasaṃhāra-rūpaṃ bheda-trayam || 209

smṛtam ūrdhvaṃ tu sahasā tad eva iha aniketanam |
kāla-grāsa-anta-dehaṃ tu sarva-dikkaṃ nirantaram ||
210

"Downward" is said to mean the knowable,
the deception of forms and so on,
the plane of duality in becoming,
hollow, drowned in attraction, aversion, and the rest.

That same is here called "transcendent",
flawless, for he transcends
the dualities of "visible" and "invisible",
he is the supreme Śiva "upward".

Thus, it has been proclaimed by Ruru:
"Downward" truly signifies
the triple division: creation, existence, and dissolution.

"Upward", here, designates the sudden, the abodeless,
whose body is the complete digestion of Time,
who pervades all directions without interruption.

Awakening is not envisioned the same way across all traditions. In a fascinating tantric text, *The Refutation of the Views of Liberation*, a dualistic tantric master of the 8th century describes around twenty definitions of awakening. Most of the time, there is no actual awakening, but simply a "liberation" (*mokṣa*) from the cycle of rebirths.

Either one realizes that nothing ever truly happened (Vedānta), or that one was never really involved or affected (Sāṃkhya), or that the self we cling to is merely a mental construction (Buddhism), or one is reborn in paradise, beside the most beautiful incarnation of God (Vaiṣṇavism). In other traditions, one is transmuted into an immortal divine body, or the deity bestows its qualities upon the soul, or one goes "into the stars" (whatever that may mean). In none of these views is there a real suggestion of a life *already awakened here and now*. The dualism remains between a flawed "here-below" and a perfect "there-above".

The ideal of embodied awakening (*jīvan-mukti*) is the contribution of non-dual Tantra. It is no longer a question of being reborn elsewhere or not being reborn at all, but of *experiencing the ocean in the drop*. Feeling the Whole in the fragment we are as individuated persons. Transcending the opposition between fleshly life and spiritual life.

This is the heart of Tantra—an ideal radically different from most Eastern and Western spiritualities, which invite us toward transcendence, but at the price of the flesh, or even our individuality.

At the heart of this non-dual contemplation, "downward" (*adhaḥ*) designates the domain of the knowable (*vedya*), a space where forms and illusions (*rūpādi-vibhrama*) play out in the theater of existence. This plane is marked by the duality of becoming (*bhava-bheda-pada*), an endless cycle of creation, existence, and dissolution—*tuccha*, "empty" in the sense that consciousness must keep its essential energy turned toward itself, lest it become lost, drowned (*vipluta*) in attachment and aversion.

This dimension, though filled with diverse experiences, is acknowledged as an expression of Light, a field where consciousness unfolds into multiplicity.

Simultaneously, consciousness transcends the opposition between "visible" and "invisible", or between the individual and the impersonal (*vyakta-avyakta-dvaya-uttīrṇa*), manifesting as the supreme Śiva "upward" (*ūrdhvaṃ śivamayaṃ param*), free from defect, a presence beyond the boundaries of form and formlessness, opacity and transparency.

This "upward" dimension is the sudden (*sāhasa*), unplaceable act, an audacity where Time itself is dissolved, penetrating all directions (*sarva-dikkam*) without pause (*nirantaram*).

This dialectic of "downward" and "upward" is an exploration of the triple division (*bheda-trayam*): creation, maintenance, and dissolution—eternal cycles at the heart of becoming. Yet within this very duality, expressed through this threefold division, resides a Presence that is more than the sum of opposites, a state that transcends time and space, where consciousness is neither frightened by becoming nor numbed by dissolution, but radiates in its absolute fullness.

In this sense, this triple duality is also a triple revelation— the *rāva*, the "wild roar" of undomesticated consciousness that laughs at its own rules.

104 – Duality Is Destroyed the Moment It Is Seen

ittham bhedamayam sarvam kālāgnyādi-śivāntakam |
tattvena vyapadeśena sakṛd yad dṛṣṭam akramāt || 211

Thus, all that is made of duality—
from the Fire of the End of Time to Śiva—
is "seen" in its true nature,
in a single stroke and without transition,
through this authentic teaching.

tatkṣaṇān nāśam āyāti tad eva advaya-cit-pade |
asparśe'sparśa-hnutā asvalpā-samparkataḥ abhitaḥ ||
212

From that instant, it is destroyed for good
in the non-dual consciousness,
beyond contact, without any dependency on contact,
without the slightest trace of duality.

Or:

From that very moment onward, this all-dual reality
is annihilated for good

in the non-dual field of awareness.
This absence of contact is an all-pervading contact.

I chase after a mirage. The moment I truly see it, it vanishes. A snake slithering in the grass terrifies me. But when I look at it closely, it dissolves—and what remains is only a rope (or a glimmering trickle of water). Such is the nature of illusion: it cannot bear to be seen.

This notion is typical of Mādhyamaka Buddhism and Advaita Vedānta. Sureśvara, the disciple of Śaṅkara (the most famous Vedāntin), defines illusion as "that which is sustained by a lack of inquiry"—that which is only "real" as long as it is not examined. The moment I approach the ghost, it fades. And this gaze that leads to nothing is in fact a gaze that opens.

So, say the Buddhist yogis. A gaze that opens is a gaze that is free. It no longer clings, it no longer contracts. It purifies and expands until it reaches its infinite perfection. It becomes Buddha—Awakened.

Indeed, life confronts us constantly with the dual structure of existence (*bheda-mayaṃ sarvam*), a spectrum ranging from the most evident oppositions to the most subtle ones. Yet this authentic teaching of the Yoginī (*tattvena vyapadeśena*) reveals that, in one glance (*sakṛt*), without stages or transitions (*akramāt*), all of this duality—*from the Fire of the End of Time to Śiva*—is seen in its truth: not as separation, but as manifestations of the same infinity, of the same indefinable Śiva, both the end and the beginning of all things, from the darkest depths of hell to the summit of divine being.

This naked seeing, once fully realized, causes an immediate dissolution (*tat-kṣaṇāt nāśam āyāti*) of all painful becoming—of the grip of birth, life, and death cycles. It is annihilated in the non-dual awareness (*advaya-cit-pade*), in a state where the duality between sensation and non-sensation (*asparśe'sparśa-hnutā*) is no longer relevant.

A state untouched by the smallest trace of duality, revealing a wondrous diversity wholly absorbed in unity—an open space of pure presence, free from the conceptual limitations of the mind.

One burst of seeing is enough to kill our projections. Even if light casts shadow, the shadow cannot resist light. Even if a room has lain in darkness for centuries, light dispels it in an instant—effortlessly, without struggle.

This idea of sudden awakening, in a single instant of genuine perception, is deeply Buddhist in tone. And so it is fitting that this final teaching ends on such a strong Buddhist inspiration.

105 – The Ultimate Teaching: …

So where is the final *chummā*?

By veiling that last secret from our eyes, I like to think the author meant to remind us that the Absolute is not something we can grasp or appropriate. Yet this is not a loss—for the treasure is the very light that illuminates these words.

And finally, the Transmitter, Niṣkriyānanda, confirms that he is the reincarnation of the legendary Durvāsa—the "Lord of Wrath"—now pacified, finding bliss in Non-Doing, after the overwhelming encounter he described at the beginning.

The final secret is the one "that cannot be written in a book." The ultimate revelation, therefore, is that of silence. What could be more eloquent, as Ramana Maharshi so often reminded us?

The last page is thus a blank page. Empty like Presence. Some may find this fanciful, but we have a precedent: the *Book of the Twenty-Four Philosophers*, an anonymous Latin text that appeared in the south of France in the 12th century. Its content echoes the oral teachings of the Yoginīs. This book recounts how twenty-four philosophers gathered one day to understand God.

Each proposed a definition, including the famous one: "God is an infinite sphere whose centre is everywhere and whose circumference is nowhere." You can see how these aphorisms resemble those of the Yoginīs, and like them, each is accompanied by a brief commentary, also anonymous.

But when we reach the twenty-fourth philosopher, we find… a blank page! This oddity puzzled scholars for centuries. One scribe even filled in the "empty" page with the text from the twenty-third philosopher. Emptiness is difficult to bear. Silence is hard to hear. And yet mysticism—devotion to the mystery—is precisely the attempt to say what cannot be said. It is only natural, then, that silence or a blank page should assert themselves in the end. Thus, in both East and West, silence is the ultimate teaching.

As the Yoginīs have sung again and again, this silence is not sterile, not dead, not empty. Emptiness is not empty. It is the listening of a music other than that of the mind. And it is also an invitation to let this melody continue within us.

Thus the greatest mystic, the greatest *yoginī* of the West, Hadewijch of Antwerp, ends her *Poems* with an invitation to continue them through the song of intimate experience. Let each of us become this *Book of Nothing*! Initiation is awakening to oneself. Every moment sustained in this spirit is transmission—a new page of this utterly secret and endless Book.

The Book is you, dear reader.

Seeds to Be Sown

I began this work of translation before the high, pure, luminous peaks of the Alps. In a valley of exceptional breadth, shaped to embrace the path of the sun. The images of the no less vast valley of Kashmir accompanied me. Again and again, I asked myself what the world of the Yoginīs might have looked like. And each time, the same answer arose: their world was the world of silence. That free sanctuary, always present whenever our heart joins the silence of the beginning—now. A single instant is enough to summon the Yoginīs. A moment of suspension. The pivot of the moment, the present moment, that absolute wonder discreetly celebrated by Plato, father of Western philosophy.

Where the heart's murmur eclipses the tumult of words, the essence of *The Elucidation of the Secret Teaching of the Yoginīs* unfurls. This dialogue between the visible and the invisible, the tangible and the untouchable, weaves a web, a *tantra*, where duality melts into the absolute singularity of consciousness, a vast sphere with no above or below, the embrace of God and Goddess who, in each instant, birth the Child that we are.

Then everything bathes in an aura of magic. This old oak table, this worm-eaten bookshelf, this worn floor, these ancient stones... This vision echoes the famous declaration of the non-dualist Gauḍapāda: the ultimate truth is that nothing is (truly) liberated since everything rests in eternal presence. In this "nonchalance filled with ardour" is revealed the sacred dance of creation and dissolution in the vast sky of consciousness, the ether shimmering through all things.

At the heart of this timeless wisdom—which returns to us in these decisive times—the reconciliation of opposing forces becomes the leitmotif of a symphony where each note—from the senses to the mind, from the tangible to the intangible—merges into the ultimate space, sensation without separation. The duality of objectivity and subjectivity resolves into a state of egoless awareness, a domain where *non-relation* (*asaṃbandha*) is the only true relationship, marking the end of one journey and the beginning of another in an eternal cycle of spiritual rebirth—for in the Infinite, there is no end, only unity without confusion.

These secret teachings, these symbols of recognition, passed down through rare and precious manuscripts, return to us after a millennium by the patience of a few scribes and the grace of the Goddess. They recount a quest for understanding beyond words, a pilgrimage beyond the limits of rational thought. I

n these texts, the Sanskrit words and verses in the so-called "vulgar" tongue open gates to realities only the heart can grasp, inviting the seeker to transmute the veils of illusion and embrace the dawn's clarity, hidden in plain sight: Love.

In this state of awakening, the *manas* (mind) becomes the servant of the spaciousness of consciousness, a shoreless sea where every wave—thought, sensation, or perception—is seen for what it is: an expression of the Infinite, a gift.

Every teaching, every Mantra and Mudrā revealed in this sacred text guides the devotee along the path of self-realization—to the full blooming of every petal. They invite us to explore the hidden dimensions of existence, where day and night, creation and dissolution, are but facets of one and the same reality, as demanding as it is loving—demanding by virtue of its deep benevolence.

This initiatory wisdom, this dialogue between the Goddess and the silent Master, between a human teacher and their disciple, unfolds as a mirror in which the essence of every soul in quest of fulfilment is reflected. The ultimate truth—that all is Love, and that in this recognition the dance of creation and dissolution becomes a celebration of the unity of consciousness—becomes the beacon guiding the seeker toward the shore of eternal peace. And yet, here, to run aground is to cast off, to be carried away into the vastness.

Thus, the secret teachings of the Yoginīs are not revealed as a body of knowledge to be accumulated, but as a call to live each moment in full awareness of dynamic unity, in resonance with all that is—and all that might not be. To plunge into that wild current, to follow the waters we are in our deepest core.

Every breath becomes a tribute, every posture of the body, every image arising in the mind. A life of yoga, of union, a unifying life, illuminating and purifying—for the divine is always already there, before all effort, before even any ideal or goal.

The yoga of the Goddess is a union of two. It is the encounter that awaits us at the end of all others, good or bad. It belongs to us—it belongs to you, dear reader—to play your part in it.

Appendix 1 : Who is Nishkriya ?

The author of the *Chummā-saṅketa-prakāśa* names himself Niṣkriyānanda (verse 224) and is named as such in the colophon. He presents himself as the reincarnation of Durvāsa (v. 223), a legendary Indian sage, the "best of sages" (*muni-vara*, v. 231). He received the revelation of the *Chummās* from Siddha-nātha (v. 8) and from the Goddess Bhairavī (v. 13a). He is a *brāhmaṇa* (*vipra*, v. 16; *dvija*, v. 20), who receives the "great transmission" (*mahā-krama*, v. 27). He addresses a disciple ("son", *putra*, v. 27; "listen", *śṛṇu*, v. 36). Niṣkriyānanda bears the marks of a Śaiva ascetic (*mudrā-dhara*, v. 232), who "wanders through sanctuaries" (v. 32) and who, like his disciple Vidyānanda, is endowed with "the infinite powers of the (Goddess)" (*tad-ananta-śakti*, v. 232). I believe this designation allows us to identify the author of the *Explication des Vātūla-nātha-sūtra*, Anantaśakti, with Vidyānanda, who receives the teaching from Bhairavī, the Yoginī, from Niṣkriyānanda, and from Siddha-nātha, who would thus be the Mad Master, Vātūla Nātha, "he who is intoxicated by the fragrance (of the Yoginī)", *Gandha-mādana* (*Vātūla-nātha-sūtras* 3).

A hymn attributed to Anantaśakti was published in 1964 by the University of Trivandrum, in southern India. Here are a few observations concerning this beautiful poem:

1. The Trivandrum edition is based on a single manuscript (C.O. 1278) from the university's library, though its provenance is not specified. However, we know that southern India, and Kerala in particular, have housed numerous manuscripts belonging to the Krama tradition. In a lecture posted on YouTube, Professor Alexis Sanderson refers to a collection that supposedly disappeared

in 1907 following a flood. Moreover, it is now known that a Kashmiri scholar—his name unknown but bearing the honorific *bhaṭṭa*, "sir"—traveled to Kerala in the 17th century and built thirteen temples there. These temples embodied the twelve reflections of Kālī within the Cycle of Consciousness (*samvit-krama*), the secret teaching at the heart of the Kālī-krama.

2. The author of the hymn appears to be Anantaśakti: *anantaśakti-kṛc cedaṃ stotram* — "this hymn is the work of Anantaśakti," as stated in the colophon.
3. It contains 104 verses written in various metres.
4. The hymn is addressed to the Goddess Tripurā, a Kaula tradition that integrates the Kālī-krama—for example, in the *Mantraraśmi-mālā*—and which also includes the solitary worship of the Goddess Parā.
5. The hymn features expressions that are typical both of Anantaśakti's commentary on the *Vātūla-nātha-sūtras* and of the *Secret Tradition of the Yoginīs* (*Chummā-sampradāya*, a fitting name for the corpus of the Yoginī's secret teachings). The language of the Krama is very distinctive, as Kṣemarāja noted. Here are a few characteristic expressions:

- Verse 1: *niruttara-camatkṛti-prasara-sāra-sambodhikā jayaty agama-jā* — "She who awakens the essence flowing from a supreme astonishment, born of revelation, is victorious!"
- Verse 4: *niruttara-icchobhaya-sāmarasyādyā mūrtir ādyā pravibhāti dīptā* — "She is the ever-shining Lamp, the primal embodiment of the fusion of the Absolute and Desire."

- Verse 5: *sphurati niravakāśā śambhuśaktiḥ svatantrā* — "Free, the energy of Śiva flashes uninterruptedly!"
- Verse 41: *oḍḍiyāṇa-para-pīṭha-saṃśrayaṃ saṃśritā niravakāśa-dharmiṇī nirvikalpa-para-dhāma-cāriṇī yā kalā-mayām ahaṃ nato'smi tām* — "I bow to her who is incarnated in the supreme seat of Oḍḍiyāna, whose being is uninterrupted, who dances in the ultimate realm beyond thought, and who overflows with energies."
- Verse 53: *nirdhāma-dhāma-vibhatrā parameśa-dhāmni* — "She manifests the domain without domain in the realm of the Supreme Lord."
- Verse 72: *prakāśatāṃ yāti nirākhyarūpā yeyaṃ parā śaktir iha stumas tām* — "We now praise that supreme Power who appears in the form of the Unspeakable."
- Verse 76: *kāpy amitātra pūjā* — "Here the adoration is without bounds."
- Verse 86: *sadā bhakṣayan niravadhi-kramākramaiḥ* — "She eternally devours, through both sequential and sudden illuminations, without end."
- Verse 101: *vibhāti tāṃ naumi bhavābdhi-madhye pronmagna-jantūddharaṇaika-dīkṣām nirdhāma-dhāma-krama-visphuliṅga-prapūritāśeṣa-dig-antarālām* — "I bow to her who shines at the heart of the ocean of becoming; she is the sole initiation that saves the submerged beings, filling all directions and spaces with sparks from the evolution of the domain without domain."
- Verse 102: *kṛtam idam aniketa-dhyāna-sādhyaika-mūrter nirupama-nija-saṃvid-devatām āyayoccaiḥ* — "This (adoration) of the unique Embodiment is realized through meditation without fixed abode, a worship offered by the

excellent ones to the unparalleled deity of their own consciousness!"

6. Furthermore, this hymn is filled with stylistic and conceptual elements found in both the commentary on the *Vātūla-nātha-sūtras* and the *Elucidation of the Secret Tradition of the Yoginīs* (*Chummā-sanketa-prakāśa*).
7. Nevertheless, the hymn celebrates the Goddess Tripurā, whom scholars generally consider to be a later development than the Krama tradition.
8. Finally, the hymn is filled with expressions central to "Kashmir Śaivism," such as *svatantra* (freedom) and *spanda* (vibration).

My hypothesis is therefore the following: Anantaśakti, author of this hymn, could also be the author of the commentary on the *Vātūla-nātha-sūtras*. If so, he was likely from southern India and composed his work after the revelation of the Tripurā tradition—that is, after the 11th century. He would then be the compiler of the *Elucidation of the Secret Tradition of the Yoginīs* (*Chummā-sanketa-prakāśa*).

Whatever the case may be, this hymn is magnificent.

Niṣkriyānanda is thus a *brāhmaṇa* who claims to have received a mystical and oral transmission from a mysterious being—an initiation that appears related to the tradition of the Krama—, who is the reincarnation of Durvāsa, and who has a disciple-ascetic.

The lineage would thus be:

The Goddess Bhairavī < Siddha Nātha < Niṣkriyānanda < Vidyānanda < Śaktyānanda < Śivānanda, etc. (the masters of the Kashmir lineage)

Durvāsa is an important figure, known for his anger and his curses. He plays a major role in several tantric lineages.

What else is known about Niṣkriyānanda?

He is the author of a poem of fifty verses on the Twelve Projections of the Goddess Kālī, inserted in chapter seven of a book from the Kaula tradition of the Goddess Kubjikā, titled *Ciñcini-mata-sāra-samuccaya* ("The Quintessence of the Teaching of the Tamarind Tree"). This title refers to a village in the Goa region, where a sacred tree stood, beneath which lived a certain Tuṣṇi-nātha, the "Silent Master." Note that the *revealers* (*avatāraka*) of the Kaula traditions are often described as silent (*tuṣṇa, mauna*). This book is the first known source to describe the four main Kaula traditions or "houses" (*ghara*): 1) the Western or original tradition, the Trika, which venerates the Goddess's Triad in her peaceful, excited, and wrathful aspects; 2) the Eastern tradition of Kubjikā; 3) the Southern tradition of Tripurā or Śrī-vidyā; and 4) the Northern tradition of Kālī, the Krama. Chapter seven, which details this last tradition, contains two points of interest: a) the poem attributed to Niṣkriyānanda and b) a brief description of Niṣkriyānanda and his disciple Vidyānanda.

The Goddess Kālī is said to have incarnated where Tamasa Muni, "the dark silent one" (i.e., Durvāsa), lived, also referred to as the King of Anger (*Krodha-rāja*, v. 158). He received the supreme Knowledge of Non-Action (*niṣkriyā-jñāna*), hence the name of his reincarnation, author of our text. This oral teaching is the *vedha-saṃkrama*, the transformative transmission of the Twelve Kālīs, relying solely on personal experience—a transmission called "the skeleton of Kālī," as in the *Chummās*, an inexplicable state (*anākhyā*). The vocabulary of this text resembles that of the *Chummās*, though it is more symbolically oriented.

Vidyānanda, Niṣkriyānanda's disciple, is most likely the person addressed in the *Chummās*, as the *Ciñcini-mata* notes he was a yogi "rich in asceticism" (*tapo-dhana*, v. 182), looking like a wild man, living in cremation grounds, engaging in nocturnal transgressive practices—again matching the *Chummās*. He and Niṣkriyānanda are said to have met in the caves of Śrīśaila, a famous sanctuary in southern India. The scene at the beginning of the *Chummās* likely takes place there.

Furthermore, Niṣkriyānanda and Vidyānanda are mentioned in a Krama tantra, the *Devī-pañca-śataka* (III, 15–16), and in its variant, the *Yoni-gahvara*. Among the human master-couples of the Kaula lineage (which the Krama belongs to), Niṣkriyānanda is listed first, along with his partner Jñāna-dīpti, "Lamp of Knowledge." It is thus logical to consider him the first human in the lineage, as other sources suggest. Next come Vidyānanda, then Śaktyānanda, and then Śivānanda, who may be an alias for Jñāna-netra, the "revealer" of these two tantras. Jñāna-netra is also considered the yogi who brought the Krama into Kashmir after receiving a new revelation in neighboring Oḍḍiyāna (now the Swat Valley in Pakistan). Jñāna-netra likely lived around 850 CE. Niṣkriyānanda could therefore be dated to around 750–800 CE. Though early, this would not be impossible for a text as sophisticated as the *Chummās*.

Indeed, the *Chummās* show influence from Yogācāra Buddhism, which holds that "everything is consciousness." As early as the 8th century, this philosophical system began translating into a non-dual tantric Buddhism (*Guhyasamāja-tantra*). This system describes the dissolution of the gross mind (*citta*) into its subtle layers in four stages—possibly influencing the Krama. The Krama too describes consciousness (*saṃvit*) as a four-phase cycle (*krama*): projection, stasis, resorption, and a fourth moment called "light" (*bhāsā*), also named "emptiness beyond emptiness" (*śūnya-atiśūnya*). The Buddhist *Guhyā-samāja-tantra* mentions similar stages: *śūnya, ati-śūnya, āloka, āloka-ābhāsa, āloka-upalabdhi,* and *prabhāsvara.* It is quite plausible that the *Chummās* belong to this same 8th-century context.

This same succession of four couples—Niṣkriyānanda to Śivānanda—is also mentioned in the *Kha-cakra-pañcaka-stotra* ("Hymn to the Quintuple Wheel of Space," vs. 116–118), likely a Kashmiri text. There, they appear in a hymn celebrating the same lineage as the *Devī-pañca-śataka,* as if each figure were a manifestation of the Goddess. Niṣkriyānanda is described as "the luminous manifestation of the rays of the Sun (of Goddess Kālī)" (*śreyaskara-karābhāse*). Two other masters are named after Śivānanda: Nityā and Mokṣānanda.

Niṣkriyānanda is also cited in the commentary on the *Vātūla-nātha-sūtras,* where reference is made to his receiving transmission from Siddha-nātha through the "natural" (*a-kṛtaka*) book of the body. Siddha-nātha is named *Gandha-mādana-siddha,* and Gandhamādana is the name of a place near the land bridge between India and Sri Lanka. This supports the theory of a southern origin for the Krama: Gandhamādana and Śrīśaila. Additionally, some mantras in this tradition are in Dravidian languages, as Professor Alexis Sanderson has noted.

Finally, Niṣkriyānanda is described at the beginning of the *Kaula-sūtras* as an incarnation of Durvāsa, "avatar of Rudra-Śiva."

But why does the Krama of Kashmir claim its origin in Oḍḍiyāna through Jñāna-netra, if it also comes from southern India through Niṣkriyānanda? I believe Jñāna-netra was a "refounder." In tantric lineages, it is common for a particularly radiant or charismatic member to reconnect directly with the original source, reviving the transmission. There are many examples of this in Tibetan Buddhism, with the phenomenon of *tertons* (treasure revealers). Moreover, the later Kashmiri Krama influenced South India through Śrīvatsa (with his *Cid-gagana-candrikā*, "Moonlight in the Sky of Consciousness") and Maheśvarānanda (with his *Mahā-artha-mañjarī*, "Cluster of the Supreme Meaning").

A verse in a tantra from the Kubjikā tradition seems to allude to this double origin:

"During the Age of Misery, Maṅgalā of the three eyes descended into the Northern cave in the land of Oḍḍiyāna. Siddha Nātha did the same in his lineage. Thus elevated (*oḍḍīya*) in his body, he gained sovereignty and became known as the Sublime Odīśa" (*Ambāsaṃhitā*, 10/165b–166a).

Siddha Nātha could be the mysterious master, also called the "silent" or "mad" master, who initiated Niṣkriyānanda and other yogis and yoginīs. The *Secret Teaching of the Yoginīs* may thus be an essential but long-ignored source of Kashmir Śaivism.

We also note, in support of this, that the *Chummās* contain all the key notions of *Spanda* (spanda, unmeṣa), *Pratyabhijñā* (vimarśa, ahaṃtā, camatkāra, svātantrya), and even Abhinavagupta (anuttara, paramādvaya). However, their philosophy differs from *Pratyabhijñā*, rejecting the notion of a supreme "I," viewing the world as magical illusion, and not valorizing speech. The very name Niṣkriyānanda goes against the more affirmative tone of other Kaula traditions. The term *niṣkriya* is used negatively, for example, in this passage from the foundational tantra of the Kubjikā tradition: "Without consciousness, my dear, everything is devoid of freedom, like a stone. Without action, without consciousness, all is like a corpse" (*Kubjikā-mata*, 4.21). While the *Chummās* do distinguish between space, which is inert (*jaḍa*), and consciousness, this teaching, full of paradox, emphasizes transcendence and negation.

To sum up, here are four essential points from this brief investigation:

- Niṣkriyānanda was a yogi from southern India who received a divine revelation at the origin of the Krama.
- He is the incarnation of the legendary sage Durvāsa.
- He stands at the origin of the Kashmiri Krama lineage, which also claims a second origin: the Yoginī Maṅgalā/Vīrasiṃhā of Oḍḍiyāna.
- He is, therefore, the overlooked source of Kashmir Śaivism.

Appendix 2: On the Manuscripts of the Chummāsaṅketaprakāśa

Manuscripts for this text are rare. To my knowledge, there are four. None of them is complete. The first page is always missing — the one that introduces the author's account of the circumstances surrounding this teaching.

There are numerous variants and obscure passages. Based on this, I have selected the versions that seemed the most reliable, while noting the others. I have occasionally proposed corrections.

It is important to remember that manuscripts were copied by hand. India's climate requires frequent copying, as heat and humidity are not favorable for preservation. The Kashmir Valley has a drier and colder climate, like that of the Kathmandu Valley in Nepal. However, texts were originally copied onto birch bark sheets, before eventually being written on paper. Finally, the copyist does not always understand what they are copying. All these factors explain the variants and the difficulty in "reaching" the original text.

The sūtras seem to be in Old Kashmiri, the language of medieval Kashmir, but this is far from certain. They may in fact be in a southern language (Telugu?), as Professor Sanderson has noted that some Mantras in the Krama tradition are in Dravidian languages. Moreover, these Mantras are preserved in the Śuddha-mālā-mantra, a Mantra practiced and transmitted in the southern Śrīvidyā tradition. Most often, these are Sanskrit words pronounced in the local way. For example, naṣṭaḥ ("destroyed") becomes niṭṭo. Words ending in -u indicate the masculine, while those in -a appear to mark the feminine. The Revelation verses are in Sanskrit and reuse words from the sūtras—or rather the Chummās—but with their Sanskrit pronunciations.

503

Finally, the text contains, within itself, thirty verses in Kashmiri, with titles in Sanskrit. I have translated these titles, which are sometimes linked to the Chummās. The verses in Kashmiri contain Sanskrit words, but the whole remains difficult to translate.

List of Manuscripts

- Benares, "BHU" = ACC. NO. – 328180
  Manuscript No. – CN. 491
  Title – Chummāsaṃketaprakāśa
  Sheet size: 13.3 x 10.3 cm
  Number of leaves: 11 and 1/2
  Condition – Incomplete
  CN. 491–493
  Manuscript found and transcribed by Mark S. G. Dyczkowski, written in śāradā script.

This manuscript presents itself, in its colophon, as belonging to Divākaratsa. A scholar by this name is placed by A. Sanderson "in the mid-10th century" (Śaiva Exegesis, p. 255), as cited by Kṣemarāja and his teacher Abhinavagupta. This may be seen as further evidence of the Chummās' antiquity relative to the Kashmir Krama tradition.

- Berlin, "B" = SBB-PK Hs no. 11387, paper, śāradā script, incomplete: begins on folio 2r, with folio 1 missing.
  Manuscript discovered by a German team.
- Rastogi, "R": a copy of a copy (?) of a manuscript belonging to Pandit Dinanath Yaksh, published in 2011, on paper, in nāgarī script, 13 folios, incomplete. "Mentioned in a list of manuscripts to be published by the Kashmīra Rājakīya Shodha-vibhāga." It continues up to Chummā 74 but contains many gaps.

- Śrīnagara, "Ś" ("ORL"): manuscript discovered and photographed in December 2024 by Ben Williams in Śrīnagara, śāradā script, incomplete, accessed late and little used.
- Sanderson Partial Edition, "S": not a manuscript, but the conjectural emendations proposed by Alexis Sanderson (Oxford), a world-renowned expert in Tantra. His proposals appear in *Mélanges tantriques*, pp. 333–344.

In total, I count 105 Chummās (including the 105th, which I believe is marked by its absence) and 30 Kathās.
Textual conjectures are indicated by the symbol "<".

Partial Bibliography

- *Chummāsaṅketaprakāśa*, ms "R", in Rastogi, Navjivan, *Kashmir Ki Shaiva Sanskriti mein Kul Aur Kram-Mat*, D.K. Printing World, 2011
- *Ciñcinīmatasārasamuccaya*, edition by Mark S. G. Dyczkowski
- *Cittasaṃtoṣatriṃśikā*, in Janārdan Paṇḍey, in *Śaivādvayaviṃśatikā*, Varanasi, 2003
- *Devīdvyardhaśatika*, edition by Mark S. G. Dyczkowski
- *Īśvarapratyabhijñāvimarśinī* of Abhinavagupta : doctrine of divine recognition, Sanskrit Text with the commentary Bhāskarī. vol.1-2, edited by K.A. Subramania Iyer and K.C.Pandey. Delhi, etc. : Motilal Banarsidass , 1986
- *Kālikakramapañcāśikā*, Niṣkriyānanda, in *Tantrāloka*, volume 3, Appendix, pp. x-x, edited and translated by Mark S. G. Diczkowsky, Amazon 2023
- *Kālikākulapañcaśatikatantra*, edition by Mark S. G. Dyczkowski
- *Kaulasūtra*, in Rastogi, Navjivan, *Kashmir Ki Shaiva Sanskriti mein Kul Aur Kram-Mat*, D.K. Printing World, 2011
- *Khacakrapañcakastotra*, edition and translation by Mark S. G. Dyczkowski, Kindle Edition, 2021
- *Kramasadbhāva*, edition by Mark S. G. Dyczkowski
- *Kularatnoddyotatantra*, edition by Mark S. G. Dyczkowski
- *Mahānayaprakāśa*, Anonymous, Trivandrum Sanskrit Series 130, 1937
- *Mahānayaprakāśa*, Arṇasiṃha, edited and translated in Appendix of Tantrāloka, volume 3, by Mark S. G. Dyczkowski, also in Kindle Edition, together with the *Khacakrapañcakastotra*, see above
- *Mālinīvijayavārttika*, Kashmir Series of Texts and Studies, 30, Shrinagar, 1921

- *Manthānabhairavatantra*, Kumārikākhanda, edited and translated by Mark S. G. Dyczkowski, D.K. Printing World, 2009
- *Pratyabhijñāhṛdaya*, Kashmir Series of Texts and Studies, 3, Shrinagar, 1911
- « The śaiva exegesis of Kashmir », in Mélanges à la mémoire d'Hélène Brunner , Ecole Française d'Extrême-Orient, 2002
- *Svacchandatantra*, Kashmir Series of Texts and Studies
- *Ūrmikaulaśāstra*, edition by Mark S. G. Dyczkowski
- *Vātūlanāthasūtra*, edited by Madhusudana Kaul Sastri, Kashmir Series of Texts and Studies, 39, Srinagar 1923
- *Vijñānabhairavatantra*, Kashmir Series of Texts and Studies
- *Tantrāloka*, edition and translation by Mark S. G. Dyczkowski, Amazon, 2023
- *Timirodghāṭana*, edition by Mark S. G. Dyczkowski
- *The Touch of Śakti*, Ernst Furlinger, D.K. Printing World, 2009
- *Yogavāsiṣṭha*, edition by Wāsudeva Laxmaṇa Śāstrī Paṇsīkar, Motilal Banarsidass, 2008

Contact

Online course
Workshops
Books

www.david-dubois.com
deven_fr@yahoo.fr
https://www.instagram.com/daviddevendradubois/